Bloodstained Narratives

Horror and Monstrosity Studies Series
Bernadette Marie Calafell, Marina Levina, and Kendall R. Phillips, General Editors

BLOODSTAINED NARRATIVES

The *Giallo* Film in Italy and Abroad

Edited by Matthew Edwards
and Fernando Gabriel Pagnoni Berns

University Press of Mississippi Jackson

The University Press of Mississippi is the scholarly publishing agency of
the Mississippi Institutions of Higher Learning: Alcorn State University,
Delta State University, Jackson State University, Mississippi State University,
Mississippi University for Women, Mississippi Valley State University,
University of Mississippi, and University of Southern Mississippi.

www.upress.state.ms.us

Designed by Peter D. Halverson

The University Press of Mississippi is a member
of the Association of University Presses.

Copyright © 2023 by University Press of Mississippi
All rights reserved

Portions of "*A White Dress for Marialé*: An interview with director Romano
Scavolini" by Matthew Edwards were previously published in *Twisted Visions:
Interviews with Cult Horror Filmmakers* (Jefferson: McFarland and Company, Inc., 2017)

First printing 2023

∞

Library of Congress Cataloging-in-Publication Data

Names: Edwards, Matthew, 1978– editor. | Pagnoni Berns, Fernando Gabriel, 1975– editor.
Title: Bloodstained narratives : the giallo film in Italy and abroad /
Matthew Edwards, Fernando Gabriel Pagnoni Berns.
Other titles: Horror and monstrosity studies series.
Description: Jackson : University Press of Mississippi, 2023. | Series:
Horror and monstrosity studies series | Includes bibliographical
references and index.
Identifiers: LCCN 2022051944 (print) | LCCN 2022051945 (ebook) | ISBN
9781496844453 (hardback) | ISBN 9781496844460 (trade paperback) | ISBN
9781496844477 (epub) | ISBN 9781496844484 (epub) | ISBN 9781496844491
(pdf) | ISBN 9781496844507 (pdf)
Subjects: LCSH: Horror films—History and criticism. | Slasher
films—History and criticism. | Detective and mystery films—History and
criticism. | Sex role in motion pictures.
Classification: LCC PN1995.9.H6 B617 2023 (print) | LCC PN1995.9.H6
(ebook) | DDC 791.43/6164—dc23/eng/20230126
LC record available at https://lccn.loc.gov/2022051944
LC ebook record available at https://lccn.loc.gov/2022051945

British Library Cataloging-in-Publication Data available

CONTENTS

Acknowledgments VII

Introduction: Argentina, the Onetti Brothers,
 and the Resurgence of *Giallo* 3
 FERNANDO GABRIEL PAGNONI BERNS AND MATTHEW EDWARDS

Part I: New Readings on Classic *Gialli*

Chapter 1: The Killer's Eye: *Giallo* and the Zoom Lens 13
 BRIAN BREMS

Chapter 2: Argento's Evil Eye: Movements, Containments, and
 the *Giallo*'s Possessive Gaze 30
 ÉMILIE VON GARAN

Chapter 3: *Death Laid an Egg*: A *Giallo* Out of Far-Left Field 48
 DONALD L. ANDERSON

Chapter 4: The Transnational *Giallo*: Jess Franco's *Paroxismus* and
 the Postmodern Crisis of Temporality 67
 LISA HAEGELE

Chapter 5: The Analog of Self-Authenticity within
 The Forbidden Photos of a Lady above Suspicion 84
 GAVIN F. HURLEY

Chapter 6: Beyond Interesting: The Affective Complexity of
 Barbara Bouchet in *Don't Torture a Duckling* 102
 ERIC BRINKMAN

Chapter 7: *A White Dress for Marialé*: An Interview with
 Director Romano Scavolini 122
 MATTHEW EDWARDS

Chapter 8: *Watch Me When I Kill* and *The Bloodstained Shadow*:
An Interview with Director Antonio Bido 129
MATTHEW EDWARDS

Part II: The *Giallo* Abroad. A Transnational Phenomenon

Chapter 9: A Kinder Capitalism: Elements of the *Giallo* in
Hong Kong New Wave Cinema 141
ANDREW GROSSMAN

Chapter 10: "But Illusions Don't Kill": An Examination of
Giallo Tropes and Gender in Satoshi Kon's *Perfect Blue* 164
SEAN WOODARD

Chapter 11: "This Is No Longer a Metaphor But a Demonstration":
The Red of Blood in *The Strange Color of Your Body's Tears* 182
SHARON JANE MEE

Chapter 12: Almodóvar Meets Gay Porn Meets *Giallo*: Rewriting Argento's
L'uccello dale piume di cristallo in *Un couteau dans le Coeur* 199
FERNANDO GABRIEL PAGNONI BERNS

Chapter 13: Warped Nests: Domestic Architecture, Transgressive
Female Bodies, and the Dissolution of the Patriarchal Domain in
1970s American *Gialli* 216
BRENDA S. GARDENOUR WALTER

Chapter 14: "Beauty Is the Only Thing":
Sex and Fantasy in American *Giallo* Cinema 233
CONNOR JOHN WARDEN

Chapter 15: The Canadian *Giallo*, or How the Italian Thriller
Influenced the Canadian Slasher Film 251
MIKEL J. KOVEN

About the Contributors 272

Index 276

ACKNOWLEDGMENTS

Matthew Edwards: This collection would not have been possible without the help of both my family and friends and the contributors who participated in this book. Particular thanks go to my Mum and Dad, and to my brothers, Paul, Mark, and Daniel. Thank you also to Patrick Prescott for continuing to support me in my writing endeavors and to my cats Mimi and Bertie. I would like to extend my thanks to the editorial staff at University Press of Mississippi for agreeing to publish this collection and for their help in realizing the project. Last but not least, a huge thank you to my wife, Johanna, for her love and support during the editing of this book.

Fernando Gabriel Pagnoni Berns: I dedicate this book to my mother, Irma, and my sister, Fabiana. To Nestor, who is always pushing me forward, and Eduardo, my incredible tango dancer/banker/film fan/voracious reader/philosopher/clown friend. My thanks to my co-editor, Matthew Edwards, for his support and more thanks to the editorial staff at University Press of Mississippi. And, of course, to all the *giallo*'s masters: Dario Argento, Mario Bava, Sergio Martino, Lucio Fulci, Luigi Bazzoni, Massimo Dallamano, and many, many others. For a new era of *gialli*!

Bloodstained Narratives

Introduction

ARGENTINA, THE ONETTI BROTHERS, AND THE RESURGENCE OF *GIALLO*

FERNANDO GABRIEL PAGNONI BERNS AND MATTHEW EDWARDS

A woman is photographed by a mysterious stranger when she walks the streets alone. Close shots of shining knives. The color red as an omnipresent presence through the *mise-en-scène*. Infantile traumas emphasized with shots of creepy dolls. Psychedelic saturated colors. Brutal murders. And a revelation involving gender confusion.

All the imaginary described above is not from Dario Argento's masterpiece *L'uccello dalle piume di cristallo* (*The Bird with the Crystal Plumage*, 1970) but from Argentinean director Luciano Onetti's *Sonno Profondo* (2013), part of his trilogy of homages to *gialli* produced with his brother, Nicolás. Interestingly, Onetti's *Sonno Profondo* is essentially an experimental film with no dialogue and with all the action seen from the killer's point of view. The film takes the grainy classic style of 1970s sleaze filmmaking so typical at the grindhouse and elaborates this to create a piece of cinema that focuses on homage, an era and a cycle: the Italian *giallo*. *Francesca* (2015), Onetti's second homage, keeps the *giallo* aesthetics but ads more plot, even if the film is overcomplicated. However, the ambiguity and the lack of a proper resolution "is fully in keeping with the sense of postmodern abstraction characteristic of the *neo-giallo*" (Towlson 2021, 24). Both Luciano and Nicolás will close the trilogy directing *Abrakadabra* (2018), revolving around a magician (Germán Baudino) who finds himself the target of a sadistic serial killer.

It may seem baffling that two Argentinean directors (filming in Argentina) have chosen the *giallo* as a narrative to pay homage, going so far as to include all the dialogues in their films in Italian. This mobility, in fact, is just another step in the transnational flux that created the *giallo* cycle in the first place. As argued by Mikel Koven, there is a cross-fertilization between the *gialli* and the German *krimi* cycle (2005, 5). The *krimi* were hugely popular films made in Germany throughout the 1950s and '60s, mostly based on novels penned by British author Edgar Wallace. With bizarre plots and bizarre criminals, the *krimi* mixed suspense with a Gothic atmosphere and the absurd, creating a blueprint for the Italian cycle. Decades later, the *giallo* will become, in turn, a blueprint for the American slasher cycle of the 1980s. As argued, "as a bridge extending into postmodern horror cinema, *gialli* have influenced 1980s, 1990s, and twenty-first-century horror by establishing the foundation for popular slasher horror movies of the 1980s and early 1990s" (Hurley 2020, 110).

Argentina and Italy share a common history, as the South American country was populated, in part, with Italian immigrants running away from poverty and war in Europe. By 1914, the Italian community in Argentina consisted of 300,000 individuals (Baily 1999, 217). As such, Italian immigrants and the receiving society were eager to construct a continuum to determine similarities and, in consequence, shape an imaginary in common (Baily 1999, 218). In terms of architecture, ideology, language, and, basically, ways of life, Argentina is very Italian, with much of the native population being descendent of Italians or Spaniards. Even one of the editors of this collection, Argentinean Fernando Pagnoni Berns, has Italian blood ("Pagnoni"). All the actors in the Onettis' films speak (or are dubbed into) Italian, but the foreign language sounds somehow "fitting" in an Argentinean film. Making *giallo* in Argentina is a logical step within the mobility proposed by the globalized world of cinema.

The *giallo filone* ("vein," meaning a corpus of films being part of a codified group but nevertheless open to experimentation and reformulation) has never been really defunct and is now brought back from the Italian 1970s via a series of tributes that recognize the intrinsic valor of a series of films previously considered as just basic exploitation. As Bruce Isaacs explains, speaking specifically of Dario Argento, the *giallo* desire is that of "interrogate the cinematic form" (2020, 114) thus taking the corpus closer to the avant-garde and the experimental cinema than to mindless sleaziness.

But what is a *giallo* film?

Giallo is not fond of concrete definitions, preferring rather the ambiguous and playful. In Italian, *giallo* means "yellow." The term makes reference to the bright colors of early mystery paperbacks published in Italy by the Milanese Mondadori. These paperbacks, which began publication in the late 1920s, mostly offered vernacular translations of authors such as Agatha Christie or Edgar Wallace. As Koven explains, "a few years earlier, Mondadori had achieved success with a series of romance novels published with bright blue covers, and so their 'giallo' series was an extension of this color-coding of popular literature" (2006, 2). Soon enough, the color yellow signified "crime" for Italian readers. Through the 1970s, this label extended itself to cinema, when Italian film audiences (and, later, abroad) adopted it as the name for a peculiar Italian sub-genre of thriller film which put the emphasis on atmosphere and the killings rather than in the case's resolution.

Like the American *noir*, a genre and/or cycle highly codified and aestheticized, *giallo* was rapidly recognized by a series of striking features and narrative and visual conventions. First and foremost, the murder itself. In contrast with the killings in *noir* cinema, mostly bloodless gunshots, the murders in *gialli* are depicted through sophisticated, cruel, bloody set pieces that, in the case of auteurs such as Dario Argento or Mario Bava, work almost autonomously from the main narrative. Long in length and filled with excessive baroquism, the murders are not just a plot point but a masterclass on the art of filmmaking.

The *gialli* presented another set of recognizable conventions: amateur sleuths, close shots of hands (that of the murderer) covered by black gloves, repressed memories, bold music scores, and lengthy titles such as *Lo strano vizio della signora Wardh* (*The Strange Vice of Mrs. Wardh*, Sergio Martino, 1971), *Perché quelle strane gocce di sangue sul corpo di Jennifer?* (*The Case of the Bloody Iris*, Giuliano Carnimeo, 1972), or *Il tuo vizio è una stanza chiusa e solo io ne ho la chiave* (*Your Vice Is a Locked Room and Only I Have the Key*, Sergio Martino, 1972). These long titles many times contained animals (mostly, as red herrings)—*L'iguana dalla lingua di fuoco* (*The Iguana with the Tongue of Fire*, Riccardo Freda, 1971) or *Gatti rossi in un labirinto di vetro* (*Eyeball*, Umberto Lenzi, 1975)—in answer to the success of Argento's animal trilogy: *L'uccello dalle piume di cristallo* (*The Bird with the Crystal Plumage*, 1970), *Il gatto a nove code* (*The Cat o' Nine Tails*, 1971), and *4 mosche di velluto grigio* (*Four Flies on Gray Velvet*, 1971). And, of course, shots of J&B Whiskey, a marker of sophisticated cosmopolitan life. Not surprisingly, the *giallo* was a response to Italy's "economic miracle" that changed the country's topography and cultural life from the agrarian to the modern after the nation opened to global tourism. Hence the travelogue narrative and the recurrent presence of airports, cars, and roads scattered through the films.

Lastly, the *gialli*'s tradition "gleefully mixes high and low culture, where you'll find flashes of artistic brilliance sharing the screen with moments of jaw-dropping squalor" (Gallant 2018). Certainly, the *giallo* pivots between sexploitation and European psychedelia on the one hand, and avant-garde experimentation on the other, thus blurring the frontiers of what is considered art and what is considered cinematic sleaze.

The *giallo filone* has three origins, each one solidifying the tropes of the genre. Arguably, it all began with Mario Bava's *La ragazza che sapeva troppo* (*The Girl Who Knew Too Much*, 1963), a film revolving around Nora (Leticia Román), a young woman who travels to Rome and witnesses a murder after, accidently, consuming some drugs. The police do not believe her since a corpse cannot be found. Several more murders follow, turning Nora into an amateur sleuth.

La ragazza che sapeva troppo established some of the cycle's tropes, chief among them the eye and vision as untrusted apparatuses. Even Nora is uncertain about what she saw and if the murder really took place. Following this black-and-white film, Bava crystallized the conventions with his groundbreaking *Sei donne per l'assassino* (*Blood and Black Lace*, 1964) where a masked, black-gloved killer starts murdering various fashion models in a desperate attempt to obtain a scandal-revealing diary.

The *gialli* got all its definitive tropes with Argento's *L'uccello dalle piume di cristallo*. In the film, Sam Dalmas (Tony Musante), an American expatriate in Rome, witnesses an attempted murder. He learns later that it is connected to an ongoing murder spree in the city and decides to do his own investigation. Soon, he and his girlfriend (Susy Kendall) are personally targeted by the killer. Argento's film gave the final defining touches to the cycle: to the eye as an untrusting witness and the black-gloved killer, the director added sexual trauma and clues misunderstood by the dark corners of the witness's mind. These three films, *La ragazza che sapeva troppo*, *Sei donne per l'assassino*, and *L'uccello dalle piume di cristallo*, shaped and formalized the *giallo* film, one of the most colorful, sexy, and complex cycles in film history.

The *giallo* film was displaced in the mid-1980s by the Italian zombie film formula, the latter more based on gore and guts than in the labyrinth-like plots of the former. Later efforts such as Lamberto Bava's *La casa con la scala nel buio* (*A Blade in the Dark*, 1983) did not receive the attention that the classic *gialli* were afforded during the heyday of the cycle, showing that audiences were demanding new forms of cinematic thrills. With Italy losing its place of privilege in European cinema through the 1980s, *giallo* became, apparently, a thing from the past.

Giallo received a renaissance of sorts after the coming of new technologies such as DVD and Blu-ray, and it was discovered by legions of horror aficionados. However, as mentioned, the *giallo* inspired and survived in the American slasher and the thriller formula of the 1980s and the 1990s and influenced many filmmakers through America, Europe, and Asia.

According to the popular site bloodydisgusting.com, "it's clear that we're in the middle of a Giallo renaissance. This colorful brand of Italian and Italian-inspired horror may never have truly gone away, but it's cool to see modern filmmakers paying tribute to masters like Dario Argento" (H. C. 2019). The reviewer is talking about Abiel Bruhn and John Rocco's weird little gem *The Night Sitter* (2018), but the mention of homage is applicable to other films as well, ranging from Yan Gonzalez's *Un couteau dans le Coeur* (2018) to *Berberian Sound Studio* (Brad Strickland, 2012), *Piercing* (Nicolas Pesce, 2018) to Hélène Cattet and Bruno Forzani's *Amer* (2009), and Sebastián Gutiérrez's *Elizabeth Harvest* (2018) to Edgar Wright's *Last Night in Soho* (2021).

The *giallo* film, indeed, has been with us since its (supposedly) demise through the 1980s. It has changed clothes, but remained a faithful companion to weird cinema. It has been transformed into other genres, into other cycles. But the heart remains "yellow."

The Book

The first section, focused on classic *gialli*, opens with Brian Brems's "The Killer's Eye: Giallo and The Zoom Lens," where the author analyzes the use of the zoom in *gialli*, using *Nude per l'assassino* (*Strip Nude for Your Killer*, Andrea Bianchi, 1975) as a case study. For the author, the zoom lens is essential at the moment of analyzing *gialli*; it is as much a part of the genre's collective *mise-en-scène* as the black-gloved killer, eroticism, or other narrative tropes. In the second chapter, E. Jacob examines the tourist gaze and the evil eye, both opening up the possibility to engage with the sites and sights of collection within Dario Argento's cinema. A final component of the analysis of Argento's *L'uccello dalle piume di cristallo* reifies the presence of colonial elements of the film and the need for a post-colonial mode of engagement with the *giallo*. Then Donald L. Anderson offers a close reading of Giuli Questi's *La morte ha fatto l'uovo* (*Death Laid an Egg*, 1968), an overlooked masterpiece. The author situates the film within the experimental tradition of the *nouvelle vague* and examines the significance of Maderna's film score. Further, Anderson analyzes the film's critique of capitalist exploitation, the rise of a mechanized workforce, and the bio-economics of developing mutated chickens as a cost-saving device. Anderson's chapter reassesses the technical and theoretical significance of Questi's film within the history of *giallo* cinema. Taking as examples two *gialli* directed by Jess Franco, the West German-Italian coproduced *Paroxismus—Può una morta rivivere per amore?* (1969) and the West German-Spanish coproduction *Der Todesrächer von Soho* (*El muerto hace las maletas*, 1972), Lisa Haegele argues that the films represent a shared European popular cinema that transgresses national boundaries and historical specificities, reflecting the new politics of European unification and efforts to form a collective European identity after the Second World War. Furthermore, she contends that the *giallo* in the "long 1968" is best understood in the context of a broader European cinema rather than purely as a "national" cinema. By examining Luciano Ercoli's 1970 film *Le foto proibite di una signora per bene* (*The Forbidden Photos of a Lady above Suspicion*), Gavin Hurley illustrates how some films use the philosophical concept of Jean-Paul Sartre's concept of "bad faith" to adhere audiences to the narrative. In the author's analysis, several plot points and narratives detail how the main character surrenders to the gaze rather than living authentically as a free individual. Next, Eric Brinkman centers on female star Barbara Bouchet, who starred in many *gialli*. The author argues that what makes Bouchet effective across *giallo* films is that the affective qualities of her performances support the central themes of the cycle: visceral thrills provided by the voyeuristic depiction of an unknown killer whose violent bloodletting is the result of psychological issues that center around sexuality. Closing the section, Matthew Edwards offers two interviews: the first with director Romano Scavolini (*A White Dress for Marialé*), and the second with cult *gialli* director Antonio Bido, who is responsible for two cult entries in the *giallo* cycle: *Watch Me When I Kill* and *The Bloodstained Shadow*.

The second section on international *gialli* opens with Andrew Grossman's essay, which investigates elements of the *giallo* in Hong Kong New Wave Cinema. He argues that Hong Kong films self-consciously "inject" foreign elements rather than seamlessly incorporate or "own" them. Hong Kong's semi-*giallo* films are not glossy appropriations of Western cinema, ready-made for easy consumption and digestion, but asymmetrical and indeed awkward mash-ups that reveal (rather than conceal) their layers and sutures. Sean Woodard explores how the homogenization of Italian *giallo* elements and those of J-Pop culture provide a platform to re-examine representations of gender, victimhood, mental illness, and the perception between fiction and reality as analyzed in Satoshi Kon's animated psychological film *Perfect Blue* (1997). Via Gilles Deleuze, Sharon Jane Mee examines Hélène Cattet and Bruno Forzani's neo-*giallo* film *L'étrange couleur des larmes de ton corps* (*The Strange Color of Your Body's Tears*, 2013) as a demonstration of cinema that is un/endurable but nonetheless absorbing through the bold use of color, the latter a literal demonstration of sensation. In his chapter, Fernando Gabriel Pagnoni Berns argues that French *giallo Un couteau dans le Coeur* (Yann González 2018) is a rewriting of the themes of Dario Argento's *L'uccello dalle piume di cristallo* (*The Bird with the Crystal Plumage*, 1975). Understanding adaptation not as a unidirectional process progressing from an original source to cinematographic illustration, but rather as a process of feedback between works and social and cultural contexts, the author uses this rewriting as a case of adaptation from film to film, analyzing how González's film queers Argento's work by revealing its indebtedness to homosexual desire and identity. Brenda S. Gardenour Walter examines the reciprocal relationships between domestic architecture, the gendered human body, and the family in three American giallo films: *Private Parts* (1972), *Alice, Sweet Alice* (1976), and *The Eyes of Laura Mars* (1978). Released in the 1970s, these films reveal cultural fears about the autonomy of women within and beyond the home, the purported breakdown of the patriarchal family, and the slippery boundaries of the human body—all of which are reflected in the collective architectural spaces depicted in each film. John Warden Connor's chapter explores the relationship between sexuality and horror dynamics within American neo-*giallo* cinema. In particular, he chooses to focus on two films, Brian De Palma's *Body Double* and Nicolas Winding Refn's *The Neon Demon*, which he argues exists within the American tradition of *giallo* more firmly than any European lineage. Our book closes with Mikel Koven exploring how Canadian produced slasher films can be considered *gialli* by means of influence. In the films selected for study, the emphasis is as much on discovering who the killer is than in trying to simply avoid being killed. Because of the demands of the mystery genre, these slasher films emphasize ratiocination to unmask the killer. Much like the traditional Italian *giallo* thriller.

Works Cited

Baily, Samuel. 1999. *Immigrants in the Lands of Promise: Italians in Buenos Aires and New York City, 1870 to 1914*. Ithaca: Cornell University Press.

Gallant, Chris. 2018. "Where to Begin with Giallo." https://www2.bfi.org.uk/news-opinion/news-bfi/features/where-begin-giallo.

Hurley, Gavin. 2020. "Giallo." In *The Microgenre: A Quick Look at Small Culture*, edited by Anne H. Stevens and Molly C. O'Donnell, 103–112. New York: Bloomsbury.

Isaacs, Bruce. 2020. *The Art of Pure Cinema: Hitchcock and His Imitators*. Oxford: Oxford University Press.

Koven, Mikel. 2006. *La Dolce Morte: Vernacular Cinema and the Italian Giallo Film*. Lanham, MD: Scarecrow Press.

Luiz, H. C. 2019. "Giallo Tribute 'The Night Sitter' Is a Dreamlike Visual Treat." *BloodyDisgusting*, August 1, 2019. https://bloody-disgusting.com/reviews/3575916/review-night-sitter-dreamlike-visual-treat.

Towlson, Jon. 2021. *Global Horror Cinema Today: 28 Representative Films from 17 Countries*. Jefferson, NC: McFarland and Company.

Part 1

NEW READINGS ON CLASSIC *GIALLI*

Chapter 1

THE KILLER'S EYE

Giallo and the Zoom Lens

BRIAN BREMS

The shower sequence in *Psycho* (Alfred Hitchcock, 1960) has been roundly credited with inspiring several generations of horror filmmakers. Before the actual killing, roadside motel operator Norman Bates (Anthony Perkins) moves a painting off the wall, revealing a peephole cut into it that looks into the bathroom where Marion Crane (Janet Leigh) is undressing for her fateful shower. Hitchcock cuts in to a close-up of Norman's eye, a shot taken from the side; the tiny glint of light from the illuminated bathroom flickers in his pupil, an effect emphasized by the black-and-white photography. Bates watches a moment. Hitchcock briefly cuts in to his point of view, revealing Marion's back, as seen by Norman, and us, through the peephole. Carrying forward the obsession with seeing that had long characterized his cinema,[1] Hitchcock uses the camera to tell his audience where and when to look.

In another universe, Hitchcock might have used a zoom lens to achieve this effect; it is not hard to imagine an alternative version of the point of view shot through the peephole, slowly zooming in closer on Marion's back as she undresses. Perhaps the restrictions of the Motion Picture Production Code would have prevented him from indulging in such prurient, seductive use of the camera; indeed, he was already pushing it considerably. By the time of the explosion of *giallo* cinema a decade later in Italy, the zoom lens would become a ubiquitous hallmark of the genre, as inseparable from the films as its black-gloved killers, mysterious narratives, and depictions of erotically charged violence. Technological advancements in the usability of zoom lenses increased filmmakers' interest in it as a tool (Hall 2018, 88).[2] Hollywood filmmakers working in the 1970s, most notably Robert Altman, used the zoom lens to such a degree that it became an identifiable part of their visual styles. Though the zoom lens was controversial among cinematographers[3] and critics alike (Hall 2018, 8, 136), the most expressive filmmakers found ways to integrate it into their work, using the zoom to create emotional or psychological effects; others simply admired its practicality, especially for shooting on location.

Giallo filmmakers undoubtedly were attracted to all of these qualities. In Hollywood cinema, according to Nick Hall's (2018) history of the zoom lens, "[t]wo main attitudes to the zoom can be detected in the films of the 1970s. Some directors used the zoom without hesitation, zooming as frequently and obviously as they wanted to. Others did their best to conceal its use—using zoom lenses as an alternative to a set of prime lenses, coordinating zoom moves to take place at the same time as pans, or simply zooming as little as possible" (137). The *gialli* directors certainly belong to the former camp, ostentatiously flaunting their uses of the zoom to such a flagrant degree that its visual presence is inextricable from the genre, a clear and identifiable marker of a *giallo*. In America, "there was no genre with which the zoom could be most closely associated" (Hall, 2018, 139), but in Italy, the *giallo* film relied on the zoom to create an intensely subjective experience for the viewer by subordinating the spectator's gaze to absolute control. The zoom lens's shifting focal point magnifies not only the objects it captures within the frame, but also the directorial hand behind the camera; it commands the spectator's look while simultaneously alerting the spectator to its manipulative function. Unlike the "invisible style" of classic Hollywood continuity that seeks to hide the seams of editing and downplay camera movement, the *giallo*'s zoom shot announces itself loudly, opening the genre and its techniques up for parody and pastiche.[4]

In this analysis, I offer a survey of the use of the zoom lens in the *giallo* film in an effort to articulate its general meanings across a number of examples of the genre, while singling out one film in particular for close reading. While the zoom lens and the *giallo* have often both been fodder for contemptuous critics, the consistent presence of the zoom lens within a number of *giallo* films demonstrates a rather sophisticated use by multiple filmmakers of then-new technology to enact genre. According to Italian cinema historian Peter Bondanella (2009), "ways of seeing or not seeing become one of the genre's basic themes," often expressed through the "frequently employed zoom shot" (375). For various *giallo* filmmakers, the zoom lens becomes as essential tool for expressing mood, carrying political ideas, creating character identification, and playing with ironic genre commentary. I will offer several cursory examples to establish how the zoom lens works across the *giallo* cycle before turning to *Nude per l'assassino* (*Strip Nude for Your Killer*, Andrea Bianchi, 1975) for a more substantive reading. For efficiency's sake, I have largely avoided extended plot summaries, but given that all the films I reference are *gialli*, the reader can make some reasonable inferences about the plots of all these films.

Most literature written on the use of the zoom lens in narrative cinema namechecks the iconic dolly-zoom shot from Alfred Hitchcock's *Vertigo* (1957), which simulates the protagonist's fear of heights whenever he looks down. While the film's technical use of the dolly-zoom has often been repurposed by other filmmakers (notably by Steven Spielberg in *Jaws* [1975]), Hitchcock's initial use of the technique has important implications for study of the *giallo* film. Because of its influence over the slasher genre (the *giallo*'s American cousin), most see *Psycho* as the foundational text for a number of Italian filmmakers working in the *giallo* tradition. To Adam Lowenstein, it "is an inescapable point of reference" for Mario Bava and Dario Argento (2016, 128). The influence extended to other directors as well, as Bondanella argues that Sergio Martino's *Lo strano vizio della Signora Wardh* (*The Strange Vice of Mrs. Wardh*, 1971) features "a shower scene that cites Hitchcock's *Psycho*" in which "the classic black-gloved *giallo* murderer slits the throat"[10] of one of the film's female characters (2009, 394). However, beyond the genre filmmakers' affinity for Hitchcock, the zoom lens also appealed to thrifty, cost-conscious producers because it "created time- and money-saving opportunities" (Hall 2018, 123).

It is unfair to dismiss the use of the zoom lens in *gialli* as little more than a cheap device, however. Francesco Di Chiara (2016) makes the argument that "the horror genre allowed the Italian film industry to experiment with new modes of production and to develop production trends aimed at the international, rather than the domestic, market" (31). Technological improvements made it easier to use the zoom lens; *giallo* filmmakers valued its efficiency, yes, but it also reflected the thematic ideas they wanted to explore. The zoom lens offered a relatively novel formal device for establishing a unique look for their films. The films' apparent overreliance on a handful of specific visual techniques are not limitations of the filmmakers, but an essential part of the *giallo* cinema's *filone*, or generic tradition (Baschiera and Hunter 2016, 6).[5] Of the tendency to embody the killer's point of view through subjective camera shots, author Mikel Koven (2006) says "repeated use of the POV camera to denote the stalking killer is more significant than merely a cliché, it underlines the 'tradition' aspect of the *filone* itself. When filmmakers use this visual signifier, particularly within the Italian *giallo* tradition, they are consciously following in the wake of previous successful *gialli* films" (147).

Though my intention is to highlight *gialli* directed by filmmakers beyond the two acknowledged masters of the genre, Mario Bava and Dario Argento, even basic awareness of the fluidity of Italian genre cinema and the concept of *filone* requires at least a cursory examination of their highly influential work. Studying numerous examples from both Bava and Argento would require a more exhaustive approach than I have time and space for here, so I will confine my analysis to Bava and Argento's uses of the zoom in *Sei donne per l'assassino* (*Blood and Black Lace*, 1964) and *L'uccello dalle piume de cristallo* (*The Bird with the* Crystal Plumage, 1970), respectively, each director's generally agreed-upon first major *giallo*. In Bava's *Blood and Black Lace*, "he pushes us to take this performative approach to spectatorship not only by exciting our sympathies for and suspicions about one character after another via the narrative, but also by prompting us—via the camerawork, editing, music, and other formal devices—to assume a variety of different, often highly unconventional points of view throughout the film" (Olney 2013, 111).

During the opening credits, Bava establishes the highly mobile camera that he will use for the duration of the film; the first instance of the zoom occurs in the film's second shot, after a dissolve to a blood-red mannequin head, wearing a black wig. The camera slowly zooms in from a medium close-up to a full-on close-up, establishing one method by which Bava will use the zoom to create meaning. It captures a facsimile of a female character, a representation of the fashion models who will become his slasher's victims, but also begins to associate the female form with both blood (the brilliant color red of the mannequin's head) and the use of the camera as the literal and figurative eye of the killer. This association continues after the revelation of the first murder, when the victim's body is discovered crammed into a closet. The shocking discovery is accompanied by a sudden zoom-out from a tight close-up of the surprised, screaming woman who finds the mangled corpse, sharply coming to rest in a medium close-up. The suddenness of the zoom creates a visual sensation not unlike the staccato Bernard Herrmann score that intensifies the stabbing in *Psycho*; Bava includes a music cue like Herrmann's just to underline the point of comparison. Its sudden change of depth also recalls the famous moment in Hitchcock's *The Birds* (1963), when the body of a mutilated farmer is discovered, his eyes pecked out; Hitchcock accomplishes the same effect with a series of three cuts that rapidly approach the man's body, culminating in a gruesome close-up. In Bava's hands, the zoom lens is "therefore able simultaneously to replicate an existing technique (the cut) while distinguishing itself from that function and carrying wider meanings" (Hall 2018, 113). The zoom would become a *giallo* convention aided by technological improvements in the zoom lens itself and because of its disorienting effect on spectators.

Bava will elsewhere use the zoom lens to emphasize important details, such as zooming away from an important handbag (supposedly containing an incriminating diary), sitting openly on a table in the center of the models' changing area, waiting for a mobile rack of fur coats to pass through the frame, and then zooming back in on the table to reveal that the handbag has been removed by an unknown party. Later, Bava zooms in on a police suspect, whose girlfriend has been killed by the murderer, sitting anxiously in the back of their parked squad car, pairing the shot with a dread-inducing sting of music underneath; at this point in the film, the shot's subject may indeed be the murderer, for the film has yet to reveal his identity. Other zooms appear throughout the film, but they largely fall into these patterns: revealing murder victims or giving a sudden emphasis on important items or pieces of information, all of which consistently act like ripple effects from the murderer's rampage. In a shot recalling the film's opening, Bava likewise concludes the film with a zoom into a red object; this time, it is the receiver of a telephone, swinging free above the bodies of the murderers (yes, two of them) who have killed one another. The film's visual design consistently uses tracking and dolly shots at will to coincide with Bava's staging of the actors, and the zoom lens is sometimes difficult to distinguish from physical movement of the entire camera; this is far from the "abuse" of the zoom lens frequently derided by its detractors, but instead aligns with what many consider to be the best practice by masking its obviousness. Through repeated, but not excessive, use of the zoom, Bava suffuses the film's narrative with the presence of his masked, black-gloved murderer. He does not literalize the zoom lens as the killer's eye, but frequently reminds the spectator of the killer's actions whenever the zoom appears, as though the murderer's impact on the film's visual pattern matches his disruptive effect on the characters within the narrative.

Throughout Dario Argento's work, he displays the influence of Hitchcock much more overtly than Bava; a number of his films take the act of looking as their subject, in the manner of *Rear Window* (1954), *Vertigo*, and *Psycho*, all of which concern voyeurism. In *The Bird with The Crystal Plumage*, Argento's debt to Hitchcock is most obvious in the opening sequence, wherein American writer Sam Dalmas (Tony Musante) witnesses an attempted murder while trapped in the glass vestibule of an art gallery. However, Argento follows in Bava's footsteps by using the zoom in the opening credits sequence; first, he zooms in on a letter being prepared by the black-gloved murderer, but then associates the killer's point of view with the zoom lens by adopting the point of view of a still camera, which captures a woman (the killer's intended victim) walking along a street in broad daylight, stopping in freeze frame as the photographer snaps her picture. From this early moment in Argento's first *giallo*, the zoom lens and the killer's eye are one in the same, establishing a pattern which a number of *giallo* filmmakers will follow. Olney (2013) calls Argento's mixed use of the camera "perspective play" and argues that it "is not unique to Argento's *giallo* films; it is a defining feature of the *giallo* as a genre" (129). In her book on Argento's work, Maitland McDonagh (1994) argues that "his camera is nervous, restless . . . it swoops and glides, slinking along corridors, crouching at the bottom of staircases, perching on rooftops" (8). Argento's use of a zoom-out from Sam, sitting in the police station while being interrogated, coming to rest in the camera's position from a wide shot in the corner of the room, would seem at first glance to confirm McDonagh's assertion that "the camera reflects no point-of-view save its own" (8).

And yet, the presence of the zoom lens suggests an eye, despite its ability, unlike the human eye, to collapse the distance between physical spaces; "here," where the act of seeing is undertaken, and "there," where the object of the look resides, are bridgeable through the zoom lens. Thomas Allen Nelson (1986) argues that the zoom lens "encourages us to interpret—and misinterpret—the intentions of both our interest and that of the artist directing the camera. Or, a zoom-in might isolate some microscopic object or actions independent of a given film's developing story and character interests. It forces us to see, to consider factors other than those consistent with the demands of narrative content" (139). In Argento's *giallo* films, the killer's hidden identity affords him anonymity that grants him nearly mystical abilities; he can appear and disappear at will, as he does in *Crystal Plumage*, when he tries to kill Sam on the street before he is warned by an old woman at the last possible moment. Indeed, the zoom lens itself, when it directly or nearly adopts the killer's point of view, has the visual effect of concealing his identity; Argento demonstrates this at one seemingly innocuous moment when the killer calls the police to taunt them. Argento zooms in on the phone and its rotary dial, stopping as the black-gloved hands enter the frame and pick up the receiver, conveniently hiding the offender's face.

As in *Blood and Black Lace*, Argento's zoom lens functions as an all-encompassing signifier of the murderer because everything in the narrative hinges on the killer's attacks, extending the visual reach of his point of view into scenes where he is not literally present. Elsewhere, Argento deliberately echoes the opening sequence's photographic use of the zoom lens (which simulated the killer's eye) during Sam's flashbacks to the attempted murder at the gallery. The quick cuts to the killing freeze, and Argento uses a post-production optical zoom to crash in on the victim's outstretched hand, reaching towards the camera. In an influential article, John Belton (1980–81) argues that "the vari-focal nature of the zoom lens, however, gives it a resemblance, in terms of its operations, to the human eye, which other lenses cannot duplicate. It maintains focus over a variety of depths. But the zoom lens is not really normal. It is a bionic, not a human, eye" (23). Though the human eye cannot perform this function biologically, the camera's zoom lens can do it mechanically, a manifestation of Belton's "Bionic Eye."

Argento's uses of the zoom are more numerous than Bava's, so a full accounting of them is impossible here, but a few general observations about his implementation show an expansion of its utility. While Bava confined his use of the zoom in *Blood and Black Lace* to a few key moments of emphasis, Argento makes the zoom lens much more expressive of the film's thematic concerns. As Sam continues to unravel the mystery, he realizes that he has misinterpreted the attempted murder in the art gallery; the victim was the aggressor and the perceived aggressor was the intended victim. The narrative twist renders Sam's powers of visual observation ineffective; he has literally not seen what he thought he saw. The consistent appearance of the zoom lens, with its constant visual adjustment, echoes this narrative concern. Argento highlights this contrast when he crosscuts two zoom lens shots: the first is a zoom-out from a painting on the wall of Sam's apartment that depicts an attack similar to the one he saw; the second is a zoom-in on his girlfriend Julia's (Suzy Kendall) eyes, staring at the painting while they embrace. Later, a sudden zoom-out from the phone in Sam's apartment reasserts the killer's presence when Sam answers it and the killer threatens Julia in a throaty whisper. Though Sam can hear the murderer, he cannot see him. Throughout *Crystal Plumage*, Argento associates the zoom lens with the unreliability of sight, a consistent theme that will reappear throughout many *giallo* films as other filmmakers imitate the genre's most successful practitioner. This meaning is embedded not only within the thematic paradigm of the *gialli*, but directly within the zoom lens itself; from Belton's perspective, "every zoom makes an epistemological statement, contemplating man's relationship not with the world itself but with his idea or consciousness of it" (1980–81, 21). Each time a *giallo* filmmaker uses a zoom, it emphasizes the shifting nature of knowledge.

Bava and especially Argento set the thematic and visual palette for subsequent *giallo* filmmakers; before turning to a detailed reading of the zoom lens and its use in *Strip Nude for Your Killer*, I want to offer some general observations of how the zoom is used throughout the genre. Director Aldo Lado opens his 1971 film *La corta notte delle bambole di vetro* (*Short Night of the Glass Dolls*) with a searching, roaming zoom of the rooftops of Prague, establishing the film's setting, but also using the lens to set up its lacerating indictment of the city's corrupt power structure; the film tells the story of journalist Gregory Moore (Jean Sorel), who finds himself on a gurney in the city morgue, unable to move his body, but very much alive. The film's flashback structure follows Moore's attempts to recall the events that have landed him among the dead, revealing a sinister conspiracy perpetrated by the city's wealthy and powerful, who have induced his paralysis in order to silence him and protect themselves from exposure. The film's second shot, taken from the ground, is also a zoom, pulling out to pick up where the film's opening zoom left off, from a low angle of the building where the first shot concluded. The zoom finishes in a courtyard where a custodian sweeps up; a few shots later, he will discover Moore's paralyzed body lying amongst the shrubbery. According to David Bordwell (1997), "This 'searching and revealing' approach, allowing the camera to scan the action and overtly pick out key details, became a significant norm of the 1960s and 1970s" (249). The pairing of these two zooms, while serving a practical function that follows basic continuity rules (establishing shot, then a closer shot), also illustrates the personal ramifications of Lado's institutional critique. Lado unites the city's corruption (represented by its buildings) and its consequences on the ground through formal repetition. Lado underlines this further when Moore, brought into the morgue, speaks in voiceover for the first time: "Dead?" he says, incredulous, while Lado's camera zooms in on his helpless, unmoving face, stopping on his frozen lips, detached from his speaking voice floating over the soundtrack.

In Lado's *Chi l'ha vista morire?* (*Who Saw Her Die?*, 1972), he once again uses the zoom to indict failing social infrastructure. In a quiet moment, Lado zooms in slowly on his protagonist, Franco (George Lazenby), as he wistfully watches a commercial on television featuring a young girl close in age to his own daughter, who has gone missing. The zoom underlines Franco's concern for his missing daughter, but reminds astute viewers of the presence of a mysterious killer; a few scenes prior, Lado has shown the subjective point of view of the killer, behind a veil, approaching the girl. The formal properties of the genre indicate, even before the narrative reveals the girl's body floating in a Venice canal, what has happened to her through its use of the zoom lens.

Two *gialli* by director Sergio Martino—*Tutti I colori del buio* (*All the Colors of the Dark*, 1972) and *Il tuo vizio è una stanza chiusa e solo io ne ho la chiave* (*Your Vice is a Locked Room and Only I Have the Key*, 1972)—demonstrate the director's characteristic excess (on display in his infamous entries in the *poliziesco* and cannibal genres), especially in their adoption of the zoom. Throughout *All the Colors*, Martino's zoom lens coincides with one of the film's key visual motifs, the ocular symbol of a Satanist cult bedeviling Jane (Edwige Fenech). Frequently, Martino will zoom-in once on Jane as she is pursued by cult members, stop, and without cutting, zoom once more, finding a new framing position and calling clear attention to the theme of watching represented by the cult's all-seeing eye. In *Your Vice*, which is loosely based on Poe's "The Black Cat," Martino consistently associates the zoom with eroticism, violence, or both. Martino will often zoom in, then out, then back in again, all within the same single shot, to align with actor blocking; however, at his more expressive moments, the lens zooms in and out to an outrageous degree, such as on an incriminating pile of papers or on the shocked face of a murderer whose crimes have been discovered. Martino often intercuts these zooms with close-ups of the black cat's eyes, suggesting its point of view repeatedly. According to Koven (2006), Martino's confrontational uses of the zoom typify a crucial *giallo* dynamic: "such visual devices lack subtlety, but that is exactly the point" (39).

In *Le foto proibite di una signora per bene*, Luciano Ercoli (*The Forbidden Photos of a Lady above Suspicion*, 1970), the zoom lens is frequently used to emphasize Minou's (Dagmar Lassander) isolation and paranoia. The camera zooms in on her in an early moment on the beach at night, after she is threatened with a knife by the film's blackmailer; she is lying in the sand after the aggressor has snipped away pieces of her dress with a knife, and the zoom underlines her victimization, a theme captured by the film's title. Occasionally, the zooms are more expressive and abstract. At one moment, the camera zooms in to a car's headlamp, which folds up from the body of the vehicle; when it turns on, the lens zooms in further until the frame is filled entirely by the light before a cut to the next scene, in a nightclub. These visual flourishes consistently align with imagery associated with the eye. Not only does the headlight resemble an eye, its entire function is to help the driver see more clearly. Ercoli emphasizes the relationship between the zoom lens and the eye further in a later scene when Minou's friend shares some boudoir photography with her; in one of the photos, she recognizes the blackmailer. Ercoli cuts between successive shots of the photographs and a pair of sudden, sharp zooms-in on Minou's eyes as she takes in the revelation. Later, when she visits the blackmailer's apartment, another zoom crashes in on a wall-mounted mask with wooden sticks protruding from its empty eye sockets, a violent image that recalls a consistent *giallo* convention: risk to vulnerable eyes.

Though *Forbidden Photos* only fleetingly contains a glimpse of the black-gloved killer and has just one extended stalking sequence, the utility of the zoom lens for exploring themes of sight demonstrates that the zoom is perhaps even a more defining genre convention than narrative content in *gialli*. The release date of *Forbidden Photos*—1970—is more or less concurrent with *Crystal Plumage*, making Argento's influence doubtful, but its similar narrative and formal preoccupation with the eyes unquestionably makes it a *giallo*. As always in *gialli*, the eyes have tremendous power because they reveal information, but that power creates risk; when these characters have seen too much, killers often strike at their ability to see by attacking the eyes—the zoom is one of the most powerful cinematic tools in *gialli* to express the discomfort with seeing.

Several directors of *gialli* use the zoom lens to link scenes in a kind of visual montage. In *Cosa avete fatto a Solange?* (*What Have You Done to Solange?*, Massimo Dallamano, 1972), a series of grisly sex murders leads to discomfiting imagery underlined by the zoom lens. In one scene, a father whose daughter has been murdered is led into a room at the hospital, and a doctor places an X-ray on a light box, showing the daughter's pelvic region with a knife jammed into it; the camera zooms in on the horrifyingly clinical image, bereft of blood and gore, leaving only the shadow of the brutal crime visible. Dallamano then cuts to the next scene, at the girl's funeral, in a close-up on the girl's bereaved father, his eyes rimmed with tears and marked by the horror he has been forced to simultaneously see and not see in the X-ray. The camera zooms back, including the girl's mother in the wide composition. Later, the zoom lens bridges the gap between a furtive peeper, as it zooms in on a hole cut in the wall of a schoolgirls' shower, with an eye surreptitiously watching them splash and giggle. Dallamano cuts into a handheld point-of-view shot from the still-anonymous killer's perspective opening an apartment door, linking the zoom lens to the killer across scenes and inviting the possibility that the mysterious peeper and the unseen killer are the same person, despite the geographic distance between the shower and the apartment complex where the killer is about to commit his next murder.

Late cycle *gialli* like *The Killing Hour* (Armand Mastroianni, 1982) and *Blade in the Dark* (Lamberto Bava, 1983) have complicated relationships with the zoom lens. For all intents and purposes, *The Killing Hour* is an American film shot in New York with a mostly American cast and crew; as a result, much of the dialogue is recorded live (as opposed to post-synchronized) and the production recalls higher-budget American thrillers like *Klute* (Alan J. Pakula, 1971), *Dressed to Kill* (Brian De Palma, 1980), and *Cruising* (William Friedkin, 1980), all cousins to the *giallo*. Mastroianni rarely uses the zoom lens, reserving it for a few key moments of emphasis. The first appears during a television call-in show conducted by a journalist when a potential suspect speaks on air over the phone; later, a slow zoom pushes in on the film's clairvoyant artist who sees the murders in her head and then draws them; finally, a medium-paced zoom on a detective realizing the killer's identity in the film's third act. Though the film's higher pretensions seem to play a role in restricting its use of the zoom, its themes of seeing—the drawings are Virna's physical manifestation of so-called second sight—most clearly come to the forefront during Mastroianni's infrequent but emphatic uses of the zoom lens. Lamberto Bava, who is Mario's son and Dario Argento's protégé, has much more fun with the conventions of the *giallo* in *Blade in the Dark*; the story is set in a country villa where a composer is working on the music for a director's horror movie, establishing self-reflexive play. Use of the zoom lens is likewise sparse, but when it does appear, it becomes a signifier of ironic commentary on the genre. The first shot after the credits is a zoom-out from a pair of garden shears, in the hands of a gardener trimming hedges—a bit of visual misdirection. Bava uses another zoom later in the film when the composer answers the phone, and his director is on the other end of the line, mimicking the whispering, threatening voice of many *giallo* killers. He is not fooled, but the use of the zoom lens ironizes the generic conventions well-established for *giallo* cinema.

For an extended case study analysis of the zoom lens in a *giallo* film, I have chosen Andrea Bianchi's *Strip Nude for Your Killer*, a lesser known entry in the *filone*, but, coming as it does near the end of the "classic period" (Koven, 2006, 7) of *giallo* cinema,[6] one that self-consciously plays with well-established conventions, including the genre's reverential attitude towards *Psycho* and the ubiquitous zoom lens. Bondanella (2009) argues that "by the time Bianchi shot the film, the *giallo* conventions established by Bava and Argento and elaborated upon by a number of directors in the early 1970s had become well codified," which explains its playful, often goofy tone (403). Taking a cue from Bava's *Blood and Black Lace*, *Strip Nude for Your Killer* focuses on the mysterious murders of a group of fashion models, and follows the traditional structure: an anonymous killer bumps off members of the cohort during elaborate murder set pieces, all the while delivering on the genre's hallmarks: graphic violence and eroticism. However, the film's approach to both often feels less serious than films by Bava, Argento, Lado, Martino, and others. It is a self-conscious, ironic *giallo* film in the way that later American slasher films acknowledge their fulfillment of genre conventions—not quite as dramatically as Wes Craven's *Scream* (1996), but in the tradition of the elaborately staged murders in *Friday the 13th, Part III* (Steve

Miner, 1982) or the notorious fake-out at the end of *April Fool's Day* (Fred Walton, 1986). Bianchi's approach simultaneously inhabits and sends up the *giallo* conventions, in keeping with the accelerated cycle that dominates Italian genre cinema, owing to their rapid pace of production and imitation.

In addition to its narrative and thematic properties, Bianchi also exaggerates the *giallo*'s formal conventions, none more obvious than his overt use of the zoom lens. Zooms proliferate in the film's opening sequence, a blue-drenched gynecology appointment filled with the kind of erotic menace that dominates *giallo* films, in which the patient dies on the operating table during an abortion. Nearly every shot zooms either in or out, the diegetic motivations tenuous at best. Such flourishes indicate Bianchi's freewheeling adoption of *gialli*'s visual signifiers, often detaching them from their larger generic meaning. However, Bianchi does still occasionally follow the visual template established by Bava, Argento, and others; the first murder sequence following the opening credits likewise uses zooms. His zooming lens trails behind a trench coat-wearing man as he is ambushed by the film's black-leather-clad killer (who also dons a motorcycle helmet), and then, after a cut, crash-zooms in on the gory wound created by the killer's blade. Bianchi carries over the use of the zoom lens into a much less overtly threatening scene by an indoor pool, wherein the film's fashion photographer Carlo (Nino Castelnuovo) spots an attractive model as she passes by his lounge chair on the deck. First, Bianchi zooms in on Carlo sitting with his friends as the model strides past, and then cuts around to another zoom as she walks away. The camera's lens slowly zooms in and out, making needless frame adjustments in the next scene, when Carlo seduces the model in the sauna.

The film's focus on photography lends a narrative motivation for the preponderance of zooms, as do the genre's larger concerns with looking. The camera freely zooms in on models posing in lingerie, simulating the presence of a still camera's zoom lens even when no photographer is present. Inside the studio, the women are subject to the camera's look; Bianchi's free use of the zoom constantly involves the spectator in the act of looking, accelerated in moments of violence. The film's female lead, Magda (Edwige Fenech), motivates the use of the zoom lens inside Carlo's darkroom, when she challenges the photographer to see her as a model, and he encourages her to focus on her photography instead. The zoom becomes contested territory, as Magda invites the camera's eye to look at her, and Carlo encourages her to use the camera's eye to do the looking instead. Their subsequent sexual encounter is likewise dominated by zooms, as the camera slowly trains on Carlo's ecstatic face as Magda drifts down to her knees to initiate fellatio. When the motorcyclist killer visits studio employee Mario (Claudio Pellegrini), her face is hidden from the camera by judicious framing, but Mario recognizes her; he calls her "darling." When Mario opens the door to his apartment, Bianchi zooms in on his face and then out again as he realizes the murderer (who initially poses no threat to him) is standing in his room. Later, the camera zooms in again on a glass of whiskey, which the killer is filling to the point of overflow; it zooms in again on Mario's suspicious face. The murder follows, a violent confrontation that plays out in handheld camerawork. However, when one of the models discovers Mario's body the next morning, the reveal feels very much like a traditional *giallo* zoom, with the camera adopting her point of view and then zooming in on the bloody body with its pants around its ankles.

Bianchi is at his most dynamic in one of the first major murders, a neat reversal of the shower sequence in *Psycho* that influenced so many of the *giallo* filmmakers and their American slasher cousins. Left alone in a house after a sexual encounter with Gisella (Amanda), Lucia (Femi Benussi) waits naked for her lover to return. An extended stalking sequence follows, inaugurated by a crash-zoom into a set of horizontal window blinds, behind which the killer presumably waits. This sequence is, at least on its surface, one of the most traditional in the film, following the stalking set piece template established by Bava and Argento and repeated by many others. However, Bianchi's knowing, self-conscious approach is playfully ironic. Lucia wanders through the house naked for the duration of the sequence, her vulnerability an exaggeration of the traditional stalking scenes that dominate *giallo* films. Bianchi likewise uses the zoom lens to exaggerated degree. After Gisella has gone and the killer begins to stalk Lucia, the zooms announce the murderer's presence. The front door creaks, and the camera zooms in on its fluttering while Lucia cautiously goes to inspect it. She finds nothing, but the camera zooms in once again when the faucet in the kitchen sink is mysteriously turned on and she goes to turn it off. The camera consistently zooms to reframe Lucia as she steps carefully through the empty house, in and out both to follow her as she walks and display the genre's penchant for gratuitous female nudity. Hearing the faucet in the master bathroom suddenly turn on, she moves to investigate it. Bianchi's camera is behind her as she moves up the two steps into the bedroom, then crashes in when she appears in the bedroom's distant mirror; it is as if, having suddenly lost sight of the nude woman, the camera must rush to keep its eye fixated on her. There is another quick zoom into the faucet as she steps into the bathroom to turn it off, and then before the camera has even really come to rest, an even faster crash-zoom-out as Lucia snaps around to her right, hearing something at the window. Bianchi cuts to a reverse shot of the slightly billowing curtain, the site of possible danger,

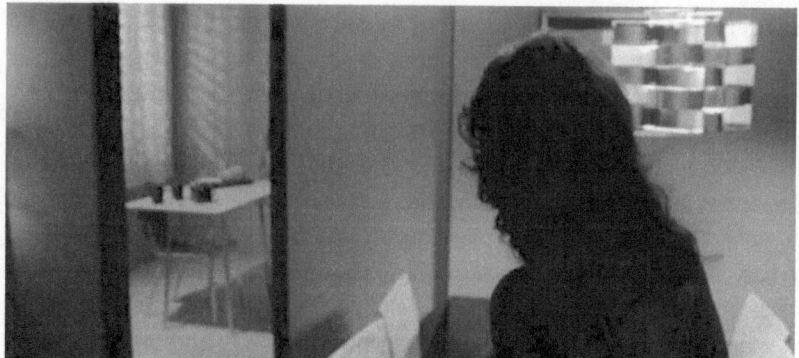

Figure 1. In *Strip Nude for Your Killer*'s most extended stalking-and-murder sequence, Andrea Bianchi's zooming camera follows the nude soon-to-be-victim Lucia (Femi Benussi) around her apartment.

in which the camera remains stable, back to the shocked Lucia, and then back to the curtain, suddenly zooming in on the black, tree-branch pattern woven into the white fabric.

Bianchi concludes the sequence with a knowing tribute to Hitchcock's *Psycho*, in which the murderer surprises Lucia while hiding in the shower. Bianchi reverses the danger: instead of Marion waiting in the shower while the murderer approaches from outside, Lucia backs up against the curtain, and the motorcyclist killer throws it aside, grabs her, and stabs her to death. However, Bianchi also employs the zoom lens to reference Hitchcock's *The Birds*, its famous approximation of a zoom lens with a series of progressively closer shots, cut together in rapid succession to simulate a pair of eyes quickly reacting to a shocking discovery. As Lucia backs away from the window in *Strip Nude for Your Killer*, she withdraws into the bathroom, moving closer to the shower where the unseen danger is hiding. In a series of shots and reverses, Bianchi captures Lucia's horrified reaction to the anticipatory danger behind the billowing curtain while, in shots from her point of view, uses the zoom lens to pull away from it. By the time Lucia has reached the shower, the camera has finished zooming away from the bedroom curtain: Lucia's fear has been focused on the wrong curtain, which the rapidly withdrawing zoom lens indicates. Bianchi restages Lucia's murder a few sequences later to comic effect, as his zoom lens tracks the stalking and killing of the nearly fully nude Maurizio (Franco Diogene), his heavyset, hairy body clad only in white briefs, in the same house; Bianchi uses a number of the same shots and the same drivers of tension, with faucets being turned on to lure the victim. Bianchi is subtly suggesting that *giallo* films are becoming rote, a simple and repeatable formula that involves nudity, violence, and zoom lenses.

Figure 2. Bianchi's zoom lens simultaneously delivers eroticism and violence throughout *Strip Nude for Your Killer*, but often does so with winking self-awareness.

Taken in total, *Strip Nude for Your Killer* feels like a radical experiment in zoom lens usage, an effort to see what happens when the zoom lens comes to stand in for a large range of cinematic effects: it replaces cuts, dollies, tracks, and montage. Like a number of *gialli*, *Strip Nude for Your Killer* is dominated by its formal properties. While its abundant zooms occasionally parody, they are indicative of the genre's propensity for excess. Lucia's murder typifies this excessive approach, with the stalking, the nudity, the violence, and the zoom usage all employed to exaggerated effect. *Strip Nude for Your Killer* is a pivotal film, coming as it does partway through the genre's life cycle, that illustrates how the zoom lens (among other *giallo* conventions) becomes a visual hallmark of the genre. Bianchi's use of the zoom shows generic imitation: he knows that in order to deliver *giallo* thrills, the zoom lens is a crucial element.

The zoom lens is an important formal signifier of *gialli*, alongside psychosexual themes and black-gloved killers as the films' conventions. Though frequently associated with the killers' points-of-view, the zoom lens also often encourages identification with victims. Olney (2013) argues, in the spirit of Carol Clover, that such techniques in Argento's work "destabilize the gendered viewing positions that often define the experience of watching horror cinema" (129). The same observation applies to numerous *gialli*, especially when the gendered identity of the killer is uncertain. Unlike Clover's argument about the deficient masculinity of killers in American horror films, the black-gloved killer in *giallo* films is often revealed to be a woman. The zoom lens is one of the genre's primary ways of calling gender boundaries into question. Laura Mulvey's influential argument about the masculine, phallic power of the cinematic apparatus through the "gaze" has often been applied to horror cinema (2001, 28–40); Mulvey herself, of course, used Hitchcock's cinema as one of her prime examples, notable because Hitchcock's influence shapes *gialli*.

At the same time, in a number of *gialli*, the presence of a female killer complicates the "gaze" considerably, especially in films where two murderers work in tandem. It is often unclear which of the murderers, the man or the woman, the camera inhabits for any given sequence, especially when the ethereal, geographically transgressive zoom lens is used. This complicates *gialli*'s "overt sensationalism and apparent misogyny" (Olney, 2013, 104); in many cases, the camera itself is actually embodying a female look and commands the spectator's subjectivity through the authoritative enunciation of the zoom.[7] Though the zoom might be used as evidence of the genre's depravity and misogyny, the sheer number of zoom lens shots throughout the *gialli* demonstrate that such a reading oversimplifies. Complex, ironic uses of the zoom in films like *Strip Nude for Your Killer* demonstrate that a number of filmmakers working in *gialli* thought a lot about how their films looked, even though the zoom lens was a cost-saving measure. *Gialli* reflect an unstable world where nothing is as it seems, a worldview underlined by their reliance on the shifting point of view afforded by the zoom lens.

Notes

1. See especially the chapter on *Psycho* in William Rothman, *Hitchcock: The Murderous Gaze* (Cambridge, MA: Harvard University Press, 1982).
2. "The tidal wave of zoom shots that appeared in feature films from the mid-1960s onward has often been attributed to the introduction of the Angenieux 10:1 zoom lens."
3. "In the pages of trade periodicals, the zoom was an inherently dangerous tool, prone to exposing the show-off tendencies of inexperienced camera operators."
4. See *The Editor* (Adam Brooks and Matthew Kennedy, 2014) and *Knife+Heart* (Yann Gonzalez, 2018).
5. "Literally translating as vein (or thread), it is best conceptualized as a trend or a current. In filmic terms, a keen awareness of commercially popular *filone* meant that producers would look to see what genre was current and try to exploit its popularity."
6. According to Koven, "approximately 1970 until 1975."
7. An important caveat: most, if not all, *gialli* directors in the classic period of the cycle are male. A truly female look, in both the characters and the directors, is impossible to discern because no examples exist.

Works Cited

Baschiera, Stefano, and Russ Hunter. 2016. "Introduction." In *Italian Horror Cinema*, edited by Stefano Baschiera and Russ Hunter, 1–14. Edinburgh, Scotland: Edinburgh University Press.

Belton, John. 1980–81. "The Bionic Eye: Zoom Esthetics." *Cineaste* 11, no. 1 (Winter): 20–27. http://www.jstor.org/stable/41686042?origin=JSTOR-pdf.

Bondanella, Peter. 2009. *A History of Italian Cinema*. New York: Bloomsbury Academic.

Bordwell, David. 1997. *On the History of Film Style*. Cambridge, MA: Harvard University Press.

Di Chiara, Francesco. 2016. "Domestic Films Made for Export: Modes of Production of the 1960s Italian Horror Film." In *Italian Horror Cinema*, edited by Stefano Baschiera and Russ Hunter, 30–44. Edinburgh, Scotland: Edinburgh University Press.

Hall, Nick. 2018. *The Zoom: Drama at the Touch of a Lever*. New Brunswick, NJ: Rutgers University Press.

Koven, Mikel J. 2006. *La Dolce Morte: Vernacular Cinema and the Italian Giallo Film*. Lanham, MD: Scarecrow Press.

Landy, Marcia. 2016. "The Argento Syndrome: Aesthetics of Horror." In *Italian Horror Cinema*, edited by Stefano Baschiera and Russ Hunter, 93–-10. Edinburgh, Scotland: Edinburgh University Press.

Lowenstein, Adam. 2016. "The *Giallo*/Slasher Landscape: *Ecologia Del Delitto*, *Friday the 13th* and Subtractive Spectatorship." In *Italian Horror Cinema*, edited by Stefano Baschiera and Russ Hunter, 127–44. Edinburgh, Scotland: Edinburgh University Press.

McDonagh, Maitland. 1994. *Broken Mirrors/Broken Minds: The Dark Dreams of Dario Argento*. New York: Citadel Press.

Mulvey, Laura. 2001. "Visual Pleasure and Narrative Cinema." In *Issues in Feminist Film Criticism*, edited by Patricia Erens, 28–40. Bloomington: Indiana University Press.

Nelson, Thomas Allen. 1986. "Through a Shifting Lens: Realist Film Aesthetics." *Film Criticism* 11, nos. 1–2 (Fall–Winter): 133–43. http://www.jstor.org/stable/44075783.

O'Brien, Adam. 2012. "When a Film Remembers Its Filming: The New Hollywood Zoom." *Journal of Media Practice*, no. 13 (September): 227–23. http://dx.doi.org/10.1386/jmpr.13.3.227_1.

Olney, Ian. 2013. *EuroHorror: Classic European Horror Cinema in Contemporary American Culture*. Bloomington: Indiana University Press.

Rothman, William. 1982. *Hitchcock: The Murderous Gaze*. Cambridge, MA: Harvard University Press.

Chapter 2

ARGENTO'S EVIL EYE

Movements, Containments, and the *Giallo*'s Possessive Gaze

ÉMILIE VON GARAN

Gary Needham's introduction on the *giallo*, written in 2002 for *KinoEye*, "begins from the assumption that the *giallo* is not so much a genre, as its literary history might indicate, but a body of films that resists generic definition."[1] While different from the Italian horror and *poliziotto* (police) genres, it can and should nonetheless be understood as an object worthy of scholarly engagement. Turning to what has arguably been defined as the "first true *giallo*," *La ragazza che sapeva troppo* (*The Girl Who Knew Too Much*, 1963; released as *The Evil Eye* in the US) directed by Mario Bava, Needham describes the opening sequence in which Nora Davis (Letícia Román) reads a *giallo* novel on an airplane. For Needham (2002), this scene represents what is "essentially a foundational gesture" culminating into the quintessential narrative elements of these films; namely the figure of the foreigner in Italy, the "obsession with travel and tourism," and the use of famous tourist landmarks from the murder on the Spanish Steps in Bava's film to the "countless deaths in or around famous squares, fountains and monuments throughout the *giallo*." The departure from its literary origins, which mainly consisted of imported translations of detective fictions like the Sherlock Holmes series, towards the emergence of the cinematic *giallo* during the "Golden Age" of Italian cinema in the 1960s, enabled a reconfiguration of the genre's previous models of rational thought and logical deduction based on their early British and American counterparts. The *giallo* reconfigures the detective novel; it moves from the rationality of the intellectual work performed by the detective to the libidinal impulses of the *giallo* killers and the "instinctive" sleuthing of the accidental witness-cum-detective. Bava's *La ragazza che sapeva troppo* also illustrates the genre's obsession with vision, which led to the rise of *testimone oculare* films, or eyewitness films, in which the protagonist witnesses a crime and reluctantly becomes amateur detective trying to unravel the mysteries of these events. Yet it is Argento's *L'uccello dalle piume di cristallo* (*The Bird with the Crystal Plumage*, 1970), in its insistence on an anti-rational logic as well as the dynamic between vision and knowledge, that arguably exploded the *giallo*'s conventions.

In his analysis of *L'uccello dalle piume di cristallo*, Frank Burke (2002) opened up a new direction in Argento scholarship whereby the forms of "social domination" through the motifs of "encagement, exploitation and compulsive accumulation," read as a representation of "colonial themes and references." Contemplating and expanding Burke's analysis of a colonial presence within the film, especially as it relates to the *giallo*'s urban locale, my engagement considers the role of the gaze in shaping movements and how this practice can be conceived of as an embodied act of translating the city. The recurrent motif of containment in Argento's cinema is considered alongside mobility, understood first as a movement, but also in its broader definition by thinking through the protagonist's position as an outsider within the diegesis. Mobility is apprehended not only through its symbolic aspects, notably through the development of an imaginary mobility, but also via the spatial navigation within these narratives as well. Specifically, the use of glass at once transparent and porous, reveals via the gaze not only the ways in which the built environment contrives and shapes movement, but how it utilizes what is "see-though" to generate an opacity through which the insidious is uncovered. This essay studies the symbolic phenomena of containment and mobility in these narratives, focusing on the manner in which Argento enunciates a discourse that rests on an act of translation of the specter of colonial histories—a term used in this context as not implying the past, but rather implicating the present.

Postcolonial theorist Ken Gelder articulated the important connection between the post- and the de-colonial and "horror *per se*." Gelder points out that, while postcolonial scholars seem more preoccupied with a higher brow form of culture, "[the] tropes of horror—spectralization, the return of the repressed, uncanny (mis)recognitions, possession (and dispossession), excess, the 'monstrousness' of hybridity—have often lent a certain structural logic to postcolonial studies," citing Homi Bhabha as an obvious choice. Despite the important nuances and differences between horror and the *giallo*, I propose a strong resonance between the two and embrace a position that aligns itself with Gelder's in this essay. Specifically, I take up Gelder's call to consider the ways in which "horror's central trope of circulation takes on new qualities" in the work of Argento, which ultimately enables "interrogations of the borders and boundaries (and especially the 'post-') of postcolonialism itself" by mapping the unfolding of "'reverse colonization' narrative[s]" (2001, 35–36).

The tourist gaze and the evil eye open up the possibility to engage with the sites and sights of collection within Argento's cinema before moving to the dynamic relationship between movements and containments. The tourist gaze here refers to a mode of looking that consumes the city, a destructive gaze produced by a set of expectations and desires projected onto the other. The evil eye, on the other hand, becomes a theoretical shorthand that speaks to a different type of consuming gaze, one that is at once reflective and reflexive of the colonial aspects at the heart of the desire for containment which animates these films. This final component of my textual analysis of Argento's *L'uccello dalle piume di cristallo* reifies the presence of colonial elements of the film and the need for a post-colonial mode of engagement with the *giallo*. While I contend that Argento does not explicitly engage in a critique of colonialism in this film, he does show an "intuitive sense of its presence, particularly insofar as it links to other things that the film seems more insistent about (hence the obliqueness of some of the colonial references)" (Burke 2002). For this reason, Argento's *Tenebrae* (1982), a return to form twelve years after his debut feature, is read through the same analytical lens in an attempt to extend these considerations to other Argento films, enabling the tracing of a lineage of thought and practice, which I believe can assist in uncovering the colonial within his and others' *gialli*.

Giallo Gazes and Tourism: Translating the City

Space, place, and time are central concepts to this engagement. At the heart of this engagement is the following question: what happens in spaces and temporalities within which mobility is not a simple, secondary effect of urbanity, but rather participates in characterizing it via the outsider's gaze?

For Iain Chambers "to think of the modern city [. . .] is to experience a perpetual translating machine" because cities are not only sites of "cultural encounters," they are also "precisely where the outside world pushes into our interiors to propose immediate proximities." The language of the city, a translating and translated space, extends far beyond the realm of the linguistic "[for] what is being 'spoken' in a mixture of asymmetrical powers is precisely the intricate accumulation of historical encounters established in the conjunctural syntax of a particular urban formation" (2011, 27). This has led me to posit that mobility and the gaze should be conceived as a dynamic and productive embodiment of the processes of translation identified by Chambers. I argue that Dario Argento, lauded by critics and scholars alike as the master of contemporary nightmares and Italian cityscapes, through his unique use of space enables such a reading and further opens up the possibility of attending to the conceptual dimensions of these films as to account for colonialism within these narratives. Specifically, I turn to the use of glass to think through opacity and transparency, not only in relation to vision, but in keeping with Chambers's "translated city" whereby the city's architecture is understood as transcending the neutrality of geometrically determined and physically defined structures and enclosures. A site of lived life, the built environment is where cultural processes, gendered transactions, and modus of sociopolitical anxieties are continually enacted.

Departing from John Urry's concept of the tourist gaze,[2] which expresses the dynamics associated with the construction of the tourist experience, as well as the complex organization of tourism and the systematic nature of its processes, this particular way of seeing becomes an appendage of mobility within the *giallo*'s urban setting. Here, tourism as an activity should be clarified, as well as the distinction between tourist as an identity and tourism as an act. If the tourist is often defined as someone who has temporarily traveled to another place, the very experience of tourism involves a period of "transition and discontinuity from the everyday world" (Turner, Turner, Carroll 2005, 294). We can therefore conceive of the tourist as a mode of being as well, one regulated by a set of actions and behaviors prescribed by the position of outsider. For Urry, the act of tourism amounts to "a leisure activity which presupposes its opposite, namely regulated and organized work. It is one manifestation of how work and leisure are organized as separate and regulated spheres of social practice in 'modern' societies" (1990, 2). Through this, his concept of the "tourist gaze" emerges; the environments within which this activity takes place become subject to this specific way of seeing. This regulated and regulating tourism emphasizes features of the landscape that further reifies the separation felt from the everyday experience. While this can effectively create a sense of alienation, it is rather in its ability to produce the extra-ordinary that Urry takes up. He writes:

> Places are chosen to be gazed upon because there is an anticipation, especially through daydreaming and fantasy, of intense pleasures, either on a different scale or involving different senses from those customarily encountered. Such anticipation is constructed and sustained

through a variety of non-tourist practices, such as film, TV, literature, magazines, records and videos, which construct and reinforce that gaze. (1990, 3)

Urry's concept therefore becomes a useful tool to articulate the manipulation of the tourist and their viewpoints in such a way that the gaze is reflective and reflexive of fantasies and expectations. Despite this gaze being most often understood as originating from a static location, it nonetheless can be mobile, for example when it is directed from insular space like the window of a train. Such environments ensure that the tourist only visually accesses what they are supposed to. Urry explains, "the typical tourist experience is [. . .] to see named scenes through a frame, such as the hotel window, the car windscreen or the window of the coach" (1990, 100). In other words, this radically different positioning ensures that the visual experience is mediated by a decidedly touristic form of vision. The suspension of reality, a vacation from the mundane, engenders a gaze which enacts a mode of viewing aligned with the cinematic.

The *giallo* is arguably the opposite; the gaze forces upon the protagonist a violent confrontation with a reality. However, considering a more nuanced approach, I would further argue that the gaze as it relates to spectatorship cannot be ignored. As such, locating fantasy and the suspension of reality becomes a complex task, as untangling this aspect of the relationship between the *giallo* and the tourist gaze requires a careful consideration of these dynamics. For Amy Corbin, the notion of cinema spectatorship itself can be thought of as a travel experience. The fundamental otherness of cinematic space enables, for Corbin, the spectator to at once experience "something distinct from their norm and the comfort of protection from this difference"[3] (2014, 314). What she identifies as a "dynamic of contained otherness" enabled by the cinematic aligns itself with the travel experience central to the notion of tourism and, as such facilitates the acceptance of questioning of the tourist gaze. Simply put, this mobile gaze provides an experience rooted in a movement that is not unlike that of the cinematic spectator. The *giallo*'s failure of the gaze provides further ground for analysis. Deception and detection are at the heart of that which drives spatial navigation. The consumption of the city, itself predicated on alienation and investigation, is mapped onto the various networks, articulations, and tensions it seeks to exorcise.

The criticism levied at Urry's concept that its emphasis on the visual fails to fully capture the tourist experience, interestingly aligns itself with the gaze mobilized in Argento's *gialli*, and arguably many others. I choose here

Figure 1. The modern art gallery of *L'uccello dalle piume di cristallo* (Argento, 1970), filled with hybrid sculptures and artifacts.

to present the tourist gaze alongside the evil eye, which generally defined is a gaze that is believed, superstitiously, to cause material harm. This becomes for me a way to articulate what I perceive as a more insidious appendage of the tourist gaze: the desire to capture. The interconnection between anthropology and art history is far from a tenuous one. David L. Hume (2013), in his genealogy of the tourist gaze, turns to art in order to clarify the material culture of tourism. The "collection of material artifacts" of visited or conquered cultures is a habit which "predates modern and contemporary tourism." For Hume, material culture was effectively changed "under the pressure of tourist gaze." Hume's analysis strengthens the intricate connection between tourism and collection. Furthermore, it elucidates the intertwined nature of a decidedly othered gaze and the arts. In other words, the activities of colonial expansion, collection, and tourism are mutually constitutive. The sights and sites of collection central to *L'uccello dalle piume di cristallo*, a gallery filled with colonial art and artifacts, are further developed later in this analysis (see image 1).

The tension between the gaze and the grotesque in the films of Argento is clearly predicated on voyeuristic and scopophilic modes of looking and seeing. Within these films, the pleasure achieved through the act of looking is derived not only from the objectification of what is being looked at, which leads to the treatment of the other as an object to be appraised, but from the anticipation of the danger emanating from this object as well. It is unknown, unknowable, and threatening. In Argento's cinema, the potential accomplishment of its knowledge and possession is thwarted by the deception of the gaze. Furthermore, the purposeful violation and/or penetration of boundaries and borders through the gaze for cinematic effect extends to the eye itself. Ocular violence, while being common in the *giallo*, is taken to an extreme level in the films of Argento. According to Ellen Victoria Nerenberg, "[t]he consequences of witnessing violence and the trauma of wounded vision is so common a trope of Argento's work that Fabio Maiello entitled his 1996 collection of interviews with Argento *L'occhio che uccide* (the assassinating eye)" (2012, 77). I instead propose that the evil eye and the tourist gaze, competing systems of vision within the dynamic relationship between seeing and not seeing, become a porous interstice whereby the literary origin of the genre, as well as its ties to imperialism and colonialism, can be explored. Hardt and Negri define colonialism as "an abstract machine that produces alterity and identity," cautioning us that "in the colonial situation these differences and identities are made to function as if they were absolute, essential, and natural" (2000, 129). The terms "colonial" and "colonialism" operate in this essay as not only theoretical shorthand to speak of a historical reality, but also, in keeping with Burke (2002), to articulate "a general tendency to relate to the world and the Other via control and subjection" which he relates to the "psychology of domination." This, I argue, can be extended to broader concerns so that the variegated political investments which shape filmic architecture can become an opening towards a more profound mediation on land itself. After all, "Argento's films point to violence indigenous to Italian locales" (Nerenberg 2012, 73). The potential power of space to embody horror cannot be divorced from its ties to the structural logic of colonial violence. The evil house, for example, has long been presented as a durational space—is wickedness laying in its very construction, embedded into its foundation. Through the theme of domestic architecture, I seek to demonstrate the emotional intertwining with and the power of cinematic illustrations of space, place, and architecture to clarify their role in articulating modern anxieties.

Film space can be conceived as providing a generative environment in which to explore the possibilities of transference. Since directors are able to practice architecture without the rules and regulations of gravity and daily life, film architecture becomes an architecture of meaning (I echo here the architectural historian Helmut Weihsmann). Because of this, film becomes an accessible medium for exploring embodied architecture where space and place are created solely for cinematic effect. Film space, therefore, becomes fundamentally an emotional space since it has the ability to render the invisible visible, whilst translating the functions of architecture into emotion and releasing the flux that is suppressed in the inert constructions of the real world. Film is perhaps an avenue through which one can experiment with the blurring of these distinct boundaries. Jean-François Lyotard writes:

The film is the organic body of cinematographic movements. It is the ecclesia of images: just as politics is that of the partial social organs. This is why direction, a technique of exclusions and effacements, a political activity par excellence, and political activity, which is direction par excellence, are the religion of modern irreligion, the ecclesiastic of the secular. The central problem for both is not the representational arrangement and its accompanying question, that of knowing how and what to represent and the definition of good or true representation; the fundamental problem is the exclusion and foreclosure of all that is judged unrepresentable because non-recurrent. (1986, 355)

For Lyotard, "Acinema" indicates that film direction, or aesthetic intentionality, and the political are at once governed by and working according to prescribed sets of rules and principles, but above all exclusions. In this sense, we could perhaps also say that political activity, like film direction, is an aesthetic act that involves the interruption of the invisible into spaces of visibility.

Gary Needham argues that while the dynamics between vision and knowledge are central to the *giallo*, it is "never to such great effect as in Argento's *L'uccello dale piume di cristallo*," in which American writer and *flaneur* Sam Dalmas (Tony Musante) who lives in Rome with his girlfriend Julia (Suzy Kendall), witnesses an attempted murder in an art gallery. The mysterious figure is thought to be an infamous serial killer. For Needham (2002),

> [the] gallery is explicitly concerned with maximizing clarity and vision: the space is minimal so there are no distractions for the gaze other than that of the crime; the doors/façade are enormous glass panels; nothing is obscured; the entire area is brightly lit. However, despite all of these supports aiding Dalmas's vision, he fails to see (or in psychoanalytic terms, he *misrecognizes*) the truth of his gaze.

Configuring Dalmas, his gaze and his movements, within Chambers's model of the translated city begins "[b]eyond the obvious threshold of translation inaugurated by the arrival of the other, the stranger" whereby he is "invariably called upon to transform" his history, culture, and understanding from which emerges the "disquieting insistence" that he too finds himself translated (2011, 28). Dalmas's movement is erratic and fails to follow the prescribed way of navigating the city. Rational movement, predicated on the "closed, idealist and metaphysical imperative—the idea of 'beauty,' the 'order' of reason, the 'rationality' of the plan, the stable 'meaning' of the discourse—is transferred into the turbulent, opened syntactical turmoil of a quotidian event" (2011, 29). Despite his position of Other and his resistance to prescribed modes of exploration, the moments of contemplation within his navigation of the city arise from the encounter with the gallery, a space of collection created for the purpose of satisfying the demands of the gaze. A rhythm emerges through the shifting dynamisms of containments and moments of *flânerie* that departs from other *gialli* set in the city. For Chambers,

> [i]f rhythm is about a regulated movement, it is clearly of an order separate from the linear flatness produced by the ocular and spatial organization of chronologies and maps. Rhythms can change. They pick up further accidents, grow emphatic and fade away. Rhythm promotes a constant return that engenders difference. Rhythm is of the body, of the historical body, of the history that produces the body and in turn is appropriated by the body. (2011, 119–20)

By bringing into the field of vision the ways in which movements and modes of mobilities within the diegetic construction of Italy as a place and space of tourism and tourist consumption, patterns emerge. This facilitates the articulation of the kinetic energy of the tourist's gaze. Such patterns betray the posture of distance adopted by Dalmas due to his position as a foreigner which necessitates a reacquaintance with space, place, and their material traces.

From the Tourist Gaze to the Evil Eye: Sites and Sights of Collection

The conceptual depth of *L'uccello dalle piume di cristallo* is often undervalued, yet in their outright denial of the sanctity of boundaries and borders whether they be bodily, architectural, or national, I identify a rich theoretical seam. Extending the colonial elements of the film past the themes of encagement and collection identified by Burke, who argues that victimization is enabled by the ways in which these modes of relationship also regulate the characters' interaction within the diegesis, I turn to the architectural use of glass to argue that every act of representation within the film should be interpreted as a simultaneous act of repression.

Interestingly, Burke turns to the correspondence between Ranieri's highrise apartment and the zoo—a "vertical arrangement of cages," as well as Consalvi's "cathouse"—"a barn in the country from which he has eliminated all access except via a ladder from a second-story window" (or another cage), to further indicate the tension between entrapment and self-containment he previously identifies. As such, Sam and Julia's apartment is at once a cage and a fortress, a trap and a sanctuary. Therein lies what Burke identifies as the subtlest yet most significant aspect of his analysis: "people encage themselves." This is reflective of Burke's use of the titular bird as a central element of his analysis as it encapsulates this argument. Not only does he translate the name of the bird with the crystal plumage, "Caucaso," to mean Caucasian, he proposes that it should be understood as a stand-in for "Whiteness" too. This leads him to argue that the most "striking example" of self-containments are provided by the killers as they don themselves in black vinyl, "a patent leather 'skin' in a radical denaturing of the self similar to that suggested by the glass feathers." He adds that it "is in this world of people radically dissociated from themselves and their world, both agents and victims of colonizing impulses, that violence, explodes" (2002). Yet, the most poignant moment of containment remains Sam's entrapment within the art gallery's glass doors.

In this moment of complicit architecture, reflective of Argento's spatial practices, the glass becomes a porous border which I read as the representation of a moment of translation. The urban locale within the diegesis reveals the space as a sight and site that conjures a "transitory exposure (Heidegger's *aletheia* or revealing), a breach in the predictable tissues of a cultural and critical discourse is temporarily achieved" (2011, 29). As the opening scene of the film, the movement that takes place here happens on two levels: first diegetically, but also through the spectator's entrance into the diegesis. This moment facilitates an understanding of buildings as mechanisms of representation, and as such, political and ideological. Stuck between the panes of glass, Dalmas is simultaneously situated as both the colonized and the colonizer. Encaged in glass despite his desire to intervene; to colonize, Dalmas finds himself impotent, his own actions having rendered him silent, helpless, and unable to participate in the violent scene unfolding before his eyes. Inside and outside therefore form a dialectics of division, hostile in their opposition and polarized in their attributes. Rather than prescriptive, the dialectic is productive. It is therefore paramount to think through the mobilization and articulation of containment from the art gallery of *L'uccello dalle piume di cristallo* to the house of *Tenebrae*. While the tourist, a subject, also finds himself contained within the gallery, the glass house reveals that it is the correlation between subject and object that should be privileged.

As previously mentioned, the gallery houses colonial art and artifacts; it also becomes the backdrop for the unfolding of the first act of violence within the film, which in turn leads to the first moment of containment. The

Figure 2. The glass house of *Tenebrae* (Argento, 1982), surrounded by a lush tropical garden, is home to journalist Cristiano Berti. The architectural elements heighten a sense of voyeurism and paranoia. Porous borders, they enable observation, but also reflection.

film features many other elements which Burke identifies as strengthening this reading, such as the Native American painting[4] in Sam and his girlfriend Julia's apartment that, rather than being hanged, sits on a sofa until it is replaced by a photo linked to the serial killer. For Burke (2002), "[l]ike the society from which it derives, the painting signifies pure expendability to Euro-American culture." There are some speculations that it is based on Pieter Bruegel's *Hunters in the Snow* (1565). The film was inspired by Frederic Brown's novel *The Screaming Mimi* (1949). In the book, the work of art that enables the solving of the mystery is a small, mass-produced sculpture of a screaming women rather than a painting. While Argento chooses a painting over a statue, the film still prominently features sculpture, which is later referenced in *Tenebrae*. The departure from this aspect of the narrative is worthy of being mined, as it enables a textual connection with Bava's *5 bambole per la luna d'agosto* (1970), loosely based on Agatha Christie's *And Then They Were None* (first published in 1939 as *Ten Little N----rs*, and then *Ten Little Indians* before it acquired its new, less offensive title). Bava's film also features what I argue is a gaze alignment with Argento's *Tenebrae* via the use of a glass house (see image 2).

Argento produces and reproduces opacity through his use of the glass, a reflective and reflexive material, in two instances: the art gallery of *L'uccello dalle piume di cristallo* and the glass house of *Tenebrae*. The shift from the public to the domestic produces an opening for a contemplation of the meaning of such a relocation. The realm of the domestic is not exempt of the exposure to and confrontation with violence. On the contrary, it becomes a space within which a violent externalization of the unconscious unfolds. For this reason, I argue, the spatialization of the return of the repressed in Argento's cinema lends itself to an analysis centered on the very colonial logic I seek to extricate. From uncanny (mis)recognition to the themes of possession and dispossession—often key to the killer's motive, as well as the "monstrousness" of their hybridity—they all demand a translation as to begin to articulate the necessity for such engagements. The uncanny correspondence between the architecture and the characters within the films of Argento has been well established. However, little reflection has been done on the ways in which the built environment and those who operate within it are mutually constitutive and constructed. There is a clear attempt to bury or hide within these interior spaces, whether they be physical and metaphorical. Operating at the level of the unconscious, such traumatic defamiliarizations are nonetheless telling, especially as they relate to concealment or purposeful obscuring of a story or history so that it might be forgotten. Yet, far from being irreducible, this opacity participates in the pleasurable aspects of the *giallo*.

The Urban Island: From Movement to Containments

In *Tenebrae*, American writer Peter Neal (Anthony Franciosa), while in Rome on a promotional tour for his latest novel, finds himself entangled in a brutal series of murders when a serial killer seems to find inspiration for his brutal killings from Neal's books. With the help of his assistant Anne (Daria Nicolodi) and young local Gianni (Christian Borromeo), Neal begins to investigate. Neal's movement through space provides yet another contrast to *L'Uccello dalle piume di cristallo*'s protagonist. Whereas Dalmas wanders through the city, aimlessly exploring Rome through a mode of navigation that aligns itself with the cinema of Antonioni, Fellini, or even Bertolucci, Neal moves with purpose. As such, he represents a departure from the other foreigners of Argento's *gialli*. Despite this, both Dalmas and Neal embody the sensations produced by the landscapes through which they move in keeping with Argento's articulation of space.

The theme of collection, much more violent here, centers around female victims rather than colonial objects, and the references to Agatha Christie and Arthur Conan Doyle, as well as the gaze alignment with Bava's *5 bambole per la luna d'agosto* through the act of stalking, provide more textual clues as to what could potentially be read as a gesturing to a colonial presence. A return to form for Argento, *Tenebrae* is set in the future. The result is a city which features a strange "architectural landscape" that becomes, for

McDonagh, a "key element in differentiating *Tenebrae* from Argento's earlier *gialli*," namely the use of "unusual architectural spaces" which create a visual "hyper-realism" that renders the environment all the more artificial. Citing an interview with the filmmaker in which he explains that he "dreamed an imaginary city in which the most amazing things happen," she regards that the film's "fictive space couldn't be less 'real,'" with its "vast unpopulated boulevards, piazzas that look like nothing more than suburban American malls, hard-edged Bauhaus apartment buildings, anonymous clubs and parking garages" (1994, 166). Furthermore, the move from Rome to its suburbs not only gives the film its desired—Kim Newman and Alan Jones (2011) term it "futuristic"—aesthetics, but also enables a fascinating dislocation and relocation of the glass house which facilitates a consideration of its significance within the genre. The home, surrounded by a luscious garden, brings to mind Hume's point that the period of heightened colonial collection coincides with the "rise of botanical gardens and menageries packed with exotic flora and fauna" (2013). More than a simple house, the glass house becomes an extra-textual object which reveals, through its location, a deeply buried past.

Loosely based on Agatha Christie's *And Then There Were None* (1939), Bava's film follows an unseen murderer who terrorizes an inventor and his guests, a group of investors, as they vacation on an island. A key aspect of Christie's novel is precisely that the violence is perpetrated on British soil. While the need to change the original title due to its offensive nature might appear obvious, literary critic and feminist scholar Alison Light argues that the title and setting of the novel, "N----r Island"[5] (later "Indian Island" and then "Soldier Island"), are integral to the work. For Alison Light, these elements "could be relied upon automatically to conjure up a thrilling 'otherness,' a place where revelations about the 'dark side' of the English would be appropriate." She adds that "Christie's location is both more domesticated and privatized, taking for granted the construction of racial fears woven into psychic life as early as the nursery. If her story suggests how easy it is to play upon such fears, it is also a reminder of how intimately tied they are to sources of pleasure and enjoyment" (1991, 91). Thus, the transposition of the glass house from the island to the Roman suburb becomes a key component of my reading of the inter-textual references within *Tenebrae*. Further to this point, as Chambers writes,

> Against a grade zero of history inaugurated by the West, its languages, disciplines, technologies and political economy, it is ethically and aesthetically possible to pose the historical heterogeneity of what persistently precedes and exceeds such a singular and unilateral framing of

time and space. In translating abstract coordinates into worldly concerns they become both multiple and mutable. In the situated realization of symbolic artifacts—the "house," the "square," the "building," the "street"—a complex historical provenance is pronounced in the shifting syntagms of an ultimately planetary frame. (2011, 29)

The glass house is no longer a simply a glass house, it becomes coordinates on which the contemplation of a colonial presence within the *giallo*, more specifically Argento's *giallo*. *Tenebrae* is set in the "manicured suburbs of Casalpalocco, a posh residential development on the southwestern edge of the city [...] and "constructed in 1962 as Italy's first 'planned community' and 'garden city.'" In addition, Casalpalocco is a "literal concretization of power, force, and violence" (2014, 9). As Siegel explains, it was intended as a "suburban simulacrum of Imperial Rome, putting under violent erasure not only the cutters of history between Imperial and Fascist eras but also any future (non-fascist) social formations" (2014, 23).

The image of the island thus extends far beyond the inter-textual potential references to Bava or Christie. Island ecologies, specifically, as they often serve as utopian sites for humans to test new world models, or as (un)natural immune systems, whose framing power offers protection from mainland living processes and factors that cannot be easily managed, further gestures to the relationship between the land and the Italian body politic.

It Came from Within

The loss of peace and protection is often at the heart of Argento's horror. It manifests as a nightmare where the loss of control over that which was once perceived as safe is the very thing that threatens. Such representations of architecture become a fundamental way to examine what happens when the spaces we build, especially those that operate within the realm of the domestic, turn on us. The *giallo*'s insistence on the urban locale amplifies the contrast between the lacking archaic Other, and the modern city, which should be considered for what it has and therefore represents: civility.

Ultimately this essay exists at the intersection of Italian *giallo* cinema, postcolonial theory, and the complicated operation of the gaze in these narratives. The reflection is enabled by the mobile subject that is the protagonist and a gaze which, in participating in the translation of the city, reveals the specters of colonialism in Italian society manifested in the *giallo*. The production of architectural fantasies achieved through the use of glass in these two films, I argue, both relate to reality and attempt to shape it. The fact that Argento's films demand "close watching" in order to appreciate their narrative and philosophical foundations arguably makes them riper for philosophical inquiries than perhaps other typical *gialli*. Furthermore, they coincide with the initiation of the de-colonialization process in Italy, a period spanning approximately twenty years—from 1955 to 1975, an aspect which has received little to no attention in the existing literature. Italian de-colonization was fairly precocious given that the loss of effective control over the country's colonies was the result of its military defeat in the Second World War. The aftermath of this abrupt end to Italy's colonial reign and empire repressed this history, which for Nicola Labanca can be attributed to the country being a fascist empire in its colonial era, "[burdening] the collective memory and contributed to a long conspiracy of silence" (2015, 120). While Labanca stresses the denial, or rather refusal, of Italy to engage with its somber history, Italian history scholar Pamela Ballinger (2019) pushes back against such claims, highlighting the ways in which the trauma of decolonization was processed in cinema.[6] For Sandra Waters, Argento's films should be contextualized within their cultural milieu, and as such, be understood as a "visual counterpoint to the social upheavals of the 1960s and 1970s [in Italy]" (2015, 159).

In his review of *L'uccello dalle piume di cristallo*, Frank Collins turns to Andrea Bini, who, in the book *Popular Italian Cinema: Culture and Politics in a Postwar Society*, notes that Argento sensed the social and political changes affecting Italy at the end of the 1960s, marked by student protests, strikes, terrorism, and countercultural political movements and situated his narratives in "cities that were unmistakably Italian" and where "communities had undergone such rapid growth and change that they had become unfamiliar and threatening places" (2011, 54). This trope is not only recurrent but perfected in Argento's cinema. Expanding on Chambers's consideration of cinema "as a means of memory" (2011, 120) by turning to Argento's films, I argue that these movements and rhythms can be conceived as the embodied practice of translation whereby the uncanny correspondence between Chambers's "translated city" and Argento's spatial practices lead me to propose, later on, an unearthing of the colonial present within these films. Burke's discussion of the "presence of colonialist themes and references in *L'uccello dalle piume di cristallo*," which he defines as "encagement, exploitation and compulsive accumulation" thus becomes the underlying thread which animates subsequent engagements with the role of the gaze in shaping mobility in these films.

This re-examination of colonial dynamics initiated by the call of scholars of the post- and de-colonial to consider the intersection of their scholarship with the field of horror, sought to untangle the claustrophobic, controlling, and dreamy dimensions of Argento's architecture with broader societal issues. I can appreciate a certain resistance to judging these films by what we would consider today's established norms of philosophical film theorization and criticism, yet would argue that time has transfigured what was long viewed as inconsequential decisions or references on the part of the filmmaker. But what I propose is not an indictment of Argento or the *giallo*, but rather an invitation to consider what an engagement that takes into consideration the colonial question might bring to the surface.

Notes

1. The essay was subsequently edited and republished in *The Cult Film Reader*, eds. Ernest Mathijs and Xavier Mendik (Maidenhead/Berkshire: Open University Press/McGraw-Hill Education, 2008), 294–300.

2. Alexia Kannas also explores the question of the tourist gaze via Urry, looking at Mario Bava's *La ragazza che sapeva troppo* and Dario Argento's *L'uccello dalle piume di cristallo*, in her chapter "Strolling the Streets: Tourists and *Flâneurs* in the Late-Modern City" in *Giallo!: Genre, Modernity, and Detection in Italian Horror Cinema* (Albany: State University of New York Press, 2020).

3. Corbin stresses the otherness of cinematic space, articulating cinema's "contained otherness that allows the spectator both the thrill of experiencing something distinct from one's norm and the comfort of protection from this difference." This aspect, which Corbin ties to spectatorship, offers a renewed entry point into the issues presented in this essay.

4. Alexandra Heller-Nicholas dedicates a chapter ("Chapter 6: Misreading Clues") to the function of painting in Dario Argento's *L'uccello dalle piume di cristallo* and *Profondo Rosso* in *The Giallo Canvas: Art, Excess and Horror Cinema* (Jefferson, NC: McFarland and Company, 2021).

5. Not censored in the original text.

6. Italy's particular relationship to its colonial past, and more broadly, colonialism itself is explored in its relationship to cinema by Pamela Ballinger who reflects on the "traumatic effects" of decolonization on the people of Italy by complicating the "frequently resort to the language of 'amnesia,' 'silences,' and 'forgetting'" to postulate a void left by decolonization in the Italian metropole." Looking to postwar Italian cinema, she takes issue with its frequent characterization as a "[failing] to deal directly with decolonization." Pamela Ballinger, "Italian Decolonization: Multidirectional Migrations, Multidirectional Memories," in *The Cultural Trauma of Decolonization: Colonial Returnees in the National Imagination*, eds. Roy Eyerman and Giuseppe Scortino (New York: Palgrave MacMillan, 2019), 43–45. She takes up Karen Pinkus's interpretation of Michelangelo Antonioni's *L'eclisse* (1962), which features a character returning to Italy from Kenya, as a meditation on the "symbolic of the displacement of memories of colonialism onto Italy's postwar 'conquest' of its urban peripheries," as an example. See Karen Pinkus, "Empty Spaces: Decolonization in Italy," in *A Place in the Sun: Africa in Italian Colonial Culture from Post-Unification to the Present*, ed. Patrizia Palumbo (Berkeley: University of California Press, 2003), 300.

Works Cited

Ballinger, Pamela. 2019. "Italian Decolonization: Multidirectional Migrations, Multidirectional Memories." In *The Cultural Trauma of Decolonization: Colonial Returnees in the National Imagination*, edited by Roy Eyerman and Giuseppe Scortino, 27–56. New York: Palgrave MacMillan.

Balmain, Colette J. 2004. "Genre, Gender, Giallo: The Disturbed Dreams of Dario Argento." PhD thesis, University of Greenwich. https://gala.gre.ac.uk/id/eprint/5795/5/Colette%20Jane%20Balmain%202004%20-%20redacted.pdf

Bini, Andrea. 2011. "Horror Cinema: The Emancipation of Women and Urban Anxiety." In *Popular Italian Cinema: Culture and Politics in a Postwar Society*, edited by Flavia Brizio-Skov, 53–83. London: IB Tauris.

Burke, Frank. 2002. "Intimations (and more) of Colonialism: Dario Argento's L'Uccello dalle piume di cristallo (*The Bird with the Crystal Plumage*, 1970)." *Kinoeye: New Perspectives on European Film* 2, no. 11 (June).

Chambers, Ian. 2017. *Postcolonial Interruptions, Unauthorized Modernities*. London and New York: Rowman & Littlefield.

Chambers, Ian. 2011. "The Translated City." *Translation: A Transdisciplinary Journal*, no. 1: 27–29.

Corbin, Amy. 2014. "Travelling through Cinema Space: The Film Spectator As Tourist." *Continuum* 28, no. 3 (April): 314–29.

Cottino-Jones, Marga. 2010. *Women, Desire, and Power in Italian Cinema*. New York: Palgrave MacMillan.

Dalle Vacche, Angela. 2008. *Diva: Defiance and Passion in Early Italian Cinema*. Austin: University of Texas Press.

De Certeau, Michel. 1984. *The Practice of Everyday Life*. Translated by Steven F. Rendall. Berkeley: University of California Press.

Franklin, Adrian and Mike Crang. 2001. "The Trouble with Tourism and Travel Theory?" *Tourist Studies* 1, no. 1 (June): 5–22.

Gelder, Ken. 2001. "Global/Postcolonial Horror: Introduction." *Postcolonial Studies* 3, no. 1 (August): 35–38.

Günsberg, Marie. 2005. *Italian Cinema, Gender and Genre*. New York: Palgrave MacMillan.

Hand, Richard. 2008. "La Dolce Morte: Vernacular Cinema and the Italian Giallo Film." *Gothic Studies* 10, no. 1 (May).

Heller-Nicholas, Alexandra. 2021. *The Giallo Canvas: Art, Excess and Horror Cinema*. Jefferson, NC: McFarland and Company.

Hume, David L. 2013. "The Genealogy of the Tourist Gaze Part 1: Art History, Anthropology and Souvenirs." Paper delivered at *Conference: International Symposium on Society, Tourism, Education and Politics*.

Kannas, Alexia. 2020. *Giallo!: Genre, Modernity, and Detection in Italian Horror Cinema* Albany: State University of New York Press.

Labanca, Nicola. 2015. "Post-Colonial Italy: The Case of a Small and Belated Empire: From Strong Emotions to Bigger Problems." In *Memories of Post-Imperial Nations: The Aftermath of Decolonization, 1945–2013*, edited by Dietmar Rothermund, 120–49. Cambridge: Cambridge University Press.

Larsen, Jonas. 2001. "Tourism Mobilities and the Travel Glance: Experiences of Being on the Move." *Scandinavian Journal of Hospitality and Tourism* 1, no. 2 (November): 80–98.
Light, Alison. 1991. *Forever England: Femininity, Literature, and Conservatism Between the Wars*. London: Routledge.
Lyotard, Jean-François. 1986. "A Cinema." In *Narrative, Apparatus, Ideology*, edited by Phil Rosen, 349–59. New York: Columbia University Press.
MacCannell, Dean. 1992. *Empty Meeting Grounds: The Tourist Papers*. London: Routledge.
Mathijs, Ernest, and Xavier Mendik, eds. 2008. *The Cult Film Reader*. Maidenhead/Berkshire: Open University Press/McGraw-Hill Education.
McDonagh, Maitland. 1994. *Broken Mirrors/Broken Minds: The Dark Dreams of Dario Argento*. New York: Carol Publishing.
Needham, Gary. 2002. "Playing with Genre: An Introduction to the Italian *Giallo*." *Kinoeye* 2, no. 11 (June): 6–10. https://www.kinoeye.org/02/11/needham11.php.
Negri, Antonio, and Michael Hardt. 2000. *Empire*. Cambridge, MA: Harvard University Press.
Nerenberg, Ellen. 2012. *Murder Made in Italy: Homicide, Media, and Contemporary Italian Culture*. Bloomington: Indiana University Press.
Newman, Kim, and Alan Jones. 2011. "Chapter 1." *Tenebrae*, audio commentary. Arrow Films.
Perkins, Harvey, and David C. Thorns. 2001. "Gazing or Performing? Reflections on Urry's Tourist Gaze in the Context of Contemporary Experience in the Antipodes." *International Sociology* 16, no. 2 (June): 185–204.
Pinkus, Karen. 2003. "Empty Spaces: Decolonization in Italy." In *A Place in the Sun: Africa in Italian Colonial Culture from Post-Unification to the Present*, edited by Patrizia Palumbo, 299–320. Berkeley: University of California Press.
Siegel, Michael. 2014. *Tenebre, Or on Neoliberalism*. New York: Wallflower Press.
Somigli, Luca. 2005. "The Realism of Detective Fiction: Augusto De Angelis, Theorist of the Italian Giallo." *Symposium: A Quarterly Journal in Modern Literatures* 59, no. 2 (August): 70–83.
Turner, Phil, Susan Turner, and Fiona Carroll. 2005. "The Tourist Gaze: Towards Contextualised Virtual Environments." In *Spaces, Spatiality and Technology*, edited by Phil Turner and Elisabeth Davenport, 281–97. Dordrecht: Springer.
Urry, John. 1990. *The Tourist Gaze*. London: Sage.
Waters, Sandra. 2015. "The Nightmarish in Dario Argento's Mother Trilogy: Spatial Oddities and Family Ties." In *Dreamscapes in Italian Cinema*, edited by Francesco Pascuzzi and Bryan Cracchiolo, 159–73. New Jersey: Fairleigh Dickinson University Press.
Weihsmann, Helmut. 1995. "Cinétecture–Film." *Architecture*. Vienna: PVS Verleger.

Chapter 3

DEATH LAID AN EGG

A *Giallo* Out of Far-Left Field

DONALD L. ANDERSON

Introduction: The Monster of Capital

In 1974, a van of teenagers picks up a "weird looking" hitchhiker along a rural Texas highway. The hitchhiker works at the local slaughterhouse and mentions how his family has "always been in meat." He complains about the "air gun" currently used to kill cattle and insists the "old way," using a sledgehammer, was better. The "new way [puts] people out of jobs" he laments. It is this early scene from Tobe Hooper's *The Texas Chain Saw Massacre* (1974) where the horror film genre directly engages the problem of automation that had undermined labor in the southern and Midwest regions of the US after WWII.[1] If *Night of the Living Dead* (George A. Romero, 1968) processed the American nightmares of racial unrest and the Vietnam War, and *I Spit on Your Grave* (Meir Zarchi, 1978) offered the violent image of a feminist uprising against the patriarchy, it was *The Texas Chain Saw Massacre* that reflected the emerging problematics of capital, labor, and automation. The cannibalistic zombies in Romero's film lacked the political symbolism of Hooper's cannibals where an out-of-work family is forced to eat its own.

Both literal and figurative cannibalism finds its way into representations of the Industrial Revolution. Marx's analysis of machines in *Capital* reveals how machines increased "the degree of exploitation." The introduction of machinery allowed laborers with "slight muscular strength" such as women and children to be included in the production of commodities.[2] Now, the workman "sells wife and child" and becomes, in essence, a "slave-dealer" (2003, 372–73). Cannibalization of one's family becomes exploitation. Mark Steven in *Splatter Capital* further highlights the theme of cannibalism in capitalism pointing out that, "capitalist accumulation is, as Marx knows, a crime whose most obvious analogue is cannibalism" (2017, 44). For Upton Sinclair, the horrors of the meatpacking industry included images of workers who

> fell into the vats; and when they were fished out, there was never enough of them left to be worth exhibiting—sometimes they would be overlooked for days, till all but the bones of them had gone out to the world as Durham's Pure Leaf Lard! (2006, 111)

The dog that accidently falls into the machine in *La morte ha fatto l'uovo* (*Death Laid an Egg*, Giulio Questi, 1968) recalls the effect of unregulated industry, while the film's finale literally copies the above scene from Sinclair's *The Jungle*. Machines as monsters and the pursuit of profit as cannibalism has a rich history in film and literature. Marx again provides a horror-film-worthy description of a factory dominated by machines describing a "mechanical monster whose body fills whole factories, and whose demon power, at first veiled under the slow and measured motions of his giant limbs, at length breaks out into the fast and furious whirl of his countless working organs" (2003, 360–61).

Six years before *The Texas Chain Saw Massacre* and 101 after *Capital*, however, *Death Laid an Egg* had already represented working-class anxieties about automation and modernization which, in this case, includes a horrific evolving farm system where chickens are mutated into bodies without heads so they are easier to produce, transport, and meet consumer demand. Guilio Questi's film signals a crucial shift in the broader thriller/horror genre that raised capitalism into a monster. I want to argue that *Death Laid an Egg* must be understood through a local historical lens recognizing Italy's far-left shift from a specific focus on antifascism to a broader focus on anticapitalism. This shift provided the opportunity for Questi to represent Italian anxieties over modernization, in particular automation and unemployment. The possibility for an anticapitalist critique of the film has unfortunately been obscured by an overemphasis on genre criticism that struggles to reconcile the *giallo* and art-house elements of the film. My broader objective, therefore, is to first re-evaluate the significance of this film in hindsight of the now recognized significance of Italian *giallo* cinema in the later twenty-first century. From here I will analyze the film's engagement with capitalism and automation as a force of terror within the context of the radical left politics of a modernizing, postwar Italy.

Too Arty for a *Giallo*, Too *Giallo* for an Art Film

Released in January of 1968 (some sources have listed the date as 1967), *Death Laid an Egg* revolves around a recently automated chicken farm owned by Anna (Gina Lollobrigida), who employs her husband, Marco (Jean-Louis Trintignant), in managing the day-to-day activities. Marco works directly with the distribution company, and it is marketing director Mondaini (Jean Sobieski) who witnesses Marco's violent (although staged) sexual fetish that includes hiring prostitutes he pretends to murder (even using lipstick for bloodied slashes across their bodies). Marco wishes to run off with Anna's younger cousin Gabrielle (Ewa Aulin). However, in typical *giallo* fashion, Gabrielle is double-crossing Marco and is involved with Mondaini. The two conspire to kill Anna and make it look like Marco was responsible. Their goal is to inherit the farm and its promised wealth following the mutation of chickens without heads or wings and installing "even better machines" Mondaini plans to purchase. Stephen Thrower describes the film as "disobey[ing] so many film-making rules it probably deserves to be considered *sui generis* but is at least tenuously a murder thriller" (1999, 64). Adrian Luther Smith's guide to *giallo* films (the first of its kind) regards the film as "compelling, but occasionally infuriating" (1999, 33) while the recent set of volumes on *giallo* cinema by Troy Howarth judge it as "perplexing as it is difficult to categorize" (2015, 82). Although recognized for its technical finesse, Questi's film is too often underappreciated; its supposed "weirdness" limits its critical appraisal in overviews of the genre.

The plot includes what seem like random themes: the chicken farm and marketing of chickens, automation, animal mutation, anxiety over modernity, a love triangle, fetishistic murder, satire of the upper class, and economic progress vs. morality. Although all critics agree *Death Laid an Egg* is more or less a *giallo*, many cannot help but make references to European art cinema and films like *Blow Up* (Michelangelo Antonioni, 1966) and the early work of Jean-Luc Godard. Of the latter, one can draw similarities between Franco Arcalli's editing and montage work and films like *Breathless* (Jean Luc-Godard, 1960) and *Pierrot le Fou* (Jean Luc-Godard, 1965). Because *Blow Up* shares some similarities with the *giallo* genre, *Death Laid an Egg* may be read as its inheritor that further synthesizes art-film-symbolism with the conventions of the *giallo*. Antonioni's use of symbolism throughout *Blow*

Up undermines the stability of meaning—in particular, the idea that sight and the act of seeing are grounds for establishing concrete reality. The film's conclusion advances this thesis when David Hemmings's character witnesses a group of mimes playing tennis with no racket or ball. Their athletic movements only suggest a game is in play. Hemmings is invited to participate in the illusion when he is encouraged to retrieve a tennis ball for the group. He throws it back and therefore surrenders to the illusive nature of sight. This scene is also a metacomment on the film's plot that revolves around the question of a possible murder Hemmings may have indirectly witnessed through a photograph.

Questi liberally borrows from *Blow Up*'s suspicions of sight. Mondaini assumes he has witnessed Marco commit murder. And at this same early point in the film, the viewer too is unaware the murder was a performance. Later in the film, the prostitutes joke that they've been killed many times in the room Marco rents to "perform" his murders, alluding to the fact that "murder" occurred but, like the mimes' tennis match, it was an illusion. There is even an impromptu fashion shoot when Marco photographs Ann and Gabrielle playfully posing with dead chickens inside the farm. This shoot is interrupted by what is later revealed (by a photo of course) to be Marco's first attempted murder where he had rigged a wrench to fall on Anna (this is instead blamed on the disgruntled workers who have lost their jobs due to the machine). Questi evokes the work of Ingmar Bergman when he films Marco and Anna together using the effect of *chiaroscuro* that shades half of their faces. He frames Marco's back from a low angle that further highlights the claustrophobic and alienating themes of the film. The symbolism in *Death Laid an Egg* links it with European art cinema, but what further establishes such a link is the film's commitment to leftist politics, something equally shared with art directors like Godard, Makavejev, and Pasolini.

Alexia Kannas's study of genre and *giallo* cinema proves informative here. She, like many recent critics of the *giallo*, prefers the term *filone* to genre. *Filone* is used to describe "films prone to consistent deviation from any established generic norm as nevertheless being part of the same discursive group" (2017, 176). *Filone* permits greater permeability between disparate films that make up a larger body of films. Gary Needham's earlier definition of the *giallo* anticipates this critical move:

> I would like to suggest that we understand it [*giallo*] in a more "discursive" fashion, as something constructed out of the various associations, network tensions, and articulations of Italian cinema's textual and industrial specificity in the post-war period. (2008, 297)

Kannas cautions critics of the *giallo* from indirectly relying on a Hollywood-centric framework that dismisses incoherent narrative, plot holes, or unorthodox camera angles as incompetency. And, as she points out, such critical moves have even been made by fans of the genre (2017, 178). There exists a similar dismissiveness made by cult film fans and critics who employ an art film-centric (rather than Hollywood-centric) framework. It's too arty for a *giallo*, but too *giallo* for an art film. It exists somewhere between *Blow Up* and Dario Argento's *L'uccello dalle piume di cristallo* (1970). The undecidability of *Death Laid an Egg* signals the porous boundary between exploitation and art. Critics like myself who came of age in the era of the video-trading circuit may recall how VHS trading lists included both art films and the sleaziest and most exploitative Italian "gut munchers." It was common to see lists that featured Godard's *Weekend* (1967) or Dusan Makavejev's *Sweet Movie* (1974) alongside *Cannibal Holocaust* (Ruggero Deodato, 1980) and *L'ultima, orgia del III Reich* (*The Gestapo's Last Orgy*, Cesare Canevari, 1977). Fans made little distinction between art cinema and horror or exploitation cinema. The single objective for fans like myself was to consume transgressive and challenging cinema in whatever "form" it came. Therefore, I find the undervaluing of Questi's film surprising given its skillful balance of exploitation, technique, leftist politics, and genre elements.

As noted by Kannas, "when framed by this Hollywood-centric understanding of hybridity, the *giallo* reads as incomplete, or as a trace of some lost or absent whole. That the *giallo* is read in terms of a kind of brokenness or fragmentation is evident even in celebratory criticism" (2017, 178). The mapping of an art film framework onto *Death Laid an Egg* also reproduces it as lacking something. Reading *Death Laid an Egg* as a "broken" art film, or an artsy *giallo*, obscures its critical importance in the history of Italian cinema, particularly the turbulent era that spans the late '60s through the '80s, when Italy was in the throes of protest, violence, and terrorism. I will now consider *Death Laid an Egg* as a symptom of this crucial period rather than as a component of a genre or *filone*. The overvaluation of genre in critical discussions of the *giallo* has severely limited appreciating the film's leftist politics and critique of capitalism.

Questi, Maderna, and Italian Communism

Antifascist groups and political parties emerged in Europe and the US following World War II, but it was the Communist Party (PCI) in Italy that proved instrumental in fighting neofascists. Readers familiar with the "Red

Scare" of the American Cold War era, and American military interventions in Latin America and Vietnam designed to undermine communism, may wonder why the PCI was so popular. In the US, communists were widely demonized during the McCarthy years, when especially those in the film industry were blacklisted following suspected communist sympathies. However, for Italy the PCI represented an "organizational format" that was "admire[d]" by "leaders of other parties" (Weinberg 1995, 23). As Leonard Weinberg notes in his study of Italian Communism:

> It [PCI] had been able to function covertly during the fascist era and then, with the collapse of the dictatorship, the PCI quickly emerged as a formidable presence all over the northern and central parts of the country. As a consequence the other mass parties, that is, the Christian Democrats and the Socialists, and parties that aspired to win mass memberships, adapted or copied many of the PCI's organizational attributes. Youth and student groups, separate women's organizations, veterans groups, party newspapers and related publishing activities, even the way in which membership in their "ruling organs" was determined, all came to resemble the PCI's structures and ways of doing business. (1995, 23)

Furthermore, the PCI "achieved widespread admiration within non-Communist circles in Western Europe and the United States because of its leaders' willingness to act independently of or even challenge the Soviet Union" (Weinberg 1995, 34). Despite the "Red Scare" in the US, any party, whether communist or not, that broke with the Soviet Union was tolerated by anticommunist administrations.

Giulio Questi was a communist and spent his early years in the resistance fighting in the mountains against the fascist Black Brigades (Ripley's Film, 2014). He also wrote for the communist magazine *Il Politecnico*. Notably, the film's soundtrack composer Bruno Maderna (who joined the PCI in 1952) also spent time with the partisans in the mountains and had participated in acts of sabotage in between finding time to compose (Fearn 1990, 332). *Death Laid an Egg* represents a collaboration of sorts between Questi and Maderna, both of whom shared leftist ideologies and similar backgrounds. And it is Maderna's participation that further differentiates the film from other *gialli* that commonly relied on composers like Ennio Morricone, Bruno Nicolai, and Riz Ortolani. No other *giallo* employed a composer principally known as an orchestral composer. Although Morricone, in particular, indulged in modernist classical approaches in non-soundtrack composition (e.g., musique concrète, col legno, sound mass), he is known for giving the sound of the *giallo* its trademark and completely tonal "lullaby" melody that is a regular feature of *giallo* soundtracks. For *Death Laid an Egg*, however, Maderna completely avoids melody and relies totally on atonal, modernist composition. Those unfamiliar with mid-twentieth-century classical music may regard the score as unrelenting and jarring. Such modernist techniques were commonly reserved for murder scenes in *gialli*, but for Questi's film, nearly the whole score (aside from the upbeat chicken music and the brief love scene) is wholly modernist. This adds to the film's regularly referenced "art-house" style.

Aside from a cantata written in 1953, a year after joining the PCI, and based on one of Antonio Gramsci's prison letters, Maderna's politics remained outside his music and he maintained the opinion that politics had little place in music insisting "musicians should do rather than say" (Fearn 1990, 319). This comment was directed at the more radical composer Luigi Nono—a pupil of Maderna's—who integrated politics into his music (most notably in the opera *Intolleranza*). Nonetheless, Maderna insisted that "I don't think I am opposed to him [Nono] ideologically, deep down: I also believe that Socialism is the future for the world" (Fearn 1990, 319). Maderna's participation in *Death Laid an Egg* bolsters the film's leftist ideology while firmly establishing its uniqueness within the *giallo filone*.

"The New Machine Arrived:" Placing *Death Laid an Egg* within Its Historical Moment

With the comment above, uttered by Marco's secretary, *Death Laid an Egg* positions itself within the anxieties over modernization in postwar Italy. The '60s and '70s marked a period of transition during an economic boom, popularly referred to as the "Economic Miracle" (*il miracolo economico*)—a direct effect of the Marshall Plan, which introduced an accelerated period of production and modernization. Released in 1968, *Death Laid an Egg* rests roughly between the end of the economic miracle and the beginning of the "Hot Autumn" (*autunno caldo*), a period of labor and student protests. This period was then followed by the "Years of Lead" (*anni di piombo*) made up of left- and right-wing terrorism. It is important to recognize the politico-historical positioning of the film in an account of its left-wing sympathies and placement within the *giallo filone*. It reflects the changes wrought by the economic miracle while simultaneously reflecting an emerging working-class consciousness that in turn anticipates the shifts in left-wing politics at the onset of the Years of Lead.

Such a positioning also represents an alternative direction the *giallo* could have taken. The *giallo* ultimately cohered around the now canonical tropes established by Mario Bava's *Sei donne per l'assassino* (1964) and further refined by *The Bird with the Crystal Plumage*. Although *gialli* do often reference anxieties and ambivalences about modernity, urbanity, and police corruption, they rarely take on a distinctly radical political position in the style of *Death Laid an Egg*. Questi's film, therefore, represents a nexus point where Questi's and composer Burno Maderna's left-wing politics gather together the above historical threads (the Economic Miracle, Hot Autumn, and Years of Lead) that made the film's politics both inevitable and distinctive. That later *giallo* films resisted such overt politics cannot be reduced to a simple preference for salacious entertainment, but rather the lack of an historical urgency captured by an overtly left-wing director.

From Antifascism to Anticapitalism

Concomitant with the growing tension of the era between Italy's rural south and urban north was a political shift in the Italian left from a specific focus on antifascism to a refocusing on anticapitalism and labor rights. Austin Fisher comments on this historical context in his study of the spaghetti western writing that, "the international student movement did not limit its definition of 'fascism' to street gangs, blackshirts and neo-Nazis. The notion of Western capitalism as a repressive system hiding behind a façade of democracy and tolerance, against which resistance was justified, was widespread amongst the New Left in Italy" (2011, 79). Even more specific is how Adam Lowenstein's analysis of the setting of Bava's *Ecologia del delitto* (Bay of Blood, 1971) evokes a fascist past obscured by property value:

> If two structuring discourses of post-war Italian cinema and society have been the politics of modernization and the national growth known as the "economic miracle," both often deployed to overlook or overwrite fascism's history, then *Ecologia del delitto* returns to the scene of the crime: land reclamation as economic engine. (2016, 136)

Lowenstein's analysis hints at the relationship between fascism and economics. Although Questi's film participates in this same discourse of anxiety over modernization, it more importantly mediates the transition for both Questi himself and left-wing politics from a politics of antifascism to a politics of anticapitalism. To better render this transition visible, consider

Questi's previous film, the famously violent western *Se sei vivo spara* (1967). The film's setting is a city whose inhabitants operate as fascist stand-ins and whose hypocrisy inspires the brutal murder of a band of thieves. As a Western, there is no explicit reference to capitalism (although the lure of gold is present); however, the film's setting suggests Nazi-occupied Republic of Salò and the brutality of the town's citizens is reminiscent of Pier Paolo Pasolini's film. *Se sei vivo spara* explores the theme of fascism by way of an insular town whose citizens maintain a violent, and hypocritical, grip on everyday life. Although motivated by a fundamentalist understanding of Christianity (and here is where a comparison to strict fascism stops), it is this religious background that nonetheless provides the means for revealing the hypocrisy of the fascists. In a particularly striking scene, the conclusion of the film finds the character Alderman (Paco Sanz) dowsed in melted gold suggesting the obsessive pursuit of gold comes at one's own peril. Ironically, it is gold that fatally preserves Alderman, rather than Alderman who, like any good capitalist, preserves (accumulates) capital. I want to read this scene as a key transition to the anticapitalist concerns of Questi's follow-up film.

Death Laid an Egg stands as Questi's own directorial move into anticapitalist discourses. He abandons the critique of fascism and begins to explore the oppressive dynamics of capitalism. This transition is historically significant. It mirrors the shift occurring in leftist politics of the time. Writing in "The History of the Red Brigades," authors Gian Carlo Caselli and Donatella Della Porta explain that, "the activities of the student groups soon extended to take in the 'worker's struggle.' Thus, between 1969 and 1970 groups emerged which sought to generalize the specific conflicts and to transform 'antiauthoritarian impulses' into 'anticapitalistic actions'" (1991, 78). Fascism in Italy was expanded to include the boss and the factory owner. What permitted this transition into a critique of capitalism was the recognition of capitalism's fascist tendencies. Quoting from *Soccorso Rosso* (1976, 175) Luigi Manconi reveals that, "among other things, 'fascism' became factory-management policy: much attention was paid to 'Fiat fascism' and to the 'hard neo-fascist line that has been imposed within the factory'" (1991, 122). In *Death Laid an Egg*, Questi's critique of automation first emerges in a left-moving tracking shot revealing the angry and solemn workers who have been put out of work due to the machine. Over this shot, Ann tersely inquires, evoking the zombies who return to the mall in *Dawn of the Dead* (George A. Romero, 1978), "Why are they coming here?" The workers stand motionless and expressionless—zombielike. Their alienation is made more pronounced behind the chain fence separating them from their work. This scene grimly substantiates the pithy comment made by the scientist who will develop mutant chickens: "man is building the machines which will make him redundant one day." Later the workers throw a rock through the window evoking the violence associated with the following decade. Commenting on such violence, Leonard Weinberg shows that "worker-management relations were often characterized by mistrust, bitterness, strikes and violent conflict with the state intervening, typically on behalf of the owners" (1995, 26).

The onset of modernity triggered the embittered violence of those displaced by its transformations. The rock thrown through the window also parallels the approval of violence as a legitimate means of protest. In Italy, violence gradually became more accepted by the radical left. This acceptance had much to do with the activities of the Red Brigades who

> identified clandestine violence as an extension of, rather than a rupture with, ordinary shopfloor class conflict. That claim made violence contiguous to legal struggles and an endogenous factory product. Furthermore, underlying the many specific justifications for attack on individual victims, certain themes recurred: that violence was the most effective way to defend class interests in general; that it could help to protect the particular interests of workers who were the victims of industrial restructuring. (Moss 1989, 85)

The machine that replaces the workers reproduces them as disposable labor, or more specifically, precarious labor. They are disposed of—Anna even says "they don't get that we don't need them"—but, more importantly, their capacity for future employment is related to a skill that is becoming automized. Guy Standing offers a complex definition of "precariat" in his book *The Precariat: The New Dangerous Class* which is too rich to succinctly sum up here, but that can nonetheless be said to "consist[s] of people who lack ... labour related security [e.g., employment security, skill reproduction security, income security, representation security]" (2011, 11). There exists no reference to union representation in the film; rather, Anna threatens to report the workers to the authorities. As laborers whose skills are limited to meat packing, their chances for locating other means of employment are minimal and likely to be met with further increases in automation and perhaps direct intervention by the state, which as Weinberg points out above, will likely side with the capitalists.

Automation and the Bioeconomics of Mutant Chickens

The representation of worker anger and retribution in the film is indicative of radical changes in employment in Italy from the 1950s through the '70s. Jobs in agriculture dropped while jobs in industry rose:

> In 1861 nearly two-thirds of the labour force worked in agriculture, with the remaining workers more or less equally distributed between industry and services. The exodus from agriculture was quite limited until the 1930s. As late as the beginning of the 1950s, over 40% of the labour force remained in agriculture. Between 1951 and 1973 agriculture's share declined sharply, with both industry and private services increasing their shares. (Giordano, Toniolo, and Zollino 2017, 9)

A consequence of labor moving into industry and private areas is a growing potential for automation to replace farm-based or agricultural skill sets. Labor that is repetitive in nature (meat processing in this case) easily lends itself to automation. It is difficult to locate accurate statistics for unemployment or jobs lost due to automation. The reason for this has to do with how one defines "unemployment," which may include those workers who are in between jobs, holding multiple part-time jobs, searching for a job, or who have begun early retirement. Nonetheless, the concern over the effects of automation on employment was a global concern for all modernized or modernizing countries. In 1967 (a year before the release of Questi's film), the *International Conference on Automation, Full Employment, and a Balanced Economy* met in Rome. One of their key objectives was to address the need for retraining and educating workers replaced by automation. According to their publication, the conference "recognizes that the development of new skills for those displaced because of automation or those hopelessly unemployed because they have no skills at all is one, if not the most, important challenge of our society today" (1967, 2). The machine that replaces the workers in *Death Laid an Egg* directly eliminates the specific skills they had developed and perfected over years of farming and agricultural work. It represents the horror of disposability visited upon a labor force unable to keep up with modernization. What is further symbolic is Marco's death by the machine. After discovering Anna's body, he decides to throw it into the machine to avoid being a suspect. Upon finding Mondaini's bracelet gripped in her hand however, he realizes it was Mondaini who killed her. Marco grows disoriented and falls into the machine's circulating blades that will turn him into processed meat. Like the family in *The Texas Chain Saw Massacre* whose

Figure 1. The headless chickens spark joy in the chemist, while Marco morally struggles with the situation.

response to a changing job market is cannibalism, Marco is consumed by his own company's pursuit of efficiency and profit required by a rising demand for chicken. The following shots of eggs moving through an assembly line and the automatic release of chicken feed for the caged chickens help illustrate that Marco's death is not only caused by the machine, but is also caused by the automated fervor that possessed the chicken company.

Part of this shift in employment in Italy has to do with the modernization of the north in stark contrast to the agricultural and rural south. Jobs in industry and private companies require retraining if they are not already being eliminated by automation (and even then, retraining for a whole other job skill set). As pointed out by the conference, not only is education important, but "geographical mobility." They continue, "the education and skill of our work force and the ability to maintain skills appropriate to the requirements of our changing technology will play an important role in our efforts to stabilize employment in years to come" (*International Conference on Automation* 1967, 2). The peasants in the south must migrate north to seek not just employment, but an education that will prepare them for the skills needed in a modernizing economy.

Upon finding the mutated chickens, Marco is immediately repulsed. For him, the logical end of automation where the product is finally reduced to its simplest, bare minimum ("nearly no bones!" proclaims the excited chemist), represents a moral rupture he can no longer tolerate.

When Marco destroys the mutant chickens, he is chastised by the president who questions how he could "suppress biological results of that importance to society and especially this company? Especially at a time of extreme difficulties like this when our productivity and commercial existence are faced with such a devastating economic crisis." Questi's film represents both the anxiety of factory owners in a period of crisis and the struggles faced by the working class as the postwar Italian economy began to radically shift from an agricultural economy to a modernized, and mechanized, private industry. The film poses the machine as a monster that eliminates jobs and consumes those that herald its importance. Questi's attitude around this time was nothing new. On March 8th, 1961 David J. McDonald then president of the United Steelworkers of America testified at the House of Representatives regarding the impact automation would have on employment. During this testimony he warns that "unless the installation of automation and technological change can be so managed as to minimize its human impact, we may well find ourselves faced with a hideous Frankenstein which can destroy the human and economic progress so laboriously built in recent decades" (*Impact of Automation* 1961, 3). Following this comment, McDonald engages in light film criticism pointing out that in the *Frankenstein* films it was the scientist who was the real monster. Such a parallel would lead one to believe McDonald was suggesting capitalism was the true monster that gave birth to automation, but he stops before arriving at such a point. Instead, he insists, "we, the creators of this monster called automation, can instead use this monster for the good of mankind . . . a great machine for good, rather than a monster for evil" (*Impact of Automation* 1961, 3). In the literature of machine versus man—from Marx's characterization of machines as monsters, to the attitude expressed above—automation is regularly described in terms of monstrosity and unmanageable horror.

    The most horrific aspect of the film is the mutant chickens referenced above. These chickens have no heads or wings and are only meat. Biology is reduced to a raw commodity by erasing those aspects unnecessary for production (beaks, eyes, tongues, wings, bones). In their voluminous analysis of empire in the postmodern age, philosophers Michael Hardt and Antonio Negri consider the effects of what they term "agricultural postmodernization" which "develops biological and biochemical innovations, along with specialized systems of production, such as greenhouses, artificial lighting, and soilless agriculture" (2004, 112). The mutation the chickens undergo in the film represents a moment for both industrial innovation and the trend of patenting biological organisms. Hardt and Negri similarly express concern over the corporate ownership of the "genetic information encased in the seed" (2004, 112). Questi's film, therefore, reaches beyond a routine Marxist critique of labor and examines the bioeconomic nature of capitalism—the development and eventual patenting of new biological organisms for capitalist exchange. *Death Laid an Egg* further reflects Hardt and Negri's analysis of the Italian economy. Alongside the film's nexus point joining the three major periods: the Economic Miracle, the Hot Autumn, and the Years of Lead, the film's bioeconomic aspect drives Questi's project into the realm of postmodern informatization where biology, economy, and privatization of a new species coalesce.

Ambivalence Is Not an Option

Capitalist production would be meaningless without the participation of a consuming class. Therefore, I want to conclude this chapter with a discussion of consumerism. Questi reserves a slightly satirical tone when observing his upper-class characters that include Anna, who lounges at the pool, and the upper-class partygoers who play the "empty room" game. The seriousness with which the factory scenes, including the disgruntled workers, are filmed is set against this other satirical voice. Satirizing the upper-class and their excessive consumption is a standard exercise popularized by Godard, Buñuel, and others described as art-house directors. The often unconscious and naïve consumption of commodity objects by those whose desires have been manipulated by marketing often find their folly revealed by satire in the domains of film and literature.

Death Laid an Egg opens in a hotel inhabited by various unidentified characters. One is preparing to commit suicide; another eavesdrops through an air vent hearing what sounds like a murder. The camera erratically pans over these figures never pausing at length on their faces. One shot crisscrosses a bearded man smoking, seemingly uninterested in establishing any role for the character. The camera remains cold and detached. Shots of the jagged edges and sharp angles of the hotel are interspersed with freeways and on-ramps littered with advertisements. With the onset of travel (a key theme of the *giallo filone*), the movement of alienated subjects of the world passing through airports, hotels, and freeways increased in the latter half of the twentieth century. Building on the work of theorist Siegfried Kracauer, Kannas points out how in *gialli* such "void-like, impersonal spaces" like hotel lobbies "become symbolic of the conditions of modernity" (2017, 10). In his analysis of what he terms "rural *gialli*," Austin Fisher reads such films as *Non si sevizia un paperino* (Don't Torture a Duckling, Lucio Fulci, 1972) as "representing and negotiating the national past in moments of crisis" (2016, 170). He further points out that, "entwined within this commentary on the onset of modernity is of course the contrapuntal framing of residual Italy from a bygone-era, whose antiquated mores cause tensions upon the arrival of the cosmopolitan protagonist" (2016, 170). Franco Arcalli arranges these shots of a modernizing landscape and architecture with a kinetic energy exemplifying the tension between a rural south and urbanizing north. This montage is better understood as a prelude to the film's interrogation of the modernizing forces of automation, disposable labor, and bioeconomics than an indulgence in art film aesthetics. Admittedly, yes, this opening reproduces the *gialli*'s travelogue refrains, but more importantly it heightens the delirium of modernity and a transforming agricultural economy. Again, it is how *Death Laid an Egg* rests upon the boundary between art and exploitation that distracts critics from reading what is right there on the screen: a leftist film in conversation with its sociocultural moment.

In *La Dolce Morte*, Mikel J. Koven analyzes what he calls the genre's "ambivalence towards modernity" (2006, 46). His explication draws out the different ways the genre problematizes or processes the sociocultural transitions endemic to modernity. Regarding the travel theme prevalent in *gialli*, Koven writes, "This is one of the areas in which the genre articulates its ambivalence toward modernity: specifically, through juxtaposition of luscious travelogue visual footage with diegetic horror and tragedy" (2006, 51). Although I agree with Koven's analysis of the *giallo* film's tendency towards ambivalence generally, *Death Laid an Egg* does not entirely share such an ambivalence. The opening discussed above illustrates many aspects pointed out by Koven, but I want to mark how Questi's politics and the political and historical urgency of the film disables it from expressing ambivalence towards left-wing politics, in particular the negative effects on labor by automation. And this is due in large part to its unique placement at the conjoining historical coordinates in Italy discussed above.

The Lost Future of *Death Laid an Egg*

If ambivalence to modernity is the common refrain of the *giallo* film, it is not only Questi's lack of ambivalence, but his indictment of the failure of modernity to make life better for everyone that further disassociates *Death Laid an Egg* from its *giallo* brethren. Modernity, for Questi, means the erasure of the working class by machines and the manipulation of nature for consumer demand. Neither the solemn tracking shot of the workers' faces as they recognize their obsolescence, or the absurd reimagining of the chicken as the "everyday man" in a desperate marketing campaign to resell the chicken

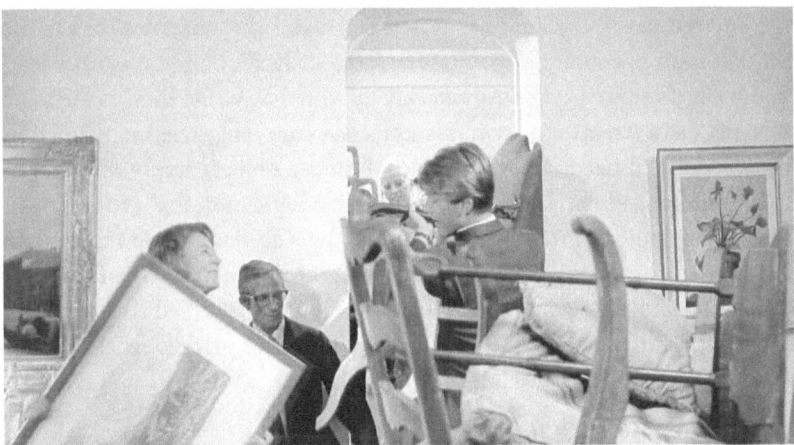

Figure 2. The upper-class partygoers empty a room to make a blank space where they can confront truth.

to consumers, would maintain their political urgency had the film feigned an ambivalent attitude toward these two outcomes of modernity. In *Ghosts of My Life: Writings on Depression, Hauntology and Lost Futures*, the late cultural theorist Mark Fisher defines "lost futures" as a haunting by the "spectre of a world in which all the marvels of communicative technology could be combined with a sense of solidarity much stronger than anything social democracy could muster" (2014, 26). In other words, a "lost future" leads us to ask why such progress in the twenty-first century did not result in a more democratic world. Fisher insists, "what should haunt us is not the *no longer* of actually existing social democracy, but the *not yet* of the futures that popular modernism trained us to expect, but which never materialized" (2014, 27). Questi's film, and his own transition from a politics of antifascism in *Se sei vivo spara* to one of anticapitalism, is a mourning of the failures of a postwar, modern Italy.

Death Laid an Egg offers its clearest example of a "lost future" during the party scene where the marketing director Mondaini asks partygoers to completely empty a room of all its contents, insisting that "there should be nothing in here which evokes emotion." The objective of this game is for two people to enter the room and trade secrets. The empty room operates as a *tabula rasa* that encourages participants to achieve a truthful purity outside the cultural influence of commodity objects.

It is therefore significant that the attendees all appear to be upper class and that the party occurs in a well-furnished apartment. Questi's condemnation of consumer society is reflected in the proclamation made by one of the attendees that they are "moving out of the web of lies"—the web being the interference of consumerist desires with assumed "pure" desires and the accumulation of material goods. The "web of lies" comment evokes Jean Baudrillard's analysis of consumer society where he writes that "in the logic of signs, as in the logic of symbols, objects are no longer tied to a function or to a defined need. This is precisely because objects respond to something different, either to a social logic, or to a logic of desire" (2001, 47). In (post)modernity, commodity objects shed their utilitarian role and assume a symbolic currency. Their role is to represent the cultural significance of their owners whose desire for an image or reputation exceed any use value. To then shed these objects is, according to the naïve partygoers, the way to reach their true selves and likewise shed the lies of their lives.

Conclusion: "There Is No Time in This Room"

If "popular modernism" anticipated the world of the *giallo* where air travel, urban infrastructure, J&B Scotch, and fashion-conscious interior décor made up of art and antiques were the norm, then it is this empty room that returns its inhabitants to the "not yet" of that modernism where interpersonal relationships relied on direct emotional connection rather than cultural currency and demonstrations of wealth. The partygoers find they were never liberated by modernism, but rather oppressed by its distractions that had distorted their existential connections with themselves and others. Their happiness was misrecognized as fulfillment, and this room, and the underlying plotline involving Gabrielle and Mondaini wanting control of the farm, demonstrate how these characters of modern times are so sad and unfulfilled.

The film's twin focus on automation and consumer society coalesce around the theme of "time." Time, for the workers, is measured by a clock-in system where labor hours are proportionately converted into wages. This is a time measured by extraction: the extraction of surplus labor from the bodies of men and women. Consumer society, however, exists within a time of consumption where, "we are living the period of objects: that is, we live by *their* rhythm, according to *their* incessant cycles" (Baudrillard 2001, 32). So, when a partygoer comments, "there is no time in this room" they are imagining themselves free from commodity fetishism. Questi directs this scene as an upper-class game the rich and leisurely play to pass the time. He deliberately places it in stark contrast to the time which brutally demarcates labor and capital.

Whether *Death Laid an Egg* is too arty to be a *giallo*, or too *giallo* to be an art film is wildly beside the point. In fact, such a query distracts from its critical role in reflecting a crucial moment in Italian leftist politics. This does not mean critics must ignore its placement within the *giallo filone*, but genre criticism too often asks what something *is* rather than what something *does*. *Death Laid an Egg* reveals the tensions of its historical moment that marked a shift from antifascist to anticapitalist activism. And in doing so both reflected, and anticipated, the horrors of automation and its disastrous effects on labor. *Death Laid an Egg* was out of left field, but more importantly, it was ahead of its time.

Notes

1. *Metropolis* (Fritz Lang, 1927) may be the earliest film to express the abuse of laborers in service of enriching the higher class. This film too places a machine at the center of its plot. However, *Metropolis* has as its descendants science fiction films like *Blade Runner* (Ridley Scott, 1982), *Minority Report* (Steven Spielberg, 2002), and others rather than films part of the horror/thriller genre.

2. Although Marx details how machines led to more employment of women and children and therefore whole families, he does describe how machines come to replace workers. See Karl Marx, *Capital*, vol.1, ed. Frederick Engels (London: New World Paperbacks, 2003), 412–21.

Works Cited

Baudrillard, Jean. 2001. "Consumer Society." In *Selected Writings*, edited by Mark Poster, 32–59. Stanford: Stanford University Press.

Caselli, Gian Carlo, and Donatella della Porta. 1991. "The History of the Red Brigades: Organizational Structures and Strategies of Action (1970–82)." In *The Red Brigades and Left Wing Terrorism*, edited by Raimondo Catanzaro, 70–114. New York: St. Martin's Press.

Fearn, Raymond. 1990. *Bruno Maderna*. Chur: Harwood Academic Publishers.

Fisher, Austin. 2011. *Radical Frontiers in the Spaghetti Western: Politics, Violence and Popular Italian Cinema*. London: I. B. Tauris.

Fisher, Austin. 2016. "Political Memory in the Italian Hinterland: Locating the 'Rural Giallo.'" In *Italian Horror Cinema*, edited by Stefano Baschiera and Russ Hunter, 160–74. Edinburgh: Edinburgh University Press.

Fisher, Mark. 2014. *Ghosts of My Life: Writings on Depression, Hauntology and Lost Futures*. Alresford: Zero Books.

Giordano, Claire, Gianni Toniolo, and Francesco Zollino. 2017. *Questioni di Economia e Finanza: Long-run trends in Italian Productivity*. Rome: Bank of Italy.

Hardt, Michael, and Antonio Negri. 2004. *Multitude: War and Democracy in the Age of Empire*: New York: Penguin Press.

Howarth, Troy. 2015. *So Deadly, So Perverse: 50 Years of Italian Giallo Films, Vol. 1*. Baltimore: Midnight Marquee Press.

Impact of Automation on Employment: Hearings before the Subcommittee on Unemployment and the Impact of Automation of the Committee on Education and Labor House of Representatives. 1961. Washington, DC: US Government Printing Office.

International Conference on Automation, Full Employment, and a Balanced Economy. 1967. New York: American Foundation on Automation and Employment.

Kannas, Alexia. 2013. "No Place Like Home: The Late-Modern World of the Italian Giallo Film." *Senses of Cinema*, no. 67. http://sensesofcinema.com/2013/uncategorized/no-place-like-home-the-late-modern-world-of-the-italian-giallo-film/.

Kannas, Alexia. 2017. "All the Colours of the Dark: Film Genre and the Italian Giallo." *Journal of Italian Cinema and Media Studies* 5, no. 2 (March): 173–90.

Koven, Mikel J. 2006. *La Dolce Morte: Vernacular Cinema and the Italian Giallo Film.* Lanham, MD: Scarecrow Press.

Lowenstein, Adam. 2016. "The Giallo/Slasher Landscape: *Ecologia Del Delitto, Friday the 13th* and Subtractive Spectatorship." In *Italian Horror Cinema*, edited by Stefano Baschiera and Russ Hunter, 127–44. Edinburgh: Edinburgh University Press.

Maderna, Burno. 1968. *Death Laid an Egg.* Fin de Siecle Media, compact disc, 52 min.

Manconi, Luigi. 1991. "The Political Ideology of the Red Brigades." In *The Red Brigades and Left Wing Terrorism*, edited by Raimondo Catanzaro, 115–43. New York: St. Martin's Press.

Marx, Karl. 2003. *Capital, Vol. 1*, edited by Frederick Engels. London: New World Paperbacks.

Moss, David. 1989. *The Politics of Left-Wing Violence in Italy, 1969–85.* London: Macmillan Press.

Needham, Gary. 2008. "Playing with Genre: An Introduction to the Italian Giallo." In *The Cult Film Reader*, edited by Ernest Mathijs and Xavier Mendik, 294–300. Berkshire: McGray Hill.

Ripley's Film. 2014. "La mia Resistenza." Uploaded on April 23, 2014. YouTube video, 4:29 min. https://www.youtube.com/watch?v=UN45Mh3zes4.

Sinclair, Upton. 2006. *The Jungle.* New York: Penguin.

Smith, Adrian Luther. 1999. *Blood and Black Lace: The Definitive Guide to Italian Sex and Horror Movies.* Cornwall: Stray Cat Publishing.

Standing, Guy. 2011. *The Precariat: The New Dangerous Class.* London: Bloomsbury.

Steven, Mark. 2017. *Splatter Capital.* London: Repeater Books.

Thrower, Stephen. 1999. *Beyond Terror: The Films of Lucio Fulci.* Surrey: FAB Press.

Weinberg, Leonard. 1995. *The Transformation of Italian Communism.* New Brunswick: Transaction Publishers.

Chapter 4

THE TRANSNATIONAL *GIALLO*

Jess Franco's *Paroxismus* and the Postmodern Crisis of Temporality

LISA HAEGELE

One of the most notorious exploitation filmmakers in postwar Europe, Spanish-born director Jess Franco (1930–2013) made approximately 200 feature films over the course of his nearly sixty-year-long career. Known by various other pseudonyms—Jesús Franco, Franco Manera, Jess Franck, David J. Khune, and more—Franco established himself as a transnational B-film director in the 1960s and 1970s, working with producers and crew in Spain, Italy, France, England, and West Germany. His large body of work represents a wide range of genres in unusual combinations, from supernatural and erotic horror to cannibal and zombie films, from women-in-prison films to nunsploitation, and many other hybrids that blend together crime, adventure, horror, sex, and science fiction. It is no surprise that Franco has only recently become the subject of scholarly attention, due not only to his "trashy," low-budget film style but also his sheer elusiveness as a director. His gargantuan filmography consists of titles in multiple languages and contains several versions of individual films, making his work notoriously difficult to trace. His films tend to frustrate conventional methods in film scholarship based on auteur theory, national cinema movements, and the commonly held division between art and popular cinema. Consistently working on the margins between nations, languages, aliases, genres, and styles, Franco is best understood as a transnational director whose work and identity as filmmaker decenter and fundamentally challenge the established boundaries and categories in postwar European cinema.

Considering Franco's penchant for sex, horror, and other transgressions, it is no surprise that he made many films in the vein of the *giallo*, a term more often associated with the violent, sexually explicit, and highly stylized crime thrillers in Italian popular cinema since the 1960s. Even before the release of Mario Bava's *La ragazza che sapeva Troppo* (*The Girl Who Knew Too Much*, 1963), considered by many to be the first *giallo*, Franco's *Gritos en la noche* (*Screams in the Night*, 1962, released in English as *The Awful Dr. Orloff*) reads much like a *giallo*, while *Der Todesrächer von Soho* (*The Death Avenger from Soho*, 1971, released in English as *The Corpse Packs His Bags*) and the slasher film *Die Säge des Todes* (*The Saw of Death*, 1981, released in English as *Bloody Moon*) follow the *giallo* format more closely (Hawkins 2000, 99). While scholarship has tended to locate the *giallo* within the parameters of Italian national cinema, history, and politics, in this essay I demonstrate how Franco's *Paroxismus* (*Paroxysm*, 1969, released in English as *Venus in Furs*), a West German and Italian coproduction, reveals the transnational dimensions of the *giallo* even in its early stages. By closely analyzing the confused and often conflicting representations of time and space in *Paroxismus*, I argue that Franco's *giallo*—as is the case with others both in and outside of Italy—articulates a crisis of temporality in the context of a unified Western Europe and globalizing postmodern world. In conclusion, I suggest that the film, though long neglected by scholars, engages with history as critically as the more esteemed European art films of its era.

The *Giallo* in Transnational Perspective

While its exact definition remains contested, scholars tend to agree on a set of formal and thematic elements that characterize the *giallo*: graphic violence, usually of a sexual nature and almost always towards women; an abundance of sex and nudity; non-normative sexualities, mostly lesbianism; sharp murder weapons; a witness to murder, often an unwitting tourist; psychological trauma and terror; fluid boundaries between dream and reality, performance and authenticity; international travel and jet-setters; surreal and stylish camerawork and set design; and ambiguous, inconclusive endings. Identifying Mario Bava's *La ragazza che sapeva troppo* and *Sei donne per l'assassino* (*Six Women for the Assassin*, 1964, released in English as *Blood and Black Lace*) as its earliest examples, scholars have tended to discuss the *giallo* specifically within the context of postwar Italian cinema and history. While Mikel J. Koven (2006) links the trauma at the heart of most *gialli* to the "defeat and emasculation of Italy in the war and under fascism" (93), Ian

Olney (2013) argues that *giallo* filmmakers "consciously modeled their films after the contemporaneous [anti-detective] fiction of Scerbanenco, Sciascia, and others, as well as certain Italian art films of the period" (107). And even though Gary Needham (2002) describes the *giallo* as a "conceptual category with highly moveable and permeable boundaries," he also locates it and its development within Italian borders, suggesting that one understand the phenomenon "as something constructed out of the various associations, networks, tensions and articulations of Italian cinema's textual and industrial specificity in the post-war period."

Despite scholars' insistence on framing the *giallo* as particular to Italian cinema, the best-known *gialli* were international coproductions involving cast and crew from several European (and non-European) countries, as was typical for European popular cinema in the 1960s (Bergfelder 2006, 10). Mario Bava's *The Girl Who Knew Too Much* and *Blood and Black Lace* are Italian, French, and West German coproductions; Dario Argento's *L'uccello dalle piume di cristallo* (*The Bird with the Crystal Plumage*, 1970) and Massimo Dallamano's *Cosa avete fatto a Solange?* (*What Have You Done to Solange?* 1972) are Italian and West German coproductions; and Lucio Fulci's *Una lucertola con la pelle di donna* (*A Lizard in a Woman's Skin*, 1971) was produced by companies in Italy, France, and Spain. Many famous *giallo* directors—Bava, Dallamano, Fulci, and Sergio Martino, among others—worked under pseudonyms reflecting the nationalities of their markets outside of Italy, demonstrating their transnational identities as filmmakers. And while David Sanjek (1994) and Ian Olney (2013) emphasize the unique focus of the Italian *giallo* on convoluted plots, improbable endings, and unreliable perspectives, the West German *Krimis*—based on the early twentieth-century novels of British author Edgar Wallace—also revolve around "nonsolution" (Gerhards 2013, 153) as the attempt to guess the identity of the perpetrator through logical reasoning is entirely or mostly futile. In its tendency to "nationalize" postwar cinemas, film scholarship has exaggerated the differences between the *giallo* and other European crime films. Given the international context in which it emerged, the *giallo* in the late 1960s and 1970s asks to be read not only within but also beyond the limits of national specificity, especially as a body of films that focuses so heavily on the transgression of generic, geographical, and ideological boundaries.

The predicament, then, is how to read the *giallo* outside of a strictly Italian context. In his work on 1970s cinema, Timothy Corrigan offers a useful model through which one might read the transnational *giallo* as reflecting a postmodern "crisis of temporality." Using David Harvey's *The Condition of Postmodernity* (1990) as an analytical base, Corrigan demonstrates how the films of Rainer Werner Fassbinder—one of the most acclaimed directors of the New German Cinema of the 1970s—stage the violent return of material histories that have been repressed by postmodern culture into the "textual present" of the film (1994, 141). Citing Harvey, Corrigan notes how "geographical localities are made to reconfigure themselves in terms of larger, often global, spaces" as a result of the "time-space compression in Western capitalism since the 1960s" (1994, 153–54). Despite its insistence on transcending the specificities of historical and cultural place, postmodern culture cannot be freed of the material histories that it tries so hard to elide. These repressed material histories and their once possible futures compete and contend for space in a single textual present—in Fassbinder's films, for example—that is "unable to accommodate so many textual presences at once" (1994, 147). Severed from a "localizing and naturalizing" context (1991, 74), the lost histories and places return, Corrigan argues, as "transcending textualities" that have lost their original meaning, now free-floating materials searching frantically for space in a textual present that collapses underneath their weight (1994, 153). Overburdened with material textualities competing for space—costumes and phrases indexing cultural myths, cinematic and literary subtexts, music recordings and song lyrics, television and radio broadcasts, and representational strategies themselves like lighting and framing—Fassbinder's postmodern films ask to be read not for any particular textual meaning but in terms of the "temporal emergency" or crisis that they stage (1994, 145). With their "exaggerated materiality of languages, images and sounds," the films frustrate readings that emphasize narrative and meaning: "The contradictory nature, overabundance, and material weight of textual fabrics in many Fassbinder films work not towards comprehension but impenetrability and incomprehension. This impenetrability in turn redirects the experience of these films from a textual reading towards a crisis of temporality" (1994, 145–46).

Corrigan emphasizes in particular the violence that returning textures and materials bring into the present. In their search for possible locations, textualities produce an "apocalypse where too many texts occupy, distract, and recuperate the present tense of a single space" (1994, 147), in which they "use up" and "assault" bodies as the "central location for [their] onslaught" (1994, 148, 142). In Fassbinder's films, bodies become subject to the forces of "textures and formulas whose very material seems to weigh on and direct certain action and perspectives" (1994, 145). Unable to redirect the mass of texts, images, and events that accumulate around them, bodies become paralyzed, "stripped of motivations and spread across the boredom of an immobile and interminable present" (1991, 183). In Fassbinder's *In einem*

Jahr mit 13 Monden (*In a Year of 13 Moons*, 1978), for example, the main protagonist Elvira undergoes sex reassignment surgery in order to win the love of Anton, the man she loves. After transforming herself into a "more desirable image" (1994, 146) for Anton, Elvira fails nonetheless and commits suicide at the end of the film. Buried beneath the sound of skipping records and surrounded by "odd circling figures from her past," the death of Elvira demonstrates how the "mounting pressure to accumulate more and more textual positions" (1994, 146) ultimately leads to the "physical slaughter of the subject within the incoherence of so much excessive material" (1991, 71). The postmodern desire to be free of material histories "speeds one to a space where one is buried in a garbage of textual relics" (1994, 146). Failing to be naturalized or absorbed into a historical logic, the textualities of lost place and time continue "irrepressibly to haunt" the present, immobilizing and exhausting bodies by the "violence of [their] continual temporal recycling" (1994, 148).

Corrigan's arguments resonate with the *giallo* as a cinema that is so preoccupied with violence, uncertainty, and issues related to time, space, and memory. In the remainder of this chapter, I argue that Franco's *Paroxismus* demonstrates a crisis of temporality associated with the "time-space compression" of postmodernity and the growing global economy in the late 1960s. Marketed to international audiences for the quickest possible revenue, *Paroxismus* is a product of the very structures that it articulates *as* a crisis. By closely reading its representations of time, space, and textuality, I demonstrate how Franco's film dramatizes the disruptions in time and space in postmodern culture of which it is also a symptom.

Transcending Textualities in *Paroxismus*

Paroxismus begins with Jimmy (James Darren), an American jazz trumpeter, on a beach near Istanbul. Frantic and out of breath, Jimmy unburies his trumpet from the sand and plays it until he notices the body of a woman washed up ashore. In a flashback, Jimmy recalls seeing the woman, Wanda Reed, at a jet-set party along with Ahmed, a "millionaire playboy," Kapp, an art dealer, and Olga, a fashion photographer. That night Jimmy witnesses Wanda's gruesome murder: in a dark cell, Olga and Kapp violently tear off her clothes, beat, and whip her, after which Ahmed slices her neck with a dagger and sucks her blood. Unsettled by the experience, Jimmy escapes to Rio de Janeiro to continue performing with his band. There he is haunted by Wanda, who kills Kapp and Olga in revenge. As Jimmy becomes increasingly drawn to Wanda, his girlfriend Rita—played by the American jazz and soul singer Barbara McNair—leaves him. He and Wanda return to Istanbul, where Wanda seduces and murders Ahmed, now a powerful sultan with reign over African lands. When Wanda tries to run from the police, Jimmy chases her into a cemetery where he stumbles across her grave. In the final scene of the film, Jimmy again runs toward a body on the beach, which he now discovers to be his own. The closing image is a freeze-frame shot of Jimmy's trumpet as it washes up ashore.

With the exception of the archetypal black-gloved killer, *Paroxismus* contains all the main aspects of the *giallo*, the most obvious of which are its incoherent plot and ambiguous ending. The film favors excess, spectacle, and performance, featuring several jazz performances with Barbara McNair as Rita and the English rock band Manfred Mann, accompanied by Franco himself on the trombone and piano. Characteristic of Franco's films, *Paroxismus* abounds in sex and violence, represented most graphically in the scene of Wanda's murder. With careers in fashion and the arts, Wanda's killers and later victims include two men and a woman, Olga, with whom Wanda—in typical *giallo* style—has sex before making her slice her wrists in a bathtub suicide. Later in the film, Jimmy considers whether Wanda is a "sick" woman on a "paranoiac trip," like many killer women who populate the *giallo*. Jimmy, like the amateur detective in many *gialli*, witnesses a brutal sexual murder in a foreign country, leading him to experience traumatic flashbacks and hallucinations as he tries to make sense of what he saw. Constantly in flux, Jimmy does not "seem fixed to a home or location" and is "always (in) between places" (Needham 2002), traveling between Western Europe, Turkey, and Brazil, spending his nights in hotels, and never mentioning a home to which he plans to return. Although Jimmy's voiceover narration should grant him some semblance of authority, his discovery of his own corpse at the end of the film calls his story and reliability into question. Finally, as Mikel J. Koven (2006) writes about the *giallo*, the film takes an ambivalent stance toward the liberalization of postwar European society and culture (53). The film represents and simultaneously exploits non-normative sexualities and interracial coupling, legalized in the United States just two years earlier in 1967.

Indeed, fluid boundaries and uncertainty lie at the heart of Franco's film, pointing toward the crisis of temporality that Corrigan discusses in relation to Fassbinder.[1] Neither we nor Jimmy can discern the boundaries dividing dream from reality, life from death, present from past. Even from the start of the film, Jimmy admits his uncertainty about when, where, and even whether the events he recounts took place at all: "It all began last year, or at least I think it did. Because at the time I wasn't quite sure what was real and what wasn't." As he begins his story, he contemplates when he may have met Wanda at the party: "Was it last week? Or last month? Or last year? When you don't know where you're at? Man, I'd tell ya time is like the ocean. You can't hold onto it." As he ponders these questions, the wealthy, stylish young socialites at the jet-set party are presented in a series of snapshot-like images. Rather than stand fully arrested as in a photograph, they appear as though they were told to freeze mid-action. Liquids in drinks are still moving and some bodies cannot remain perfectly still. The past—of which Jimmy is uncertain to begin with—seems to be stuck in an immobile present; as David Harvey (1990) writes about the shifts in postmodern time and space, "past experience gets compressed into some overwhelming present" (291). The past and present are collapsed into each other; the past *is* an always present tense because, as Jimmy's confusion suggests, it has not been integrated into the context of historical temporality. Detached from the trajectory of historical time, bodies—in this instance, the partygoers—are immobilized and stripped of motivation, permanently poised in limbo in an interminable present tense. In a postmodern world ruled by jet-setting and fashion, consumption, and the increasing ephemerality of things, time—"like the ocean"—is ungraspable and too vast to be controlled, in constant motion and spread out over the totalizing, flattened surface of a global present.

Jarring and seemingly out of context, Wanda's murder at the party lends itself, beyond the mere shock factor of sexploitation and violence, to interpretations based on the violent return of material textualities into the film's textual present. Moving through the frozen partygoers, Ahmed greets Wanda at the entrance to the party before leading her to a dungeon-like space. While the eerie glockenspiel melody associated with Wanda continues to play over the soundtrack, the next scene contrasts sharply with the party scene in its *mise-en-scène*. Replacing the contemporary, stylish designs of the party space is a dimly lit, cave-like interior featuring a chandelier, candelabra, and plenty of ominous shadows and flickering lights. The clash of historical temporalities that are conveyed in the visual styles of each space—one contemporary, the other gothic—is paralleled by the characters themselves. Olga is a contemporary fashion photographer with a chic, minimalist studio; Kapp is an art dealer with a modern, baroque-styled home; and Ahmed is a vampiric millionaire playboy and sultan from an ancient world. The fact that all three characters traffic in images—Olga in fashion, Kapp in visual art, and Ahmed in opulence and extravagant displays of wealth—emphasizes their embodiment of a textuality as opposed to some "authentic" material history.

In their initial appearance in the film, Olga, Kapp, and Ahmed are presented individually in close-ups against a flat red background, as though they are loose images that have not yet been integrated into the fabric of the film text. Entering as "transcending textualities" into the film's story, they attack Wanda in a scene whose sheer brutality and visceral nature underscore the brute material force and urgency of their violent return. Ahmed slowly grabs the dagger to slice Wanda's neck in a series of medium and close-up shots. These shots are briefly interrupted by a similarly framed close-up of Ahmed in a shimmery gold turban, which flashes three times in two sets that are some seconds apart. Moments before Wanda's murder, the insert—a single image of Ahmed from what appears to be a foreign place in a distant past—implies that Wanda's murderer is the image itself, a repressed, "culturally dislocated" textuality that, through its frantic and jarring repetition, is desperately vying for space in the present (Corrigan 1994, 150). The most graphically violent scene of the film, the murder of Wanda marks a moment of "temporal emergency" in which repressed material textualities return into the global present—as allegorized by the jet-set party—where they attack and slaughter bodies in their struggle to reclaim a place in the textual space (Corrigan 1994, 145). After they kill her, they return to their "places" in the text: Kapp returns to his mansion, Olga is busy in her studio, and Ahmed becomes the sultan again in his ancient palace.

During the remainder of the film, Wanda avenges her killers, representing on some level the return of a repressed material history caught up in the vicious cycle of one textuality violently taking the place of another in order to recover meaning—however temporarily, if not impossibly—in the textual present. The exaggerated materiality of Wanda's images, repeated throughout the film, underscores her status as a textuality searching compulsively for a localizing context. Washed ashore as a scarred, wet, naked corpse, she enters the film literally as dead weight, wrested from her original temporal context and devoid of meaning (see image 1). After they have sex for the first time, Jimmy asks her, "Who are you?" to which she replies, "I don't know." Jimmy responds contemplatively: "Oh I see. No names, no dates, and no stories. This is the beginning and the end." Wanda continues: "For me, everything ended a long time ago." Wanda does not have a personal identity or past; instead, she is a textual relic that has been displaced from history only to enter into the temporal emergency of a single global present, or, as Jimmy describes it, "the beginning and the end." The sequence ends with a zoom-in to a close-up of Wanda's face looking directly into the camera, followed by a zoom-out of a painting of a water goddess, possibly of the Yoruba deity Oshun, being paraded through the crowds at the Rio Carnival.[2] By linking Wanda to a painting of a divine religious figure, the match cut gestures toward Wanda's own timelessness and material textuality, even implying

Figure 1. Wanda's dead body washes up into the textual space.

that Wanda is a manifestation of that particular mythology returning into the textual present of the film.

Wanda's fur coat also emphasizes the materiality of her image. While her name alludes to the character Wanda in Leopold von Sacher-Masoch's famous novella *Venus im Pelz* (*Venus in Furs*, 1870), the alternate title of the film, the connections between Franco's Wanda and Sacher-Masoch's Wanda are weak. Franco's Wanda tortures Ahmed at the end of the film in a sadomasochistic act of violence, but she represents the earlier Wanda mostly to the extent that she wears a fur coat, that is, on a textural as opposed to a symbolic level. Aside from the fact that she speaks very little throughout the film, Wanda dons various other outfits and disguises that exaggerate the materiality of her image: shimmery silver tights and stiletto heels, a sparkly silver dress and handbag, and a hairstyle that varies between blonde bouffant curls, a dark brown bob, and long blonde tresses. From her cold, wet skin to her soft fur and glistening, radiant surfaces, Wanda's presence in the film is a textural one with little semantic value.

For Jimmy, Wanda represents in some respects a kind of postmodern utopia that liberates him from the material burdens of time and place. Describing his time with her, he notes: "[It was] like today was tomorrow and there never was a yesterday . . . it was like time just didn't exist anymore. The real world had suddenly vanished, and I was hypnotized." When she appears to Jimmy for the first time after her death, he follows her out of the jazz club through a garden plaza to a house where they have sex. A dreamy, romantic music score with saxophone and strings fills the soundtrack, while the camera whirls around the couple from above in shots that are connected through soft, slow dissolves. Intercut with shots of them embracing are several folk portrait paintings presented in zoom-ins, extreme close-ups, tilts, and rack focus shots. Reminiscent of an eighteenth- or nineteenth-century European painting style, these anonymous artworks depict young women and children. One woman resembles a Spanish soldier in her navy blue uniform with red and gold stripes; another plays a ukulele; and one of the last paintings shows what appear to be siblings adorned in rose bouquets. Like Wanda herself, the strangely out-of-place portraits seem to figure in as transcending textualities in a space that Jimmy experiences as timeless. No longer anchored down in their original historical places, the paintings are imbued with new life, presented with motion-filled shot techniques and placed in a physically intimate, dynamic sequence. Inserted between and across the images of Wanda and Jimmy's sexual union, the textualities seem to coexist peacefully in a single space of harmony and transcendental bliss, sentiments that are enhanced by the soft lighting and gentle smiles on the painted figures' faces.

Despite this impression of peaceful coexistence, *Paroxismus* illustrates the impossibility of that postmodern utopia. Wanda's art-filled room is not impervious to the violence of returning material histories; indeed, the odd placement of the paintings in the sequence draws attention to the very violence of their extraction from their original histories. With their modest, placative facial expressions, the women in the paintings unambiguously point toward gendered oppression, while the female soldier evokes the violent histories of European colonialism in South America. These textualities therefore ironically contradict the notion that the textual present can be liberated from the devastating meanings of the past. Similarly, the film ironically undercuts Jimmy's naïve vision of a present unfettered by the materials of the past, of which he tries to convince Wanda toward the end of the film: "I told her the past didn't matter. To forget everything. All that counted was what was happening now." At that moment, however, the sounds of the carriage driver whipping the horses signal the return of Wanda's traumatic past in which Olga and Kapp violently whipped her before her death. That past returns, that is, as an acoustic textuality that, contrary to Jimmy's wishes, irrepressibly pervades the present.

Furs, Trumpets, Sounds, Mirrors: The Battles of the Textualities

Coming back from the dead, Wanda derails Jimmy's sense of time and place. Jimmy's "trauma"—the term used by David Harvey (1990, 286) to describe the experience of the radical reconfigurations of time and space in postmodernity—arises in connection with the compression of time across the surface of global space, which Wanda's return evidences. When he first sees her on the other side of the Atlantic since her death in Istanbul, he exclaims in voiceover: "It was this Wanda. She was dead! I found her body on the beach in Istanbul. How could she suddenly walk in through a doorway in Rio? It was crazy!" Perplexed, Jimmy walks the streets of the carnival "to try to make sense of what was happening. But nothing added up. She was dead. Or was she alive? Was I dead? Or was I alive?" Jimmy ponders these questions in a close-up shot superimposed over footage of the carnival, where crowds of people in elaborate costumes celebrate, dance, and play music. Several soundtracks overlap and compete with each other, including Jimmy's voice, festive samba music, and Wanda's non-diegetic glockenspiel motif. With its conflicting and overwhelming images and sounds, the scene expresses Jimmy's confusion and disorientation. Jimmy is no longer able to orient himself; even Rio is an image disconnected from place, emphasized by its distant, touristic point of view offering a stereotypical portrayal of Afro-Brazilian culture and traditions. Moreover, Jimmy is never embodied in the space of the carnival, which, presented only in documentary footage, seems discontinuous with the story of the film. In a sense, Wanda's return shatters the world that Jimmy knew, and he is now unable to navigate through the disparate images and texts that had been his temporal and spatial markers.

After their first sexual encounter, Wanda continues to traumatize Jimmy by disrupting his sense of time and place. Sweaty and startled, he awakens from a nightmare in which images of Wanda from both earlier and later in the film flash on-screen, leading him to call out her name repeatedly in his sleep. He wakes up to find Rita on his bedside; she tries to comfort him by reorienting him geographically: "Jimmy, you're dreaming. This is Rio, not Istanbul." The overwhelming material weight that Wanda brings into the global present—exemplified by the transitory space of the hotel room—is symptomatized not only by Jimmy's feverish sweat but also in Rita's desire to let Wanda's body take the place of hers. Jealous of his affections for Wanda, Rita begs Jimmy, "Tell me, how did she hook your mind? Please show me. Let my hands be her hands, and my lips her lips!" Conflicted between deferring and succumbing to Wanda's presence, Jimmy retorts: "Don't say that, don't ever say that!" In the end, Rita buckles under Wanda's pressure and leaves Jimmy, forced to relinquish her place to Wanda in a textual present that cannot accommodate both.

Wanda's material presence dictates Jimmy's movements over which he loses control. Compelled to follow her out of the nightclub, he observes,

"I wanted to run, but I had to follow her. I was trapped in a whirlpool that kept sucking me in deeper and deeper. Where was I going? Why was this happening to me? Why couldn't I fight it?" Similar to the first scene in which he approaches Wanda's corpse on the beach, Jimmy is presented in choppy slow-motion shots with lens filters that create watery, wave-like effects. Given that Wanda washes up ashore as a saturated corpse, the watery effects of the images seem to indicate her point of view as her material presence takes over the film text, restricting the movement of bodies within it.

In particular, however, Wanda usurps Jimmy's place in the textual present by keeping him from playing his music. Her textuality, in other words, suppresses and ultimately replaces his. After his experience in Istanbul, Jimmy complains to Rita: "I want to get back to my music, but something keeps stopping me. I can't play my horn anymore!" By talking with her about what happened, Jimmy eventually begins to recover from his trauma and returns to the jazz club to play his trumpet: "Slowly I was getting back on solid ground. My music was in the groove. It was great!" As that precise moment, however, Wanda enters the club, her non-diegetic music motif gradually drowning out Jimmy's music in the diegesis. Invading the textual present from the outside, Wanda's non-diegetic textuality, that is, tries to take the place of a diegetic textuality. As jazz fusion, a popular music style in the late 1960s combining jazz, rock, and funk, this diegetic textuality represents in its cultural hybridity the global present that Wanda interrupts. Staring at her in disbelief, Jimmy drops his trumpet to his side, just as he does when he first discovers her corpse, and remarks in voiceover: "Suddenly I felt all the life being drained out of me." As Wanda continues to push him out of the film text, Jimmy, robbed of his horn, loses his autonomy, sense of self, and subjectivity: "A guy like me without a horn, well, it's like a man without words."

Among the *giallo* characteristics through which *Paroxismus* stages a crisis of temporality—trauma, travel, ambiguity, and stylistic excess—the violent murders articulate the crisis most forcefully. Wanda kills Kapp—who moves through global space as easily as she, for he also suddenly appears in Rio after Istanbul—in her first effort as a transcending textuality to reclaim through murderous violence the space stolen from her by her murderers. Her textual presence in Kapp's mansion is announced by the off-screen sound of her footsteps, which interrupts and takes over the classical piano piece that Kapp is playing, just as her music motif does to Jimmy's music. Kapp looks toward the foyer where he sees her standing seductively in her shimmery silver tights and fur coat. When he rises from his seat to greet her, she disappears only to reappear again in another room, sitting still on a chair and facing the camera as though posing for a fashion shoot. The camera cuts to Kapp and back to

Figure 2. Kapp struggles to breathe in the presence of Wanda.

the same shot of Wanda, who disappears again when Kapp tries to approach her. Upon retreating to his bedroom, Kapp sees Wanda's reflection in a mirror while she lies on his bed and caresses herself in a sexually provocative way. As Kapp begins to undress her, her reflection is divided across two mirrors, her feet in one and the top half of her body in the other. Kapp proceeds to enter the frame and bends down toward the bed to kiss her, but the tilt of the camera reveals that she is not there.

Kapp becomes increasingly overwhelmed when he sees Wanda's doubled reflections and mirroring of already mirrored reflections. As the images of Wanda flash on-screen at an ever-greater frequency, Kapp appears to be suffocating, turning red and gasping for air (see image 2). At the same time, the refrain of the music score is repeated at an accelerating tempo while taking on new instrumental and rhythmic textures. As these images and sounds begin to crush Kapp, the last image that he sees of Wanda is her scarred dead body, the same image that appears to Olga and Ahmed shortly before their deaths. Just as Ahmed's image slaughters Wanda in the beginning of the film, so, too, does Wanda's dead body—whose scarring and listlessness emphasize the materiality of the image as well as the violent nature of its return—ultimately kill Kapp in a suffocating death. The music stops and, as in all the scenes in which Wanda commits a murder, the chorus of Rita's song—"Venus in Furs will be smiling"—plays three times while Wanda again dons her eponymous fur coat, concluding the sequence with the material overdetermination of kitsch. Like Olga and Ahmed, whom Wanda kills without actually touching them, Kapp is a victim of too much materiality that breaks through the global space—instantaneously from one side of the Atlantic to the next—and into a textual present to reclaim place.

As the film approaches its end, time and space become more tightly compressed and the narrative begins to break down. Among her other murders, Wanda's killing of Ahmed, her last victim before Jimmy, brings most strongly into relief the anarchic and endless recycling of textualities devoid of meaning. The sequence begins in a palace where Ahmed seems to have recuperated his place in the textual present after he—or more precisely, his image—kills Wanda early in the film. When Wanda first enters the palace, shots of Ahmed before he stabs Wanda in the first murder sequence flash on-screen, including the images of him picking up the dagger and the same close-up of him in a turban, now flipped in a mirror image along a vertical axis. In a scene already overloaded with the exaggerated materiality of these recycled images, Ahmed begins to tell Wanda a legend—reminiscent of Sacher-Masoch's *Venus in Furs*—in which a "slave girl" in this very palace torments a sultan, her new master, to death. He explains to Wanda that she is now "more qualified" for the role as "slave girl" than when she first appeared to him "a long time ago." While he lies on his bed and narrates, the camera tracks Wanda as she moves behind him. In the same take, the camera pans right to Ahmed entering the room before panning further right toward Wanda, now topless and bejeweled in the role of the sultan's "slave girl." The shot contains multiple temporal registers and conflicting textualities. In the same space and in one take, Wanda appears as her "present" self in her fur coat and as the "past" enslaved woman in the palace, while Ahmed is on his bed but also assumes the role of the sultan about whom he narrates. Wanda, the "slave girl," torments Ahmed, the sultan, in a moment that is narrated as past but is merged with—and therefore becomes—the present. As in Wanda's murder scene, the past and the present occupy one turbulent and confused space in which various material textualities—relics of legends, cultural myths, and literary texts—perpetually attack each other only to be slaughtered and replaced by another. The overembellished, campy *mise-en-scène*, replete with shimmery surfaces, rapid cuts, zoom-ins, rack focus shots, and recycled film stock, emphasizes the impenetrability and chaos of a space overwrought with textual violence. In this continual cycle, Wanda's story of revenge, then, is redundant, a vacant narrative trope that she occupies in order to reclaim her place in the text.

Ultimately, however, Wanda's textual presence overburdens the film, leading to its implosion in a frenzy of stylistic excess and narrative collapse. Chasing her into a cemetery, Jimmy searches frantically for Wanda in a sequence that consists of fast-forward and slow-motion shots oversaturated with shades of red, yellow, blue, pink, green, purple, and various other color combinations. High-pitched sounds and overlapping soundtracks, both new and reused, accompany the shots, most of which are handheld, out of focus and barely legible. Jimmy spots Wanda's fur coat lying on the ground next to a gravestone that reads: "Wanda Reed. A young beautiful stranger washed on to our friendly shores with only death as a companion. May she find peace in her final resting place." While Wanda appears to have recovered a place in a "foreign" textual present—literally becoming text on the gravestone—the narrative, unable to accommodate her weighty presence, breaks apart and returns back to the very beginning. Like a broken record that returns repeatedly to the same place in its compulsive attempt to move forward, the film returns to the place where it began. Again, Jimmy knocks on glass windowpanes in a beach house—as though trying to escape the cycle—before running toward the beach to look for his trumpet. This time, however, Jimmy discovers his own corpse rather than Wanda's, as though he has been expelled from the textual present upon its collapse and now returns as the debris of a transcending textuality. In retrospect, then, the haste with which Jimmy recovers his horn at the beginning of the film stresses his sense of urgency in relocating himself in the text through the subjectivity that musical expression affords him. At the same time, his weakness and inability to catch his breath point toward the physical toll that the continual temporal recycling of textualities takes on bodies, crippling and exhausting them until they become a burdensome, mutilated mass. The last image of the film is a freeze-frame shot of Jimmy's trumpet washed up ashore. Trapped in an interminable present and alone in the frame, the trumpet is dislocated from time and place, a material object ejected from the textual space in which it took on meaning as music-maker. Jimmy's trumpet and Wanda's remaining fur coat are the debris of failed emplacements, drifting across the limitless expanse of global temporality and washing up as strangely misplaced objects into foreign texts that cannot support them.

Since treating the *giallo* as a serious object of study, scholars have tended to disagree on how to categorize the phenomenon, whether as a style, cycle, genre, or *filone*, the Italian word for strand, current, or trend. While Gary Needham (2022) emphasizes that the *giallo* represents a "body of films that resists generic definition," Ian Olney (2013) argues that such an approach is not particularly helpful because the *giallo* "becomes at once all things and nothing" (105). In order to understand the *giallo* film, Olney stresses that "we need to recognize the importance of its generic and historical dimensions" (105). *Paroxismus* offers an alternative reading of the *giallo* that mediates these discussions. While the *giallo* pushes into the direction of a genre with its set of identifying narrative and stylistic features, Franco's film demonstrates that the *giallo* is ultimately precisely about the impossibility of becoming a genre. As *Paroxismus* shows us, the *giallo* is a genre that one might best describe as a *failed* genre, unable to organize the disparate and conflicting images, signs, and sounds of lost places and histories across global space within the formulaic parameters of genre. As a body of films that focuses so heavily on violence and trauma, the *giallo* faces particular challenges in finding a shared language of trauma in the context of postwar Europe, thus returning to some unidentifiable, vague or unknowable traumatic past. With its focus on fluid boundaries, stylistic excess, visceral violence, and temporal and spatial disorientation, the *giallo* challenges the very concept of borders according to which genre functions. Extending across national limits, the *giallo*, as Franco's film indicates, tries to cover *too* much space and *too* much time, leading to the collapse of narrative logic and an excess of confounding texts and materials in a moment of, to return to Corrigan, "generic desperation" (1991, 137). In a sense, then, the Italian term *giallo* points ironically to its own failure to limit itself to nation and genre, emerging symptomatically during a postmodern crisis of time and space. But the generic failure of the *giallo* is precisely what lends it its subversive energy. As a product of a globalizing Western European film industry, Franco's *giallo* turns against, in some respects, the very structures that made it, not only by insisting on the impossibility of its generic uniformity, but by celebrating alterity, materiality, and incongruity at the expense of a clean and coherent narrative. Franco's *Paroxismus* embraces the disjunctures, interruptions, and uncertainties of postmodern temporality, transforming them into an aesthetic that came to define the *giallo* in the following decade.

Notes

1. Locating the *giallo* at the transition between modernism and postmodernism, Alexia Kannas (2021) similarly emphasizes the "pervasive anxiety" (68) that permeates the *giallo* world, one that is plagued by a "decadent dementia" and an inability "to shift gear or move forward" (69).

2. For more on the role of paintings in the *giallo*, see Alexandra Heller-Nicholas's *The Giallo Canvas: Art, Excess and Horror Cinema* (Jefferson, NC: McFarland and Company, 2021).

Works Cited

Bergfelder, Tim. 2006. *International Adventures: German Popular Cinema and European Co-Productions in the 1960s*. New York: Berghahn Books.

Corrigan, Timothy. 1991. *A Cinema Without Walls: Movies and Culture After Vietnam*. Rutgers, NJ: Rutgers University Press.

Corrigan, Timothy. 1994. "The Temporality of Place, Postmodernism, and the Fassbinder Texts." *New German Critique*, no. 63 (Autumn): 139–54.

Gerhards, Sascha. 2013. "Ironizing Identity: The German Crime Genre and the Edgar Wallace Production Trend of the 1960s." In *Generic Histories of German Cinema: Genre and Its Deviations*, edited by Jaimey Fischer, 133–56. New York: Camden House.

Harvey, David. 1990. *The Condition of Postmodernity: An Enquiry into the Origins of Cultural Change*. Cambridge, MA: Blackwell.

Hawkins, Joan. 2000. *Cutting Edge: Art-Horror and the Horrific Avant-garde*. Minneapolis: University of Minnesota Press.

Heller-Nicholas, Alexandra. 2021. *The* Giallo *Canvas: Art, Excess and Horror Cinema*. Jefferson, NC: McFarland and Company.

Kannas, Alexia. 2021. *Giallo! Genre, Modernity, and Detection in Italian Horror Cinemas*. Albany: SUNY Press.

Koven, Mikel J. 2006. *La Dolce Morte: Vernacular Cinema and the Italian* Giallo *Film*. Lanham, MD: Scarecrow Press.

Needham, Gary. 2002. "Playing with Genre: An Introduction to the Italian Giallo." *Kinoeye: New Perspectives on European Film* 2, no. 11 (June). https://www.kinoeye.org/02/11/needham11.php. Accessed October 29, 2021.

Olney, Ian. 2013. *Euro Horror: Classic European Horror Cinema in Contemporary American Culture*. Bloomington: Indiana University Press.

Sanjek, David. 1994. "Foreign Detection: The West German *Krimi* and the Italian *Giallo*." *Spectator* 14, no. 2: 82–95.

Chapter 5

THE ANALOG OF SELF-AUTHENTICITY WITHIN *THE FORBIDDEN PHOTOS OF A LADY ABOVE SUSPICION*

GAVIN F. HURLEY

Luciano Ercoli's 1970 film *Le foto proibite di una signora per bene* (*The Forbidden Photos of a Lady above Suspicion*) offers a unique *giallo* that can be overlooked in favor of better-known *gialli* released in 1970, including Dario Argento's *L'uccello dale piume di cristallo* (*The Bird with the Crystal Plumage*, 1970) and Mario Bava's *Il rosso segno della foglia* (*Hatchet for the Honeymoon*, 1970). Although *Forbidden Photos* does not receive much fanfare today, the film was quite successful in its 1970 Italian release. It was well received by audiences on its opening night—and gathered substantial profits thereafter ("Forbidden" 2006).

While *Forbidden Photos* credits two screenplay writers, Ernesto Gastaldi claims that he solely penned the *Forbidden Photos* screenplay ("Forbidden" 2006). Gastaldi (1997) wrote numerous *giallo* screenplays, including many of Sergio Martino's *gialli* such as *La coda dello scorpione* (*The Case of the Scorpion's Tail*, 1971) and *Lo strano vizio della Signora Wardh* (*The Strange Vice of Mrs. Wardh*, 1971) (54–56). Like many Sergio Martino's films, *Forbidden Photos* specifically exhibits Gastaldi's *giallo* writing signature. Unlike more well-known *gialli*, such as the work of Argento, Gastaldi's screenwriting does not hide small details within plots, intending them to be overlooked (45–46)—such as details witnessed at murder scenes or subtle pieces of evidence. Instead, Gastaldi's writing emphasizes motives and actions of characters. In this way, Gastaldi's (2015) *gialli* requires fuller engagement from the viewer to decode characters' intentions (10). Accordingly, Gastaldi's *gialli* feature thrilling character-driven plots, rather than shocking horror or murder set pieces.

Forbidden Photos is a typical character-centered Gastaldi *giallo*. The film focuses on a complex blackmailing plot rather than various murders; therefore, it more closely resembles a "suspense thriller" rather than a "murder mystery" (Koven 2006, 68). Accordingly, it does not exclusively rely on black-gloved killers stalking prey. Instead, it offers a psychosexual cat-and-mouse game between a web of unreliable characters. Viewers must decode the motives of characters, rather than try to solve the identity of a single killer.

In its complexity, *Forbidden Photos* is a valuable *giallo* to examine, specifically as an interior analog for the exterior rhetoric of the genre. It offers strata of meta-commentary wherein both Gastaldi and Ercoli represent the rhetoric of the *giallo* genre as a whole.[1] Particularly, *Forbidden Photos* illustrates how *giallo*, as a genre, plays with viewers' expectations when adhering them to the fiction; simultaneously, *giallo* can also persuade viewers to reflect upon the worlds constructed by *giallo* itself. As this essay illustrates, these worlds can be understood as simulationally aesthetic. As explained by rhetorician Barry Brummett (2003), such worlds can be understood as Baudrillardian (6–7)—or, as coined by Kendall L. Walton (1990) in *Mimesis as Make Believe*, "reflexive representation" (117). The art becomes self-referential and self-contained. According to Brummett (2003), the elements of reality, representation, and simulation are intertwined as a "trialectic"—and bound together rhetorically (20–24). As such, the fictional worlds can synthesize aesthetics, experience, and rhetoric. They do not literally represent the reality outside of the art, but instead, communicate their own dreamy worlds that audiences experience—and are rhetorically invited to contemplate.

To better investigate the rhetoric of reality, representation, and simulation within *Forbidden Photos*, this essay peels back several layers. This essay first briefly outlines the concept of "bad faith" as it is evidenced in the film. Then it traces how rhetorical commentary is represented in the plot and characters of *Forbidden Photos*—presumably, within the elements of Gastaldi's vision. After this broadband analysis, the essay more closely analyzes the rhetorical commentary within the symbolic style of *Forbidden Photos* such as setting, props, and even cinematography—elements of Ercoli's vision. Finally, the essay applauds the film's rhetorical imagination. Its conclusion acknowledges the playfulness of the film—and of *gialli* in general—and how built-in rhetorical reflexivity can connect audiences to the genre.

"Bad Faith"

Forbidden Photos illustrates the existential concept of "bad faith" in action—specifically, in the character of Minou. However, the film also analogously highlights the role of bad faith within *giallo* viewers themselves. Ultimately, this bad faith can serve as a touchstone to help trace the rhetorical operations of *Forbidden Photos* as well as *giallo* films in general.

Coined by existentialist Jean-Paul Sartre ([1943] 1993) in *Being and Nothingness*, bad faith is "a lie to oneself within the unity of a single consciousness. Through bad faith a person seeks to escape the responsible freedom of Being-for-itself" (547). In bad faith, one abandons their freedom, autonomy, and individual responsibilities. Sartre more explicitly illustrates bad faith in action within his 1944 play *No Exit*. In this play, three characters are trapped in an unknown room—presumably Hell—without an exit. They begin to depend on each other and shun their own individuality. In sum, the play reveals the human tendency to neglect individual autonomy and define one's Being through other people. For example, rather than being confident with her own individual existence "for itself," the play's character Estelle requires a mirror so she can ensure that she exists. When she relies on another character, Inez, to act as her "mirror" and describe her appearance, Estelle depends upon someone else to define her. This indicates her bad faith: her lack of self-autonomy. Toward the end of the play, the third character, Garcin, is given the choice to finally leave the room of his own free will, but he does not. Again, Sartre illustrates bad faith, the refusal to accept and act as a free individual human being.

Forbidden Photos's characters orchestrate much of the film's representational and reflective bad faith. The film's small cast of characters includes Minou (Dagmar Lassander), Peter (Pier Paolo Capponi), Dominique (Nieves Navarro), an unnamed "blackmailer" (Simon Andreu), a friend named George (Salvador Huguet), and several police officers. Despite the small cast and the relatively slow pace of the action, the plot is quite complex. Peter, who is the husband of Minou, hires a "sex fiend" to blackmail and manipulate his troubled wife into killing herself so he can receive insurance money to pay off his business debts. Specifically, he designs a way to exploit Minou's existential inauthenticity and drive her to suicidal despair. Throughout this serpentine *giallo*, viewers witness Minou's existential struggle to freely preserve her own sense of self amidst this subjective turmoil. Ultimately, the film illustrates Minou as a victim of her own bad faith.

Resembling *No Exit*, *Forbidden Photos*—through the main character of Minou—offers a compelling representation of bad faith. However, unlike *No Exit*, *Forbidden Photos* does not end in despair. Rather, it ends with Minou reclaiming and empowering her authentic self. Throughout much of the film, Minou relinquishes her authentic self, allowing substances (cigarettes, alcohol, and tranquilizers) as well as other people to suppress her innate freedoms. From the very beginning of the film, she embraces being the object of a "gaze"—specifically, her husband's "gaze." For example, throughout the beginning sequence of the film, she routinely looks to the framed photo of her husband, wondering what he would think of her. She even carries the photo around the house with her and places the framed photo on her bed while she paints her toenails. Her reliance on Peter's gaze throughout the film becomes increasingly problematic for her.

Both Peter and the blackmailing "sex fiend" (who is being controlled by Peter) project their Being onto Minou. A blackmailing plot is a common narrative strand within *giallo* films; however, the multilayered strata of blackmailing and accompanying power dynamics are more unique to *Forbidden Photos*. Specifically, the blackmailer controls Minou because he pretends to know that her husband has committed murder. This false information gives him power over her but only as much as she relinquishes her power to him. And he substantiates his information with fabricated proof: an audio recording of Peter speaking about his participation in a murder plot. Looking to protect her husband from the recording, she accepts the blackmailer's proposal: that he will give her the recording once she has sex with him. After he reveals that the recorded conversation was fake, he blackmails her again with the photos of their sexual encounter. Since Minou does not want to taint her relationship with her husband, she once again surrenders to the demands of the blackmailer—despite the fact that she originally had sex with the blackmailer only so she could defend the reputation of her husband. Ultimately, she loses control as the film unfolds. To use Sartre's terms: she increasingly defines her own Being through other people's Being. Rather than living authentically as a free individual, Minou surrenders to the gaze of Peter, then the blackmailer, and finally to Peter once more since she does not want her husband to see the "forbidden photos."

After the blackmailing unfolds, Minou begins to unravel. Peter secretly interferes with events and places in her life so that Minou begins to doubt her reality. For instance, she takes Peter and the police to the blackmailer's lair, only to discover an empty apartment and no blackmailer. Throughout the film, others cannot corroborate her experiences with the blackmailer. Confused and frustrated, Minou then contemplates suicide to desperately reestablish control and end her pain. Finally, at the end of the film, viewers discover that most of her bad faith was meticulously engineered by Peter to make her mentally unstable and drive her to suicide.

Overall, Minou surrenders her authentic Being to drugs, alcohol, dependence on her husband, money, luxury, and the maintenance of her reputation. But, after she is almost killed by the blackmailer and Peter is shot dead, Minou is reborn and shatters her spell of bad faith. Dominique, as Minou's confident friend, rescues Minou by uncovering Peter's scheme and bringing the police to Minou and Peter's house.

Unlike Minou, Dominique fully celebrates her own autonomy, something that is specifically evidenced by her confident sexuality. For example, when audiences first encounter Dominique at the dance club, Minou introduces her to Peter's friend George. Although Dominique and George have just met, Dominique flirts with George and dances intimately close to him. Her outward ambition indicates her confidence and security with herself. Similarly, at the end of the film, the police commissioner mentions that another police officer will drive Dominique home from the crime scene. Without reservation, she proposes to be driven home by another officer: one who is younger and more attractive. Again, this indicates her self-assuredness and well as her confident assertion of power.

Dominique is not only motivated by lust; she is rational and deliberate, too. This imbues her with an understated ethical code despite her sexual spontaneity. For instance, during the tell-all interview with the commissioner at the end of the film, Dominique explains that she had earlier logically deduced that Peter was behind the events. However, if she had spoken too soon about his crime, then Peter would have known that *she* had known. Therefore, she had to time her actions accordingly. Dominique is not only an example of a woman who is confident and driven, but she is also patient.

Dominique is difficult to read. Although she has sexual relations with Minou's husband, she also ironically models compassion and friendship toward Minou. She frees Minou from her "bad faith" by decoding Peter's scheme; moreover, she also picks up Minou from the hospital in the last scene of the film. After watching the entire film, viewers can assume that Dominique's illicit sexual relationship with Peter may have been carried out so that Dominique could dominate him and unlock his scheme. This domination is suggested through her physical position of power on the bed—that is, straddling Peter—in a scene that reflects their affair.[2] At the end of the scene, Dominique commands Peter to leave her house via the back entrance.

Once Minou is freed from the hospital at the end of the film, Dominique asks her how she is feeling. Minou cheerfully responds with "never been better," presumably, with Peter out of her life. Revisiting her commitment from the beginning of the film, Minou more confidently vows to avoid taking tranquilizers and drinking whisky. Then, George suddenly tells Minou that she is financially sound—that is, she is financially free to pursue her own ambitions. She gets in the comfortable car with Dominique and drives off into the city. The camera pans back implying endless possibilities for Dominique and Minou.

Throughout *Forbidden Photos*, it becomes clear that all characters are connected to Peter: Minou is Peter's wife, Dominique is Peter's illicit lover, the blackmailer is hired by Peter, and George is Peter's friend and colleague. However, viewers of the film are meant to specifically identify with Minou. As the main character who occupies almost every scene of the film, Minou serves as the identifiable character surrogate.

Minou's subjective state provides an outward analog of the audience's subjectivity while experiencing the film itself. In this way, Minou can analogously represent the viewers, while Peter can analogously represent Gastaldi and Ercoli. Similar to how Peter employs the blackmailer to manipulate and seduce Minou, Gastaldi and Ercoli symbolically use characters and actors to manipulate and seduce their viewers. As such, the film mirrors the rhetorical operations of the genre. Like the power held by Peter and the blackmailer, *giallo* films powerfully seduce viewers toward willfully abandoning themselves in service to the art. But in *giallo* film, viewers also wrestle with their own authenticity. The films deceive and manipulate them until finally they are liberated at the end by a guiding hand of truth, which returns autonomy back to the viewer.

However, the concluding scene of *Forbidden Photos* may imply that it may not be that simple. The curious last line of the film may suggest otherwise: that the viewer had their autonomy stripped not by a manipulative Peter, but rather by Dominique and Minou themselves. When driving in the car in the last scene, Dominique asks Minou if she wants to go to Copenhagen to take some more erotic pictures. The joke seems a bit odd—almost in bad taste—considering that the photos almost led to Minou's traumatic death. Yet, despite the inappropriateness of the comment, Minou and Dominique laugh about the photos as they drive away. According to an interview with Ernesto Gastaldi, this final interaction was not meant to be an innocent gesture or a bad joke. Gastaldi deliberately crafted this dialogue to add another potential twist or "reversal" to the plot ("Forbidden Screenplays" 2006). He sought to give viewers one more possibility: that Dominique and Minou were pulling the strings of the narrative the entire time. It opens the option that the two women planned the series of events, perhaps as an elaborate way to dispose of Peter.

As a meta-commentary on the genre, the film's final twist may suggest that *giallo* films with open-ended or ambiguous conclusions can still hold the audience captive to its power. The film has the power to release—or not release—the viewer from its spell. Even after the final credits, *gialli* can stoke bad faith in their audience, never truly revealing the truth, never truly giving autonomy back to the viewer. Through this last line of the film's dialogue, Gastaldi flexes a last bit of muscle: the playful dominance of the *giallo* over the audience.

Ercoli's Rhetorical Stylistics

Forbidden Photos may represent the attractiveness of bad faith in *giallo* films, but how does *Forbidden Photos* specifically connect viewers to this representation? How do Luciano Ercoli's stylistics reflect *giallo* as a genre? How might the director's cinematic style inspire viewers to meta-cognitively ponder their own *giallo* experience?

The film's meta-commentary becomes clear once viewers begin to identify with Minou as their character surrogate. Once viewers see themselves in Minou and recognize their own "bad faith" as *giallo* participants, then viewers can begin to question their bad faith. Ercoli rhetorically signals this connection between viewer and Minou at the beginning of the film so that viewers can assume an active, reflective participant role rather than a passive, recipient role.

Ercoli begins the film by partnering aesthetic images with deep reflective attitudes and hedonistic undertones. This approach establishes that *Forbidden Photos* will not only be an aesthetically rich film peppered with hedonism but will also be a reflective film for the main character—and by association, be reflective for the viewer who is meant to identify with the main character. In short, the first images and sequences importantly establish the fictional world—as well as the headspace—wherein viewers are situated. It places viewers in a particular framework wherein the specific rhetorics operate.

The film's beginning credit sequence brims with representations of pleasure, art, and reflection. As the film opens, Ennio Morricone's dreamy *bossa* lounge music plays in the background. The camera pans down from pagan wall ornaments of beast faces to ones of human figures depicted in ancient Greek/Roman style. The camera continues to pan down to several scallop shell ornaments that protrude from the wall, and finally viewers see Minou smoking a cigarette, naked in a bathtub (see figure 1). As communicated by the pagan imagery of shells, water, and a naked woman with red hair, viewers may connect Minou with Venus/Aphrodite, the goddess of erotic love, as popularly understood by Botticelli's famous Renaissance painting "Birth

Figure 1. Behind the open credits text, Minou stares up at the shells and pagan imagery while she relaxes in the bathtub and smokes a cigarette.

of Venus." This pagan symbol of deistic power and erotic love suggests the potential erotic freedom and the potential innate power possessed by Minou: strength that will be unlocked later in the film. Smoking a cigarette in the bath, Minou thoughtfully looks upward toward these pagan ornaments, which the viewer has just observed. Here, via inner monologue, she contemplates her own freedom. She vows to quit smoking, drinking, and "taking those tranquilizers." In a broad sense, she ultimately ponders her own power as an individual: the power to reclaim more authentically humanistic pursuits—ones often endorsed by ancient pagan Greek and Roman philosophy and mythology[3]—rather than relying on external chemical means.

Furthermore, Minou's inner monologue delivers the first words of the film. Since the audience can hear her thoughts, Minou again projects herself as the identifiable character-surrogate. The reflective nature of her inner thoughts establishes that the film will also require self-reflection from the audience. This dimension promises that *Forbidden Photos* will be a reflective film for the viewer.

Through her inner monologue, Minou dedicates herself to temperance; however, her justifications undercut her quest for self-authenticity. She vows to stop smoking, drinking alcohol, and taking drugs because it will make Peter, her husband, happy. Minou unknowingly replaces her *recognized* inauthenticity with *unrecognized* inauthenticity. Not only does she seemingly ignore how her husband controls her, but she also seems to willingly embrace it. This concession is clearly illustrated when she sits on the bed with the picture of Peter and paints her toenails after the bath. She motivates herself to change because Peter wants it, not because she wants it. Represented by her repeatedly gazing into the mirror in the first few scenes, the film suggests that she has the means to recognize self-authenticity. However, she misuses the mirror to make herself look attractive for Peter, rather than authentically examine her own Being.

Resembling Minou's initial subjective position, viewers are escorted into self-reflection as well. The film seems to urge viewers to self-reflect on their own *giallo* viewing experience as a whole. In other words, Ercoli does not seem to require viewers to identify with specific dimensions of Minou's life, such as an overbearing husband situation or a substance abuse issue; instead, he rhetorically invites viewers to reflect on the *giallo* genre itself—to ponder their bad faith as *giallo* viewers.

Resembling Minou's misunderstood freedom when dominated by Peter, viewers may misinterpret their freedom within the *giallo* viewing experience. After all, viewers are bound to the writer and director's narrative, rhetoric, and aesthetics, and become entangled in knots of bad faith. Viewers voluntarily give away their self-authenticity when immersing in *giallo* fiction, a genre that they know will deliberately toy with their expectations for the duration of the film.

Furthermore, after Minou establishes that she needs to stop drinking and using drugs to satisfy Peter, Minou proceeds to ignore her commitment anyway. Following the bath, she immediately pours herself a glass of whisky and takes tranquilizers. She commits to self-authenticity, but her commitment is thin. She willfully gives her autonomy away to another person (Peter) and to temporary pleasures (alcohol and drugs). Similarly, *giallo* viewers give away their self-authenticity to the director/writer of the art and also to the temporary pleasures of the art itself. The *giallo* genre particularly depicts aesthetically pleasurable visuals and music, while likewise depicting characters' hedonistic behavior such as sex, drinking, dancing, and so forth. Therefore, like Minou, viewers become transported to an aesthetically pleasing world where they are vicariously swept up by sex, alcohol, and drug use. As such, they can lose their sense of self when watching *giallo* films. Just as Peter wants Minou to lose control of her self-authenticity, directors of *gialli* want viewers to lose themselves in the aesthetic and pleasurable excesses, and as a result, suspend their self-authenticity.

Minou craves self-authenticity. Ercoli makes this clear from Minou's first lines of the film. And from the pagan wall ornaments, he seems to suggest that she is strong enough to reclaim self-authenticity. Still, at the beginning of the film, her surrounding excesses immediately tempt her—and she freely succumbs to them. Ercoli illustrates these excesses by showing how Minou lounges in a warm bath, paints her toenails, pours herself a drink, sits down in her living room surrounded by art deco furniture and fashion magazines, and takes pills to fall asleep. In the same way, *giallo* films figuratively pamper

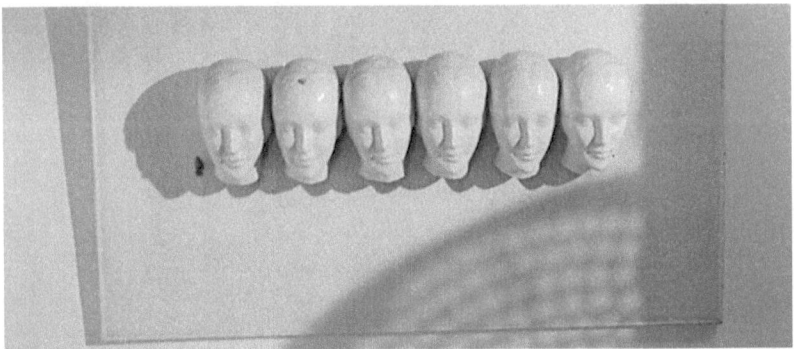

Figure 2. Wall art of six smiling mannequin heads that can represent the audience of the film.

the audience with excess: intoxicating them on aesthetics, pleasures, and escapism. In a way, viewing audiences resemble the wall ornament high up on Minou's living room wall: an ornament that Ercoli pans to once Minou takes a tranquilizer and falls asleep. The wall ornament presents a row of six smiling mannequin heads set upon the wall. Although this in-film art can represent Minou's (or viewers') fragmented subjectivity, it can also represent a smiling audience looking out at the scene—much like a front row of a movie theater. The heads on the wall smile identically and artificially: much like pacified audiences of stylish *gialli* (see figure 2). Accordingly, *Forbidden Photos* audiences surrender their subjectivity for the artificial subjectivity of Minou, replace their values with the values of the narrative, and become happily enamored by the style of the film.

The Rhetoric of Danger

Although Minou perceives security in her stability with Peter, she also seems to crave variation, excitement, and danger outside of the house—and outside of Peter. Her cravings are evidenced through her substance abuse—which offers escapism from boredom—as depicted in the beginning credit sequence of the film. Yet, these artificial substances and domestic luxuries are not enough for Minou. She yearns for stimulation outside of the house and with other people. Her cravings for excitement resemble cravings that fuel viewers of *giallo* films: the touristic hungers for something interesting, such as the rushes of violence, thrills of exposed skin, and joys of beautiful people, beautiful music, and beautiful surroundings and fashion.

Minou initially indicates her desire for variation after she bathes and paints her toenails. She sits next to a full-size mirror, so viewers see two

Figure 3. Minou's internal struggle with authenticity in front of the mirror.

representations of Minou implying a reflective double-sided nature to the character: one side is domestic and committed to Peter, the other side is wilder and craves independence. Her inner monologue/dialogue supports this double-sided nature while sitting by the mirror (see image 3). She thinks, "Dominique is right, I should change how I look"; then she reveals more of her chest by removing a white tie from her dress. After the realization, she admits she should change her look because it is "the way you [Peter] like it." From this monologue/dialogue, viewers witness Minou's yearning for variation and excitement, but viewers also witness how she undercuts her overall quest for authenticity. After all, she does not change her dress for herself, but because Dominique told her to do so—and because her husband will like it.

Following the dress alteration, Minou fantasizes about a way she can assume power over Peter. She constructs a fake story that she can tell Peter about "falling in love with another man" and insisting that they must get a divorce. The inner monologue reveals Minou's hunger for individual agency in their marriage. Yet, viewers never see her execute her plan. She never tells her husband the fake story. Furthermore, if viewers look closely, Minou even reverses the previous alteration to her dress. Without overtly signaling it to the audience, the tie that she had earlier removed from the dress returns to the garment in the next scene—which means that she replaced it. In other words, like the fantasy about falling in love with another man, she does not follow through with defiantly modifying her dress.

Ironically, the blackmailer cuts the very same tie in her dress—along with the remaining ties—when he assaults her on the beach. And, instead of a fake story about cheating on her husband, Minou eventually cheats on her husband with the same blackmailer. The blackmailer pressures Minou to enact the same actions that she fantasized about in the privacy of her home. However, he perverts the fantasies. He psychologically manipulates her to enact her fantasies against her will and in excessive ways. Through Minou's altered dress and her story about falling in love with another man, viewers catch a glimpse of Minou's cravings for control and agency. However, Peter (through the commissioned blackmailer) undercuts Minou's power by commandeering both actions and perverting them. The cutting of the dress on the beach serves as a perverted form of the alteration of the dress in the house. Instead of modestly altering her clothing, the blackmailer cuts all of the ties to her dress, violently against her will. Instead of an innocent fantasy about falling in love with man who is not Peter, Minou is coerced by the blackmailer into having sex with a man who is not Peter. Clearly, these encounters with the blackmailer do not directly unfold from her bad faith—since Peter commissioned the blackmailer to assault his wife as she innocently wandered the beach—but once Minou enters the blackmailing plot, her bad faith provides openings for others to take advantage of her. As a result, her downward spiral gains momentum.

In short, this downward spiral resembles the experience of the *giallo* viewer. In a particular way, *giallo* films coerce viewers to take part in consecutive uncomfortable experiences. The danger and excitement are thrust onto them through a perverse fiction that is crafted by a screenwriter and director. In many ways, the violent thrills enact the rhetorical purpose of the genre. Unlike other genres, *giallo* films specifically usher viewers into complexly deceitful tales of sex and murder. Much like Minou, who leaves the house and becomes swept up in a murder and blackmailing plot, the viewer is swept away from the comfort of their reality into taboo and aggressive excitement. And although bad faith may not fuel the initial viewing experience, it can open avenues for the film to manipulate viewers as they become immersed in the *giallo*.

The viewer is escorted from comfort into danger: specifically, from the security of their subjective and reflective reality toward wilder aesthetic elements (music, fashion, style), and ultimately into the open world of possibility and danger (the murder plot itself). Minou depicts this movement in the first several minutes of the film. When she finally leaves the bathtub and stylish living room, Minou is portrayed distant from the camera and viewer. She is depicted as far away, wandering the dark beach. Through this scene sequence from bathtub to beach, Ercoli depicts Minou as increasingly distant from the camera with each subsequent scene. The spaces and locations increasingly expand as well: from the bathtub's confines, to the larger bedroom, to the even larger living room, and finally to the wide beach with its vast ocean. This increasing distance simulates how Minou opens her possibilities toward a world outside of her comfort zone, which is not unlike viewers' experience of the *giallo*'s open fictional world of possibilities. As in any fiction, participants become swept up into a wider fictional world. However, the world of *Forbidden Photos*—a world that viewers know through Minou's eyes—is ultimately controlled by a deceptive character (Peter). This scheme can represent how Ercoli and Gastaldi play with the viewer. The viewer enters an anxious game—much as Minou enters an anxious game.

To this end, like all *gialli*, *Forbidden Photos* subverts traditional or conservative means of entertainment. The film alludes to this subversion—as well as the audience's attraction toward such subversion. This attraction is spotlighted when Minou sits in the bar after the beach assault, presumably seeking safety from the blackmailer. Here, Minou joins the two men at a table and watches a monotonous traditional card game. Waiting for Peter, she becomes increasingly bored and drunk. When Peter finally arrives, viewers see him through a jagged broken window of a bar. Then, viewers momentarily see Minou through the broken window—from Peter's perspective outside of the bar. Eventually, Peter calls to her through the window. This scene is curious. Rather than Peter meeting her inside the bar, he calls to Minou so she has to leave the bar. Excited to see him, Minou leaves the safe space and runs back into the dangerous night and into the arms of the deceptive Peter. Again, this scene appears to mirror how viewers, through the character of Minou, similarly greet the seemingly safe (but actually dangerous and deceptive) narrative with open arms. Moreover, it represents how *giallo* viewers leave the confines of their monotonous reality to engross in the fictional reality of a *giallo* narrative: opening themselves up to a range of sharp-edged possibilities—and concurrently, they are curiously comforted by it. They freely exchange their own authenticity and identity for that of the writer, director, and the dangerous narrative itself.

The filmmaker of the *giallo* places the viewer under its treacherous spell—much as the blackmailer places Minou trapped under his treacherous spell. This representation is revealed when Minou first meets the blackmailer on the beach. Here, Minou asks, "What do you want here?" to which the blackmailer replies, "You." This response can be interpreted as direct-addressing audiences of the film. Specifically, the *giallo* itself wants to acquire or adhere "you"-as-viewers to the narrative genre. This aim is a primary purpose of the *giallo* filmmaker. It seems deliberate that Ercoli's blackmailer also stares directly into the camera as he stalks Minou on the beach. If the blackmailer represents the filmmaker (or even the genre as a whole), the point of view represents the filmmaker (and genre itself) stalking the audience by looking directly at them. And the blackmailer is clear about his methods. Much like the filmmaker and the genre in respect to the audience, he "is not going to use force"; rather he wants her to "beg him" and "plead for his kisses." The blackmailer repeats this point later in his apartment lair, stating that he wants Minou to "surrender" her "mind" and "long" for his "love." Much as Peter and his hired blackmailer control Minou's narrative, the filmmaker controls the viewer's narrative experience but also needs them to genuinely desire the experience. Resembling how the blackmailer dubiously gets Minou's consent to have sex, *giallo* filmmakers dubiously acquire rhetorical assent from the audience. The films do not physically assault viewers, but rather, in many ways, mentally dominate viewers into assent. Accordingly, on the beach, the blackmailer confesses to Minou that, "he knows her." This knowledge may suggest how deep the directors and writer of *gialli* thoroughly know their audiences. In many ways, *giallo* filmmakers use audiences' appetites for danger, adrenaline, and domination to seduce them into the narrative itself.

Much like Peter's plan to manipulate Minou, *Forbidden Photos* and *giallo* films inscribe Being onto viewers. Viewers become pawns swept along by the danger, the thrill of voyeurism, and the aesthetic bombast. Moreover, like Minou, viewers agree to give themselves to the film. Paying for admission in the movie theater, viewers literally pay money to be controlled by the filmmaker. Clearly, viewers are not being blackmailed, but they engage in a type of exchange. Viewers surrender to the film. They spend money and time for the opportunity to do so, and in exchange, *gialli* grants them access into worlds of pleasure, danger, and deceit.

Rhetoric, Genre, and Play

The analysis of *Forbidden Photos* reveals rhetorical play. In a way, *gialli* persuade audiences to suspend their authenticity to better adhere them to the narrative and genre. The innovative playfulness within *Forbidden Photos* uncovers dynamic rhetorical possibilities that can operate within other *giallo* films as well.

One playful dimension revolves around rhetoric and genre. Twentieth-century American rhetorician Kenneth Burke ([1950] 1984) explains that rhetoric involves symbols used by "human agents to form attitudes ... in other human agents" (41). According to Burke, since humans are symbol-using beings, rhetoric uses symbols to influence symbolic action (41–43). Genres play a functional role in organizing the use of symbols. Genres help categorize the symbols in ways to effectively operate within given occasions. These categories help shape audience expectations, which can help streamline audiences' communicative connections and experiences. Therefore, if audiences are aware that they are watching a *giallo*, they expect narrative elements such as murder, suspense, black-gloved killers, red herrings, stylish visuals, and so on. These elements compose the genre of *giallo* film. Most *gialli*, including *Forbidden Photos*, makes use of these elements; however, as demonstrated throughout this analytical essay, *Forbidden Photos* differs from other *gialli* since its narrative elements can symbolically comment back upon the *giallo* genre itself.

The overlapping genre elements can provide insight into how *Forbidden Photos* aligns with genre conventions while rhetorically acting as "meta-commentary"—or a means of commenting back on its own operations. When tracing the complexity of genre functions, literary theorist Mikhail Bakhtin specifically notes primary and secondary genres within his "The Problem of Speech Genres" essay (Bawarshi and Reiff 2010, 26). He notes that primary genres work horizontally with reality, while secondary genres work vertically with other genres (26). For example, saying "Hello?" when picking up a phone call would be considered part of the primary genre of a phone call; however, a phone call recorded and used in a cross-examination of trial would be considered a secondary genre (26). Secondary genres can be quite complex. They do not merely absorb and rearrange primary genres; they also absorb and rearrange other secondary genres (26).

Bakhtin explains that a novel—or, for the purpose of this essay, any fictional work—re-assimilates realities into its own reality (Bawarshi and Reiff 2010, 26) Accordingly, it can recontextualize multiple genre realities to form its own cohesive fictional reality (26). The cultural use of the realities, like the phone call genre, disappears into the fiction. The real-life "use-values" of the repurposed genres become destabilized (26–27). As such, secondary genres, such as novels and films, provide arenas for genres to comment on one another (27). In this way, *Forbidden Photos* acts an arena for genre commentary; however, instead of commenting on other primary and secondary genres, it comments back on the "use-function" of its own genre. *Forbidden Photos* absorbs secondary genre in an innovative manner that makes it a unique *giallo*. It does not merely present itself as a member of the genre; instead, it *re-presents* the genre by providing commentary about how the genre works. The film spotlights the purposeful rhetorical decisions made by *giallo* directors and writers—as well as the general appeal of the genre. In short, *Forbidden Photos* offers a rhetorical meta-commentary into the rhetoric of the *giallo* genre. This innovative re-appropriation of rhetoric and genre toward a type of commentary can be viewed as a playful use of genre that suspends its authenticity to the genre by also acting as a meta-commentary.

As an analysis of the film demonstrates, *Forbidden Photos* also offers a rhetoric of bad faith and domination that is fundamentally playful. Such playfulness (facilitated through the fiction) serves a crucial function because it can soften any potential ethical breach associated with the bad faith. Unlike Minou in *Forbidden Photos*, who could have been powerless for her entire marriage, viewers recognize (by the nature of the form of film) that they are only giving away their power for one to two hours. This recognition implies that viewers will be set free at the end of the film notwithstanding any domination experienced.

Although Minou and Dominique complicate the ending of *Forbidden Photos* with their cryptic dialogue, *gialli* generally set viewers free at the end of the films. The final truth frees viewers from the cloud of mystery and deception. Moreover, viewers become literally freed because the fiction has concluded. Interestingly, such final emancipation is often indicated with main characters departing in vehicles in the last scenes of *gialli*. For example, Julie Wardh (Edwige Fenech) drives away with the police at end of *The Strange Vice of Mrs. Wardh*, Greta Franklin (Barbara Bouchet) leaves in train at end of *Alla ricerca del placere* (*Amuck!*, Silvio Amadio, 1972), and Michel Aumont (Simon Andreu) boards in a plane at the end of *La morte cammina con i tacchi alti* (*Death Walks on High Heels*, Luciano Ercoli, 1971). Similarly, *Forbidden Photos* also uses the departing vehicle trope to illustrate Minou's freedom. The fictional departure suggests that the audience is potentially free from the grip of the rhetorical narrative. It signals to the audience that the whirlwind of deception has dissipated, and viewers can regain their original freedom and agency.

Conclusions

Effective *giallo* films offer carefully orchestrated and seductive domination. The films absorb viewers into their narrative experiences—and, initially, they persuade willing viewers to freely give their assent. Deeper elements of *giallo* can play with viewers' psyches as well. For instance, as noted by Ian Olney (2013), Mario Bava's iconic *Sei donne per l'assassino* (*Blood and Black Lace*, 1964) destabilizes viewers' experiences, facilitating a "performative approach to spectatorship among viewers" (115). Such fragmentation placed within a well-crafted anti-detective story instills a sense of "vertigo" in the viewer—and in this sense, Olney suggests that an appeal of *Blood and Black Lace* does not merely consist in solving a who-done-it mystery, but rather "in surrendering oneself to it" (115). In this way, the film can exhibit power over the viewer. It first persuades a viewer to adhere and assent to the experience, but then dominates them within the experience itself.

Forbidden Photos offers a similar type of narrative domination as represented by Minou being dominated by Peter. But, unlike *Blood and Black Lace*, the film symbolically delivers a revealing meta-commentary on why and how such domination rhetorically operates. In other words, alongside the plot deception, *Forbidden Photos* represents the spellbinding rhetoric that *giallo*, as a narrative genre, presents to its viewers. Resembling Minou, *gialli* viewers are often nudged into adopting particular beliefs, aligning their loyalty with particular characters, and falling victim to deceptive twists. This temporary assent can pull viewers from their own set of values wherein they freely relinquish their own self-authenticity and freedom. Unlike typical murder mysteries, *giallo* is generally lush with comfortable Apollonian aesthetics (fashion, music, beauty, order, stylish cinematography) as well as risky Dionysian frenzy (alcohol, drugs, sex, chaos, and adrenaline). As evidenced throughout *Forbidden Photos*, *giallo* films' "set pieces"[4] often lead viewers into frenzied portrayals of sex, drug use, alcohol consumption, dancing, and violence—the conventional elements of any *giallo* film. Consequently, when viewers assent to the cinematic experience, they assent to such hedonistic values portrayed in the fiction—if only for the duration of the film. Pleasure-seeking offers a key ingredient of the genre's distinctiveness. It can make the genre more appealing than typical murder mysteries and thrillers. Dionysian elements seduce audiences into its alluring web, so that viewers, like Minou, spiral into bad faith without realizing how the writer, filmmaker, and film playfully dominate them.

Notes

1. In the "Forbidden Screenplays" interview from Blue Underground's 2006 *Forbidden Photos* DVD release, Gastaldi notes that he and Ercoli worked well together on the film—and that Ercoli was quite loyal to Gastaldi's screenplay.

2. Via the character of Dominique, *Forbidden Photos* may be interpreted as a feminist narrative that celebrates female empowerment. This interpretation is important to recognize, but it extends outside of the scope of this essay.

3. Such as principles of *eudemonia*, excellence, truth, and virtue, which are integral to ancient Greek philosophy, specifically the work of Plato and Aristotle.

4. The Dionysian frenzy in *giallo* films can be partially attributed to the typical "set pieces" within Italian cinema. According to Mikel Koven (2015), a set piece within *giallo* film focuses a particular murder scene, sex scene, or dancing scene for extended periods of time (126).

Works Cited

Bawarshi, Anis S., and Mary Jo Reiff. 2010. *Genre: An Introduction to History, Theory, Research, and Pedagogy*. West Lafayette, IN: Parlor Press.

Brummett, Barry. 2003. *The World and How We Describe It*. Westport, CT: Praeger.

Burke, Kenneth. 1950 (1984) *A Rhetoric of Motives*. Berkeley: University of California Press.

"Forbidden Screenplays—Interview with co-writer Ernesto Gastaldi." 2006. In *The Forbidden Photos of a Lady above Suspicion*. [1970] 2006. Directed by Luciano Ercoli. West Hollywood, CA: Blue Underground, DVD.

Gastaldi, Ernesto. 1997. "What are Those Strange Drops of Blood in the Scripts of ... Ernesto Gastaldi?" Interview by Tim Lucas. *Video Watchdog*, no. 39.

Gastaldi, Ernesto. 2015. "What Is a *Giallo*?" In *So Deadly, So Perverse: 50 Years of Italian Giallo Films*, edited by Troy Howarth, 10–11. Baltimore, MD: Midnight Marquee.

Koven, Mikel. 2006. *La Dolce Morte: Vernacular Cinema and the Italian Giallo Film*. Lanham, MD: Scarecrow Press.

Olney, Ian. 2013. *Euro Horror: Classic European Horror Cinema in Contemporary American Culture*. Bloomington: Indiana University Press.

Sartre, Jean-Paul. 1943 (1993). *Being and Nothingness*. Translated by Hazel E. Barnes. New York: Washington Square Press.

Sartre, Jean-Paul. 1944 (1989). *No Exit and Three Other Plays*. Translated by Stuart Gilbert. New York: Vintage.

Walton, Kendall. 1990. *Mimesis as Make-Believe: On the Foundations of the Representational Arts*. Cambridge, MA: Harvard University Press.

Chapter 6

BEYOND INTERESTING

The Affective Complexity of Barbara Bouchet in *Don't Torture a Duckling*

ERIC BRINKMAN

"[Giallo] is the story of a threadbare cinema that achieved something in spite of itself."
—LUCIO FULCI[1]

In the introduction to his *The Haunted World of Mario Bava*, genre critic Troy Howarth insists that, for whatever flaws Bava's films might possess, "they *all* have points of interest" (Howarth 2014, 15; emphasis in original). Howarth has several arguments for why this is true, including that Bava's films eschew conventional narrative storytelling in order to emphasize "vivid visual images" with the "eye of a master painter" (ibid.). That Howarth would seek to elevate the lowbrow medium of the originator of *giallo* film by invoking a highbrow art form is hardly surprising, yet poetic descriptions of Bava's films as "perverse dark comedies" fail to help us comprehensively grasp their enduring appeal (ibid.). I agree with Howarth that reviewers rarely understand the appeal of genre films from directors like Bava and often resort to condescension in order to condemn to "a life of critical scorn and neglect" work they do not have the tools to fully appreciate (ibid.). However, there are better methods to draw attention to the virtues of *giallo* film that do not depend on directorial comparisons with painters and operas,[2] but rather in paying attention to what actually draws interest from genre fans. For example, the performances of the female actors in these films, like the work of their directors, continue to receive widespread appreciation from fans decades after their films have been completed. Many of them, from actors such as Barbara Bouchet, Anita Stringberg, Edwige Fenech, Florinda Bolkan, and Dagmar Lassander, continue to draw lasting interest because they offer complex, multifaceted performances in ways that current scholarship on *giallo* has failed to give enough attention. As an exemplar for how this particular form of criticism can function, this essay will focus on Barbara Bouchet's 1972 performance in Lucio Fulci's *Don't Torture a Duckling* (*Non si sevizia un paperino*), because Bouchet's performance in Fulci's film is both compelling and affectively complex. This in turn supports the film thematically, especially in that the complexity of her performance credibly maintains her positionality within this *giallo* film as a red herring. Like Sharon Stone's breakout role in *Basic Instinct* (Paul Verhoeven, 1992), Bouchet is able to maintain viewer interest within the film by believably representing herself as possessing the potential to be both an innocent victim and a violent, murderous killer.

A Renewed Interest in *Gialli*

Gialli, characterized by the set pieces; stylish visuals; psychosexually disturbed, black-gloved killers; grisly murders; and abundant plot twists like those in *Don't Torture A Duckling* are gaining renewed attention as the technology to transfer and reproduce 2K and 4K scans to DVD and Blu-ray disk becomes more readily available. This material change has led to an explosion of releases of *gialli* titles on prestige format Blu-ray discs, with companies such as Arrow, Severin, Vinegar Syndrome, and Synapse marketing these films as horror to fans of the genre. Since 2018, Arrow alone has released *The Bird with the Crystal Plumage* (*L'uccello dale piume di cristallo*, 2018), *Deep Red* (*Profondo rosso*, 2018), *Torso* (*I corpi presentano tracce di violenza carnale*, 2018), *The Case of the Scorpion's Tail* (*La coda dello scorpione*, 2018), *What Have They Done to Your Daughters?* (*La polizia chiede aiuto*, 2018), *The Cat O' Nine Tails* (*Il gatto a nove code*, 2018), and *Strip Nude for Your Killer* (*Nude per l'assassino*, 2019). Severin and Synapse have similarly released transfers of titles such as *All the Colors of the Dark* (*Tutti I colori del buio*, 2019), *Phenomena* (2017), and *Tenebrae* (2016), while Vinegar Syndrome has released three boxed sets of "Forgotten *Gialli*." HD transfers are also available for *A Lizard in A Woman's Skin* (*Una lucertola con la pelle di donna*, 2016), *Don't Torture A Duckling* (*Non si sevizia un paperino*, 2017), *Blood and Black Lace* (*Sei donne per l'assassino*, 2016), and many others.

Stylistically, the renewed interest in *gialli* has inspired several contemporary directors to emulate the narrative and visual style developed by Italian directors in the 1970s. Rian Johnson's 2019 *Knives Out* claims influence from *giallo* films, as did the more directly influenced Hélène Cattet and Bruno Forzani's neo-*gialli Amer* (2009), *The Strange Color of Your Body's Tears* (2013), and *Let the Corpses Tan* (2017). Yann Gonzalez's *Knife + Heart* (2018) has also been described as a "campy homage to *giallo*," due to its stylish visuals and leather-clad killer (Suber 2019). While the interest and promotion of such films often centers on marketing the names of prominent directors to horror genre fans, this chapter will instead focus on the roles female actors play in driving the continued interest in fifty-year-old Italian genre films.

Although female actors who performed in *giallo* films have received little scholarly attention, genre magazines that cater to the interests of fans of the horror genre have not let their work go unnoticed. While the academic interest and marketing for these films tends to highlight the name of the director, magazines will generally interview both actors and directors in order to increase sales by catering to the interests of genre fans, which continues unabated, up to over half a century after their performances. British and American magazines such as *Scream*, *Rue Morgue*, *Horror Hound*, and *The Dark Side* regularly contain interviews and feature cover art that highlight the importance of "scream queens" to their business model, and a quick perusal of the back catalog of *Videoscope* reveals a history of interviews and features on actors such as Linda Blair, Mary Woronov, Mamie Van Doren, Adrienne Barbeau, and Caroline Munro. *Shock Cinema* recently featured an interview with Sybil Danning (Kirst), highlighting her appearances in vernacular films such as *Battle Beyond the Stars* (Jimmy T. Murakami, 1980), *Operation Thunderbolt* (Menahem Golan, 1977), *Chained Heat* (Paul Nicholas, 1983), and *The Concord: Airport '79* (David Lowell Rich, 1979), and *Cinema Retro* published a "girl power" issue in 2019, with articles focusing on women in film and interviews with Marianne Koch, Stefanie Powers, and Pamela Green (Rodgers 2019). Similarly, *Scary Monsters* published an issue that focused exclusively on "Scream Queens, Horror Heroines, and Femme Fatales" with a featured article on the female actors that have appeared in Hammer films (Smeraldi 2019).

While a detailed treatment of "scream queens" is beyond the scope of this chapter, by focusing on the female actors that appeared in and continue to drive an interest in genre films, in particular *gialli*, I will demonstrate how affect theory provides a methodology to explain this continued fascination. Drawing on affect theorists such Brian Massumi, Laura Podalsky, and Eugenie Brinkema, I focus on emotional and physical responses to these films as affect, here defined as embodied pre-socio-linguistic response. Affect, in this context, is a description of bodily sensation as it occurs before being constrained by predetermined socio-linguistic emotional categories. The sensation of a racing pulse and a feeling of adrenalin are not cognized as anger or fear until we recognize it as such and either fight or run away; before that moment, as affect, it has the potential to result in either—or both—responses.

Whereas the way marketing efforts of genre magazines often seem to interpret fan appreciation of female actors as based primarily on their appearance, the physical attractiveness of these actors by itself cannot explain the continued interest in their performances. More precisely, the continued interest in particular performances across the oeuvre of these actors, well-established within their genres, suggests that the interest in actors such as Bouchet, Strindberg, or Fenech goes beyond their physical appearance; that is, it is possible to compare the effectiveness of these actors across their own films. For example, while Fenech appears nude in several of her films, they do not all share the same level of fan and critical appreciation: films such as *All the Colors of the Dark* are receiving transfer to 2K Blu-ray and increased attention, while her appearances in Italian sex comedies such as Mariano Laurenti's *Naughty Nun* (*La bella Antonia, prima Monica e poi Dimonia*, 1972) and Marino Girolami's *Lover Boy* (*Grazie . . . nonna*, 1975), in which she also appears undressed, languish for all intents and purposes as forgotten. Bouchet also appears undressed in both the *giallo* film *Don't Torture a Duckling* and in Fernando Di Leo's *poliziottesco* film *Caliber 9* (*Milano calibro 9*, 1972). Yet Bouchet's performance in *Duckling* is far more compelling: where in *Caliber 9*, Bouchet's major contribution to the film is to appear in a table dance scene (shot sideways so that her body fills the length of the screen), her ability to play a complex character in *Duckling* thematically supports the action and meaning of the film. Therefore it must be the case that there are other factors involved, such as the individual performances in different films. It can also be argued that at least as often, if not more so, when a film is successful, it is the affective labor performed by the actor that results in audiences finding it appealing, since it is also true that many of the films directed by some of the even more well-known Italian directors, such as Fulci, were often critical and commercial failures.

The Appeal of *Giallo* Film

Genre critics have also often turned to auteur theory to try to explain the appeal of *giallo* films to their fans. Howard, for example, has written book-length treatments of Mario Bava and Lucio Fulci, Tim Lucas has also written about Bava, and Stephen Thrower has covered Lucio Fulci and Jess Franco (Howarth 2014; Howarth 2016; Lucas 2007; Thrower and Grainger 2015; Thrower 2019; Thrower and Fulci 1999). Although in an interview in the Blu-ray extras accompanying the Arrow release of *Don't Torture a Duckling* Mikel J. Koven references the fact that *giallo* fans can list the filmographies of directors like Fulci, in his *La Dolce Morte: Vernacular Cinema and the Italian Giallo Film*, he explicitly argues that the goal of his monograph is not to put "Lucio Fulci, Sergio Martino, and Aldo Lado into the same revered echelons as Dario Argento and Mario Bava" (Koven 2006, v). Rather, in the field's first book-length scholarly treatment of *giallo* films, he makes an important contribution to their study by viewing them through the lens of vernacular cinema, which takes into account the promotion and distribution of *giallo* films to often distracted audiences with "divided attention" (Koven 2006, 33). According to Koven, in the theaters in Italy that screened these films, audiences expected to also be able to do other activities, such as converse with one another, at the same time that they watched the film. Films shot for vernacular cinemas are meant to provide a "context for social interaction": rather than trying to maintain an audience of quiet spectators enthralled by filmic spectacle, vernacular films provide a context to socialize, occasionally attempting to re-capture the audience's attention with eye-grabbing set pieces that contain scenes of graphic violence or sex (Koven 2006, 27).

In the same way that Koven's description of vernacular cinema helps us understand *giallo* films on their own terms, this chapter will argue that the continued interest in these films by genre fans is at least in part due to the enduring appeal and significance of the performances of female actors within the genre. In fact, it is often their affectively complex interpretations of their roles in these films that often represent the best of type in the genre, and therefore the films with the most interest from fans. Films such as Fulci's *Don't Torture a Duckling*, Sergio Martino's *Your Vice Is a Locked Room and Only I Have the Key* (*Il tuo vizio è una stanza chiusa e solo io ne ho la chiave*, 1972), *All the Colors of the Dark* (*Tutti I colori del buio*, 1972), and Luciano Ercoli's *Forbidden Photos of a Lady above Suspicion* (*Le foto proibite di una signora per bene*, 1970) continue to draw genre fan interest almost fifty years after their release dates, and it is not accidental that all include strong performances by their respective female leads. An excellent example of such a performance is Bouchet's role in Fulci's *Don't Torture a Duckling* (*Non si sevizia un paperino*, 1972), because Bouchet's charisma and talent enacting complex desire and motivations shine through in every scene in which she appears.

Barbara Bouchet in *Don't Torture a Duckling*

Barbara Gutscher was born in 1943 in the Nazi-occupied Reichenberg, Sudetenland. Following World War II, she emigrated from Germany to California with her family, having been granted permission to immigrate to the United States as a displaced person. As a teenager she performed as a dancer on a local television show in Five Points, and moved to Hollywood as an adult to work in the film industry there, changing her name to the more Anglo-centrically acceptable "Bouchet." After achieving some success as a model and actress in television commercials, she landed roles on *Star Trek* ("By Any Other Name," Marc Daniels, 1968) and played Miss Moneypenny in the James Bond spoof *Casino Royale* (1967).

Hoping for better opportunities abroad, Bouchet found the acting success she was looking for in Italy, appearing in several notable roles in both *poliziotteschi* such as *Caliber 9* and *giallo* films such as Paolo Cavara's *The Black Belly of the Tarantula* (*La tarantola dal ventre nero*, 1971), Emilio Miraglia's *The Red Queen Kills Seven Times* (*La dama rossa uccide sette volte*, 1972), and *Don't Torture a Duckling*. What makes Bouchet's performances more or less effective across these films with different directors is the complexity required of the different roles she was asking to play: some directors will give her more or less material with which to work. So it is primarily her performances within *giallo* films that provide her better opportunities, because she acts from within their genre conventions: visceral thrills provided by the voyeuristic depiction of an unknown killer whose violent bloodletting is the result of psychological issues that center around sexuality. We see these moments especially in a film such as *Don't Torture a Duckling*, perhaps aesthetically the best film of the three *gialli* in which she appears and in which she has the largest part, and also the performance in which her character portrays pedophilia, drug use, obvious sexuality, and a potential for murder, but who also ends up finally being the lead female hero of the film.

Don't Torture a Duckling has several features typical of *gialli* and several that are not. Like all *gialli*, it is a thriller centered on discovering who is behind a series of gruesome murders. In this film, however, Fulci and his cinematographer, Sergio D'Offizi, like to use long shots to establish that the film is taking place in the country, both qualities atypical of *gialli* as a genre. The most important aspect of the film for my purposes, however, is the film's use of red herrings. Misdirection is common enough across almost any kind of thriller, but in *Duckling*, Fulci throws in almost the entire cast: we are given hints that the killer of several local boys might be the local man with an intellectual disability, Giuseppe Barra (Vito Passeri); the local witch, La Maciara

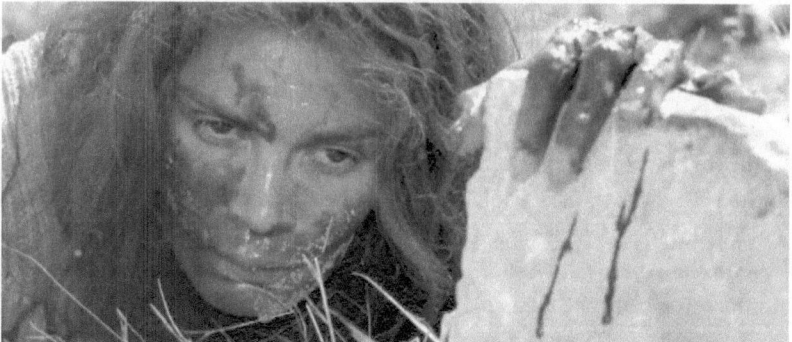

Figure 1. Bouchet must maintain interest in the film even after the graphic (yet moving) murder of La Maciara.

(Florinda Bolkan); the young female outsider who has had drug problems, Patrizia (Bouchet); and the mother of the local priest and a young girl with disabilities, Aurelia Avallone (Irene Papas). In the end, we discover that it is the local priest, Don Avallone (Marc Porel), who has been killing the boys.

The film cycles through each of these characters as the potential killer, beginning with Patrizia and then eliminating the others one by one until revealing the plot twist that the local priest is the killer.[3] The police are already holding Giuseppe when another murder is committed, so they realize he cannot be the killer. A local mob, believing La Maciara to be the killer, beats her to death with chains in a moving set piece that establishes her as a victim instead and potentially forms the basis of a critique of rural backwardness. After her death another boy is murdered again, clearing her also of suspicion and revealing her to have been the target of small-minded prejudice and rural town superstition. Next Patrizia is caught lying to the police about her continued drug use, and suspicion falls heavily on her, until big city reporter Andrea Martelli (Tomas Milian) begins to suspect the local priest's mother, who is covering up the fact that her hearing-impaired and nonverbal daughter is pulling the heads off of dolls as a way to convey that she has seen who is committing the murders. When confronted, however, Dona Avallone begs Andrea and Patrizia's help to save her daughter from her son, the priest Don Avallone, who has been murdering the local boys to "save" them from themselves; that is, with a sort of *Catcher in the Rye*-style belief in their innocence, he murders them before they can "fall." To save the girl, Andrea and Patrizia engage in a physical battle with Don Avallone, who finally is thrown from a cliff and dies the requisite gruesome death.

What is relevant for the purposes of my argument, however, is how the film is able to sustain the viewer's interest in multiple iterations of looping back to another red herring. Many *giallo* films, such as Bava's *Blood and Black*

Lace (1964) and Umberto Lenzi's *Eyeball* (*Gatti rossi in un labirinto di vetro*, 1975), also use multiple red herrings—in both virtually everyone except the police is a suspect—but neither of those films contain performances on the level of Bolkan or Bouchet. In fact, in many ways, Bolkan's performance of La Maciara's murder is the center of the film. Yet it occurs well before the end of the story: the film continues for more than another thirty-five minutes as Fulci moves past it and generates continued interest in a new set of red herrings until the final reveal. He is able to do this by relying on the talents of the second of his star actors, Bouchet, whose affectively complex performance intertwines with the interest and catharsis of the film from the murder of Bolkan's character and continues it to the end.

The Efficacy of Affect

Although there are several strands of affect theory,[4] in this chapter I will be focusing on Brian Massumi's definition of "affect" as the biological response to sensation that often exceeds our socio-linguistic capacity to describe it. In fact, affective responses can exceed us in multiple senses: they are often beyond our control, and they also exceed us in the sense that they may be read by others (Hurley 2010, 11–18).[5] Additionally, this framing of the way in which affect exceeds emotion can also be extended to include the way affect exceeds the limited confines of the experience of watching a single film: as Sara Ahmed has noted, affect is "sticky" and iterative and often follows us outside the strict confines of the original space in which it is induced (Ahmed 2004, 89–92). Each successive viewing reinforces the original affect of the initial experience and raises questions about why and what possible benefits viewers experience from such spectatorship, rewarding repeated viewings in different and multiple contexts.

In order to get at affective responses to the *giallo* films I discuss, I will often have to rely on my own experience. It is difficult to know someone else's affective response to a performance and, in fact, I will argue that often academics, reviewers, and audience members frequently misread the affective responses of others.[6] However, audience reception theory has finally begun to engage with audiences in order to rectify this potential oversight, and, wherever I can, I will mention the affective responses that I have access to, such as those recorded by audience members in blogs and product reviews or those reported by academics or reviewers. The title of this chapter is inspired by just such as investigation: reading through an Amazon review by "From the Mind of Tatlock" of the Arrow Blu-ray of *Don't Torture a Duckling*, under the subheading of "Interesting Elements," the reviewer listed a few of the actors and included the following description: "Barbara Bouchet. Beyond interesting actually" (customer review 2017).

Bouchet's performance is "beyond interesting" because her performance affectively exceeds socio-linguistic emotional categorization. As described by Massumi in his introduction to *Parables for the Virtual*, affect defined this way is a process that operates over time, what Massumi calls a "body—(movement/sensation)—change" continuum. Deploying Zeno's paradoxes of movement as a metaphor (Massumi 2002, 6), he likens affect to the movement/change the body experiences over time as a process continuum. Conversely, emotions are fixed states: they are ideological, linguistic endpoints we apply as descriptions of sensation after we experience it in order to try to make sense of it. In other words, because the body in motion cannot coincide with itself (a body in motion is not the same in that it does not stay in the same space and changes over time) (Massumi 2002, 4), the physical, material body is unreal unless it is thought of as existing over time, the "real incorporality of the concrete" (Massumi 2002, 5). Emotional categories, such as joy, anger, sadness, or fear, therefore, are socio-linguistic and fixed, and therefore cannot accurately describe the actual sensation of a body in flux. In order to accurately describe sensation then—instead of merely containing it—we must look for descriptions outside of our known, perhaps too safe, regimented emotional categories. According to Laura Podalsky:

> Brian Massumi makes the following distinction between affect and emotion: whereas affect is embodied intensity, emotion is "the socio-linguistic fixing of the quality of an experience which is from that point onward defined as personal . . ." Massumi (following Deleuze) allows for other qualities of experience that are as yet untethered to social and linguistic structures. (2011, 12–13)

In other words, affect as a description of sensation that can move amidst/between/across all of these categories, can more accurately describe the initial sensation I experience upon viewing Bouchet's performance, as it operates outside of the socio-linguistic containers I might later use to describe/contain it. I call this response *affective complexity*: prelinguistic responses to stimulation that are difficult to describe through singular or simple socio-linguistic emotional categories.

Affective complexity is significant technology for interpreting the performances within vernacular cinema, since it allows us to understand audience response through the body as a way to find nodes outside of the normal rigid structured positioning of emotion, to find the gaps in Massumi's theoretical no-body's land, which exists outside of established binary positions within the hegemonic structure enforced by dominant class, racial, and patriarchal ideology (Bruns 2000, 6). By avoiding binary ideological representations, I am searching for a way to describe analog rather than digital response: a range instead of an on-off set of descriptors.[7] Emotions, such as anger, happiness, or sadness, exist as on/off binaries and well-defined points within the continuum of affective possibilities, but are limited in what they can convey and therefore have the tendency to function to conservatively reinforce structures already in place.[8] These points, clearly demarcated within cultural norms, are easily described by extant language that exists within well-defined instances of cultural expectations, as containers that exclude more complex possibilities.

Affect, conversely, exists as a range amidst/between/across these seemingly sometimes contradictory endpoints, thus articulating new possibilities as instances within an unstructured continuum, an infinite number of points that have not been defined within a hierarchal predetermined structural context. Therefore, I will take as axiomatic Massumi's insistence that a body in motion does not coincide with itself—the real versus the virtual, abstract understanding of the same—which forces us, as we to try to engage with the reality of the virtual body, to think about the latent rhizomatic indeterminate multiplicity of its affect: the virtual body exists as an analog sea of undefined experience full of points that exist both within and without the borders and boundaries of the defined endpoints that exist within well-known, well-defined male-dominated white supremacist hierarchal cultural structures. That is, during singular instances when the unabstracted body coincides with materialist sensation, these are the well-defined interstices we recognize as "emotion," but when we consider the material body in the abstract, as a body in motion across time—such as during a performance—we can regard that range of motion/change as potentially possessing affect that operates outside of the well-known or defined structures that operate to contain and regulate affective responses.

In its relation to variation while in motion, the body is similar to the phase-shift that occurs as matter changes to energy and vice versa, capturing the "potential—process—event" dynamic discussed by Foucault as *incorporeal materialism*. Drawing on Foucault here allows Massumi to focus on the body as a process: it permits us to see that the abstracted body over time still has a material presence, something that must be understood in order to grasp those aspects of the body that function as the "real incorporeality of the concrete" (Massumi 2002, 5). In other words, it is critical for us to understand how the abstracted body still functions outside of the ideological formulations of canned emotional responses in order to distinguish when we are talking about it in its real materiality: the "virtual" is the real here because it allows us to distinguish between socio-linguistic formulation of states and the actual sensatory experience of the body over time.

Affect, by allowing us a more accurate description of the range of sensory experience of which the body is capable, therefore also allows for the possibility of feeling outside of existing hierarchies. While focusing on process does not deny the ontological status of possible endpoints along the path of sensation, it rather highlights those emotional descriptions to be "limited to a particular dimension of the real." Affect in contrast exists outside of these binary endpoints as real and contains the potential for what Massumi calls "miraculation," but what I interpret as heightened experience: that is, the ontological experience of becoming outside of our known, perhaps too safe, emotional categories, a process focused on change that is already available in the present moment, one that we often instead relate to the prescribed boundaries of the vague paradoxical invention of our ready-made culturally constructed socio-linguistic containers (Massumi 2002, 13). Thus, I am looking for something sensatory on the grid of self-coinciding bodies in moments of disjunction, an affective in-betweenness with intensity that exceeds the well-defined emotional containers of fear, disgust, desire, or aversion. These affective responses include sensation, perception, and memory, and have the potential to give the viewer a sensory experience outside the normal: becoming that leads to an ontological process that exists outside of existing cultural structures (Massumi 2002, 14).[9] I will also argue that this added complexity, which I will describe in relation to the performances of female actors, allows for more complex interpretations of vernacular films, in particular interpretations that provoke and interest genre fans, because it allows them to feel outside of simple, well-defined emotional responses and experience something sensatory off the preconceived socio-linguistic grid.

However, Eugenie Brinkema's criticism of the "turn to affect" is correct: ultimately the deployment of affect theory is of limited value if it cannot also perform the more practical and rigorous task of an application to close reading (Brinkema 2014, xi–xvi). Additionally, an understanding of the affective complexity generated by an actor such as Bouchet will help us recognize the work they are doing, work that has heretofore remained unrecognized as the performance of the previously marginalized emotional labor of women.[10] Therefore, I turn now to a close reading of Bouchet's performance in *Don't Torture a Duckling* in order to demonstrate how her performance works within the genre conventions of *gialli* in order to create the possibility for an affectively complex audience experience.

Barbara Bouchet's Affectively Complex Performance in *Don't Torture a Duckling*

What affective complexity in particular accomplishes in the context of Bouchet's performances in *giallo* films is the suggestion to the audience of a complex character whose motives, like the affect her performance generates, are often complex, multiple, and uncategorizable. This maps onto the *giallo* convention of a psychosexual mysterious killer very effectively, as part of the enjoyment of watching these films are the sensational explanations for the motivations behind the bizarre murders committed in this genre of film.

Therefore, in Fulci's *Don't Torture a Duckling*, the indeterminacy of Bouchet's motivations as Patrizia support the film thematically. As an outsider (Patrizia has evidently been sent to this small town to keep her away from drugs), she immediately seems suspicious to the local townspeople. Fulci is questioning idyllic rural traditions and claims that modernity is polluting and corrupting of the same by demonstrating that the idyllic countryside has problems of its own.[11] When the innocent La Maciara is suspected and beat to death by a mob of townspeople seeking "justice," her death is such a striking set piece and so central to the film thematically that the danger is that the final third of the film could be read or experienced as anticlimactic. Instead, because of the investment in and affectively complex performance of Bouchet also as a suspicious outsider, she continues to build tension and investment for the film's audience until the final scene, as we wonder whether she is the killer or a potential victim of either the killer or the murderous townsfolk.

Bouchet also maintains the audience's interest by being "beyond interesting" in that we never really know who her character is or what her motivations are: instead, we are always guessing about her intentions and motivations through and even beyond the end of the film. Her affectively ambiguous and indeterminate performance begins from the first scene in which she appears: after watching the mysterious opening scene in which unidentified black hands stick pins in voodoo dolls, we are introduced to Bouchet's character, Patrizia, who is living upstairs from one of the soon-to-be-murdered Catholic schoolboys, Michele.[12] As he heads upstairs to bring her some orange juice, in her first appearance in the film, she appears naked and apparently tries to seduce little nervous Michele. She asks him to bring the tray closer ("I won't bite you"), but she also appears to possibly be just trying to embarrass him. She asks him "Are you upset seeing a nude female?" and then taunts him and calls him a liar when he responds to her question, "How many girls have you had?" by answering, "Lots." She holds his cheek and tells him he is "full of shit." When his mother calls him, she taunts him again by saying, "Go, obey your momma," and when he falls retreating from the room she emasculates him further by laughing at his ungraceful exit.

How are we to understand this scene? The film opens with Michele and his friends Bruno and Tonino trying to watch some men have sex in a cabin with several prostitutes, establishing early that the director is interesting in looking and its effects on the characters and, by extension, on the audience through their gaze. Depending on one's inclinations, Bouchet's naked body could certainly be read as sexually arousing, yet the effect of her extended nude scene is to humiliate little Michele. Peeping on Bouchet as the little Catholic schoolboys hoped to peep on the men paying prostitutes for sex is certainly more complicated than it first appears, and yet it is also clearly meant to titillate the members of its audience that desire women. The camera lingers on Bouchet's nude body from several angles, closing with a sequence of shots that include showing orange juice run down her naked torso (a shot that is inserted again later in the film), fragmenting her body and making it less subjective and more available as an object intended for pleasurable viewing—an image that was also used heavily in marketing the film. Yet, succumbing to this positions the viewer in the role of the boys peeping at the beginning of the film and aligns the viewer with Michele, who has been humiliated (and will be murdered for this "fall" from grace). Titillation, admiration, humiliation, and fear are contradictory emotional responses, so from her first appearance in her opening scene the viewer is asked to navigate an emotionally complex space: does the viewer identify with Michele and accept humiliation in order to enjoy following his gaze? An individual audience member can always distance themselves from both, but the way the film is shot invites the viewer in. Already Bouchet's performance requires an affectively complex explanation of the viewer's response to the scene, as Bouchet's performance is able to walk the line between these possibilities without ever giving us an easy answer: is she trying to seduce, humiliate, or endanger Michele? Is the viewer, like Michele, in peril from engaging in this kind of gaze? Having watched the scene multiple times over repeated viewings, the "sticky" affect of the scene continues to suggest all these possibilities.

Contemporary spectatorship of the film is even more complex, as our knowledge of the #MeToo movement also affects our response to the issues raised by the staging of this scene. To what degree might Bouchet have been coerced into performing this scene? A difficult question that deserves consideration. Or we might go the opposite direction: despite the possibility of reading the scene from the perspective that Patrizia is taunting Michele, what if the viewer, like Michele, is meant to view her body in that her actions

Figure 2. Is Patrizia (Bouchet) seducing, humiliating, or threatening little Michele?

can be read as her trying to teach him a lesson in sex positivity and female agency? Her bold refusal to be embarrassed at the male gaze on her body offers a reclamation of agency, and she states unequivocally her control of who and when someone is able to look.

My own experience of watching this scene is feeling uncomfortable: what is she trying to do? Is she trying to arouse a young boy, or is she trying to teach him a lesson of some kind? I find it impossible to come to any final, determinant conclusion: she may or may not have any of the intentions I have ascribed to her. Her final motivation is unknowable and therefore uncategorizable: her motivations, as well as the sensations and affect she provokes in the viewer, evade final simple categorization, and we must understand her performance as somewhere between or alongside all of these possibilities of arousal, embarrassment, fear, agency, and discomfort.

When we see her again later in the film she questions another child similarly. After asking him if he will change her flat car tire, she follows this with: "Which would you prefer, a kiss or money?" Offering sexual labor in exchange for the physical labor of changing a car tire, she insists again on her own agency and the value of that labor. But this act also lends itself again to the suspicion that she may have an ulterior interest in these boys. She clearly understands that her sexuality gives her power over them, and we are left to believe that she might very well be the psychosexually disturbed murderer of these children, luring their attention with her sexuality and then perhaps killing them. Perhaps she is killing them in some kind of sadistic need for the attention she never received from her father, who exiled her to this small backwoods town, ostensibly in order to curb her drug habit. As an audience member watches the film initially, they might experience arousal but also suspicion and distrust—again, perhaps even fear. While by the finale of the film we learn something different about her, her later behavior does not necessarily contradict or relieve the tension we feel from her earlier scenes, even with repeated viewings, because her performance in the film never gives us an answer about whether or not she is a pedophile. What is her interest in young boys and buying a doll for the mute girl wandering around town? Narratively these questions are left unresolved, and viewers are left to ask these and other questions even after multiple viewings, leaving sticky affect that colors each repeated attempt to resolve them. For me, the shock, confusion, shame, excitement, and disgust I feel at watching Bouchet as Patrizia seems to attempt to seduce or humiliate a young boy in the opening to *Don't Torture a Duckling* cannot be reduced to one of those singular emotional categories, and that experience also follows me outside of the initial experience: that is, each successive viewing adds to, reinforces, or redefines in some way all the previous iterations.

There are multiple ways in which Bouchet maintains an ambiguous motivation for the character of Patrizia throughout the film. In addition to the indeterminate sexual intentions she manifests towards the young boys, her performance also embraces her role as an outsider, reinforces her appearance as a red herring, and as "the helper." As an outsider to the local community, the film viewer is set up to identify with the local townspeople who have lost children and therefore feel inclined to be suspicious of Patrizia's motivation for lying to the police, because of her struggle with drug addiction. Yet, like La Maciara, the viewer is also set up to respond to and feel empathy for her because of the unfair ostracism she faces from the town for being an outsider. Suspicion and empathy are oppositional emotional categories, so in order to fully experience the film a viewer must be willing to engage with these different sensations, possibly forming an affectively complex response themselves.

According to Koven, the helper is a figure within the genre conventions of *gialli* that can participate in a range of behaviors and outcomes: they can assist the amateur detective; solve the crime themselves, intentionally or unintentionally; or turn out to be a "false" helper, often the killer themselves—like Don Alberto, who as the local priest pretends to help but in the end is revealed to be the murderer (Koven 2006, 88–90). Patrizia floats back and forth during the film as the helper, who assists Andrea, as the amateur detective figure, solve the crime; as the main suspect; and as a potential love interest. One minute she is teasing Andrea and appears sexually alluring, but in the next the audience sees her playing the role of a potential suspect and drug addict. Finally, she ends up a fellow combatant: as Andrea is losing a physical confrontation with Don Alberto, she leaps in and intervenes, giving Andrea time to recover and eventually overcome the priest. She believably

Figure 3. Patrizia saves the day.

plays all these disparate roles because she is simultaneously all and none of them, embodying an indeterminately affectively complex performance that refuses to be reducible to villain, victim, or ingénue. That is, the affect of the different aspects of her role exceeds the limited genre and socio-linguistic categories that are usually employed to describe such a performance. The viewer might feel shock, disgust, or even anger at her "seduction" of Michele, yet also feel aroused by her appearance or admiring of her self-assertiveness. They might empathize with her struggle with drug abuse or blame and judge her. Yet without her help, Andrea would not have solved the crime or have been able to save Dona Avallone's daughter. Shock, disgust, anger, arousal, empathy, judgment, and gratitude are different, non-complementary socio-linguistic categories, so any single emotional category would fail to accurately describe the affect Bouchet conveys or the experience of watching her performance.

Along with embodying the complexity of her role as Patrizia, Bouchet maintains the space to enact this difficult to define exploration of sensation and affect by avoiding the overacting that often accompanied the performances of other actors playing female killers or potential killers. For example, when Laura Craven-Toranni (Valentina Cortese) confesses to the murder of her sister and husband in Mario Bava's genre-founding *The Girl Who Knew Too Much* (*La ragazza che sapeva troppo*, 1963), her performance is unconvincing because she has given no previous indication of her potential for violence before that scene. It is also easy for the viewer to distance themselves from the character of Laura, since her final over-the-top performance suggests mental illness rather than an identifiable motivation for her actions. Conversely Bouchet's performance as Patrizia hints at drug abuse, non-normative sexuality, and potential violence, but when confronted in the police station by officers—although upset—she does not sob or scream her lines the way Cortese delivers hers in her final exposition in Bava's film.

As Koven has argued, *giallo* films are generally less interested in narrative and more explicitly concerned with sensation (Koven 2006, 37–38). Bouchet's ambiguous, affectively complex performance maintains the tension in *Don't Torture a Duckling* by keeping us constantly in doubt about her motives, which she never explains. This leaves us feeling unsettled, with a complicated view and affectively complex feelings towards her character, a convincing impersonation that resists many of the stereotypes that often accompany a representation of the femme fatale or ingénue in film. This, in turn, also supports the general themes of *Don't Torture a Duckling* as *giallo*: like the plot, her unsettling behavior leaves the spectator guessing and her motives inscrutable until the final moments of the film.

Conclusion

Howarth argues in his introduction that Bava's "intelligence" as a filmmaker takes two forms: his ability to make more with less through stylishly crafted visuals, and "his utter conviction that film is an emotionally charged *visual* medium." Less concerned with meeting expectations of what "realistic" film should look like, as the progenitor of *giallo* film, Bava was invested in the "power of the image" and the "emotions that these visuals provoke" and their ability to "shock, surprise, startle and enrapture" (Howarth, *The Haunted World*, 17). Certainly, film as a visual medium has the power to enrapture the viewer, but Howarth ignores the fact that the "visuals" that constitute these images contain the forms of living, breathing actors. This chapter accounts for the presence of these actors, however, by drawing attention to the complexity of their performances.

Koven critiques an aspect of Linda Williams's seminal essay "Film Bodies: Gender, Genre, and Excess" by pointing out that her argument that horror, pornographic, and melodramatic films have different effects from comedy ignores actual audience reception. If it is the case that the "body genres" sometimes provoke fear, arousal, and emotion in the viewer through identification while comedy often produces laughter through disidentification (laughing "at" rather than "with" the clown figure), it is also true that various circumstances within the "body genres," such as unconvincing acting or special effects, "cheesy music," or inaccurate dubbing, might also encourage a viewer to disidentify with the characters onscreen (Williams 1991). By ignoring the different possibilities for diverse effects within the set pieces in genre films, she fails to account for them as they actually function within these films (Koven 2006, 123–25). If not always in equal amounts, *giallo* films can invoke all four of Williams's categories of the bodily excess, through either identification or distancing. *Don't Torture a Duckling* contains nudity (Patrizia's "seduction" of Michele), gore (Father Don Alberto's explicit gory death as his head collides with the side of the cliff as his body falls), and attempts to horrify or make the audience upset (at the beating death of La Maciara), all of which the audience can either feel empathetically towards the film, or consider it from a distance, in the process provoking fear, arousal, emotion, or laughter. By making available both modes of spectatorship and all four of the responses of the "body genres" to viewers, *giallo* films offer a kaleidoscopic panoply of choices with which to engage with these films, which therefore also reward viewers who engage in repeated viewings with this range of sticky affect. The affectively complex responses that Bouchet's performances evoke in the viewer of her films supports this exploration of sensation, which is what genre fans are looking for in them: by being indeterminate, yet also affectively stimulating, she helps to create a film-watching experience that exceeds a viewer's socio-linguistic categories and stays with them, sparking conversation and continued desire for social interactions with other fans, the directors, and the actors long after even multiple viewings of the film.

Notes

1. Antonietta De Lillo, Marcello Garofalo, and Lucio Fulci, "Dr. Lucio Fulci's Day for Night," *A Lizard in a Woman's Skin*, Mondo Macabro, Blu-ray, 2015.

2. Howarth compares Bava to a painter and then proceeds to compare him to the "mature masterpieces" the opera: "Bava's films are compelling, unique and operatically stylized" (ibid., 16).

3. For more on the killer priest as "false helper" in *giallo* film, see Koven, 66, 90. Michael Sevastakis, in his *Giallo Cinema and Its Folktale Roots: A Critical Study of 10 Films, 1962–1987*, discusses via Vladimir Propp's morphology of Russian folklore the fact that "clerical garb" makes a priest "inconspicuous and at the same time approachable" to his fictional victims (85).

4. I identify three main branches, which sometimes overlap but often do not: Gilles Deleuze, as further developed by scholars such as Brian Massumi (2002); Silvan Tomkins, followed by Eve Kosofsky Sedgwick (2003); and various scholars such as Bruce McConachie or Amy Cook, who have applied cognitive/neurological research as a heuristic to understand performance (Shaughnessy 2013).

5. Erin Hurley also describes how affect exceeds us in a biological sense. This however reads as more of an emotional flattening than an exceeding description of affect theory, and as such is less germane to this project.

6. For an excellent discussion of how reviewers misread an audience's laughter in response to a screening of *Schindler's List* (Steven Spielberg, 1993), see John Bruns, "Laughter in the

Aisles: Affect and Power in Contemporary Theoretical and Cultural Discourse," *Studies in American Humor* 3, no. 7 (2000), 5–23.

7. Similarly, Valerie Traub describes how she is looking for "broadband" mode of feminist practice: "Introduction—Feminist Shakespeare Studies: Cross Currents, Border Crossings, Conflicts, and Contradictions," 30. Thank you to Dr. Jennifer Higginbotham for this reference.

8. Psychologists are still debating whether it is possible to feel happy and sad at the same time, even when subjects report feeling this sensation. See A. Pawlowski, "Is It Possible to Feel Happy and Sad at the Same Time?" (*Today.com*, May 11, 2018).

9. Massumi defines intensity as the experience of the self-referential aspect of sensation, the relationship between the somatic sensory feeling of having a feeling and the self.

10. For a brief discussion of affect and the marginalization of the emotional labor of women, see Sara Ahmed, *The Cultural Politics of Emotion*, 1–16. For a full-length treatment, see Arlie Russell Hochschild's *The Managed Heart: Commercialization of Human Feeling*.

11. For an introduction, see Troy Howarth's *So Deadly, So Perverse: 50 Years of Italian Giallo Films, Vol. 1*, 190, and also the linear notes to the 2017 Arrow release of the film. For a specific discussion of Fulci's treatment of modernity in the film, see Koven, 112–13.

12. Unfortunately, no one has been able to recover the names of the actors who played the three boys, Michele, Bruno, and Mantino.

Works Cited

Ahmed, Sara. 2004. *The Cultural Politics of Emotion*. Edinburgh: Edinburgh University Press.

Brinkema, Eugenie. 2014. *The Forms of Affects*. Durham, NC: Duke University Press.

Bruns, John. 2000. "Laughter in the Aisles: Affect and Power in Contemporary Theoretical and Cultural Discourse." *Studies in American Humor* 3, no. 7 (2000): 5–23.

Customer review, Amazon. October 6, 2017. https://smile.amazon.com/Torture-Duckling-2-Disc-Special-Blu-ray/product-reviews/B0719DZHPL/ref=cm_cr_getr_d_paging_btm_next_3?ie,=UTF8&reviewerType=all_reviews&filterByStar=positive&pageNumber=3.

Howarth, Troy. 2014. *The Haunted World of Mario Bava*. Baltimore, MD: Midnight Marquee Press, 2014.

Howarth, Troy. 2015. *So Deadly, So Perverse: 50 Years of Italian Giallo Films, Vol. 1*. Baltimore, MD: Midnight Marquee Press.

Howarth, Troy. 2014. *Splintered Visions Lucio Fulci and His Films*. Baltimore, MD: Midnight Marquee Press, 2016.

Hurley, Erin. 2010. *Theatre and Feeling*. New York: Palgrave Macmillan, 2010.

Kirst, Brian. "Sirens, Virgins, Warriors and Queens: An Interview with Sybil Danning." *Shock Cinema*, no. 55 (2018): 3–9, 47.

Koven, Mikel. 2006. *La Dolce Morte: Vernacular Cinema and the Italian Giallo Film*. Lanham, MD: Scarecrow Press.

Lucas, Tim. 2007. *Mario Bava: All the Colors of the Dark*. Cincinnati, OH: Video Watchdog.

Massumi, Brian. 2002. *Parables for the Virtual: Movement, Affect, Sensation*. Durham, NC: Duke University Press.

Pawlowski, A. 2018. "Is it Possible to Feel Happy and Sad at the Same Time?" *Today.com*, May 11. https://www.today.com/health/it-possible-feel-happy-sad-same-time-t128850.

Podalsky, Laura. 2011. *The Politics of Affect and Emotion in Contemporary Latin American Cinema: Argentina, Brazil, Cuba, and Mexico*. New York: Palgrave Macmillan.

Rodgers, Diane A. 2019. "Women in Film." *Cinema Retro*, no. 44: 18–25.

Russell Hochschild, Arlie. 2012. *The Managed Heart: Commercialization of Human Feeling*. Berkeley: California University Press.

Sedgwick, Eve Kosofsky. 2003. *Touching Feeling: Affect, Pedagogy, Performativity*. Duke University Press.

Sevastakis, Michael. 2016. *Giallo Cinema and Its Folktale Roots: A Critical Study of 10 Films, 1962–1987*. Jefferson, NC: McFarland and Company.

Shaughnessy, Nicola, ed. 2013. *Affective Performance and Cognitive Science: Body, Brain and Being*. New York: Bloomsbury.

Smeraldi, Don A. 2019. "Scream Queens, Heroic Heroines, and Femme Fatales." *Scary Monsters*, no. 113 (Summer): 72–101.

Suber, Devan. 2019. "'Knife + Heart' is a Queer Romp through Giallo." *The Triangle*, no. 5 (April). https://www.thetriangle.org/entertainment/knife-heart-is-a-queer-romp-through-giallo.

Thrower, Stephen. 2019. *Flowers of Perversion: The Delirious Cinema of Jesús Franco*. London: Strange Attractor Press.

Thrower, Stephen, and Antonella Fulci. 1999. *Beyond Terror: The Films of Lucio Fulci*. Fab Press.

Thrower, Stephen, and Julian Grainger. 2015. *Murderous Passions: The Delirious Cinema of Jesús Franco*. London: Strange Attractor Press.

Traub, Valerie. 2016. "Introduction—Feminist Shakespeare Studies: Cross Currents, Border Crossings, Conflicts, and Contradictions." In *The Oxford Handbook Shakespeare and Embodiment*, edited by Valerie Traub, 1–38. Oxford: Oxford University Press.

Williams, Linda. 1991. "Film Bodies: Gender, Genre, and Excess." *Film Quarterly* 44, no. 4 (Summer): 2–13.

Chapter 7

A WHITE DRESS FOR MARIALÉ

An Interview with Director Romano Scavolini

MATTHEW EDWARDS

Film director Romano Scavolini is the director of one of the most underrated, and least known, *giallos* to emerge out of Italy: the wonderfully haunting *A White Dress for Marialé* (*Un bianco vestito per Marialé*, 1972), starring Evelyn Stewart and Ivan Rassimov. As a child, Marialé witnesses her father murder her unfaithful mother and her lover (who dies heroically by twisting naked in the air in a pirouette with his tackle exposed as it flaps about against his thigh) before turning the gun on himself. Ten years later, and clearly disturbed by this event, our traumatized protagonist now lives in a dilapidated castle with bully husband Paolo (Luigi Pistilli), who keeps her confined to the building by sedating her. When Marialé invites a series of friends over, much to her husband's annoyance, things begin to unravel very quickly. The guests include her former lover Massimo, arguing couple Semy and Gustavo, and hedonistic free-loving trio Mercedes, Joe, and Sebastiano. When touring the castle, the group stumbles across a series of strange outfits in an underground crypt, including the white dress Marialé's mother wore while killed. Putting on these new guises kicks off a passionate masquerade dinner and a wild, surreal, and flamboyant orgy, fueled by alcohol and their perverse desires. When the dust settles, all is not what it seems as one by one the guests are picked off by an unknown murderer. The film asks the viewer to untangle the threads to guess the killer in the midst. *A White Dress for Marialé* is a superb and underrated *giallo* that is visually arresting, atmospheric, and surreally horrifying. This unsung Euro-horror is a critique of the male violence and oppression towards women and '70s hedonism. What is surprising is that such an accomplished film has bypassed many *giallo* fans watchful gaze.

I had the pleasure of interviewing Romano Scavolini about his seminal contribution to the genre. I thank him for giving up time to be interviewed for the collection and for sharing his memories and experiences on the making of this *giallo* classic.

Matthew Edwards: How did you get involved in film?

Romano Scavolini: My professional experience is more extensive than just writing and directing *A White Dress for Marialé* and *Nightmares in a Damaged Brain*. Before directing *A White Dress for Marialé*, I did more than fifty short films and documentaries. During that time, at the age of eighteen, I went to Germany working as a "stevedore" on the Neckar River that crosses the city of Stuttgart, and while working, during the weekends, I wrote, directed, acted and produced my first film *The Ravaged One*. It took eighteen months to finish shooting the film and then I returned to Italy, where I established myself in Rome. I had to wait till 1964 to shoot my first short film *The Quiet Fever*, while in the meantime the only copy of my first film, *The Ravaged One*, became lost in the cellars of a New York Post Office. *Quiet Fever* won numerous prizes worldwide as a powerful essay on human violence. The film's commentary included five poems by Dylan Thomas. Finally, in 1966, I made my first (second in my count) professional full-length feature *Blind Fly*, considered a controversial pictorial analysis of aimless violence brought on by the central character's lack of motivation and purpose in life. The film was obstructed and censored by the Italian government and "banned forever." Nonetheless, the film made the rounds of major international festivals eluding the government order hidden inside diplomatic luggage. The film promoted me to the ranks of a "cult" filmmaker. The next year, I wrote and directed *The Dress Rehearsal* (1968), a "Joycean" film exploring multifaceted aspects of the making of film through innovative editing and structure, and then I realized "a-non-film" or, if you prefer, "a voluntary abandoned project in the making," titled *Entonce* (1969). Then I thought that my experience as a filmmaker was at an end. So I went to Vietnam as a freelance photographer (I voluntarily surrendered to the idea of not bringing with me a film camera but only two still cameras) in order to "be physically there," where I could see with my own eyes the real horror of modern time. I was wounded, hospitalized in a South Vietnamese camp and when released, I returned to Rome. I continued to survive but only as a DP on various "genre" films, even working with Gideon Backman on a "special" on Federico Fellini. Then I started my own production company [Lido Film Company], and after a while I was almost forced to write, direct, and produce a number of films on a broad range of subjects such as *A White Dress for Marialè*.

ME: You have spent time as a photographer and documentarian in war-torn regions such as Vietnam. How has this experience shaped you as a person and would you say it shaped your cinematic vision in any way?

RS: The experience in Vietnam, like any other experience of horror, can never relate to the experience that you live witnessing the same horror depicted in a movie. While in a theater the viewer knows that what he sees is fiction; the horror that has a real-life spectator, has a radically different consequence in your consciousness. Although it is inevitable that in the theater the spectator identifies with the images on screen, in real life all the existential parameters collapse. In Vietnam, as in any other human tragedy, "being there" is [means] everything; while watching a movie it is pure "appearance." The fact is that while at the movies, unconsciously, in every viewer coexist two different entities that assist to the show immersed in the darkness of the theater: the first one is the viewer who "sees" the film. The second entity is the one who "observes within" the reactions of the first one. This event did not take place in real life. Because the emotions that the spectator feels when he witnesses real horror "stain" his consciousness in a completely different way as when watching a movie. In short, while watching a movie the spectator enters in a state of "hypnagogic" consciousness, a state of semi-hypnosis that is closer to a state of a dream that is different from the waking state. In the theater the viewer is immersed in a sort of schizophrenic state of mind which ends as soon as the lights of the theater turn on. My experience in Vietnam has been the typical experience of those who were transferred dramatically and suddenly from his living room watching the news on television on the war in Vietnam War to the "front line" of the same war. And to answer your question, I must say that my experience of the Vietnam War did not affect at all my choices while making a film. Quite the contrary: in *Nightmares in a Damaged Brain*, for example, the scenes of horror I did emphasize them just because I was always conscious of the fact that the "viewer" is an "atypical" witness of all kind of violence as they appear on screen. The viewer of a horror movie, even though he identifies with what he sees, knows that at the end what he saw did not even stain the screen, but they will go away as a dream that vanishes on awakening. The "front line" of the war in Vietnam never vanished from my consciousness; it is there every day as a "continuum" in space and time reminding me that I was "immersed in the flesh and blood in the horror."

ME: Your 1972 film *A White Dress for Marialé* is a terrific *giallo* and I consider it one of the most underrated Italian films of the seventies, along with *Footprints on the Moon* (1975, directed by Luigi Bazzoni). How did you become attached to the project?

RS: *A White Dress for Marialé* [aka *Spirits of Death*] is an atypical project of my filmography. The fact is that I had previously produced a film with my brother Sauro, and I was in debt by a lot of money. I had no ongoing project that was able to cover my debts, so I agreed to direct, photograph, and also execute the production of the film with an associate of mine. This is the reason why I have often said that the film is not mine. The screenplay they submitted to me was terrible. It was written by two B-movie scriptwriters, and the cast had already been decided. In order to direct and photograph the film, I asked to rewrite the screenplay, but I was only allowed if I agreed to not delete or make changes to the existing characters. They gave me two weeks to rewrite it. I rewrote the full screenplay but I didn't sign it, because the two writers denied me this. The budget was contained; therefore I had to make a number of choices to carry it out, trying not sell myself out entirely, but rather, doing everything to make it a horror film of a high standard. Not only did I rewrite the script to the extent that the production had imposed upon me and manage the photography, but I was also the camera operator and I only had a three-week shooting schedule.

ME: I understand that you weren't initially thrilled with the script, in that it was a more conventional horror film. What changes did you administer to the script?

RS: Right now, I do not remember exactly the scenes I had rewritten, but I can assure you that the script that I was given to be read had to be thrown in the trashcan. It was not my kind of story, and all the tragedy that took place in that castle was very far from my taste. I remember that I tried to instill in the plot a kind of "psychoanalytic" dimension by acting on the central character of the film, and by opening the movie with a flashback in which Marialè, as a child, witnesses the murder of his mother by his father. This single scene has characterized all the changes that I later made to the script.

ME: Talk us through the production of the film. Did you experience any technical challenges or difficulty during the shoot?

RS: As I told you, I have held various positions: from the executive producer to the rewriting of the script, direction of the photography, and also the cameraman; I had to do all this in three weeks. The first decision I made was to pre-light all the interiors so that I could be free to move the camera 360 degrees without limits. To be able to run safely without repeating too many slates meant that I was able to spend many hours with the actors. We did rehearsal after rehearsal of all the scenes scheduled for the day. Consider that, for more than half of the film, the group of actors was always in front of the camera. Rehearsals for hours with the actors, and choreographing their movements, allowed me to stay physically behind the camera and shoot in controlled time even complex scenes. Also many people do not know this, but I shot the film in "widescreen format" using a perforations system that was used at the time in Italy called "2P." I used a camera whose shutter was "modified" to impress "half frame" of a full 35 mm, at a time. Half of a 35 mm frame impressed is equal a rectangular image similar to a 16:9 format, which was then converted into CinemaScope format only in postproduction. Today the film is released on Blu-ray and I can tell you that at least, photographically, it's absolutely top quality.

ME: The opening of *A White Dress for Marialé*—when Marialé's father shoots his unfaithful wife and her lover in the woods, while Marialé is forced to watch—is sublime. I thought that sequence was beautifully shot and edited. Were you pleased with the way you realized this scene?

RS: I consider the opening scene of the film very important because all the tragedy that overshadows the whole plot sheds a significant light on everything else. Marialé witnesses the murder of her mother but also her father's suicide, not seen but perceived throughout the sequence. I wanted to open the film with idyllic images: the lovers flirting under the shade of an ancient tree while the light of the sun wraps around the romantic scene as a painting of Degas. Then the arrival of the car, the soft steps of the woman's husband in the grass, then the shot. I asked the young actor to die spouting into the air like a wounded fawn. I did not want a double homicide with blood, but only two red spots on the woman's dress. She's still fully dressed, and apart from the nudity of the young lover, she had always taken a very pure attitude.

ME: Another fantastic sequence is when the characters converge inside the underground chamber with the mannequins. That scene oozes style and atmosphere and a real sense of foreboding horror. How did you set about visualizing that sequence?

RS: Among all the props that enrich the film, Marialè's dress occupies the most important place. The film's title clearly states it: Marialè's dress is the central core of the story. With this in mind, I thought that the "clothing" of Marialè's mother but also other clothing and customs, could assume a meaning. With this in mind, I created the sequence in the basement filled with dummies because I wanted to specifically point out that Marialè had developed her illness throughout the years by creating a whole imaginary world to surround herself with imaginary people (dehumanized dummies) who wear clothes that could have been those of her mother forty years before. Her guests are inclined to visit the castle till they go down to the basement. Meanwhile, one of guests, hidden among the dummies, wears one of the dresses and has assumed the frozen posture of a dummy. This sequence has offered me the chance not only to describe one aspect of Marialè's syndrome, but also to start the sequence (which I consider the best of the film) of the orgiastic-blasphemous "last dinner" in which, wearing various clothes found in the basement, all the guests (to the exclusion of Marialè's husband), make themselves up each of them assuming the mask of their own idiosyncrasies.

ME: The film is seemingly a deliberate clash of cultures. On one hand, you have this new era of hippie free love and hedonistic attitudes juxtaposed with the gothic castle setting. The film is seemingly about the death of the free-love generation. What was your angle on the film?

RS: Your comments before the question implies what you think about the cultural and narrative structure of the film. But this film has only offered me the opportunity to highlight the corruption of the morals, the idiocy of mankind, the ambiguity of all passions, the lack of compassion, the dominance of greed, the sexuality lived as pure blasphemous vice, and ending without offering any positive final. In fact, the film was violently opposed by the Vatican, and though it was very successful at the various openings, it was withdrawn from circulation by the distributor [who was] fearful of judiciary complaints.

ME: Talk us through the feast/masquerading orgy scene. How did you direct the actors in that sequence?

RS: The orgy, or better to say "the last supper" in blasphemous key, represents the best part of the entire film. I set out to design the scene as a series of in-camera-taking long sequences accompanied movement of the actors with a song that I loved very much, played by a pop group called "Iron Butterfly" entitled "IN A GADDA DA VIDA" (which in post-production was rearranged by the Fiorenzo Carpi). As I said earlier, I choreographed the entire sequence with all the actors repeatedly, then I placed the camera on a three-wheeled platform that was free to be moved by two technicians and I shot the series of sequences, as I said, in-camera-taking long shots, while the camera was dancing with the music.

ME: I loved Semy's [Shawn Robinsons] underwater death in the film as she is repeatedly bludgeoned in the swimming pool. Talk us through the filming of that sequence.

RS: While the entire film was shot in a castle in Rome's suburbs, to shoot underwater we were forced to move to a soundstage with a pool that had portholes for filming purposes. Shawn Robinsons was an extraordinary professional, and in that sequence, she worked with a great disposition although she was forced to stand in the water, at night, for a few hours. In addition to the pool sequence, we also shot in studio the sequence of the "scorpions." Those are very peculiar animals and needed to be treated under close supervision by an expert, as the scorpions' venom could be deadly.

ME: Composer Fiorenzo Carpi and conductor Bruno Nicolai's score is truly magnificent and one of the best the *giallo* genre has to offer. Were you pleased with the music?

RS: Few people know that the "theme" of Marialè was chosen (I do not know by whom) to accompany the first flights of the Concorde; one with a French flag from Paris and the other with the English flag, from London, 21 January 1976. Fiorenzo Carpi's score is still unmatched today. I followed the whole process until the recording in the studio with the orchestra conducted by Bruno Nicolai.

ME: You have stated publicly that you wished it didn't belong on your own filmography. Do you still feel this way? Personally, as I stated earlier, I consider the film to be a brilliant piece of filmmaking.

RS: Thanks very much. I consider myself an author and as such I consider only those films that I've written from the first page to the last. After the writing comes the realization, and most of the time what has been written does not correspond 100 percent to what has been imagined. Each author has always two films to come to terms with: one is what he imagined to shoot, and the second is what he is able to translate into images. It is increasingly the case that the two films never fit together. But the reasons are too long to engage in this type of explanation now. Marialè is one of three films in my filmography that I did not conceive, imagine, create, write, etc. The film does not even belong to the genre I love, that of stories that I feel close to my sensibility. But I consider myself a professional and as such I think that *A White Dress for Marialé* is a good packaged product for the market and if there are people out there that appreciate it then I am satisfied.

ME: How was *A White Dress for Marialé* received critically upon release in Italy? Are you surprised that the film has become a cult film in both America and Europe, since its release on DVD?

RS: As I said, the film was instantly a box-office success and well accepted from critics quiet attentive to its revolutionary content, but as soon as the film hit a large audience it was violently criticized by the Vatican and by a bigoted and hypocritical religious people who asked that the film be withdrawn from the theaters as it was in contempt of religion and morality. So it was withdrawn by the distributor. In Italy, the movie is practically unknown even if there are various requests for it to be released again. I don't really care.

Chapter 8

WATCH ME WHEN I KILL AND THE BLOODSTAINED SHADOW

An Interview with Director Antonio Bido

MATTHEW EDWARDS

Although not as well-known as other directors of *giallo* cinema, Antonio Bido's contribution to the genre should not be understated. Responsible for two cult-classic *gialli* films of the late 1970s, *Watch Me When I Kill* (*Il gatto dagli occhi di giada*, 1977) and *The Bloodstained Shadow* (*Solamente nero*, 1978), the latter set in Venice, both shockers reveled in the tropes and motifs associated with the yellow-peril genre. In *Watch Me When I Kill*, a knife-wielding maniac is slicing down (or drowning) his victims, not through a crazed bloodlust but as a means from stopping a deadly secret escaping into the public domain. Following on from this murder mystery, which also boasted a pumping soundtrack from prog-rockers Trans-Europe Express, Bido lensed the *giallo* masterpiece *The Bloodstained Shadow*, a film centering on a young college professor who, upon returning to his childhood home in order to visit his Catholic brother, becomes caught up in a violent wave of murders that rocks the local community. Both atmospheric and intricate in plot, expertly utilizing the evocative setting of Venice and the surrounding islands, the film once again showed Bido's expertise in handling *gialli* material and in subverting *giallo* tropes and motifs readily associated with the genre. In November 2019, I had the pleasure of interviewing Antonio Bido about his films and the story behind the filming of these *giallo* favorites.

The following interview was kindly translated from Italian into English by Roberto Curti.

Matthew Edwards: Your first foray into the world of *giallo* cinema came with the underrated (in the UK and the US, certainly) *Watch Me When I Kill*. How did the opportunity arise to direct the film for Elis Cinematografica and WeBi Cinematografica?

Antonio Bido: First of all, let me say that regarding *Il gatto dagli occhi di giada* being underrated, I have to disagree with you. When the film came out, it got good reviews—sometimes very good ones—in almost all of Italy's most important newspapers, and box-office grosses were very good too. In fact, they were superior to those of any other thriller made in that period, save for Dario Argento's ones. I think that it grossed 576 million *lire* in a couple of months, which I think now would amount to 3 million Euros. Anyway, the opportunity arose from a financing I obtained in Padua, from a friend's father who was an industrialist. He provided part of the budget, while P.A.C. provided the rest of the money and purchased the film for distribution.

ME: Talk us through the genesis of turning Vittorio Schiraldi's story into a workable screenplay. Did the script for *Watch Me When I Kill* undergo various rewrites? I ask as you are partly credited with a writing credit along with Roberto Natale and Aldo Serio.

AB: I wrote the first draft with Vittorio Schiraldi, who penned the original story. The producer then demanded a revision of the script in order to make the film a little bit more in line with the trends of the moment. There were rather strong arguments with the producer, who hired a couple of screenwriters—Aldo Serio and Roberto Natale—to revise the script. After these clashes, eventually I accepted a compromise: the revision was good as long as it would make the film more "Argento-like," but the second part of the story, after Corrado Pani's character moves to Padua, wasn't to be touched at all. It was the most personal part of the film, where you can see the "real" Antonio Bido, the one that will come to the fore in *Solamente nero*. Anyway, even though the first half is the result of said compromise, I managed to put my personality in it.

ME: Stylistically, how did you approach the filming of *Watch Me When I Kill*? Were you given free reign by the producers to tackle the material in a way that you saw fit?

AB: Once we agreed on the final script, on set there were no impositions on the part of the producer. I was free to shoot and do as I pleased. I had no problems at all.

ME: Talk us through the production of the film? Did you encounter any problems during the shoot?

AB: I was very young, twenty-five or twenty-six—the film was released in 1977, but I started shooting it at the end of '75, maybe early '76 [note: actually April 1976]. On the first day of shooting, I realized that everyone on set was older than me, the d.o.p., the art director, the cameraman... I was a kid, and a little fearful among all these experienced professionals. The first scene was the one with Bianca Toccafondi and Fernando Cerulli, when Bianca is sitting and Cerulli is at the window behind her. I decided to do a tracking shot, a rather unusual choice, and after we wrapped the scene the d.o.p. came to me and said, "So you do know how to shoot!" From then on I didn't feel a kid anymore, and the crew respected me for they understood I knew my job. You see, quite often first-time directors had no clue at all and the d.o.p. used to help them a lot... from their uncertainties, it was clear they didn't know how to make a movie, and when this happened the crew took advantage of that and put the director under their feet, so to speak.

ME: When one thinks of *giallo* cinema, the films tend to be exploitive in tone with graphic violence. In contrast, *Watch Me When I Kill* is restrained in terms of the explicitness of the violence on screen. The film plays out more as a murder mystery than a straightforward horror film. In many respects, the film comes across as an anti-*giallo*, subverting the elements that viewers are used to in "*giallo* cinema." Would you agree with this and was that a conscious decision made by you prior to filming?

AB: I agree with you. *Il gatto dagli occhi di giada* is rather restrained in terms of graphic violence, especially regarding blood-letting which is almost absent. I think there is only some blood in the opening scene in the pharmacy. It was a precise choice on my part, as was emphasizing the grotesque rather than the horrific.

ME: The "anti-*giallo*" feel to film for me is best represented during the scene when Giovanni Bozzi [Fernando Cerulli] is strangled to death in the bath. Normally, in *giallo* cinema, the victim would be a pretty young woman. In *Watch Me When I Kill*, the only naked flesh we see is of a middle-aged man. Were you deliberately trying to subvert audience expectations?

AB: My idea of emphasizing the grotesque is perfectly summarized by the bathtub murder, where that ugly, skinny, pale-looking, middle-aged man is exactly the opposite of the beautiful naked women you used to see in movies at the time. Incidentally, I didn't want (and they didn't even ask me) to put a sex scene in the film. I tried to be as original as I could, in order to detach myself from what other filmmakers had done... and I think I managed to, especially in the scenes set in Padua.

ME: Two of my favorite moments in the film are the death scenes with Esmeralda Messori [Bianca Toccafondi], when her head is shoved in the oven and when Giovanni Bozzi is murdered by our gloved killer in the bath to the sound of Verdi's *Dies Irae*! Talk us through the filming of those scenes.

AB: These were the two most difficult scenes to shoot. With the bathtub scene, I wanted to create a tense atmosphere through various types of shots, and it wasn't easy, because the actor had to stay in the water for hours . . . so, sometimes we had to let him out or else his skin would wrinkle. We had to stop filming several times for various issues: the water was getting too cold and we had to add hot water, the actor's penis became visible underwater and we added more foam to hide it . . . now this makes me laugh, but then it was exhausting! And I was worried I couldn't finish the scene on schedule, because I had many different shots in mind, and each one required time. Moreover, it was very difficult to give the illusion of the man being strangled with the shower hose. You couldn't squeeze it too much around his neck because it hurt, and there was also the chance that the hose might break. . . . As for Esmeralda Messori's death, the real problem was not shooting the scene but the makeup. Bianca Toccafondi had to undergo a makeup session lasting some hours, and then, when she finally saw herself in the mirror, she refused to shoot. The makeup artist came to me, desperate: "Antonio, Ms. Toccafondi doesn't want to do the scene because she looks ugly . . ." So I talked to her, almost in tears: "Please, you're such a great stage actress . . ." "Antonio, I look so awful with this makeup, I look like a monster . . ." "Bianca, you are ruining me if you don't shoot this scene. I must absolutely shoot it this way, because if the makeup doesn't look nasty enough the scene just won't work the way I want it to . . . " So, in the end I talked her into doing the scene, without having to resort to the producer (who would threaten to sue her, break the contract, etc., and meanwhile the film would halt). I guess she took pity on me because I was a kid.

ME: One of the most outstanding elements of *Watch Me When I Kill* is your expert use of sound in the film in terms of heightening the tension and horror. I don't think you have been given due credit for this, especially your use of layering sound (the answer phone messages/the scene when Lukas has an audio engineer to decipher the answering machine message).

AB: Let me say that your questions are very original, because people usually ask me the same things over and over! So, thank you for this. As for the use of sound, it's very important as you noticed, and it wasn't emphasized enough by critics. People talk about the music, but not about the other sound effects we used in the film. The sound design took lots of time and research.

ME: Trans Europa Express's soundtrack greatly amplifies the feel and mood of the film, too. How did they become involved in the film?

AB: I didn't involve Trans Europa Express in the film personally. The editor, Maurizio Tedesco, was friends with Mauro Lusini and told me, "Antonio, I know a musician who would be perfect for the movie," and he introduced him to me. Immediately a great chemistry was born between us, Mauro sent me a demo with the film's main theme which I liked very much, and so I entrusted him with the score. Trans Europa Express were actually a duo: Lusini and his collaborator Gianfranco Coletta.

ME: Another facet of *Watch Me When I Kill* that stands out to me, and other scholars, is that it is the only *giallo* that deals with the Holocaust. By doing so, again you subvert the ending. When the killer is finally unmasked, and the motives behind his killing spree, the degree of sympathy you held for the victims dissipates. In a sense, the audience is being challenged as to whether or not the killer was justified in his murder spree. For me, the finale brings forward a magnitude of questions relating to wartime guilt and retribution. Was that your intention?

AB: Yes, you have centered the point perfectly. The theme of the Holocaust is a very strong and unusual one for a thriller. At that time, *gialli* were about psychopaths who started killing people, there were no strong motivations usually. I think one of the strongest and most original elements of my film is this emphasizing of the motives behind the murders. As you said, in the end the murderer is revealed to be a victim, and the victims are revealed in turn to be the real victimizers. There is an inversion of roles.

ME: You followed up *Watch Me When I Kill* with the better known *The Bloodstained Shadow*. What are your memories working on this film and how did it come about?

AB: Yes, today *Solamente nero* is the better known of the two, but at the time of its release it grossed half as much as *Il gatto dagli occhi di giada*. It was only decades later, when it came out on video, DVD, and Blu-ray all over the world that it became more popular. *Solamente nero* is the ideal continuation of the Padua segment in *Il gatto dagli occhi di Giada*. It is a more authorial film, more attentive to atmosphere and feelings, and therefore more nuanced. It is a more personal work, and perhaps more original in a way. It was born from my own idea, and we didn't have any imposition whatsoever on the story and script. I was free to write the movie the way I wanted.

ME: One of the most memorable aspects of the film is its evocative locations in Venice and the surrounding islands. You make excellent use of the city's canals and waterways and stylistically the film has a gothic grandeur about it. Like *Don't Look Now* [1973], you use Venice perfectly as a backdrop for the unfolding murder mystery. Were you pleased with how the film turned out, and your use of Venice? Production-wise, was it an easy shoot?

AB: I am very satisfied with the Venice setting. I tried to portray an unusual Venice, and to achieve that I shot mostly in the isle of Murano, in the Venetian lagoon. Only a few scenes were shot in Venice. I used lesser-known locations, so to speak. Production-wise, it was quite complicated, because the crew stayed in Venice and every morning we had to move to Murano, which is rather distant. So we had to load boats and motorboats with the equipment and so on, and it was not easy. Moreover, this meant wasting time which could have been used for the actual shoot. Shooting in Venice is not simple, but it was worth it.

ME: Compared to *Watch Me When I Kill* the violence is cranked up a notch or two, in terms of bloodletting. Yet one aspect that struck me was that the film features a death similar to your first *giallo*, where an unfortunate victim has her head pushed into an open fire. Was that merely a coincidence or a nod to your earlier *giallo*?

AB: Well, perhaps there is more violence in the film, maybe not in terms of bloodletting. Surely the murder scenes are more violent . . . as for the choice of having Stefania Casini's mother burned alive in the fire, I don't know if it was a conscious reference; certainly it seemed to me the cruelest thing the murderer would do on that occasion.

ME: Again, your use of editing is an interesting facet of your films. In particular, the scene involving Don Paolo and the falling crucifix is expertly done, in my opinion. Do you have an idea before shooting how these scenes will play out or are they mainly constructed in the editing suite?

AB: I agree with you, I love the crucifix scene very much. It's suspenseful and very effective. I had envisioned all the shots and angles prior to filming, not in the script but in my notes. Each day I wrote down how I would shoot the scenes in order to know how they would be edited. It is very important for a director to know beforehand how a scene will be put together in the cutting room, otherwise editing becomes a tough job. I wanted the scene to be structured and edited exactly that way, so I shot all the various angles to achieve the rhythm and suspense I wanted it to have. Otherwise it would have been impossible to construct it in the editing room.

ME: *Giallo* films have a tendency to show religion from two differing viewpoints: on one side the church cannot be trusted, on the other a place of sanctuary from the vices of the world. However, in *The Bloodstained Shadow* there seems to be a struggle between these two concepts. That the brutal killer transpires to be a man of the church, yet despite his horrific actions he is wracked with guilt and that he has let down those who have looked up to him. Despite being a murderer, he openly challenges the wealthy child molester. He clearly is a man of morals. I thought this "struggle" was an interesting area to explore in the film. Was this your intention when writing the screenplay?

AB: Very interesting question and one nobody has ever asked me before. Somehow I always wanted to give a reason behind the murders, not merely human madness but deeper motivations. In *Il gatto dagli occhi di Giada* the motive was the Shoah, and the film ended with the victims becoming the murderers. Here, as well, Don Paolo is a complex character. He kills people, but he does so because his moral sense is so strict that he cannot accept that his ignominious murder be discovered. It's a twisted logic, I admit it, and it comes from a twisted mind, but he is not a psychopath. He kills following his own morals, and his being torn between temptation and salvation somehow reflects my own attitude toward religion.

ME: What was it like working with Stefania Casini and Craig Hill, who was exceptional as Don Paolo?

AB: Working with Stefania was beautiful. She was a lovely girl, nice and professional, very collaborative. We got along very well, and we're still friends nowadays. I interviewed her for my autobiography, *I miei sogni in pellicola* [*My Dreams in Film*; Bido is referring to his own 2019 documentary/autobiography: https://www.imdb.com/title/tt11587298/?ref_=nm_flmg_dr_1], and she had many nice things to say about shooting the film. It was a pleasure working with Lino Capolicchio and Craig Hill as well. The only difference was that Casini and Capolicchio were very experienced actors, whereas Craig Hill had never played a similar role before, he was used to playing Western characters, and so the first days I struggled a bit to make him "enter" the character. But once he did he was just great, insuperable. A beautiful cinematic face, perfect for the role. I'm very, very satisfied with his casting as Don Paolo.

ME: The love-making scene involving Stefano and Sandra, and the previous romantic scene prior, for me is the only misstep in the film. There was an awkwardness to the scene that actually slows the rhythm, tension, and suspense you had built up to that point. If you were to go back to the film now, would you cut that scene?

AB: Yes, I agree with you. If I could go back in time, I'd cut the whole scene, and the previous one as well, their boat trip. I didn't put any sex scene in *Il gatto dagli occhi di giada*, as was customary back then, and I don't remember why I put one in *Solamente nero*. I tried to shoot it in an elegant way, not vulgar. But undoubtedly it doesn't have anything to do with the film, and it could have easily been cut.

ME: Like many *gialli* fans, I loved the cinematic death of Dr. Aloisi on the canal. Talk us through the filming of this scene.

AB: That was a very complex one to shoot. It took two days to light the two hundred meters of canal . . . back then it wasn't like nowadays, when you can film almost in the dark. We had to use many lights and there were hundreds of meters of cables all around. And the water was very cold, because it was late February. Sergio Mioni, who played Aloisi, was not only an actor but also a professional stuntman, and was cast for the role because he could play that scene himself. It would have been impossible to shoot it with a stunt double, because I had to do the close-ups and so on . . . Mioni was a great professional, but nevertheless we had to stop filming every now and then because he almost fainted, for the water was icy. We pulled him out of the water, took him to one of those Murano glass furnaces so that he'd warm up a bit, and when he felt better he went back in the canal again. There was also a protest on the part of some Murano citizens because I wanted the motorboat to ride fast through the canal, but it made tall waves which damaged several boats anchored along the canal. As you watch the scene closely, you'll see some boats slamming violently against the banks. At some point I was afraid I wouldn't be able to finish the scene . . . I think the producer later paid for the damages.

ME: Talk us through your choice of music in *The Bloodstained Shadow*. Stelio Cipriano's eerie melodies and electronics, performed by Goblin, are used to startling effect. At times there is a sparseness, solitary piano before shifting gears to the thumping, or ominous, synths or bass groves. I thought the music was used effectively in building the tension in the film and when used as musical equivalents of "jump scares." Talk us through the sound design of the film.

AB: The music is truly beautiful. Cipriani did a great job, with the collaboration of Goblin and especially Claudio Simonetti, who contributed to the arrangements with his Moog during the recording session. I had several meetings with Cipriani to decide how the various themes and cues would be. He made me listen to them, we discussed, changed something here and there, etc. And I attended the recording session in the studio. In his final interview before passing away, which is included in my autobiography *I miei sogni in pellicola*, Stelvio acknowledged the collaboration with Simonetti, which was very nice about him. He said that their collaboration made the result much better.

ME: Finally, how were both films received in Italy, upon release? Are you proud of what you achieved and what is the winning formula on creating a *giallo*?

AB: *Il gatto dagli occhi di giada* performed very well at the box office, it was among the top-grossing films for several weeks, and was one of the most successful Italian *gialli*. *Solamente nero* grossed about half as much, possibly because of bad publicity and distribution. It came out in the summer, and moreover the genre was waning, people were getting tired of it. But it sold well all over the world, just like *Il gatto dagli occhi di giada*, which even came out theatrically in the United States, something very few Italian films managed to do.

The winning formula for a good *giallo* is not easy to put down. The director must have a particular sensibility because he must know exactly the pacing a *giallo* must have. It's all based on suspense, on rhythm, on camera cuts. If you miss one of these elements, the scene is no longer scary. It needs lots of attention and skill. That's why I chose to make my first feature film a *giallo*. It was not an easy task, but it allowed me to prove I had the skills to be a director.

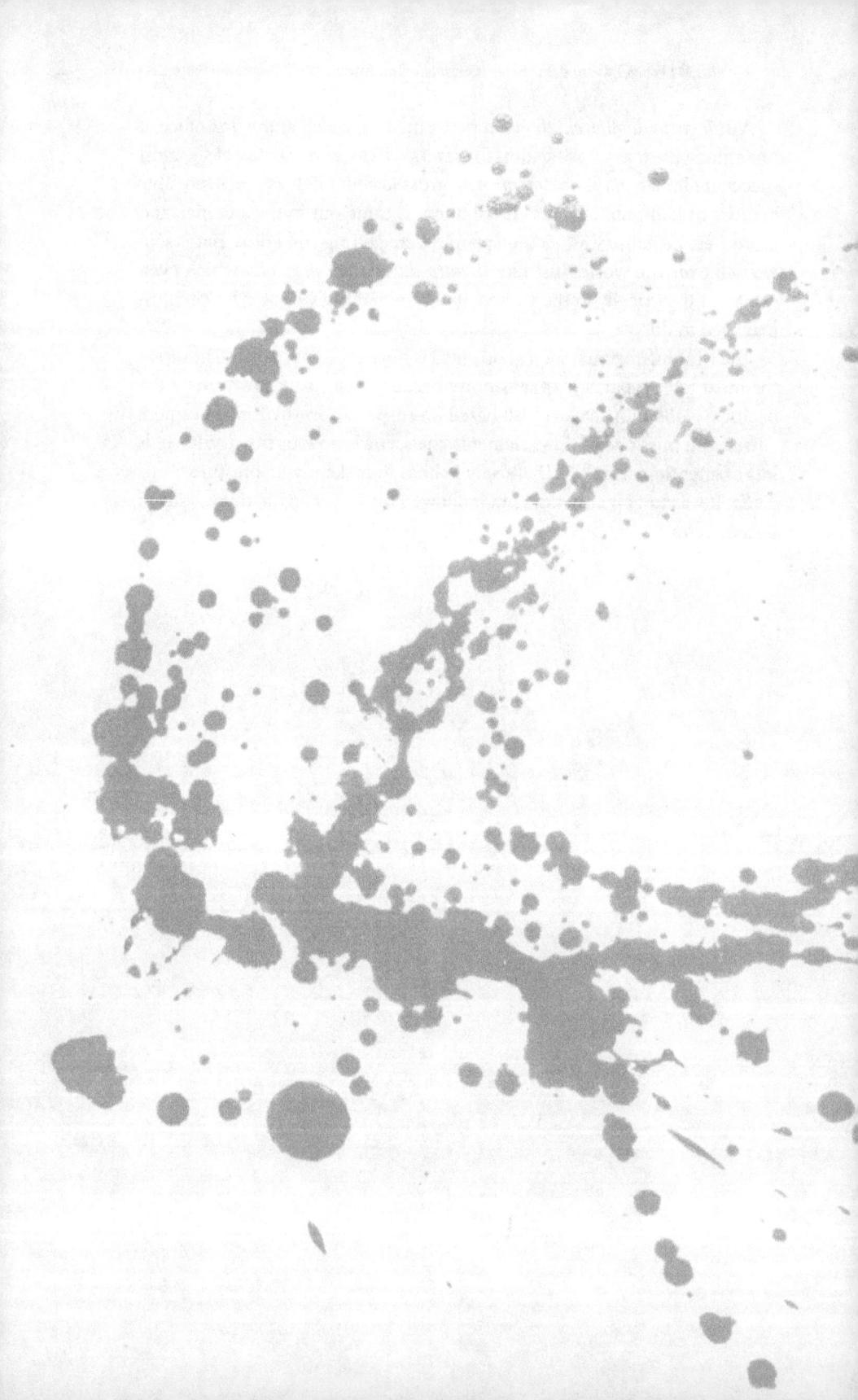

Part II

THE *GIALLO* ABROAD

A Transnational Phenomenon

Chapter 9

A KINDER CAPITALISM

Elements of the *Giallo* in Hong Kong New Wave Cinema

ANDREW GROSSMAN

Introduction: Hong Kong Cinema and the Transnational Problematic

The thrusts of postcolonial theory and identity politics have encouraged us to demonize the practice of cultural appropriation: it is an arrogant kind of politico-economic violence, absorbing social and aesthetic differences into capitalism's all-consuming, inescapable sway. The shifting economic tides of the twenty-first century have shown us that omnivorous cultural appropriations are no longer the exclusive domain of American capitalism. Boasting the world's biggest audience of pop-culture consumers, China now shapes the tastes and boundaries of worldwide cultural production, appropriating Hollywood's glossy action-movie conventions for its own political purposes. But contemporary Chinese blockbusters don't merely feature propagandistic messaging and nationalistic heroes. Their bloated, homogenized style disavows the unpretentious local color and narrative economy that characterized the heyday of Hong Kong cinema. Today, Hong Kong directors must oblige the mainland's globalized aesthetic and succumb to a so-called transnationalism that, too often, is little more than an acquiescence to Hollywoodized image-making. What mainly distinguishes today's slick Chinese action films from their Hollywood counterparts are the former's political censorships and a jingoism that would make Rambo green with envy.

Yet the now-ubiquitous labels of transnationalism and cultural appropriation are hardly one-dimensional. There are degrees of transnationality, each with its own levels of moral and aesthetic culpability. This essay provides a case study in what could be called a limited or "localized" cultural appropriation: New Wave Hong Kong cinema's piecemeal borrowing of elements from the Italian *giallo*. This trend unusually exemplifies how a local film culture might adopt foreign elements without seamlessly folding them into totalized, organic wholes. Consequently, Hong Kong's genre hybrids provide a less ideological version of the transnationalism now endemic to commercial Chinese-language cinemas. Hong Kong cinema's appropriation of *giallo* themes is perhaps an unlikely example, for Italianate styles and Cantonese cinema share few overt similarities. If the *giallo* exudes decadence, sensuality, and chic (if sometimes reactionary) thrills, the HK New Wave emphasized grit, realism, and a raw, noirish style. Rather than adapt to foreign styles, the films examined here weave *giallo* elements incongruously, even abruptly, into existing templates within HK cinema. Philip Chan's *Night Caller* (1985), for instance, adapts *giallo* themes to the *policier*, yet does so far less smoothly than Italian films that, like Massimo Dallamano's *What Have They Done to Your Daughters?* (*La polizia chiede aiuto*, 1974), straddle the *giallo* and the *poliziottesco*. More idiosyncratically, Leong Po-chih's *He Lives by Night* (1982) and Long Jiang's *The Red Panther* (1983) adapt *giallo* imageries to the HK horror-comedy formula popular in the 1980s. Kuei Chih-hung's *Corpse Mania* (1981) provides a most unusual example, injecting *giallo* imagery into the costumed universe of the Shaw Brothers studios.

In describing these films' cultural borrowings, this essay consciously uses verbs like "adapt" and "inject" rather than "fuse" or "synthesize." In the examples discussed, Hong Kong styles coexist with imported influences asynchronously, without forming glossy hybrids fit for transnational distribution and consumption. Paradoxically, the films' failures to neatly suture foreign influences become a success in purely cultural terms, for the films signify not greedy appropriations but selective and modest ones that imitate Italian models *only to a self-conscious degree*. Making little effort to create organic unities, these generic mashups betray the artificiality of their own structures, allowing audiences to see raw pieces of narrative unimpeded by a totalized form. These *giallo*-esque films thus offer a kind of puzzle on a formal level as well: their narrative building blocks are so nakedly visible that audiences could easily rearrange them in their minds, imagining differently structured films altogether.

Part One: The Philosophy of the Detective Genre in Relation to the *Giallo*

Much as HK's New Wave often borrowed from the *giallo*, so did the *giallo* appropriate foreign elements, namely patterns in the English detective story. Yet the detective story and the *giallo* share only superficial similarities. Like classic detective novels, *gialli* present their murder mysteries within insular environments, such as university campuses or isolated villas, not only to limit the number of potential suspects, but also to circumscribe the investigative spaces in which heroes can reasonably discover truths. As in English mysteries, the *giallo*'s killings usually occur in upper-class milieus, whether aristocratic or nouveau riche. This emphasis on "blueblood" killings surely carries an implicit class commentary. It is no accident that Agatha Christie never wrote (to my knowledge) a whodunit set within a decrepit inner-city tenement. The poor are already the economic victims of unjust societies; it would be gratuitous to subject them to a second, far more trivial victimization at the hands of a knife-wielding lunatic. The decadent bluebloods who populate the *giallo*, however, fully deserve their gruesome fates and seem naturally predisposed to bumping one another off. Presumably, the *giallo*'s proletarian target audience would enjoy seeing the demise of a decadent aristocracy that—especially after the revolutionary throes of 1968—had outlived its usefulness.

Generally, the *giallo* attempts to negotiate two opposing literary traditions: detective fiction, whose deductive logic and criminological insights stem from post-Enlightenment empiricism, and gothic horror, whose irrational shocks and supernatural enigmas impede or confound the exercise of human reason. By straddling and often conflating the two traditions, the *giallo* makes us momentarily forget that detective stories and horror stories are thematically opposed. Simply put, detective stories champion the triumph of logic over chaos, while horror stories, exploiting broadly what Keats called "negative capability," revel in fears for which reason alone cannot account. In his classic *Harper's* essay "The Guilty Vicarage," W. H. Auden suggests that detective stories, unlike thrillers, "provide the magical satisfaction" of "being dissociated from the murderer" (Auden 1948, 412). This satisfaction becomes a moral illusion that sanitizes the nasty business of detective stories, whose bloody murders are basically indistinguishable from those of gothic thrillers. As *gialli* increasingly favored gothic elements and dispensed with the detective formula's moral dissociations, the genre's thematic overtures to detection became something of a ruse. Typically, the *giallo* establishes the groundwork for a mystery but withholds sufficient clues to solve it, instead revealing the killer in a "shock" ending, in the manner of Hitchcock's *Psycho*. Whereas Agatha Christie deluges readers with dozens of interlocking clues, most *gialli* provide only three or four—enough to create the semblance of a mystery but hardly enough for either protagonists or audiences to truly piece things together. In *Deep Red* (*Profondo rosso*, 1975), for instance, Dario Argento reveals a split-second glimpse of the killer during the initial murder and then distracts us with dreamlike audiovisual flourishes: creepy dolls, a childhood nursery song, and close-ups of eyes, keys, and locks, none of which provide solid groundwork for Holmesian deduction. If we guess the killer, it is only because we remembered that split-second glimpse Argento should never have given us.

Stories of detection are inherently conservative fantasies in which the investigating hero, representing conventional morality, reinstates social order through the exercise of Enlightenment reason. In his elegant self-confidence, the detective comes to signify the hopeful human capability for reason itself. The word "hopeful" is crucial, however, because the sleuth's superingenuity is usually a narrativistic sham. Sherlock Holmes and Hercules Poirot depend on the contrivances of a prodigious knowledge and perception unavailable to the average—or even above-average—inheritor of Enlightenment wisdom. To counterbalance this superhumanity, mystery writers often marginalize or pervert their heroes, as if admitting the detective's ratiocinative brilliance is only the flip side of a neurotic personality. Doyle made Holmes a lonesome drug addict, a tunnel-visioned plumber of minutiae blissfully unaware of the order of the planets. Similarly, Christie made Poirot an irritating, egotistical eccentric, a Socratic *eiron* who critically observes social follies and passions without partaking in them.

Unlike the virile, two-fisted hero of hardboiled crime fiction, the sleuth of classical detective fiction is isolated sexually. Holmes and Poirot are notoriously chaste not because they are prudes but because they are peerless sublimators, transferring mundane (sexual) energies into amazing feats of intellection. Existing between the detective story and gothic horror, the *giallo* slides toward the eroticism of the latter, a tendency surely reflecting changes in popular tastes. As John Cawelti suggests, "perhaps the majority of people ... will rather quickly lose interest in a [detective] structure that is predominantly rational and will prefer their mysteries served up as a sauce to heroic or erotic action."[1] (Cawelti 1976, 43) Unfortunately, the *giallo*'s eroticism tends to engage Freudian clichés, a problem that occasionally plagues the HK examples examined below. While *giallo* killers are sometimes motivated by revenge, money, or jealousy, the genre disproportionately links homicidal tendencies to childhood sexual trauma.[2] In Argento's *Four Flies on Grey Velvet* (4 *mosche di velluto grigio*, 1971), the killer is a gender-confused woman whose father raised her as a boy; in Lucio Fulci's *Don't Torture a Duckling* (*Non si sevizia un paperino*, 1972), a mad priest kills young boys to spare them adulthoods of sexual sin; in Lamberto Bava's *A Blade in the Dark* (*La casa con la scala nel buio*, 1983), the killer is a transvestite whose gender confusion is conflated with murderous psychopathy; and in Bava's subsequent *Delirium* (*Foto de Gioia*, 1987), the killer is driven mad by lifelong incestuous desires for his sister, a former nude model. Thankfully, Argento's *Deep Red* doesn't bother to explain the killer's mania; we only learn that the killer's spouse once planned to commit her to an asylum, allowing us to fill in the specifics.[3]

Freud was doubtless the greatest detective writer of all, but countless *gialli*—such as Sergio Martino's 1973 *Torso* (*I corpi presentano trace di violenza carnale*)—entirely misunderstand his theories of sexual trauma, particularly the primal scene, often employed as a catch-all explanation for homicidality. The primal scene is certainly pertinent to studies of detection narratives, but not because the accidental sight of parental coitus can belatedly send boys into knife-wielding frenzies. Freud's 1908 essay "On the Sexual Theories of Children" reminds us that the primal scene merely explains our fascination with mysteries—it marks our first, stumbling foray into sleuthing. Because a repressed, bourgeois society insists on lying to children about the facts of sex, children learn to mistrust adult authority and suppose (often correctly) that the world is a series of mysteries that must be decoded, not intuitively but analytically. Thrillers caricature Freud's androcentric primal scene as a source of adulthood violence because the coitus-witnessing boy, kept ignorant of female anatomy, assumes the female partner is a mutilated man suffering from a penile lack. Misperceiving intercourse as the violent assault by a superior man against an inferior, deformed one, the boy thus adopts "a sadistic view of coition" (Freud 1908, 18). The boy broods over this initial confusion, as Freud says, but *mere brooding* cannot predict or instigate latent homicidality. Freud does claim, rather hyperbolically, that the boy's "first failure [to discern heterosexual coitus] has a crippling effect on the child's whole future" (Freud 1908, 14), but one toddling failure hardly predisposes him to a life of misconstrued sadism. Rather, the boy turns his confusion into "the prototype of all later intellectual work directed toward the solution of problems" (Freud 1908, 15), laying the groundwork for a heroic (if sublimating) Holmes, not an unhinged killer. Vulgarizing Freud's myth, some *gialli* assume the boy remains forever in a stage of arrested development, ensuring an impotent, villainous future.

If horror clichés take the primal scene as an infantilizing curse, the Holmesian mystery commits a contrary error, idealistically believing that adult reason will solve any intellectual problem. In its positivistic assumptions, the classical mystery presumes that every killing is rational, intelligible, and discoverable. One wonders how Holmes might explain the killings in R. W. Fassbinder's *Why Has Herr R Run Amok?* (1969) or Chantal Akerman's *Jeanne Dielman* (1975), wherein murders are not goal-directed enterprises but nihilistic symptoms of Camusian alienation. In its conservative naiveté, the murder mystery identifies "crime" not as the *mass* killings of warlike or unjust societies but as the machinations of individual deviants who can be surgically rooted out. As Cawelti argues, the "detective restores serenity to a traditional image of middle-class social order by proving that the disruptive force is not in the social order itself but in the particular individual motives of a relatively marginal, 'least-likely' person" (Cawelti 1976, 101). Auden similarly suggests that whodunits are escapism not merely because they morally dissociate readers from killers, but also because they attempt to exorcise society's sins by scapegoating single deviants, while greater social injustices go unexamined.[4] To their credit, *gialli*, like Poe's tales, rarely provide tidy senses of closure or reassurances that order will return after lone killers are unmasked. Indeed, *A Bay of Blood* (*Ecologia del delitto*, Mario Bava, 1971), *Torso, Deep Red*, and *Tenebrae* (Dario Argento, 1982) spill so much blood that the mere revelation of a killer's identity cannot restore our faith in an ordered, orderly moral universe.

Emphasizing the erotic thrill of criminal transgression, the neogothic *giallo* finally parts company with detective fiction, a genre steeped in law-and-order conservatism. For Auden, the whodunit makes the beauty of brilliant detection and the morality of social order indistinguishable: "The job of the detective is to restore the state of grace in which the aesthetic and the ethical are as one" (Auden 1948, 409). Yet the detective can only effect order in a fantastically sanitized world in which he—an intellectual who transcends the policemen and civil servants who assist and legitimize him—embodies the potential for grace and commands the faith of the people. In the *giallo*, where society is inexorably avaricious, impulsive, and sadistic, redemption seems an impossible goal.

Part Two: *Giallo* Influences in the Hong Kong *Policier*

Unlike nearly all other New Wave movements, the Hong Kong New Wave of the late 1970s and early '80s disproportionately drew upon established genres: the *policier* (e.g., *The System, The Servants, Cops and Robbers*); the gangster film (*The Club, Coolie Killer*); supernatural horror (*House of the Lute*,

Life After Life, *The Imp*); and films about disaffected youth (*The Happenings*, *No Big Deal*). Practically every other cinematic New Wave rebelled against old forms, and when French, Japanese, or Brazilian New Wavers engaged established genres, they did so in terms of ironic metanarrative or subversive pastiche—consider Godard's *Breathless* (1960) and Truffaut's *Shoot the Piano Player* (1960), the mid-1960s films of Suzuki Seijun, or Glauber Rocha's anti-Westerns *Black God, White Devil* (1964) and *Antonio das Mortes* (1969). The HK New Wave was unique, arguably, because it used genre films not as ironic points of departure but as legitimate testing grounds for stylistic and thematic innovations. In place of irony, one finds in HK's New Wave a balance of naturalism and cynicism and an overriding belief that genre filmmaking can bring order to disparate, chaotically paired, and deliberately unsynthesized stylistic elements.

The HK New Wave's sense of urban realism makes it an unlikely breeding ground for *giallo* influences. Furthermore, HK thrillers, often beholden to implicit notions of Confucianst fate, seldom pretend to the British detective story's "fantastic" empiricism, as do many *gialli*. Nevertheless, HK's New Wave produced a string of gritty mysteries and police procedurals that borrowed both directly and indirectly from *giallo* traditions. Many of HK's *giallo*-esque thrillers emphasize tortuous police investigation, thus dovetailing with the narrative designs of *The Bloodstained Butterfly* (*Una farfalla con le ali insanguinate*, Ducio Tessari, 1971), *Don't Torture a Duckling*, *What Have They Done to Your Daughters?*, and other *gialli* whose plots mirror those of *poliziotteschi*.[5] Others, such as the spoof *Heaven Can Help*, employ the "adventurer" model of some *gialli*, such as *Deep Red* or *A Blade in the Dark*, wherein amateur sleuths investigate killings in the absence of legal authorities. The more artistic, enigmatic thrillers of HK auteurs, meanwhile, largely dispense with sleuthing altogether, using the template of the murder mystery to deflate the genre's reductive assumptions about truth-seeking.

As HK's *policiers* moved *giallo*-esque procedurals from Italian villas and piazzas to the colonial city's cramped government housing estates, the class commentary implicit in the Italian model underwent a transformation. When a killer bumps off crochet-playing, nymphomaniacal elites in Ferdinando di Leo's inept *The Beast Kills in Cold Blood* (*La bestia uccide a sangue freddo*, 1971), we assume that upper-crust decadents are getting their just desserts. In their emphasis on social realism, however, HK directors usually examine a desperate underclass condemned to block housing. As such, the police procedural model becomes both a narrative and thematic device, as roving cameras investigate the societal conditions of proletarian toil and lawlessness. The HK films examined here tend to downplay the element of mystery-solving, perhaps because there isn't an immoral societal underbelly to expose. Living in dire poverty, the films' characters already understand that the true villain is socioeconomic injustice, a crime for which no single psychopath could be scapegoated. In lieu of mystery-solving, one finds the implicit (yet omnipresent) specter of fate, perhaps the most immobile, implacable value in Chinese culture.

For the present discussion, the vague term "thriller" isn't especially edifying, as it historically has embraced everything from bloody Jacobean tragedies to Todd Slaughter movies. Emblematic of varying styles and sub-genres, the HK films under discussion can be called "pseudo-*gialli*." Overall, these HK variants are not authentic *gialli* on three accounts. Firstly, they frequently supplant the *giallo*'s overtures to positivistic detective fiction with retrograde notions of fate. Secondly, they graft *giallo* themes onto local HK film styles. Thirdly, they largely deal with working-class characters rather than educated or decadent elites (Patrick Tam's *Love Massacre* is a rare exception). Notably, these pseudo-*gialli* span a variety of stylistic approaches: films such as *The Secret*, *Love Massacre*, and *Before Dawn* are very much the opaque, noirish products of New Wave auteurism, while *The Red Panther*, *Heaven Can Help*, and *Night Caller* retain the comic-sentimental tone and expositional conventions of commercial HK cinema. In general, these films absorb the *giallo*'s stylistic traits but *not* its themes, replacing the willfulness of detection with fateful (if not fated) conclusions.[6] Unlike Italian *poliziotteschi*, in which rogue policemen oppose institutional corruption, HK procedurals—including those without *giallo* influences—usually glorify the heroic lives of police inspectors.[7] Though partly an effort to restore confidence in a police force wracked by corruption in the late 1960s, this law-and-order propaganda also echoes the values of martial brotherhood typical of Chinese action cinema. In the context of detective fiction, this sense of collectivism supersedes and disintermediates the individualistic Holmes archetype, who enforces order through a pursuit that straddles public duty and private entertainment.

The following discussion, in no way exhaustive, limits its focus to *giallo-esque* films of the early HK New Wave: roughly, from the late 1970s through 1985. Certainly, not every film with a lurking slasher should be categorized under the umbrella of "*giallo*" or "pseudo-*giallo*." For instance, HK's "category III" films might employ police procedural frameworks—as do *Dr. Lam* (1992) and *The Untold Story* (1993)—but their politically symbolic sadisms are a distinct phenomenon. Psycho-thrillers such as Lee Siu-wa's *Crazy Blood* (1983) and Oli Nicole's *Blood Call* (1988) might occasionally recall Italian suspensers but lack the *giallo*'s telltale ingredients (e.g., mysterious identities, police procedures, and/or elaborately staged serial killings). Ho Fan's erotic thriller *Expensive Tastes* (1982) certainly does evoke the *giallo* in its Freudian fixations, Mario Bava-esque color schemes, and bizarrely staged sequences of female terror, but it lacks the mystery elements and procedural-legal framework that link the films examined here. Tsui Hark's *The Butterfly Murders* (1979) is often recognized for its *giallo*-esque tendencies, but its foundations in the *wuxia* genre move it beyond the present discussion. Importantly, the HK examples are never direct clones of *gialli*, even if *He Lives by Night* and *Heaven Can Help* go beyond "homage" and enter the realm of parody. Overall, the present discussion examines how *giallo* tropes had influenced the HK New Wave without overtaking it, as HK filmmakers rarely appropriated Italian motifs wholesale.[8]

If Italian *gialli* are basically horror films reframed as detective stories, HK's pseudo-*gialli* are foremost police procedurals that center around the search for psychopathic killers. While Italy's procedurals often critique the institutional corruption prevalent in regional politics, HK's procedurals usually adopt a naïve law-and-order stance, excepting Peter Yung Wai-chuen's unglamorous, almost neorealistic *The System* (1979), which evokes much of the cynicism (if none of the theatricality) of Sidney Lumet's police noirs.[9] Though HK (and Taiwanese) cinema produced countless police procedurals in the late 1970s, it makes sense to begin with Alex Cheung Kwok-ming's *Cops and Robbers* (1979), in which police oppose not organized criminals but the sort of rampaging deviant endemic to the *giallo*. The theme of self-evident fate (as opposed to mystery) is announced over the credit sequence, as schoolchildren play cops and robbers while singing a song that suggests one's role in the game is predestined. Here, the serial killer is a gun fetishist rejected by the police academy for being cross-eyed (a cruel twist of fate). When policemen kill his brother, he becomes a trigger-happy maniac, and the film morphs from a competent *poliziottesco* into a suspenser with surprisingly horrific overtones, especially when the psycho kidnaps a cop's young son and torturously shears off his hair. The prolonged climax features one of the most memorable one-on-one confrontations in all of Hong Kong cinema. After an exhausting chase, the gun-wielding killer pursues an unarmed cop into a cul-de-sac. A tense, two-minute standoff passes before the cop rushes the killer, only to fortuitously trip and evade the killer's final bullet (again, fate). In a frenzied, cathartic rage, the cop dashes out the killer's brains in unexpectedly realistic fashion, a scene that prefigures the desperate violence of Tsui Hark's *Don't Play with Fire* (1980). Like many HK procedurals, the film adopts an uncritical pro-police stance, reinstating institutionally the social order that, in Auden's ironic scheme, is otherwise realized by an individual, "graceful" sleuth.

Figure 1. The primal scene strikes again. *The Savior*.

Ronny Yu's *The Savior* (1980), released eight months after *Cops and Robbers*, is perhaps the first New Wave procedural to explicitly borrow *giallo* themes.[10] Though it shares with *Cops and Robbers* sharp editing, adroit location photography, and Teddy Robin Kwan as a producer, the film is dramatically uninspired, alternating violent murders with subsequent police investigations. In Yu's film, inspecting police pursue a prostitute slasher scarred by a variation on that old bugbear, the Freudian primal scene. At age ten, the killer witnesses his father's dalliance with a hooker; shortly thereafter, his mother, a crazed religious fanatic, slashes her throat with a razor before the boy's eyes. Having learned that women are either home-wrecking tramps or sacrificial lambs, he has little choice but to mature into a misogynistic, erotophobic psycho. Clumsy attempts at psychoanalytic symbolism arise when the son's treasured killing blade is discovered within a wooden crucifix hung above his dead mother's portrait. The film does add a twist by having the killer's wealthy father participate in the killings; when he discovers his son's predilection for mutilating sex workers, he hires a black-gloved assassin to bump off witnesses. In the finale, the father attempts to calm his son, now trapped on a rooftop and surrounded by police. Rather than surrender, the son, now mad beyond repair, accidentally impales his intervening father, thus completing the ill-fated Oedipal design.

Writer-director-star Philip Chan, a former police detective, clearly intended his *Night Caller* (1985) as an homage to the *giallo*, and it's a far nimbler knockoff than *The Savior*. The film begins as a beautiful model, Jessica, is approached by an offscreen figure (presumably her lover) clad in regulation dark coat and black gloves. The mysterious figure suddenly

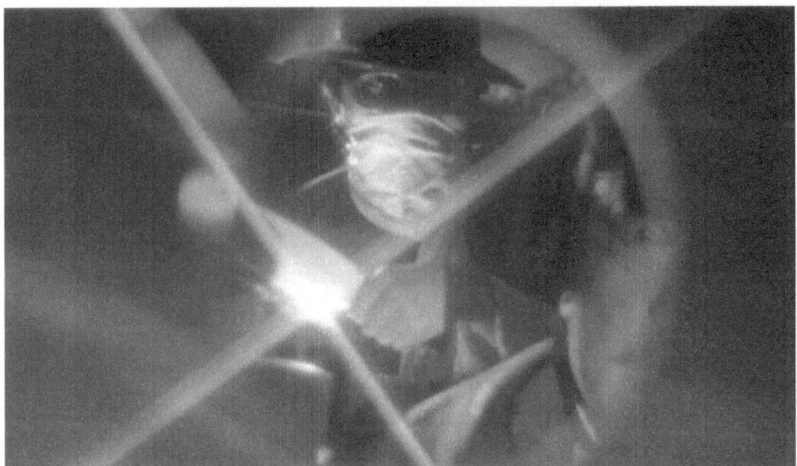

Figure 2. *Giallo* imagery in Hong Kong. *Corpse Mania.*

slashes her to death in an Argento-like set piece embellished with blue-hued chiaroscuro and a melodramatic lightning storm. In the following police procedural, a senior detective (Chan) is abetted by a rookie partner and a perky female subordinate. Further murders plague Jessica's modeling agency (a closed society), but the film abandons any pretenses to mystery by openly revealing the killer as a bisexual woman whom Jessica betrayed. When the killer and her male accomplice kidnap Chan's young partner and sadistically torture him at length, the film becomes a more conventional urban thriller, as Chan and his female sidekick must rush to the young partner's rescue. In its emphasis on protracted male (rather than female) suffering, *Night Caller* has something in common with the martial arts film, but as in the *giallo*, the suffering is highly eroticized. In a bizarre scene, the shackled, bleeding young cop, stripped to the waist, sits below the female killer as she wallows in a mud bath and narrates her doomed lesbian affair with Jessica. More unusual, however, is the current of sentimentality that runs throughout the narrative, from the police officers' brotherly relationships to the mental anguish of Jessica's young daughter, traumatized after witnessing her mother's butchery. The screenplay's labored sentimentality—at times approaching melodrama—diffuses the film's brutality, much as lowbrow comedy disrupts the *giallo*-inspired antics of *He Lives by Night* and *The Red Panther*, discussed below.

The sadomasochism implicit in *Night Caller* is illustrated more graphically in prolific horror director Kuei Chih-hung's *Corpse Mania* (1981), a rare example of a period film pseudo-*giallo*. A Shaw Brothers production that relocates the *giallo* to the set-bound, costumed *mise-en-scène* typical of the studio, the film takes place during China's post-revolutionary warlord era, when residual feudalisms contrasted with ascendant modernity.

Here, a police procedural transpires in 1930s Guangzhou, where lantern-filled brothels comprise a mysteriously closed society and policemen have recently adopted Western investigation techniques. Like *The Savior* and *Night Caller*, *Corpse Mania* prematurely reveals the identity of its maniac: a morose necrophile named Li, who hides behind dark glasses and pines for Hongmei, a lovely yet tubercular courtesan. Knowing Hongmei will soon die, Li buys her freedom from a brothel-keeper only so that he can indulge in imminent necrophilia. In an arresting, artistically framed sequence, Li lies naked alongside Hongmei's bloated, maggot-spilling corpse, as the film presents the necrophiliac encounter (both a transgression and a mortification) as languorously erotic rather than repellent. After Li is released from an asylum, police suspect him in newly discovered atrocities, at which point the film's procedural elements take center stage. *Corpse Mania* is a rare HK pseudo-*giallo* to retain a legitimate mystery—a delivery boy possibly adopts Li's guise and kills in his stead—but, as in many *gialli*, identities are revealed not through the audience's reasoned investigation but in an expository denouement, in which the killer's sudden confession provides a Gordian-knot solution to the narrative's refusal to divulge sufficient clues.

Part Three: The Pseudo-*Giallo* and New Wave Auteurism

Though situated within HK's New Wave period, the films discussed so far derive from standard detective conventions, and directors such as Ronny Yu (*The Savior*) and Kuei Chih-hung (*Corpse Mania*) are confirmed genre filmmakers. But HK auteurs were also influenced by the *giallo*, even when their films advanced local styles and, once again, emphasized the pull of fate over the exercise of free will. Importantly, the three auteurist films discussed—*The Secret*, *Before Dawn*, and *Love Massacre*—borrow *giallo* motifs but veer far from generic formulae. Adapting techniques borrowed from European art cinema (and sometimes classical Hollywood), these films craft deliberately opaque narratives that balance cool cynicism and raw sensationalism. The films' opacities undermine their ostensible positions as mystery-thrillers (Italianate or otherwise), offering enigmas without answers, appearances without depths, and irrational violences that yield no orderly (or ordering) truths.

Based on a documented 1970 HK murder case, Ann Hui's *The Secret* (1980), a key work of the New Wave, begins with thematic overtures to fate. As paper dolls are ritually burned in a Buddhist temple, the film crosscuts jaggedly across spatially diverse characters, as if they all were subject to destinies (and deaths) the film had prearranged. The narrative proper begins as police discover two blood-soaked corpses, a male and female, hanging in the woods. In a dank, gelid autopsy chamber, we see the bodies examined in extreme forensic detail. Hui then cuts (without clear spatial logic) to a blood ritual in which the dead woman's grandmother decapitates a chicken—even in the modern world, ancient religion (i.e., fate) abruptly intervenes, much as outmoded tradition coexists with modern detection in *Corpse Mania*.

Within its murder mystery, the film somewhat perfunctorily includes a red herring—a mentally unbalanced vagrant and his overprotective mother might be the killers—and needlessly alludes to Nicolas Roeg's 1973 *Don't Look Now* (a mysterious girl runs about in a bright crimson coat). Yet a standard plot synopsis fails to capture the unnerving, disorienting style Hui brings to the narrative. Though superficially a thriller, the film's opacity and objectivity show a kinship with the French New Wave. Expositions are missing or deliberately cut short, forcing viewers to intuit relationships; scenes and individual shots end with befuddling abruptness; and the narrative builds through distant events that objectively unfold, rather than through a progression of intimately lensed plot points. Hui's almost cubistic editing effectively violates the crime genre the film ostensibly inhabits. As Hui edits the mystery plot into unchronological shards, content becomes form, and viewers must probe the film's mysteries by piecing together not diegetic clues but the film's own fractured structure. Furthermore, in finally revealing its mystery, the film narrates events from multiple perspectives, offering the relativism of *Rashomon* in lieu of the focal truths sought by Holmesian deduction.

Like *The Secret*, Clarence Ford's *Before Dawn* (1984) is an idiosyncratic mystery that alludes to *giallo* motifs without becoming a generic specimen itself. Unlike Yim Ho's *The Happenings* (1979) and Patrick Tam's *Nomad* (1982)—other stylized New Wave films about alienated youth—*Before Dawn* has a chic quality redolent of Hollywood melodramas. Something of a "lost" work in Ford's prolific output,[11] the film begins with a visual allusion to *The Secret*, as police discover a naked murder victim in a nighttime forest. This time, the sexually abused victim is male, marked by bloodied buttocks. The film centers on the homoerotic relationship between two former classmates, a crossdressing gay prostitute and a young man suffering from a complex Oedipal relationship with his mother, an aging whore. The *giallo* element, here given a gay twist, is mostly submerged until the last act, when the young prostitute's pimp is revealed as the kinky killer—who winds up taking his own life, denying possibilities for justice or revenge. Much of the film focuses on the prostitute's Oedipally conflicted friend, whose self-abnegating mother (Deanie

Yip) regrets her life choices in a long, sentimental climax that occupies more screen time than the killer's demise. Decentering the film's sex thriller component, Ford concocts a masochistic puzzle with diverse influences, from *Stella Dallas* (1937) to the overheated melodramas of Douglas Sirk and Lino Brocka.

If *Before Dawn*'s hothouse atmosphere betrays the influence of Sirkian melodrama, and if *The Secret*'s structural fragmentations owe something to Alain Resnais and Jacques Rivette, Patrick Tam's *Love Massacre* (1981) follows in the footsteps of Michelangelo Antonioni. The film constitutes a pictorial essay unique in mainstream HK cinema. Narrating at aloof distances, Tam objectively posits his characters in geometric landscapes often framed at 180 degrees, recalling the pictorial alienations of Antonioni's *Red Desert* (1964) and, in scenes set in the California desert, *Zabriskie Point* (1969). Unusual for being set in San Francisco, *Love Massacre* is a rare HK thriller to focus on well-educated, bourgeois professionals. The story begins as mentally unstable Joy slashes her wrists when her partner Louie threatens to leave her. The film's following section limns the relationship among Joy, Louie, Ivy (Joy's caring roommate), and Joy's brother following her suicide attempt. The quadrangular relationship is only superficially belied by scenes that suggest linearity. A POV rollercoaster ride, drives along empty highways, and Joy's trail of footsteps in the desert (an image that bookends the film) suggest purposeful journeys that contrast with the swirling, irrational violence that eventually overwhelms the characters.

After Joy dies in a car accident, the film refocuses on her brother, a homicidal paranoiac fixated on unrealized incestuous desires for Joy (he even luxuriates in her coffin before she's buried). Rather than truly psychologize his characters, however, Tam treats them as Artaudian cyphers, as desubjectivized beings choreographed in abstracted landscapes; at one point, in fact, Ivy is seen reading Artaud. When characters observe Rothkos in a museum, Tam frames them within or alongside the monochromatic canvases, as if they were the artworks' accessories, not their overseers. Artwork accrues overtly symbolic value when the brother, teetering on the brink of madness, begins to doodle erratically beyond the boundaries of his lined sketchbook—an indication that he is no longer a controlled object but a manic *cum* willful subject seeking to dominate others. In the film's final act, the brother turns murderous, stalking nubile female students in a dormitory in a lengthy sequence evocative of both *gialli* and post-*Halloween* slashers. In the dreamlike climax, the murderous brother, seemingly in a trance, hands Ivy his bloodied dagger and implores her to "help him," whereupon she plunges the blade into his stomach—a fated conflation of murder and suicide in a film that refuses to resolve its enigmas realistically.

Initially, *Love Massacre* seems an exceptionally arty film that uses the framework of a thriller without providing many thrills. The film also presents manic characters but refuses to psychologize them meaningfully. In a routine thriller, the killer's unfulfilled incestuous desires would be equated (inanely) with homicidality, but *Love Massacre*, so intricately composed, is hardly routine. The scene in which Ivy conspicuously reads Artaud, however, might inspire viewers to analyze the film beyond generic frameworks. Though not overly violent, the film is indeed coldly "cruel" in the Artaudian sense. When Artaud proposed his controversially named Theater of Cruelty, he insisted that it did not primarily intend to promote "merciless bloodshed and [the] disinterested, gratuitous pursuit of physical suffering" (Artaud 1958, 102). The "cruelty," rather, resided in an actor or director's strict refusal to engage in humanistic realism. Artaud imagined a cinema that "was directly opposed to psychological interpretations" (Murray 2014, 96) and "in which even psychology would be devoured by the action" (Saillet 1958, 153). Director Tam seems to follow Artaudian designs not only by exteriorizing characters' jagged mental states through their harsh, geometrical environments, but also by making the killer a psychologically impenetrable—or simply empty—cypher. Indeed, in the film's second half, he descends into a robotic, trancelike state unshaken by even his final murderous rampage.

The specter of Artaud reappears in the deliberately strange scene in which the killer angrily, nonsensically scribbles past the borders of his notebook. Clearly, the killer cannot express his thoughts coherently or even legibly—a problem that haunted Artaud his entire life and which, in Murray's view, catalyzed the very idea of his Theater of Cruelty. Murray traces the theme of artistic paralysis to Artaud's unrealized film scenario *Eighteen Seconds* (*Les Dix-huit seconds*), whose suicidal protagonist "has become incapable of reaching his thoughts" and cannot "translate [ideas] into appropriate gestures and words" (Murray 2014, 97). For Artaud, the "impossibility of producing work [was], perversely, what generate[d] text," as he began to write prolifically about his own creative paralysis (Murray 2014, 13). These writings, in turn, would partly form the foundation of a "cruel" theater intent on demolishing literary history. The killer of *Love Massacre* unfortunately has no such real-world ambitions, nor can he write himself out of his mania. When he scribbles beyond the boundaries of his notepad, he enters irrational spaces that promise freedom but yield only impotent frustration. Unable to sublimate his frustration into artistic performance, he can do little but succumb to the murderous demands of the *giallo*-esque genre in which he is ensnared.

This brief digression into Artaud is admittedly fanciful, entailing some speculation perhaps beyond director Tam's intentions. Nevertheless, the film itself proffers the "clue" of Artaud, and we should follow this clue faithfully, rather than assume Tam merely engages in pretentious namedropping. We can likewise follow the film's allusion to Rothko: much as Rothko's endlessly layered colors cumulatively form the surface of his canvases, so are these characters' internal layers tantamount only to surface appearances. To dig deeper would reveal only paler shades of the surface, proving that appearance reveals rather than conceals reality. Though Tam generously provides the antirealist avenues of Artaud and Rothko, we could well make an assertion without them: *Love Massacre*, and to a lesser degree *The Secret* and *Before Dawn*, abandons the pretense of detection and truth-searching that underpins *gialli* and mysteries in general. In *Before Dawn*, inspecting police simply stumble across the suicidal villain's corpse; *The Secret* begins with police procedures but soon slips into *nouvelle vague* fragmentations; and *Love Massacre* offers no ordering or legalistic presence at all, only the surface behavior of characters teetering at the edges of their own personal abysses. Though borrowing the premises of mysteries, these films dispense with centered, truth-seeking heroes and intentionally deny audiences final catharses of reason and order.

Part Four: Comic Variants in HK's Pseudo-*Giallo*

If the procedural and auteurist films discussed thus far make sideways allusions to *giallo* tropes, that has largely been the point: HK directors, at their most idiosyncratic, had selectively borrowed elements from *giallo* without imitating or appropriating the genre wholesale. We can also discern a third, sometimes more obvious *giallo* influence in certain HK thrillers with decidedly comic tones and without auteurist pretentions. In films such as *The Red Panther*, *Heaven Can Help*, and *He Lives by Night*, bumbling farce and quasi-suspenseful *giallo*-isms become only two ingredients (among many) mashed together in the slapdash, off-the-cuff style common to early '80s HK filmmaking. The results are not so much pastiches but multiple competing pastiches existing within a single film—arguably a symptom of young, overzealous filmmakers trying to balance emergent local styles with an influx of cosmopolitan and transnational influences.

Of course, terror and comedy have often sat side by side. Shakespeare plays Hamlet's encounter with the gravedigger for dour humor, and Walpole inserted into *The Castle of Otranto* foolish scenes of servants spooked by what they believe are ghosts. This sort of comic relief isn't merely a respite for the audience. Once the terror itself is placed "in relief," it seems all the more terrific and can return refreshed, with escalating intensity. Authors and audiences tacitly understand that "relief" entails a certain calculus: if comic moments drag on too long, the terror irretrievably weakens and fades. Totally ignoring proper rules of relief, HK's comic pseudo-*gialli* make no attempt to judiciously subordinate comedy to horror, often to their detriment (assuming the film's horror elements are intended to be genuine and not another form of absurdity). In these films, comic and horrific scenes not only carry equal weight, but are alternated so abruptly that audiences expecting effective thrillers are bound to shake their heads in frustration. This deliberate lack of synthesis, not merely an eccentricity, opposes the prime motive of detective fiction, which, as Auden suggests, contrives to *fuse* moral judgment and rational order—elements erased by these films' excessive, narratively *unwarranted* absurdities.

Few films juxtapose comic and horrific elements more bizarrely than Long Jiang's *The Red Panther* (1983). Unlike, say, the early films of John Landis or Peter Jackson, the film rarely attempts to blend unlikely comic surprise and unlikely horrific shock; these contrary elements are instead rudely coupled, with the pathos of horror and the alternate pathos of comedy seldom intersecting. The plot concerns a creeping psycho in requisite black gloves who anaesthetizes victims before performing unnecessary surgeries and vivisections. Opposing the killer is the film's comic hero, a womanizing detective who tends to his nagging mother and suffers from chronic hemorrhoids. The underdeveloped mystery depends on the assumption that the killer, a skilled anesthetist, is a practitioner associated with a local hospital, which provides the mystery with a "closed" society. Only once do comedy and horror effectively mingle: a mentally unstable murder suspect wanders into a party at an old folks' home, and elderly partygoers must gingerly placate him while nervously trying to flee. The synthesis is short-lived, as comedy and horror crudely diverge in the finale. The killer, exposed as a female doctor denied a medical license because of her immigrant status, kidnaps and etherizes the hero, now in the hospital awaiting hemorrhoidal surgery. He eventually breaks his bonds and impales her with a bundle of scalpels; in her last dying breath, she stabs him in his ulcerous rump. The film ends with a freeze-frame of the hero clutching his buttocks and leaping in pain—not only a ludicrous conclusion but a bizarre manifestation of "fate," if we assume his posterior lesions were destined for surgical intercession.

Even more farcical is David Chiang Da-wei's *Heaven Can Help* (1984), an outright spoof that situates *giallo* motifs within the candy-colored, gimcrack production design typical of Cinema City studios. The film even includes a stylized, mock-Argento scene in which a trench coat-wearing killer stalks a beautiful woman, splits her head with an axe, and shoves her face through a plate glass window (recalling a similar image in *Suspiria*)—a spectacle revealed as bogus action on a movie set. Essentially a supernatural farce, *Heaven Can Help* imagines a world akin to HK horror-comedies like *The Dead and the Deadly* (1982) and *Mr. Vampire* (1985), wherein spirits and humans commingle through unstable boundaries that barely separate metaphysical and physical worlds. Eric Tsang's hero, a sad sack named "Down Hill," learns from a fortune teller that fate has doomed him to a short, luckless life. Indeed, he loses his fiancée, his job, and his life (in a freak car accident) in a single day. Guardians to hell's entrance send him back to earth but also warn him that he'll return to hell when three strangers he's fated to meet are murdered by a slasher, who'll then murder Tsang as well. Returned to earth, he quickly finds himself in mock-*giallo* scenarios, stumbling farcically through the three murders. In the finale, Tsang manages to defeat the killer through some lethal slapstick—a rare instance in Chinese cinema of fatalism happily foiled. Undoubtedly, one advantage of the farcical approach is that, by spoofing rigid genre conventions, one can change the rules of the game.

Like the aforementioned *Night Caller*, Leong Po-chih's *He Lives by Night* (1982) begins with a set piece steeped in *giallo* mystique. As a French showgirl in white stockings saunters down a blue-lit alleyway, the director summons pulsing electronic music, stark backlighting, pouring smoke, and billowing multicolored draperies, cribbing every cue from the *giallo* playbook. Suddenly, an unseen assailant wielding a box-cutter slashes apart the dangling draperies and strangles the woman with her own stockings. Almost immediately, farce intervenes in the shape of a portly, pipe-smoking police detective (Kent Cheng), who arrives to the tune of bouncy music. The heroine, a tomboyish DJ (Sylvia Chang), is meanwhile harassed by a lunatic fan, who keeps in his bedroom a blowup sex doll plastered with a photo of her face. We know the lunatic is a (pointless) red herring, however, because the film has already identified the real killer as a man in drag, perhaps echoing Michael Caine's transgendered slasher in *Dressed to Kill* (Brian De Palma, 1980). The explanation for the killer's shifting gender identity is even less convincing than the psychobabble of De Palma's film. In a flashback, the killer witnesses his wife cuckolding him with a male transvestite. After murdering both of them, he (nonsensically) begins to don women's clothes (as if he were cuckolding himself?) and sets out to kill salacious nightwalkers. Despite Arthur Wong's stylish cinematography and a moody, Goblinesque score, the film drags terribly in its "comic" sections and is rife with fake jump scares. The disjunction between lowbrow Cantonese slapstick and Argento-ish horror is jarring, but the filmmakers *accentuate* rather than disguise their tonal shifts, as if defiantly refusing to smoothly synthesize "local" humor with imported European elements.[12]

In reviewing these three manifestations of *giallo* motifs—generically procedural, auteurist, and comic—we've seen how HK cinema had incorporated transnational influences in messy, non-unitary, and decidedly anti-Aristotelian ways. One might argue that these borrowings are exploitative, insofar as they exploit other filmmakers' ideas for profit, but they are never wholesale appropriations or unreformed imitations. While the artistic merits of some of these pseudo-*gialli* are debatable, the films do signify how a local cinema might import ideas without attempting to absorb them outright, as unrestrained capitalism often does (e.g., Bollywood plagiarisms of Hollywood films). That many of these films are connected rather loosely by the *giallo* thread only demonstrates how extensively that thread had been woven throughout multiple genres, styles, and auteurist approaches within HK's New Wave.

In the interest of semiotics, the present essay has put aside film directors' intentions, which can often be misleading or unfulfilled, and has assumed that HK filmmakers were aware of one another's *giallo*-esque borrowings (which seems an inescapable conclusion). As suggested earlier, the non-unitary structures of many films discussed, especially the comedies *He Lives by Night* and *The Red Panther*, would be considered failures by conventional standards, as they careen from style to style and theme to theme with reckless abandon. These films don't merely delight in grafting discrete genres onto one other; they don't care about the sloppy disjunctions that obviously would result. Even the oft-present theme of fate fails to glue the narrative pieces together. Yet this apparent failure can be perceived as a kind of perverse success, if we see the films' ragged structures as the irreverent outcome of HK filmmakers transplanting European film tropes onto local styles *but also happily violating* the unitary narrative forms from which those tropes are taken. The films' layers of genre are palimpsestic only superficially, because each layer of the palimpsest is blatantly legible and (more or less) separable. Because they arose within a colonial film culture, these happy violations carry an additional weight. The films' schismatic layers demonstrate how filmmakers can juxtapose local and foreign themes within a single work without reproducing the capitalist rhetorics of absorption and recuperation, as the borrowed elements remain blissfully unabsorbed.

Conclusion: Allegorizing the Aesthetics of Unification

An examination of foreign influences in forty-year-old Hong Kong genre films could well seem frivolous when the former colony's sovereignty and very identity are presently under violent assault. The mass protests precipitated by proposed amendments to the Fugitive Offenders Ordinance, which would have extended the mainland's legal reach into the Hong Kong Special Administrative Region, were a last-ditch attempt to salvage democratically the "one country-two systems" policy that the PRC persistently betrays. In the midst of these protests, begun in March of 2019, the central government deployed an old tactic used throughout China's centuries of internal rebellion: blame the revolutionaries for stirring up the pot and frame the resultant violence as a problem of local control. By November of 2019, chief executive Carrie Lam was absurdly blaming students on the campuses of Hong Kong Polytechnic and Chinese University for inciting and escalating antipolice violence. In fact, pro-democracy activists at Hong Kong Polytechnic had to dig secret tunnels to flee a campus surrounded by the HKSAR's militarized police, now obliged to follow mainland directives.

In light of police brutalizing unarmed protestors, one can only wonder how average Hong Kong citizens now view the trite pro-police propaganda of 1980s detective films. It is one thing to know in the abstract that movies' law-and-order fantasies are only fantasies; it is quite another to be bludgeoned on the head with that realization. Controversially, luminaries such as Jackie Chan, Eric Tsang, and Alan Tam, probably keeping an eye on their wallets, have defended HK police at the expense of pro-democracy interests. At a private banquet in February 2020, pro-police celebrities regaled police chief Chris Tang Ping-keung, who remarked to Jackie Chan and prolific B-movie actor Alex Fong, "I learned everything from you . . . I didn't know how to be a policeman, [but] I learned it while watching your [detective] films" (Mok). Though meant as a flattering joke, the comment exposes the popular fear that the militaristic propaganda of police movies is more than empty rhetoric. When Auden characterizes detective fiction as escapism, we should remember that he makes a moral judgment, not an aesthetic one. As detective fiction "dissociates" us from the murderer, we become so closely associated with the detective hero that we fail to see how legal authorities facilitate a corrupt status quo of elites and scapegoats. Of course, hard-boiled fiction and noir offered skeptical detectives rather than conformist ones, but skepticism alone, lurking in dark alleys and dingy saloons, could not disrupt the noble policeman's status quo. Had Sherlock Holmes more of a class consciousness, we might have sidestepped detective fiction's law-and-order delusions long ago.

The order and orderliness of detective fiction function as a microcosm of the legal and political strategies that bind together citizens of an obedient society. Throughout its history, China's centralized government has excelled at such strategies, unifying geographically and ideologically disparate populations through laws packaged in the neo-Confucian rhetorics of harmony and stability. These strategies have changed little over the centuries, whether China was coping with modernity, postmodernity, or its own internal crises of capitalism. As China's neo-authoritarianism eventually produced neoliberal power, China and its film industry have emerged as culturally imperialist forces themselves. Hollywood studios have been rightly criticized for deliberately sidestepping narratives that might ruffle the feathers of PRC apparatchiks. Self-censorship has become the most cost-effective business model, as Hollywood blockbusters must cater to mass audiences in China, the world's largest market. We can only be thankful for small resistances, such as Quentin Tarantino's refusal to cut from *Once Upon a Time in . . . Hollywood* (2019) the Bruce Lee segment that so galled Chinese censors.

While the allegory of "unification" shouldn't be stretched beyond its breaking point, we do necessarily engage the sociological underpinnings of the cultural works we analyze. As Hong Kong's unique identity is threatened with erasure by a totalitarian—and totalizing—mainland unwilling to honor the "one country-two systems" model, the less oppressive, less omnivorous cultural appropriations found in HK's pseudo-*gialli* could resonate on multiple levels. The freewheeling, "non-unitary" mode of HK filmmaking in the 1980s represented a moment when local artists were under no social or political pressure to conform to a unified aesthetic (even though their police films, paradoxically, were themselves conservative fantasies). This polystylistic tendency has largely been lost, as directors in what is now the Special Administrative Region are beholden to mainland hegemonies of production and self-censorship. In recent years, the trend towards unity—both political *and* aesthetic—has only intensified. A recent spate of homogenized, monothematic films by Hong Kong directors that glorify the People's Liberation Army—such as Andrew Lau's *The Founding of an Army* (2017) and Dante Lam's *Operation Red Sea* (2018)—would have been unthinkable even in the early 2000s. Such films exemplify the paradoxes of steamrolling Chinese capitalism, which produces commercial, utterly disposable fictions with Hollywoodized production values. While New Wave HK directors' chaotic genre mashups may initially seem like mishaps, historical quirks endemic to a particular film movement, we might in retrospect appreciate their disunities as signs of an idiosyncratic freedom lost in the march of transnational "progress."

Notes

1. By the 1980s, erotic violence would predominate the genre: e.g., Fulci's *The New York Ripper* (1982) and Soavi's *Stage Fright* (1987).

2. Certain *gialli* are self-conscious of the genre's pseudopsychological clichés. The hero of Argento's *Tenebrae* (1982) writes thrillers that critics call misogynistic and exploitative. When a sniveling critic asks him why he connects sexual deviants and violence, the hero observes that his novel's gay character is well-adjusted and "perfectly happy," while the killer is the real deviant.

3. A few *gialli* do go beyond pseudopsychology and attempt to handle sociocultural issues. Sergio Martino's *Your Vice is a Locked Room and Only I Have the Key* (1972), for instance, addresses gendered and political themes absent from garden-variety *gialli*. In the opening, a misanthropic, racist professor who hosts orgies of young hippies humiliates a black female guest, claiming she is from the "colonies." In her defense, the hippies sing a liberating chant, "Daughter, Free Yourself."

4. Thrillers that do examine social problems could thus transcend their genre. Powell's *Peeping Tom* (1960) implies that the real villain is not a single sociopath but a cultural obsession with scopophilia, thus implicating the audience as well.

5. Other foreign influences predate the *giallo* trend. Mid-1970s HK and Taiwanese police-detective films owe something to *Dirty Harry* (1971) and contemporaneous French *policiers*.

6. Mystery elements in 1970s HK cinema were rarely connected to the empirical detective tale. Prolific *wuxia* writer Ku Lung, for example, fills his stories with enigmas, yet these tend to be impenetrable, metaphysical mysteries revealed through epiphany, not deduction.

7. Many contemporaneous HK procedurals were unrelated to the *giallo* (e.g., *0.38* [1980], *Gun is Law* [sic] [1983], *Cop of the Town* [1985], etc.). As the HK gangster film rose to prominence in the late 1980s, the police genre eventually accrued some much-needed skepticism, yielding films that addressed the police corruption scandals of the 1960s and early 1970s, such as *Lee Rock* (1991) and *The Powerful Four* (1991).

8. Filmmakers beyond HK obviously have created their own pseudo-*gialli*. Ram and Rono Mukherjee's thriller *Haiwan* (1977) borrows freely from Argento, and Partho Ghosh's *100 Days* (1991) transplants Fulci's *The Psychic* (1977) into a song-and-dance Bollywood masala. However, the HK examples constitute an unusually concentrated trend within a narrow timeframe (the early 1980s).

9. Lacking any *giallo* elements, *The System* falls outside the scope of this essay, though its cynicism makes it more interesting than most HK procedurals.

10. 1980 also saw the release of *The Servants*, co-directed by Ronny Yu and Philip Chan. Though not obviously influenced by *gialli*, its story of cops pursuing a razor-wielding sociopath has passing similarities with other films discussed.

11. Released only on Hong Kong VHS, *Before Dawn* remains obscure. A revival might prompt a re-evaluation of Ford's deferred auteurism.

12. Though some camera movements in *He Lives by Night* echo those in Argento's *Tenebrae* (1982), Leong Po-chih's film was actually released several months earlier.

Works Cited

Artaud, Antonin. 1958. *The Theater and its Double*. Translated by Mary Caroline Richards. New York: Grove Press.

Auden, W. H. 1948. "The Guilty Vicarage." *Harper's Magazine*, vol. 5. https://archive.harpers.org/1948/05/pdf/HarpersMagazine-1948-05-0033206.pdf?AWSAccessKeyId=AKIAUXG2GD7CYHBPPE7E&Expires=1582443839&Signature=BafO05pOrXySeaaiGbzGEsvy%2BoU%3D.

Cawelti, John G. 1976. *Adventure, Mystery, and Romance*. Chicago: University of Chicago Press.

Freud, Sigmund. 1908 (2014). "On the Sexual Theories of Children." Translated by D. Bryan. Originally published in *Sexual-Probleme* 4, no. 12 (December): 763–79. White Press/Kindle edition.

Mok, Danny. 2020. "Videos of Hong Kong Police Officers Dining with Jackie Chan and other Pro-Establishment, Anti-Protest Entertainers Go Viral." *South China Morning Post*, February 18. https://www.scmp.com/news/hong-kong/society/article/3051053/videos-hong-kong-police-officers-dining-pro-establishment.

Murray, Ros. 2014. *Antonin Artaud: The Scum of the Soul*. London: Palgrave MacMillan.

Saillet, Maurice. 1958. "In Memoriam: Antonin Artaud." *The Theater and its Double*. Translated by Richards. New York: Grove Press.

Chapter 10

"BUT ILLUSIONS DON'T KILL"

An Examination of *Giallo* Tropes and Gender in Satoshi Kon's *Perfect Blue*

SEAN WOODARD

Satoshi Kon's *Perfect Blue* (1997) has been lauded for its animation style and intricate narrative. The film is imbued with horror elements as it explores the psychological breakdown of its main character, Mima Kirigoe. Mima is a singer who leaves her J-Pop supergroup CHAM! to become an actress. While shooting a television series entitled *Double Bind*, Mima loses her grip on reality as a stalker begins murdering people around her. Since the film's theatrical release, British journalist and anime scholar Andrew Osmond notes that numerous critics have compared Kon's adaptation of Yoshikazu Takeuchi's novel to Alfred Hitchcock's thrillers and Dario Argento's *giallo* films (Kon 2018). While Kon admits that *Perfect Blue* was not influenced by either directors' work, he welcomes audience interpretations of the film (Kon 2018). Kon's comment about Argento's films draws comparison to the thematic and narrative structures that populate his directorial debut; his openness to interpretation allows scholars the opportunity to view his psychological thriller through the lens of the *giallo*—an Italian genre of murder-mystery films known for their convoluted plots, elaborately stylized murder set pieces, and exploitative depictions of violence and sexuality.

As *giallo* studies have increased, film journalists and scholars have examined thrillers from other countries bearing similarities to *gialli*. Troy Howarth (2019) notes in the third volume of the *So Deadly, So Perverse* series that a definitive tome of *giallo*-inspired films may not be feasible; however, he includes selections from major countries that illustrate their influence (11–12). Furthermore, *giallo* and folklore scholar Mikel J. Koven (2018) shares similar views that many modern *giallo* homages only appear to mirror the genre's style: "With all respect to films like *[The Strange Color of Your] Body's Tears* and *Amer* and that *giallo* nostalgia film, they're copying the style. They're not copying the content. What they're not doing is updating them to contemporary sensibility." Although not included in Howarth's text, *Perfect Blue* arguably represents the ideal *giallo*-esque film that Koven describes: a film that critiques the originating country's contemporary culture.

Prominent global filmmakers, such as Guillermo Del Toro, have praised *Perfect Blue*'s intricate plotting and interplay between reality and unreality. Del Toro (2015) stated in a tweet, "PERFECT BLUE by Satoshi Kon. A *Giallo* for all. And, dare I say it? Perhaps one of the most intricate ones ever made. In any medium." The film shares particular elements with Argento's early *gialli* period from 1970 thru 1975, Lucio Fulci's *Sette note in nero* (*The Psychic*, 1977), and Francesco Barilli's *Il profumo della signora in nero* (1974).

To illustrate a gendered reading of *Perfect Blue*, I will first contextualize the film in the *giallo* tradition through Koven's theory of vernacular cinema. Second, I will elucidate how *giallo* tropes—such as phallic murder weapons, hysteria plots, and sexualized violence—appear in the film's narrative; I will also compare Kon's film with seminal *gialli* to identify narrative and thematic connections. Third, my discussion of these tropes will inform a feminist reading of the film—interacting with Linda Williams's examination of gender in horror and thriller films, Barbara Creed's theories of the monstrous-feminine, and Carol J. Clovers's discussion of the Final Girl trope—that confirms Mima's traditional *shōjo* image as vulnerable and fragile.

In a slim eighty-one minutes, *Perfect Blue* explores topics such as toxic masculinity and the voyeuristic gaze; private versus public personas; the extreme psychological pressures thrust upon J-Pop stars from professional colleagues and fans; and the advent of the internet. Scholars of the film have examined Mima from a traditional *shōjo* (young girl image) perspective. Coco Zhou (2015) states,

> characterized as "selfish, irresponsible, weak, and infantile," the *shōjo* image has become pervasive to the point of defining the Japanese national character in the postmodern era. . . . By the late twentieth-century, the concept of *shōjo* has been rearticulated as both a phenomenon of Japanese consumer culture and a model of Japan, which to some critics meant a state of passivity, commodification, and narcissism.

However, positioning Mima instead as a *giallo* protagonist allows one to examine these topics in relation to her gendered autonomy in a manner that may not be immediately evident if viewed solely through an anime lens. Within this context, the type of murder set pieces and the notions of female hysteria and sexual violence that are common to the Italian *giallo* film provide a platform to re-examine representations of gender, mental illness, and the perception between reality and unreality in *Perfect Blue*. Mima's psychological health deteriorates until she is confronted by the stalker-killer who has been plaguing the television set of *Double Bind*. Even though Mima displays characteristics of a Final Girl as a *giallo* protagonist, the ambiguous ending unfortunately solidifies her as a traumatized victim of the events, rather than a full-fledged heroine.

The Italian *giallo*'s status as genre has been the subject of conjecture among Italian cinema scholars. While Mario Bava's *La ragazza che sapeva troppo* (1963) arguably represents the beginnings of the genre before its traits became codified in films by Argento, Umberto Lenzi, and Sergio Martino, there is disagreement regarding whether to view the *giallo* through historical or generic terms or as a body of films whose tropes evade generic categorization (Heller-Nicholas 2021, 27–50; Kannas 2020, 9–37). As an extension, scholars debate the degree to which *giallo* is distinguished from the horror genre. In *Euro Horror: Classic European Horror Cinema in Contemporary American Culture*, Ian Olney traces the burgeoning scholarship of the genre, arguing that placing these types of films in a historical or generic context is essential to defining this popular movement of Italian cinema. While Olney (2013) concurs with Gary Needham on the genre's malleable nature, he believes that the "*giallo* film possesses a strong generic identity and that an understanding of this identity affords us a clearer picture of its relationship with horror cinema in general, as well as an explanation for its cult popularity among contemporary American viewers" (106). Olney continues by positing that the genre's origins can be traced to the popular detective novel.

From a narrative standpoint, the genre is rooted in both the mystery-thrillers of Agatha Christie, Cornell Woolrich, and Edgar Wallace, while also borrowing aspects of Edgar Allan Poe and Sir Arthur Conan Doyle's detective fiction (Olney 2013, 106; Bondanella 2009, 372). In *A History of Italian Cinema*, Peter Bondanella notes some of the *giallo*'s shortcomings, particularly how some plots fail to make rational sense. He admits that red herrings abound in *giallo* plots, and that they can often confuse or frustrate viewers while simultaneously manipulating them "with stunning visual effects built around the set-piece extravaganza" (Bondanella 2009, 376). These set pieces are privileged by the combination of "dramatic visuals and music—in set design, color photography, special effects, sound tracks, and editing" (Bondanella 2009, 375–76) Each *giallo* director's visual flair often contradicts (or elevates, depending on the person with whom you speak) the formulaic elements of popular fiction, thus placing *gialli* in a contended liminal space between "low" and "high" art.

This distinction arguably relates back to the international influences on the *giallo*. In *La Dolce Morte: Vernacular Cinema and the Italian Giallo Film*, Mikel J. Koven (2006) suggests that the *giallo* should be seen less as a genre, and more so as *filone*, "a cluster of concurrent streamlets, veins, or traditions" (6). The primary *filone* elements that constitute the narrative framework of classic *gialli* are as follows: the first consists of the amateur detective, where the protagonist witnesses a crime and attempts to solve it; the second involves a police investigation, borrowing elements of *poliziotto* films; and the third centers around criminal activity, the plot more closely resembling "suspense thrillers" where antagonists extort the protagonist through blackmail or murder (Koven 2006, 6–8).

Koven furthers his definition of *giallo* by contextualizing the genre in the vein of vernacular cinema. Recognizing the *giallo*'s exploitation origins, Koven uses the term as a means to distinguish this set of films "without adhering to the bourgeois criteria of classical narrative, intellectual abstraction, and elitist notions of 'the artistic,'" while replacing categorical nomenclature such as popular or mainstream cinema (2006, 33). He concludes that vernacular cinema must be formulaic in terms of narrative; consistently simplistic in its locales and character behavior; and, unlike "high" art, viscerally demanding of the audience to form a personal relationship with the plot and elicit an immediate emotional response to the film's images (2006, 38–40).

Kon's film qualifies as a vernacular cinema text. While its narrative introduces dream logic and constantly keeps the audience guessing what sequences constitute as reality, the red herrings and ambiguous visuals do not detract from the basic plot structure of the film: (1) Mima leaves CHAM! for an acting career; (2) she sheds her virginal pop idol image; (3) she begins losing her sense of reality after an unknown stalker begins committing murders; and (4) she identifies the killer and defends herself in a final confrontation.

In addition, the locales of the film are relatively few. The viewer observes Mima in her bedroom or shooting the television series either on location or in the studio. Occasionally, scenes differ in location when key people close to Mima are murdered. For example, one murder occurs in a parking garage elevator, while another takes place in an apartment.

Apart from the murder set pieces and the controversial simulated rape scene, the film's style rarely distinguishes itself with a visual flare. The animation is simply drawn—almost garish in its appearance—and resembles the gritty pulp underpinnings of the story, in comparison with other directors' animation styles. According to Kon (2007), "It isn't that I tried to make the drawings sensational as such, but I wanted the drawings to effectively flow smoothly during the eighty minutes of the film. Rather than have one scene stand out, I hoped that the story would be delivered well." For these reasons, an anime of this sort would arguably not be considered "high art."

As an extension, the medium of anime can be differentiated from the works of Akira Kurosawa, Yahujirô Ozu, and others celebrated Japanese directors due to how anime is experienced by audiences. In *Anime: A History*, Jonathan Clements (2013) writes, "The performative action is what happens in the text—the activity of the characters as viewed by the audience. The representative event is the impact of the text on the world around it—the way it is remembered by the audience in the realm of 'artistic heritage'" (8). Clements additionally notes that

> [m]any writers are often apt to imagine that anime has magically appeared out of nowhere in the late 1980s, unaware of the precedence of 'hidden imports' in overseas markets during the previous decades. All too often, it is assumed that reaction and reception to anime in the author's homeland is a universal constant both there and in every other country . . . Although there was a degree of transnational rationalization in the globalized late 1990s and early 2000s, particularly after the introduction of the Digital Versatile Disc (DVD) made simultaneous, or near-simultaneous multiple-language releases of the same object much more likely, the narrative of anime history before the DVD is widely different from territory to territory. Sometimes, the reactions were less about the content than about its performative context. (177)

Clements's statement draws a parallel between anime and the *giallo*'s ability to cultivate performative spectatorship. According to Olney (2013):

> Euro horror movies foster performative spectatorship in two ways. On the one hand, they prompt it because of how they were originally made. As we have already seen, practical necessity forced Euro horror directors to pursue an unprecedented blend of cheapness and sensationalism in their work, marking them as quintessentially postmodern filmmakers.
>
> On the other hand, Euro horror movies foster performative spectatorship because of the way in which they are now watched. The

remediation of Euro horror cinema—its translation from celluloid to video, and from video to digital format—and its repurposing as home entertainment has had an enormous impact on how contemporary American viewers engage with Euro horror films. Although Euro horror spectatorship has always been marked by a uniquely interactive relationship between text and audience, the performative dimension of this relationship has been intensified by these recent technological and cultural developments. At the same time, the performative dimension of Euro horror spectatorship has been amplified by virtue of the perspective from which these movies are now viewed by fans. (43–44)

After discarding plans to shoot *Perfect Blue* as a live-action film, Kon thought that the animated product would be relegated to the home video market. However, the film managed to secure a theatrical release and placement in international film festivals before being released on DVD, where many viewers were introduced to the film.

Now that *Perfect Blue* has been established as part of the vernacular cinema tradition, it is important to define which *filone* the film belongs to. As a *giallo* protagonist, Mima does not fit the role of an amateur detective. The plot's intricacies and the film's editing make the performative spectatorship of Mima's experience an internal one. As she imagines a virtual representation of her J-Pop self in reflective surfaces and reads a fictionalized diary of her life on an internet homepage, the audience experiences her confusion and observes her different personas fragment and battle for dominance. Furthermore, Mima remains, for the most part, physically unscathed until her climactic confrontation with the killer; instead, Mima's mental health remains in the foreground. Mima worries about her safety (as does her female manager, Rumi), but she does not actively engage herself to determine the killer's identity. Unlike the amateur detectives in Argento's *L'uccello dalle piume di cristallo* (1970) and *Profondo rosso* (1975), Mima remains removed from the investigative proceedings. Nor does Mima receive any aid from the police during this time. The absence or incompetence of the police in tracking down the killer in *Perfect Blue* is a trope that is common in multiple *gialli*. In this case, Mima assumes the role of the protagonist in the "suspense thriller" *filone*. Koven (2018) states,

> Starting in the mid-1960s, you had a bunch of other filmmakers trying to cash in on Bava's success by exploring what I call the "hysterical *giallo*," which are movies about trying to drive somebody insane in order to get an inheritance or something. Usually there's much

adultery going on and love triangles. And this carries through the *giallo* through the late 1960s.[1]

In *Perfect Blue*, the "hysterical *giallo*" antagonist—who is revealed to be Mima's manager, Rumi—wants two things. The first is for Mima to not abandon her J-Pop image. When this goal is no longer attainable, given Mima's trajectory to become a successful actress despite the mental duress she is subjected to, Rumi's second option is to assume Mima's identity both mentally and physically. Rumi not only believes she is the real Mima, but also dresses up in the role, similarly to how Norman Bates transforms into his mother in Alfred Hitchcock's *Psycho* (1960), a film that furthers Susan Napier's (2006) comparison between Satoshi Kon and Alfred Hitchcock.[2] To fully achieve this, Mima must be eliminated since Rumi believes only one Mima can exist. Once her life is directly threatened, Mima declares she is the real one in a brief display of agency that is previously not present.

Unfortunately, Mima's declaration of knowing who she is during the penultimate scene does not constitute a satisfying character arc: this one display of advocacy is not enough for her to rise above the victimization she endures. This victimization is first seen at the beginning of the film when Mima gives her final performance with the group CHAM! The performance is intercut with Mima traveling on the train and running errands. She finally reaches her room, which appears to be the only space where we see Mima with all her masks removed. This introduction delineates the initial display of Mima's private and public personas. According to Napier (2006),

> This opening sequence established a number of important themes in the film. The first is that perception cannot be trusted. Again and again throughout the narrative, Kon sets the viewer up, sometimes by showing what appears to be a real sequence only to pull back to show that it is happening on television or on stage . . . The second theme, or perhaps constellation of themes, concerns identification, the gaze, and the problematic role of the pop idol. These themes are signaled by 'fan boys' who discuss Mima in a disturbingly possessive way. (23)

Watching the CHAM! performance is a security guard named Uchida, also known as Me-Mania/Mimania, who is a fan of Mima. In a sexually voyeuristic POV shot, Mima is framed within his cupped hand—a gesture that foreshadows the pornographic violence that she will endure (see image 1). This suggests that Mima, as well as her image, belongs to him. Her persona has been commodified by those who idolize her.

Figure 1. Me-Mania framing Mima in his cupped hand in *Perfect Blue*.

Mima serves as a representation of a Japanese *shōjo*, which critics often categorize as a young female character often delineated by weakness or passivity (Zhou 2015). Napier (2006) notes that the *shōjo*'s vulnerability "is of particular significance to contemporary Japan, underlying the fact that the country is intensely aware of its rather anomalous place among nations—economically powerful but militarily vulnerable, with its centuries old traditions seemingly threatened from both within and without" (26). When Mima announces that the next song will be her last, she becomes visibly timid when fans react negatively. A small group begins taunting her. When Uchida confronts them, they bloody his face. Visibly upset, Mima cannot finish her announcement, so another CHAM! member finishes relaying her message of pop idol retirement. Napier notes,

> Mima's decision is pivotal for the plot, as the more or less harmless obsession of the generic fan boys transforms into a psychotic over-identification on the part of the two other characters, Mima's mentor Rumi, an older woman who was herself a former pop idol, and a grotesque looking concert security guard who, as his fan-obsession mounts, begins to call himself "Mimania" (a play on "Mima" and "Mania"). To Rumi and Mimania, Mima's decision to abandon her innocent and cute pop idol persona is not simply a disappointment, it is a betrayal. (2006, 23)

When Mima returns home, she receives a call from her mother. She questions her daughter's decision to become an actress. This exchange is crucial to understanding Mima's minimal agency in the film. While she is firm in her explanation as to why transitioning into an actress is viable for her career, she is arguably feigning the agency of her decision. Mima deflects the question by repeating what sounds like a rehearsed public relations response: that the pop idol image is suffocating her and that her mother does not understand the industry. We then see Mima ignoring Rumi's advice by being eager to please the producers of the *Double Bind* television show. Brushing off the implications of how performing a rape scene or being photographed nude could taint her public image, she arguably does not understand the gravity of such decisions. In effect, her mental health suffers for the sake of appearing professional.

Mima begins seeing a virtual pop idol version of herself in mirrors and windows as filming progresses. This virtual version also communicates with her as a speaking avatar on the Mima's Room homepage, where Me-Mania fabricates a daily diary of Mima's routines. In "Screening Interiority: Drawing on the Animated Dreams of Satoshi Kon's Perfect Blue," Meg Rickards (2006) argues that Mima's

> angst is about shedding her safe image as a squeaky-clean pop idol and embarking on the unpredictable career of an actress—a move that solicits disapproval from her mother, for one. It seems clear that Mima's *doppelgänger* is a direct result of her trauma around becoming an actress, and after all, what is acting, but displacing one's own identity?

As Mima sheds her virginal pop idol image, Me-Mania and Rumi—unbeknownst to the audience at this early stage that she is the killer—become outraged. She sends an ominous fax to Mima and then mails a letter bomb to the television set. The letter explodes when Mima's agent, Mr. Tadokoro, attempts to open it. After Mima poses for Murano's scandalous nude photo shoot and shoots *Double Bind*'s rape scene, Mr. Tadokoro and the show's screenwriter, Takao Shibuya, are both found dead.

Feminist critic Linda Williams (1999) equates sexually gendered violence in the horror film with pornography: "Feminist critics of pornography often evoke similar figures of sexual/textual violence when describing the operation of this genre" (271). Elucidating upon Robin Morgan's "pornography is the theory, and rape is the practice" slogan, Williams writes that women are exploited for pornographic value; the horror genre glorifies female victimization, which then can manifest itself in reality; and women remain the predominate victims (ibid.). While horror films are populated with female victims, Koven (2006) argues that the "*giallo* is fairly egalitarian in its choice

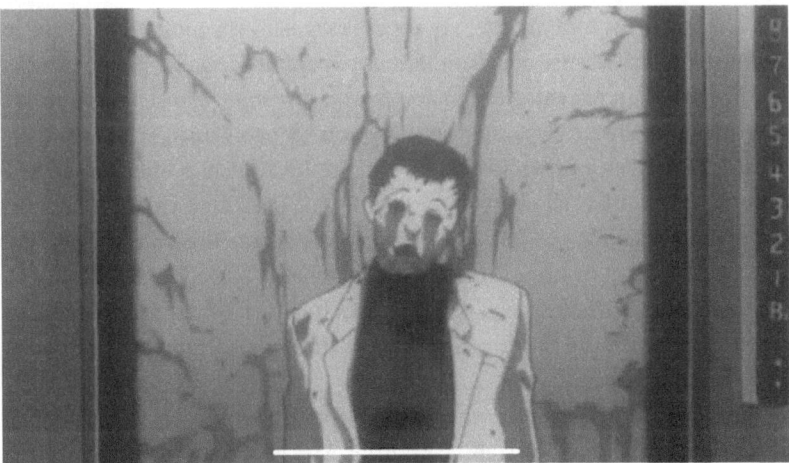

Figure 2. Takao Shibuya's body in an elevator with his eyes gouged out in *Perfect Blue*.

of victims: the vast majority of the films surveyed feature killings of both men and women in pretty equal measure. It would be fairer to argue that, rather than misogynistic, the *giallo* is a misanthropic genre" (66). Koven further elaborates on the relationships between killers and their victims in *giallo* films:

> In many of these films, there is no apparent connections between the victims, and the hunt is for a serial killer. Sometimes, however, the connection between the victims is the link that leads directly to the killer: it may be revealed that all the victims know a specific person, perhaps the amateur detective or the first victim, or it may be that the victims all knew the killer's secret somehow. Sometimes the victims all worked together, studied together, traveled together, or belonged to the same criminal gang. (66)[3]

Perfect Blue's victims all work together with Mima on *Double Bind*. Rumi considers these men responsible for tarnishing Mima's image. Their dismemberments—the gouging of their eyes with a phallic screwdriver—are presented in shocking murder set pieces.

The first killing shows *Double Bind* screenwriter Takao Shibuya arriving in an underground parking garage. Getting out of his car, he finds a bloodied note that spells "Double Bind" in cut-out letters. The garage is silent, save for the eerie lyrics of the CHAM! song, "Angel of Love." When he calls for the elevator, the doors open to reveal a portable boombox blasting the song. The scene then cuts to show his body sprawled upon the elevator floor with his eyes gouged out.[4]

Perfect Blue's second murder sequence is arguably the most *giallo*-esque in its construction because of its similarities to psychic Helga Ulmann's (Macha Méril) murder in Argento's *Profondo rosso*. In *Profondo rosso*, Ulmann serves as a guest panelist at a parapsychology conference. During the event she senses the presence of a murderer sitting in the audience. She later admits over the phone that she knows the identity of the killer. Going to answer her apartment door, she hesitates because she senses the murderer on the other side. The door bursts open, and a hatchet is buried in her flesh. The intruder towers over Helga as she attempts to crawl away, repeatedly bludgeoning her with the hatchet. She crashes through a window, glass shards imbedding in her neck.

Similarly, in *Perfect Blue*, the photographer Murano answers a knock at his apartment door, revealing Rumi or Me-Mania disguised as a pizza delivery person. As Murano pays for the pizza, he is stabbed in the eye with a screwdriver. Recoiling in pain, he falls back into the room as the killer advances, stabbing him repeatedly with the weapon. The scene is intercut with flashbacks to the nude photoshoot, implying that his death is a result of his pornographic objectification of Mima. As the scene continues, we see Mima in place of the killer, further distorting our concept of reality.

In "An Eye for an Eye," Linda Williams (1994) discusses characteristics of the eye in Argento's *Opera* (1987): the eye is the "supreme organ of violation not just because of what it does, but because of what it is: grotesquely penetrable, soft, liable to cry, bleed, respond with discharge, exquisitely sensitive to light and touch. In the world of schlock horror, the eye is asking for it" (16). The knowledge that Rumi is orchestrating the murders inverts the trope of the masochistically male-centric phallic murder weapon. By gouging out their eyes—symbolically castrating them through a violent raping of their eye sockets, which recalls Barbara Creed's discussion of the male fear of castration[5]—she eradicates the voyeuristic gaze that both sexually objectifies and sullies Mima's pop idol image.

While Final Girls in slasher films often have phallic power to counter and defeat their attacker, Rumi's use of the screwdriver identifies her as what Creed defines as the monstrous-feminine. As her manager, Rumi is protective of Mima; in counseling her, Rumi can be considered a surrogate mother who oversees her adoptive child's professional well-being. Aside from their brief telephone conversation, Mima's mother remains absent for the rest of the narrative. As Creed (2015) states,

> we can see abjection at work in the horror text where the child struggles to break away from the mother [or stepmother], representative

of the archaic maternal figure, in a context in which the father [or mother] is invariably absent.... In these films, the maternal figure is constructed as the monstrous-feminine. By refusing to relinquish her hold on her child, she prevents it from taking up its proper place in relation to the Symbolic. (44)[6]

Rumi's own psychosis mirrors that of *Double Bind*'s fictional serial killer, whom, as is noted by one of the characters, has dissociative identity disorder: "In other words, 'multiple personality syndrome.'" All those crimes took place when she was some other persona." If Rumi is a mother figure, but also believes she is the real Mima because of dissociative identity disorder, then the mother personality must protect its child personality. This creates a clear distinction in Rumi's mind—the real Mima must perish so the figurative Mima can be preserved. Once a former pop idol, Rumi's past trauma informs the catalyst—the psychosexual pornographic violence against Mima—for her actions. This connection between the antagonist's past and present relates her to the female killers in Argento's early *gialli*, *L'uccello dalle piume di cristallo*, and *4 mosche di velluto grigio* (1971).

In *L'uccello dalle piume di cristallo*, Monica Ranieri (Eva Renzi) is assaulted by an unknown person. Ten years later, she sees a painting of the event that triggers her psychosis. This time she identifies with the attacker's persona. During the final confrontation with writer and amateur detective Sam Dalmas (Tony Musante), Monica traps him under a modern art instillation full of spikes. Film critic and Argento scholar Maitland McDonagh (2010) states that until the police rescue him, "all the emasculated Dalmas can do is wiggle silently like a worm on a hook" (40). Monica's position above him and her slicing of his face with a knife inverts the phallic power complex and compounds his temporary castrated state. She later is kept under observation in a mental hospital, like Rumi in *Perfect Blue*.

In *4 mosche di velluto grigio*, Roberto's (Michael Brandon) wife Nina (Mimsy Farmer) relates her traumatic childhood. She was committed to a mental institution after her abusive stepfather forced her to identify as a boy. Although her stepfather's death allegedly cured her gender confusion-based psychosis, Roberto bears a resemblance to her stepfather. This triggers her childhood trauma; by seeing Roberto as a surrogate for her stepfather, she must kill him to achieve a semblance of sanity and gender identity again. McDonagh (2010) notes that as Nina states her intention to watch him die slowly, "she gestur[es] to Roberto with his own gun (one might invoke again the Lacanian model of possession of the phallus granting access to the power of speech here, but it's almost too obvious to mention) while he cowers against a wall" (84). In *Perfect Blue*, Mima is confronted by her virtual "other"; however, the virtual Mima's voice changes and her reflection reveals Rumi wearing an approximation of Mima's CHAM! costume. While Rumi in *Perfect Blue* does not explicitly detail her trauma to Mima, her declaration that she is the real Mima, along with her physical transformation, solidifies this alternate reality in Rumi's mind. In addition, the umbrella she uses to attack Mima positions Rumi in a phallic-empowered state to announce that she is the authentic Mima.

Rumi's reveal as the killer through a mirrored surface also recalls dialogue spoken in Argento's *Suspiria* (1977), a supernatural thriller erroneously considered a *giallo* by many critics and scholars. When discussing Helena Markos, a Greek immigrant believed to be a witch, psychiatrist Frank Mandel (Udo Kier) tells Suzy Bannion (Jessica Harper) that he is convinced the act of identifying as a witch is an extension of mental illness. He states, "Bad luck isn't brought by broken mirrors, but by broken minds." While being chased by what at first resembles her virtual avatar, Mima sees Rumi's true self reflected, signaling a rare instance where she distinguishes reality.

Until this point in the narrative, Mima—with her fragmented reality and deteriorating mental health—parallels the characters of Silvia Hacherman in Francesco Barilli's *Il profumo della signora in nero* and Virginia Ducci in Lucio Fulci's *Sette note in nero*. In *Il profumo della signora in nero*, Silvia (Mimsy Farmer) experiences hallucinations linked to childhood trauma surrounding her mother's suicide. In one flashback, she witnesses her mother having sex with a man who is not her father; it is unclear whether the act is rape. Years later, Sylvia returns to the ruins of her childhood home, where she is assaulted by her stepfather Nicola (Orazio Orlando). She smashes a brick against his head in order to escape. However, her sanity is called into question when she attempts to explain what happened to her boyfriend Roberto (Maurizio Bonuglia). Nicola's body and any signs of struggle are nowhere to be found, leading the viewer to believe she hallucinated the entire incident.

Similarly, *Sette note in nero*'s clairvoyant protagonist, Virginia (Jennifer O'Neill), experiences premonitions of her murder accompanied by a mysterious ostinato, a repeated series of melodic notes. While she embodies the role of the amateur detective and is assisted by her psychologist (Marc Porel), her descent into madness leads to her inevitable Poe-inspired fate of being sealed behind a wall alive. The fact that her husband (Gabriele Ferzetti) is the perpetrator recalls the misogynistic underpinnings female protagonists in horror films experience as their bodies are physically and mentally mutilated by male killers.

In many ways, Satoshi Kon's addition of the online persona to *Perfect Blue*'s script presages the detrimental effects of social media and the necessity to create the semblance of perfection via a public online persona. According to Craig Norris (2012), "Computer screens, mirrors and windows become surfaces onto which characters project their alter egos or reveal their 'true' face" (73). He continues, "The mobile, elastic and volatile identities offered within *Perfect Blue* replicate the concerns of identifying too heavily with mass media products and ideals of celebrity. Here the experience of identification via mass media can be an unsettling experience. While it helps form identity it also immediately questions that identity through multiple and contravening identifications" (74). As her fictitious doppelgängers torment her, Mima regresses into herself. This arguably confirms the feigned advocacy she displays during the phone conversation with her mother and through the eager-to-please persona she exhibits on *Double Bind*'s male-dominated set. She allows herself to be convinced by multiple men that the changes to her character are necessary for the story and Mima's image as a serious actress. Her accommodating, traditional *shōjo* image betrays any notion of her self-advocacy.

In the penultimate sequence, Mima awakens in Rumi's apartment, which is uncannily decorated as Mima's room. Rumi them attacks her. The elaborate set up—Mima climbing out through her window, followed by a tense chase along rooftops and the streets below—heightens the suspense common to both thriller and *giallo* genres. Their confrontation seems to position Mima as a Final Girl; however, many of Mima's characteristics and her lack of agency defy such a reading. Writing about the *giallo*'s distant cousin, the American slasher film, Carol J. Clover (2015) states: "The one character of stature who does live to tell the tale is in fact the Final Girl. She is introduced at the beginning and is the only character to be developed in any psychological detail. We understand immediately from the attention paid it that hers is the main story line" (44). This introduction to the commonly gendered horror trope initially seems to describe Mima. As *Perfect Blue*'s protagonist, Mima's character arc suggests psychological depth on the surface, even as her persona fragments. However, Mima does not adhere to the next set of criteria that defines a Final Girl: "She is intelligent, watchful, levelheaded; the first character to sense something is amiss and the only one to deduce from the accumulating evidence the pattern and extent of the threat; the only one, in other words, whose perceptive approaches our own privileged understanding of the situation" (44). Although intelligent, Mima's weak, accommodating nature and psychological downturn betrays her sense of watchfulness and levelheadedness. Although Mima survives an assault from Me-Mania—which could have been a hallucination—on the last day of shooting *Double Bind*, her inability to distinguish between reality and unreality allows Rumi to take her by surprise. Mima's reaction to Rumi's attack is one of fright and self-preservation. Granted, she does experience a moment of lucidity to declare herself the real Mima before she breaks free from Rumi's grasp. When Rumi chases Mima into the street, she temporarily experiences a deer-in-the-headlights moment. As a truck approaches, she envisions its headlights as spotlights upon her and imagines the sounds of a cheering crowd. Mima's decision to push Rumi out of the path of the oncoming vehicle shows the burgeoning sense of responsibility and sympathy Mima has for Rumi in the moment. However, it is not enough to qualify her as a successful portrayal of a Final Girl.

The last scene solidifies this reading. Mima, now a successful actress, visits Rumi in a mental hospital years later. While many commenters on the film view this moment as one of Mima distancing herself from her past trauma and being able to heal, Satoshi Kon's interpretation of the scene provides a crucial counterpoint. Kon partially agrees with this sentiment of Mima healing. In the series of lectures conducted by Runa Nagai, Kon acknowledges that Mima grows more mature and develops a stronger sense of self. However, he doesn't believe "it's as clear cut as that, to have a personal development by saying goodbye to our past selves. . . . It's not like once we grow once, we don't need to anymore. You go through a series of having your old values destroyed, enduring hardship, and making something out of all that. I think it's a never-ending process" (Nagai and Kon 2007). To illustrate his point, Kon addresses the final shot of the film. Two nurses debate whether they witnessed Mima visiting the hospital. Mima states, "No, I'm real!" as she gets into her car and looks directly into the rearview mirror—an action reminiscent of the ending to Martin Scorsese's *Taxi Driver* (1976). Kon believes this final shot creates a certain ambiguity. Despite being the film's director, he is not convinced as a viewer of Mima's admission.

Furthermore, the ambiguity surrounding Mima's final line of dialogue hinges on which version of the film viewers experience. As with the Italian *giallo*, worldwide audiences often first experience anime content in a dubbed version. In particular, a distinct differentiation in the voice acting between the original subtitled Japanese language track and the English export language track for *Perfect Blue* heightens the ambiguity of Mima's statement. In the Japanese version, the viewer clearly hears Mima's voice utter the words. However, in the English dub, the voice that repeats the phrase is that of the voice actor who portrays Rumi. This stark contrast arguably negates reading Mima as a recovered trauma survivor.

As a psychological thriller, Satoshi Kon's *Perfect Blue* represents a labyrinthine excursion into the notions of public and private personas in a narrative that constantly questions the concepts of reality. Structurally, the film's narrative mirrors the third "suspense thriller" *filone* of the traditional *giallo*, given how Mima's manager Rumi terrorizes Mima. The murder set pieces also position *Perfect Blue* as a modern *giallo*-esque film. The use of a phallic screwdriver as murder weapon and accompanying violent visuals are reminiscent of seminal *gialli*. In addition, viewing the film in the vein of the Italian *giallo* also encourages further discussion of many of the film's themes, including personas, gender norms, and sexualized violence. To position Mima as a *giallo* protagonist, specifically through the lens of feminist film theory, allows scholars to examine how the narrative's events affect her. Unfortunately, Mima remains a somewhat static character, who is merely a target of psychosexual violence. Mima's weak *shōjo* traits ultimately prevent her from displaying any pretense of self-agency and leave her in a victimized state at the film's conclusion. Avenues for further research can potentially include additional feminist readings, a Lacanian analysis of *Perfect Blue*'s characters and visuals, and an exploration of the soundtrack as a *giallo* film score, among other critical approaches.

Notes

1. Koven also mentions that there are instances where the "hysterical *giallo*" mixes with one of the two other types. The first example includes the protagonist in Fulci's *Sette note in nero* being driven insane by premonitions of her own death and therefore must act as a detective to identify the killer before her life is taken. The second combines the insurance-scam plot of the classic *giallo* with the exotic locales and heightened eroticism that populate the post-Argento *gialli*, as in Sergio Martino's *La coda dello scorpione* (1971). While elements such as these intersect in subsequent films, given the profitability of the *giallo*'s formulaic structure, directors incorporate them to position their most recent films as more sensational than previous offerings.

2. In her discussion of the gaze, Napier draws comparisons between the works of Satoshi Kon and Alfred Hitchcock. Using a feminist theory lens, she elucidates the male-centric view of the performative nature of their female characters. However, she notes that Kon's gaze shifts in later works to what may instead be interpreted as collaborative or bisexual in nature, and that, taken as a whole, his oeuvre addresses the negative implications of the male gaze.

3. Koven notes that the term "serial killer" is a problematic one in terms of Italian history and language; it is primarily understood, and is a commonplace word, in an Americanized context. For a more in-depth discussion, see pp. 97–99.

4. Numerous film critics have drawn comparisons between this sequence and a similar scene in Brian De Palma's "Americanized" *giallo*, *Dressed to Kill* (1980); however, the connection appears merely tangential.

5. See Barbara Creed, "Horror and the Monstrous-Feminine: An Imaginary Abjection," in *The Dread of Difference: Gender and the Horror Film*, ed. Barry Keith Grant (Austin: University of Texas Press: 2015), 37–67. Echoing Julia Kristeva's *Powers of Horror: An Essay on Abjection*, Creed states that "horror film's obsession with blood, particularly the bleeding body of woman, where her body is transformed into the 'gaping wound,' suggests that castration anxiety is a central concern of the horror film—particularly the slasher sub-genre. Woman's body is slashed and mutilated, not only to signify her own castrated state, but also the possibility of castration for the male. In the guise of a 'madman' he enacts on her body the one act he most fears for himself, transforming her entire body into a bleeding wound" (46).

6. Bracketed text mine.

Works Cited

Bondanella, Peter. 2009. *A History of Italian Cinema*. New York: Continuum.

Clements, Jonathan. 2013. *Anime: A History*. London: Palgrave Macmillan.

Clover, Carol J. 2015. *Men, Women, and Chain Saws: Gender in the Modern Horror Film*, 2nd ed. Princeton: Princeton University Press.

Creed, Barbara. 2015. "Horror and the Monstrous-Feminine: An Imaginary Abjection." In *The Dread of Difference: Gender and the Horror Film*, 2nd ed., edited by Barry Keith Grant, 37–67. Austin: University of Texas Press.

Del Toro, Guillermo (@RealGDT). 2015. "PERFECT BLUE by Satoshi Kon. A Giallo for all. And, dare I say it? Perhaps one of the most intricate ones ever made. In any medium." Twitter, October 23. http://twitter.com/realgdt/status/status/657657457238515713?lang=en.

Heller-Nicholas, Alexandra. 2021. *The Giallo Canvas: Art, Excess, and Horror Cinema*. Jefferson, NC: McFarland and Company.

Howarth, Troy. 2019. *So Deadly, So Perverse: Giallo-Style Films from Around the World: Volume Three*. Baltimore: Midnight Marquee Press.

Kannas, Alexia. 2020. *Giallo!: Genre, Modernity, and Detection in Italian Horror Cinema*. Albany: State University of New York Press.

Kon, Satoshi. 1997. "Interview with Director—Satoshi Kon." *Perfect Blue*. UK: Anime Limited, Blu-ray.

Kon, Satoshi. 2018. "Interview: Satoshi Kon." Interviewed by Andrew Osmond. *All the Anime*. https://blog.alltheanime.com/interview-satoshi-kon/.

Koven, Mikel J. 2018. "All the Colors of Giallo Cinema: An Interview with Mikel J. Koven." Interview by Sean Woodard. *Drunk Monkeys*, August 7. http://www.drunkmonkeys.us/2017-posts/2018/8/7/film-all-the-colors-of-giallo-cinema-an-interview-with-mikel-j-koven.

Koven, Mikel J. 2006. *La Dolce Morte: Vernacular Cinema and the Italian Giallo Film*. Lanham, MD: Scarecrow Press.

McDonagh, Maitland. 2010. *Broken Mirrors/Broken Minds: The Dark Dreams of Dario Argento*. Minneapolis: University of Minnesota Press.

Nagai, Runa and Satoshi Kon. 2007. "Lectures by Satoshi Kon." *Perfect Blue*. UK: Anime Limited, Blu-ray.

Napier, Susan. 2006. "'Excuse Me, Who Are You?': Performance, the Gaze, and the Female in the Works of Kon Satoshi." In *Cinema Anime: Critical Engagements in Japanese Animation*, edited by Steven T. Brown, 23–42. New York: Palgrave Macmillan.

Norris, Craig. 2012. "*Perfect Blues* and the Negative Representation of Fans." *Journal of Japanese and Korean Cinema* 4, no. 1 (January): 69–86. http://dx.doi.org/10.1386/jjkc.4.1.69_1.

Olney, Ian. 2013. *Euro Horror: European Horror Cinema in Contemporary American Culture*. Bloomington: Indiana University Press.

Rickards, Meg. 2006. "Screening Interiority: Drawing on the Animated Dreams of Satoshi Kon's Perfect Blue." *IM: Interactive Media E-Journal of the National Academy of Screen and Sound*, no. 2: 1–21. http://www.imjournal.murdoch.edu/au/?media_dl=447.

Williams, Linda. 1994. "An Eye for an Eye." *Sight and Sound* 4, no. 4 (April): 14–16. https://login.ezproxy.uta.edu/login?url=https://www-proquest-com.ezproxy.uta.edu/docview/1305514900?accountid=7117.

Williams, Linda. 1999. "Film Bodies: Gender, Genre, and Excess." In *Feminist Film Theory: A Reader*, edited by Sue Thornham, 267–81. New York: New York University Press.

Zhou, Coco. 2015. "Girl as Sign: Epistemology of the *Shōjo*." *Flow Journal*, November 22. https://www.flowjournal.org/2015/11/girl-as-sign/.

Chapter 11

"THIS IS NO LONGER A METAPHOR BUT A DEMONSTRATION"

The Red of Blood in *The Strange Color of Your Body's Tears*

SHARON JANE MEE

Introduction

Writing in *Cinema 1: The Movement-Image* on Jean-Luc Godard's formula "it's not blood, it's red," Gilles Deleuze suggests that color is affect itself (1986, 118). The color-image is characterized by affect that absorbs the image and its spectators: "the colour-image does not refer to a particular object, but absorbs all that it can: it is the power which seizes all that happens within its range, [...] absorb[ing] not only the spectator, but the characters themselves, and the situations" (Deleuze 1986, 118). This is a theory of color (of "colorism") that puts color in the body of the spectator, or rather, in the changing states or qualities of the material and affective spectator as color bleeds from the image and absorbs the spectator (Deleuze 1986, 118).

Here, my concern will be with the affective expression of blood (-red) in neo-*giallo* film. The affective expression of blood in cinema *as* red means that I am concerned with the intensities of color rather than the material, blood. That blood is red is also to "speak and show literally" (Deleuze 1989, 183). Between *Cinema 1* and *Cinema 2: The Time-Image*, Deleuze moves from an affective understanding of red (-blood) to a consideration of how color as an "unlinked" category, operating in a "free indirect discourse and vision" by which images follow one another with no associative continuity, serves to "demonstrate" thought (1989, 186–88). That is, in *Cinema 2*, to "speak and show literally" is no longer found in the "association" or "attraction" of images, but in the "false continuity" of a demonstrative series of images characterized by the "this and then that" and the interstice—the void—"BETWEEN" (Deleuze 1989, 179–80). By conceptualizing films' employment of the interstice to produce the montage-rhythm of the split screen, I want to continue Deleuze's work on affect to consider how the expression of blood as red in the color-image—what I suggest is color's ability to "speak and show literally"—accounts for the sensible encounter that the spectator has with the image and the split between images (Deleuze 1989, 183). The interstice between images, I will contend, is the space into which color bleeds. The movement of blood in the body is the minimal condition of sensation. In cinematic terms, the affective expression of blood that characterizes the spectator's sensible encounter with the color-image refers to an open diastole-systole that is not simply in the image but in the relation between images produced by intensities (here, color) that bleed into the interstices between images, between characters, between situations, between film and spectator, seizing and absorbing.

This essay does not suggest that it is only blood which defines the *giallo* film, however, it will contend that the *giallo* film uses blood of a particular hue in particular ways. For Deleuze, the "unique tone of blood" means that we are no longer in the realm of metaphor, but in that of demonstration (1989, 182–83). I will contend that blood in *giallo* film does not simply propel the plot of the murder mystery forward but is a demonstration of affect. Blood (-red) is a demonstration that reveals the murder mystery to characters, as well as spectators, in sensible encounters. The red of blood in images of *giallo* film is that which "show[s] literally" (Deleuze 1989, 183). "Show[ing] literally" in this context, does not mean that *giallo* film is a cinema of bloody excess, like a gore film (Deleuze 1989, 183). Rather, the red of blood in the *giallo* film contributes to an architectural aesthetics.[1] Just as the movement of blood in the body is structured by the chambers of the heart and arterial passageways, the *giallo* film is structured by sensible encounters with its bloody tableaus. Thus, the aesthetics of the *giallo* film is found in the architecture or arrangement of situations and scenes of murder, the literal (and grandiose) architecture of the apartment building in which the murder mystery is set, and the psychological "architecture" of the characters and the way traumatic encounters from the past inflect the present.

This essay will examine Hélène Cattet and Bruno Forzani's neo-*giallo* film *L'étrange couleur des larmes de ton corps/The Strange Color of Your Body's Tears* (2013) as a demonstration of affect that is absorbing, but nonetheless un/endurable. Where *The Strange Color of Your Body's Tears* may be considered a neo-*giallo*, I will outline the reasons for this, alongside the attributes that recall the *giallo*. The red of blood is a demonstration of affect, but, at the same time, it bleeds into the interstices between the split screens of the film, between walls in the apartment building, between women named Edwige, Barbara, Dora, and Laura, between past and present, and between film and spectator. The color red in this film's bloody tableaus at once seizes and absorbs the image and the spectator, while bleeding into the interstices.

The Strange Color of Your Body's Tears (2013)

The Strange Color of Your Body's Tears (2013) is Cattet and Forzani's second feature-length film after *Amer* (2009). Both *Amer* and *The Strange Color of Your Body's Tears* are homages to *giallo* film and can be situated within the aesthetic of neo-*giallo*. In fact, it is as an homage—though Cattet and Forzani reject the term—that I will define *The Strange Color of Your Body's Tears* as a neo-*giallo* (Ellinger 2018, 45). Cattet and Forzani, who are both from France but now live and work in Brussels, brandish a sensual and colorful aesthetic in their films that uses, Cattet notes, "*giallo* iconography as a tool for subversion" (Ellinger 2018, 45). Thus, in the way that Forzani suggests that they "reinterpret and re-use the *giallo* language" we may think of their films akin to a shattering and re-piecing together of motifs through split screens and cyclic and repeated scenes such as the scene of Barbara (Anna D'Annunzio) in *The Strange Color of Your Body's Tears* where glass is broken to pierce the skin in the way that glass is shattered over Julie Wardh's (Edwige Fenech) body in Sergio Martino's *Lo strano vizio della signora Wardh/The Strange Vice of Mrs. Wardh* (1971) (Ellinger 2018, 45–47).

The Strange Color of Your Body's Tears is about a telecommunications executive, Dan Kristensen (Klaus Tange), who arrives home from a business trip to find his wife, Edwige (Ursula Bedena), missing. The door of their apartment is locked from the inside and there is no evidence of a struggle. Dan calls the police and is helped in his investigation by Detective Vincentelli (Jean-Michel Vovk). In Dan's frantic search for his wife, he is introduced to various tenants in his apartment building: a "crazy old woman" living on the seventh floor who relays to him the story of the disappearance of her husband, Paul; the woman, Barbara, living in apartment number 7, who, in an erotic encounter, drugs him and crushes glass into his chest; the landlord, Dermont, who threatens him with eviction; and the bearded man who, it is revealed, lives in the spaces between walls and in other people's apartments when they are not there. As Dan and Vincentelli uncover clues that provide evidence that a tenant, Laura, is responsible for the murders, they also uncover boyhood traumas caused by the mysteries of older women.

While the murder scene of Edwige in *The Strange Color of Your Body's Tears* is shot in black-and-white, it is the colored and fragmented style of the murder of a tenant by a dark-haired woman, the slicing of the bearded man's throat with a razor blade, the splash of blood when Vincentelli shoots Barbara, and the stabbing of Dan (in the top of the skull) and Vincentelli (through the back of the head so that the blade protrudes from his mouth) that are reminiscent of the tableaus of *giallo*. In Dario Argento's *giallo* films, the scenes of murder offer bloody tableaus wherein bodies of victims are creatively sliced or stabbed with blades and found in their architectural settings often pooled in garishly red blood. As in numerous *gialli*, *The Strange Color of Your Body's Tears* has the investigators arriving too late to scenes of the murder. In Cattet and Forzani's neo-*giallo* film, the red of blood also indicates how trauma is an arrival too late to understand. This is the trauma of Dan who, at a young age, had a relationship with the older Dora, and the trauma of a young boy who had observed the adolescent Laura bleeding between her legs.

The title of *L'étrange couleur des larmes de ton corps/The Strange Color of Your Body's Tears* indicates color intensities. This *strange color* suggests that here, *body's tears* may refer to the sanguineous fluid of blood. However, Anton Bitel (2014) notes a double entendre: "For while in normal usage the French '*larmes*' can only denote lachrymal secretions, its English translation 'tears' might additionally, depending on how it is pronounced, evoke the rips, holes, wounds, splits and gashes that will form a recurrent, eroticized motif in the film" (66). The "rips, holes, wounds, splits and gashes" that are evoked by this pronunciation of tears are the knife wounds in the body but also the labia of the model in the softcore magazine, *Plaisir*, which appears as a smile and had traumatized Vincentelli as a young boy (Bitel 2014, 66). This alternative pronunciation from the body's tears to the tears (rips) that are made in it is made conspicuous, when, in the final credit sequence, the "*couleur*" in the title is changed to "*douleur*" (ibid.). The "strange color" passes into the "strange pain" made by tears in the body in *L'étrange douleur des larmes de ton corps*. This double entendre is further found in the blue teardrop earrings and green pendant, and most notably in the red, green, and blue teardrop rings that are gifted to the dark-haired woman by a tenant of the building. Through the surveillance video that is secreted in every apartment in the building, the bearded man witnesses the dark-haired woman use the colored teardrop rings to tear the skin of the tenant; the rings are turned to the palm of the hand and used to claw the chest of the victim. In this double entendre, teardrops tear, and the tears made in the body cause a "strange pain" that drives the body back to traumatic scenes from one's childhood. Thus, the strange color of your body's tears is rather the "mental anguish and physical pain" felt in the traumatic exposing of the body's fears (indicated by the English subtitle of *L'étrange douleur des larmes de ton corps* given in the final credit sequence as *The Strange Color of Your Body's Fears*) (Bitel 2014, 67).

Giallo is no stranger to childhood trauma. Trauma has been known to plague murderer or presumed murderer (Dario Argento's *4 mosche di velluto grigio/Four Flies on Grey Velvet* [1971] and *Profondo rosso/Deep Red* [1975]), victim (Martino's *Tutti i colori del buio/All the Colors of the Dark* [1972]), and detective (Argento's *Non ho sonno/Sleepless* [2001]) in *giallo* cinema. Such films signify the return of trauma using childhood toys and music. The child's toys that the murderer's gloved hand moves over in *Profondo rosso* are reminiscent of *The Strange Color of Your Body's Tears* and the child's toys that Edwige has hidden in a striped hat box. In *Profondo rosso*, a toy mechanical boy enters the room prior to Professor Giordani (Glauco Mauri) being stabbed by the murderer. In both *Tutti i colori del buio* and *Profondo rosso*, it is children's songs which attend the murder sequence—in *Profondo rosso* from a record player, and echoed in *The Strange Color of Your Body's Tears* by the tape reel that Dan finds in the striped hat box.

Trauma in these films is also aligned with the figure of the mother, childbirth, or menstruation. In *Profondo rosso*, the childhood trauma of Carlo (Gabriele Lavia) is caused by the murderous actions of his mother. In the title sequence of *Tutti i colori del buio*, the nightmare that Jane Harrison (Edwige Fenech) has is of a woman giving birth and a strange mechanical toothless fairy. In *The Strange Color of Your Body's Tears*, blood from the knife that stabs into Edwige's nether regions spills onto a young girl's dress.

The Strange Color of Your Body's Tears shares an aesthetic by which we can situate it within the contemporary milieu of *giallo* films. The color red is prominent in these films, signified by the red block letters in the title sequence of *The Strange Color of Your Body's Tears*. However, the *giallo* aesthetic is not simply found in red, but extends to the elaborate Art Nouveau architecture, mural paintings, and stained-glass windows reminiscent of Argento's *Profondo rosso* and *Suspiria* (1977). In Cattet and Forzani's neo-*giallo*, the color scheme of red and yellow is found in the décor in Dan's apartment. Yellow rubber gloves are worn by Detective Vincentelli. Of course, *giallo* is Italian for "yellow" and, as a genre, takes its name from the yellow covers of the cheap paperback mystery novels popular from the 1930s (Koven 2006, 2).

The black leather gloves, black hat, and trench coat worn by the murderer are also an oft seen motif in Argento's *giallo* films, including *L'uccello dalle piume di cristallo/The Bird with the Crystal Plumage* (1970), *4 mosche di velluto grigio*, and *Profondo rosso*. In her essay, "The Argento Syndrome: Aesthetics of Horror," Marcia Landy writes of Argento's films: "The films share a codified visual language in relation to the murderer, involving disguises as part of the legacy of horror, figured in literature and film: black gloves; a mask, a cloth, a stocking or a floppy hat covering the face; a long black coat; and often shot from the rear or from the view of the victim, but not from the viewer, until exposed" (2016, 99). This is also the visual language of Cattet and Forzani's neo-*giallo* film as in the scene in which the bearded man follows a woman who wears long black leather boots. She is shot from the point of view of the bearded man and as though from snapshots taken with a camera. In *The Strange Color of Your Body's Tears*, the black hat is a black bowler found in a striped hat box. Red leather gloves and a trench coat are worn by a mysterious woman in the apartment building. Characters in this neo-*giallo* even share names with actresses from *giallo* films. Dan's wife, Edwige, shares her name with prominent actress, Edwige Fenech, who stars in Martino's *Lo strano vizio della signora Wardh* and *Tutti i colori del buio*, as well as Giuliano Carnimeo's *Perché quelle strane gocce di sangue sul corpo di Jennifer?/Why Those Strange Drops of Blood on Jennifer's Body* (1972) (Bitel 2014, 66). Barbara, in turn, shares her name with actresses Barbara Bouchet (Lucio Fulci's *Non si sevizia un paperino/Don't Torture a Duckling* [1972]) and Barbara Bach (Paolo Cavara's *La tarantola dal ventre nero/Black Belly of the Tarantula* [1971] and Aldo Lado's *La corta notte delle bambole di vetro/Short Night of Glass Dolls* [1971]).

The *giallo* takes its conventions from murder mystery and detective stories. While the cinematic form of the *giallo* film emerged in the 1940s—if we are to consider Luchino Visconti's *Ossessione* (1943) a *giallo*—and flourished in the 1960s (Needham 2003, 135–36), it is as an homage to the visual language of *giallo* by which I define the neo-*giallo*. Such visual language also has affective force. In these films, the murder mystery is visually depicted via scenes of bloody murder. Such scenes are either partially witnessed by protagonists or the dead bodies of those murdered are discovered later by protagonists/detectives. Thus, the murder mystery of the *giallo* film proceeds via the sensible encounters that the protagonists/detectives, as well as spectators, have with these bloody tableaus.

The Red of Blood

In *The Strange Color of Your Body's Tears*, it is the red color of blood, including menstrual blood, that has affective expression. Writing in *Cinema 1* on the affective intensities of color, Deleuze muses in a footnote: "in what sense are there aesthetic a-prioris, in what sense are they nevertheless created, like a particular nuance of colour in a painter?" (1986, 231). Such a question is prompted through Deleuze's discussion of the affection-image, and the way affective intensities are not yet representation. For Deleuze, colors have an "immediate and instantaneous consciousness," through "the quality of a possible sensation, feeling or idea" (1986, 98). As Deleuze writes, while affects are the expression of a particular space or time, they are also independent from it:

> The affect is independent of all determinate space–time; but it is none the less created in a history which produces it as the expressed and the expression of a space or a time, of an epoch or a milieu (this is why the affect is the "new" and new affects are ceaselessly created, notably by the work of art). (1986, 99)

My intention is to understand the affective intensities of film cinema, specifically, the expression of the red color of blood in film cinema, particular to a specific history, epoch, or milieu of cinema.

The red of blood in *giallo* film is not only of a particular hue, it also plays a particular role in these films. This role could be said to go beyond the *giallo* image's specific milieu to recall the history of Italy embedded in its cultural milieu. Landy (2016) writes that Argento's films are "a brand of scattershot narratives soaked in the blood pouring through past centuries of vicious Italian history, culture and fine art" (98). This "vicious Italian history" is the history to which Adam Lowenstein (2016) refers when he argues that Mario Bava's *Ecologia del delitto/The Ecology of Murder* (1971) responds to an era of fascism in Italy (131–33). The film's setting in the bayside landscape of Sabaudia is meaningful for grounding Bava's film in Italy's history. Sabaudia is a coastal town on land reclaimed from the mosquito-infested Pontine Marshes after draining—what Lowenstein contends was "one of fascist Italy's most ambitious and significant public works projects" (2016, 131). The blood that is spilled in *Ecologia del delitto* pools over this claim of land. Lowenstein writes: "[F]or Bava to select Sabaudia as the central location for *Ecologia del delitto* is tantamount to performing a reclamation project of his own: restoring death and impurity to a landscape Mussolini had 'redeemed' from death for agricultural fertility and purified fascist productivity" (2016, 132). Thus, it could be argued that blood injects the landscape in *Ecologia del delitto* with a "new" (even subversive) affective encounter that plays over the space–time of fascism. The spectator's sensible encounter with blood in this film expresses a "new" affect. While affect may be the "expression of a space or a time, of an epoch or a milieu," the affective encounter with cinema is always a "new" encounter that the spectator has with the image (Deleuze 1986, 99). Cattet and Forzani's subversive neo-*giallo*, in this sense, provides "new" affective encounters with *giallo* iconography (Ellinger 2018, 45).

Taking affect's independency from space–time, what is significant about Deleuze's meditation on the aesthetic *a priori* is the revision that he makes to Kant's *a priori* in the way *a priori* concepts are imposed on sense impressions by reason. In the preface to Mikel Dufrenne's *The Notion of the A Priori*, Paul Ricoeur (1966) writes: "Even if space and time are the *a priori* of sensibility, they underlie the construction of the mathematical sciences; thus we may conclude that for Kant all *a priori* are doomed to intellectuality" (ix). The aesthetic *a priori*, on the other hand, is concerned with affective expressions of the world which open the subject (immediately) to sensation. When writing in *Cinema 1* on Godard's formula "it's not blood, it's red," Deleuze suggests that color is affect itself: "Colour is [...] the affect itself, that is, the virtual conjunction of all the objects which it picks up" (1986, 118). The red of blood is an aesthetic *a priori* inasmuch as it has intensities that communicate affect. Color is not the concept "red," or simply a "being" red, rather red has the *absorbing* power of color (Deleuze 1986, 118). Deleuze writes: "If states of things become movement of the world, and if characters become the figure of a dance, this is inseparable from the splendour of colours, and from their almost carnivorous, devouring, destructive, absorbent function" (1986, 119). In cinema, color has the force of intensities of affect that devour and absorb the characters, situations, and spectators of the film.

For Charles Sanders Peirce (1960), red has a "quality of feeling" (150). He writes: "there are certain qualities of feeling, such as the color of magenta, the odor of attar, the sound of a railway whistle, the taste of quinine, the quality of emotion upon contemplating a fine mathematical demonstration, the quality of feeling of love, etc." (ibid.). For these aesthetic *a prioris*, here, qualities of feelings, it is not *form* that is *a priori*, but affective expressions which are not yet realized. As Peirce writes: "A quality of feeling can be imagined to be without any occurrence, as it seems to me. Its mere may-being gets along without any realization at all" (1960, 151). In *The Strange Color of Your Body's Tears*, before the dark-haired woman uses the colored teardrop rings to tear the chest of the tenant, the color of her eyes takes on the color of the rings in turn: red, green, and blue. During Dan's erotic encounter with Barbara, she gives him a drug which makes his mouth turn blue, and he hallucinates three women—Barbara, Edwige, and the dark-haired woman—color-filtered in the film in red, green, and blue. Color is used for its quality of feeling. However, for *giallo* film's color-images, such qualities are also originary impressions of the milieu. That is, red enters the milieu of *giallo* film, providing the spectator with sensorial encounters which predict murder.

Originary impressions are comprised of impulses or energies that are not yet actions. For Deleuze, such impulses bring complexity to affect's independency from space–time. In *Cinema 1*, Deleuze writes of the originary world of impulses and energies:

> The originary world is therefore both radical beginning and absolute end; and finally it links the one to the other, it puts the one into the other, according to a law which is that of *the steepest slope*. (1986, 124)

As "both radical beginning and absolute end," the originary world of impulses is cyclical (Deleuze 1986, 124). It is the return to the scene of the murder for the traumatized victim/witness which most exemplifies cyclical impulses in *giallo* (Needham 2003, 138). In *The Strange Color of Your Body's Tears*, this cyclic "image of time" is also found in the cyclical editing of the film (Deleuze 1986, 124).

In a scene about midway through *The Strange Color of Your Body's Tears*, Dan repeatedly wakes in bed to his intercom buzzing. He answers it to become victim, murderer, and witness to his own murder. Each time that the events are replayed, Dan gains a different view, confronting himself in each of these roles. In the first instance, Dan answers the buzzing intercom to view himself in the video, speaking from the front door. The second time he wakes in bed to his intercom buzzing, the Dan at the front door urgently tells him there is somebody in the apartment who wants to kill him. As he steps away from the intercom, he is slashed with a razor blade from behind. The third time he wakes in bed to his intercom buzzing, he approaches himself sitting in a chair. He touches this Dan, and the body of this Dan flops to the floor with gashes at his back. He turns to see another Dan enter the door and jump out the window. The intercom buzzes and the Dan in the apartment watches another Dan rise from the bed before slashing him in the back with a razor blade. The cyclical editing of this scene reminds us of the movement of blood in the body and the cyclical pulse and draws the viewer back to the affects of blood and breath.

The cyclic editing of this scene in *The Strange Color of Your Body's Tears* also has a devouring or absorbent function. In his book *Francis Bacon: The*

Logic of Sensation (2003), Deleuze summons rhythm as the vital power that unifies the multiplicity of the senses, and by which we might think of the devouring or absorbent function of the cyclical diastole-systole of the pulse:

> It is diastole–systole: the world that seizes me by closing in around me, the self that opens to the world and opens the world itself. Cézanne, it is said, is the painter who put a vital rhythm into the visual sensation. (42–43)

Both seizing the subject and opening the self to the world, this rhythm of diastole-systole is an envelopment of the subject and the world. This is a theory of sensation, whereby the "self [. . .] opens to the world and opens the world itself" (Deleuze 2003, 43). The opening to sensation in *The Strange Color of Your Body's Tears* is expressed through the rhythm of the breath and the rhythm of the knife, which both precede the red color of blood. It is the rhythm of the breath that opens the architectural spaces of rooms in the building, and the rhythm of the knife that opens bodies.

In this neo-*giallo* film, there is a confusion between inside and outside. The knife that pierces the insides of the body allows for opening, discovery, but also escape—an opening of skin, discovery of sensation, and escape of blood from the body—just as the architectural maze of the building with passageways behind walls provides new ways for opening, discovery, and escape. The bearded man says to Dan: "Your wife pushed the limits of her body, to find what was hiding inside. Instead of finding what she was looking for, she discovered Laura. [. . .] Your wife wanted to escape. She got caught where Laura had opened a new way for her, where Laura keeps her secrets." However, the knife and the passages behind walls do not, in the end, provide escape, but rather absorption (and thus, destruction) via sensation.

It is not simply an expression of red blood that is found in *giallo* and neo-*giallo* film, but an affective expression in the body of the spectator in their relationship with the image. Color-images, Deleuze writes, "'absorb,' and absorb not only the spectator, but the characters themselves, and the situations, in complex movements affected by the complementary colours" (1986, 118). Where the color-image is an open image that absorbs and devours spectators, characters, and situations, the color-image describes the experience of sensation itself (Deleuze 1986, 118). By this definition of sensation, rather than a sensible *being* within which sensings (*aisthêseis*) are concealed like soldiers in a wooden horse as Plato's *Theaetetus* dialogue suggests (Chappell 2013), the sensation of red is found in an open state of relations or an opening to possibilities. Thus, we could say that blood (-red) in this neo-*giallo* film refers to an open diastole-systole that puts red not simply in the image but in the relation between images and their relationship with the spectator. Like Deleuze's color-image, the moment of sensation is not a being-in-the-world. The moment of sensation can instead be described as a mutual *becoming* in the sensory manifold.

The Power of Red to Endure the Interstices

That blood is red, and this red is blood, is to "speak and show literally" and, one might say, to "speak and show" affect (Deleuze 1989, 183). In *Cinema 2*, Deleuze elaborates on Godard's formula "it's not blood, it's red":

> The formula in *Weekend*, "it's not blood, it's red," signifies that blood has ceased to be a harmonic of red, and that this red is the unique tone of blood. One must speak and show literally, or else not show and speak at all. If, according to ready-made formulas, the revolutionaries are at our doors, besieging us like cannibals, they must be shown in the scrub of Seine-et-Oise, eating human flesh. If bankers are killers, schoolchildren prisoners, photographers pimps, if the workers are being screwed by their bosses, this has to be shown, not "metaphorized," and series have to be constructed in consequence. If it is said that a weekly does not "stand up" in its advertising pages, this has to be shown, literally, by tearing them out so as to let us see that the weekly no longer stands upright: this is no longer a metaphor but a demonstration. (1989, 182–83)

For Deleuze, when blood ceases to be a "harmonic of red" for a red that is the "unique tone of blood," we are no longer in the realm of metaphor but that of demonstration (1989, 182–83). Given the quandary of literally showing blood, it is the gashes of red in *giallo* cinema that demonstrate affect. This is a demonstration that reveals the murder mystery in sensible encounters. The slicing of the bearded man's throat with the razor blade is a slicing that occurs across split screens, such that the split screen is a demonstration of the splitting of body tissue that spills blood at the same time as the bearded man's mouth splits open and spills blood (see figure 1). The gash on the decapitated head of Edwige recurs as a gash on Dan's own head: a gash that the camera zooms into as if to "show literally" trauma in this splitting open of the brain (Deleuze 1989, 183).

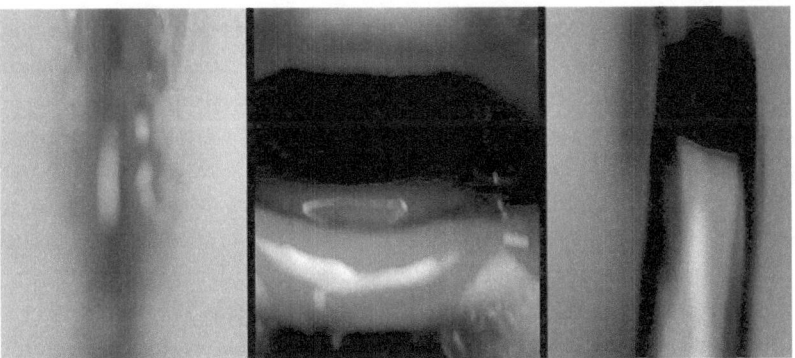

Figure 1. The slicing of the bearded man's throat across split screens (Cattet and Forzani, *The Strange Color of Your Body's Tears*).

However, to "speak and show literally" is also to "speak and show" the relation between images: a cinema where color bleeds from the image flooding the space between (Deleuze 1989, 183). The interstice is what Deleuze describes as the "BETWEEN, 'between two images,' which does away with all cinema of the One. It is the method of AND, 'this and then that,' which does away with all the cinema of Being = is" (1989, 180). In the space "BETWEEN" the fractured self is released from the "sensory-motor schemata," indeed, from that which is un/endurable (Deleuze 1989, 180, 203).[2]

In *The Strange Color of Your Body's Tears*, split screens—and the interstice between images—"sometimes [. . .] denote fractured identities, sometimes [. . .] suggest skewed perception, and sometimes simply [. . .] looks exquisite (Edmond and Heller-Nicholas 2018, 5). The interstice splits characters, space, and time; it is the AND which endures in these split screens as vertigo floods the split. The endurance of the AND is a bleeding between characters split across screens from left to right (left eye of Dan and right eye of Vincentelli), and across screens from top to bottom (eyes of Vincentelli and mouth of Dan). The endurance of the AND is a bleeding of a black void into the space of the apartment, when the apartment and a black void are split across screens from left to right, and right to left. And the endurance of the AND is a bleeding of the past into the present—or rather, a bleeding of the "missed encounter" into the present—that occurs in the psychology of trauma (Lacan 1981, 55). The three characters—Dermont, Dan, and Vincentelli—are split across screens and paired with the photograph of a woman: the dark-haired woman, Edwige, and Barbara. In the triple split screen, fragments become evidence of Laura: a photograph in the "Laura" album, a number 7 on a sheet of paper turned upside down to reveal an "L," and Vincentelli's digital image on his phone of the sleeping woman with dark hair.

The rhythmic splicing to produce a spattering of split screens opens the image to a rhythmic diastole-systole. The rhythmic diastole-systole is an opening of the self, seized by the sensations of the world. The opening—and fracturing—of the self describes a fall into sensation that is a fall in BETWEEN: "a spacing which means that each image is plucked from the void and falls back into it" (Deleuze 1989, 179). In doing away with the "Being = is" of the image (Deleuze 1989, 180), the interstice is also the crisis of the imperceptible; this is the imperceptibility of qualities of feeling derived from red and confusion as to whether the blood is the character's or the spectator's. The interstice—the "this and then that" of split screens—exposes this point of crisis, the point at which red bleeds from the image and the spectator is absorbed into the fracture between affects in images, by which cinema is "no longer a metaphor but a demonstration" (Deleuze 1989, 183). That is, red is not a metaphor in *giallo* film, but rather, it demonstrates affect.

In *The Strange Color of Your Body's Tears*, the interstice is found in the architecture of the building in which Dan resides. The labyrinthine Brussels apartment, with its passageways and space between walls, is a complex site of crisis that mirrors blood vessels in the body and the "inner architectonics of a damaged brain" (Bitel 2014, 67). The film draws us into the crisis of space and time through its kaleidoscopic spirals, spiraling records, and spinning bodies. Such psychedelia has affinity with Jesús Franco's films *Vampyros Lesbos* (1971) and *Sie tötete in Ekstase/She Killed in Ecstasy* (1971). The hallucinations of the protagonist are also key to *giallo* films such as *Una lucertola con la pelle di donna/Lizard in a Woman's Skin* (Fulci, 1971) and *Lo strano vizio della signora Wardh* (Martino, 1971). *The Strange Color of Your Body's Tears* signals the dream-state of the protagonist when, in the opening sequence, Dan is asleep on the plane between Frankfurt and Brussels and the camera zooms into his sleeping face, and later it extends to hallucinations from Dan's erotic encounter with Barbara when she gives him a drug that turns his mouth blue. However, it is the architecture of the traumatized mind with which this film is most concerned. In *The Strange Color of Your Body's Tears*, the creaking open of the kaleidoscopic architecture of the building and its stained-glass windows is like a cracking open of the "architecture" of the mind to reveal trauma.

In Cattet and Forzani's film, the architecture of the building assumes the form of the "architecture" of the body so that walls in the apartment building seem to breathe and bleed. A scene close to the beginning of the film exemplifies the way in which architecture in this film contributes to an aesthetics of breath and blood. When Dan arrives home from a business trip in Frankfurt to find his wife, Edwige, missing, he panics and randomly

Figure 2. A Brussels apartment breathes and bleeds; Paul listens with a stethoscope (Cattet and Forzani, *The Strange Color of Your Body's Tears*).

presses the intercom button for each apartment in the building. While he disturbs several neighbors, one neighbor responds and tells him to come to her apartment on the seventh floor. On entering the apartment, Dan finds the neighbor—a "crazy old woman"—seated, wearing lace gloves and a veil that conceals her face. She tells him about her husband, Paul, who was a doctor and who also disappeared. Reciting the events, the woman tells Dan about the days before her husband's disappearance. Paul was newly retired. Lying in bed together, the woman and her husband hear breathing that seems to emanate from the walls. During the day, the sound of breathing closes in on Paul. He stands in the room, twisting and turning, hoping to determine its source. On the second night after his retirement, lying in bed they hear a scream from the apartment upstairs. The woman suggests calling the police. Paul binds her to the bed and gags her using bandages. Employing a stethoscope and pressing it against the ceiling, Paul listens to the sounds in the apartment above (see figure 2). The woman struggles against the bandages, and her husband, Paul, injects her with a sedative. He drills a hole into the ceiling using a hand drill. Given the correlation between the architecture of the building "with its Escher-like labyrinth of *trompe-l'oeil* perspectives, paradoxical passageways and hidden recesses" and Dan's mental state, the placement of the hole seems significant (Bitel 2014, 67). The ceiling is painted with an Art Nouveau mural of a long-haired naked woman, and the hole is situated at her temple—where one might drill a hole in the cranium for trepanation. We hear the breath of the building through that hole. Putting his finger into the hole, Paul touches blood.

The woman wakes to find Paul calling down to her. He is in the apartment upstairs and she can see his eye peering through the hole. He asks her to hand him some matches. She stands on the bed and pushes lit matches through the hole in the ceiling and then uses the stethoscope to listen to his movements, occasionally knocking on the ceiling and calling his name. A burnt match falls from the hole and suddenly, urgently, Paul's eye appears at the hole, and he asks for more matches to see his way out of the apartment. She hands him several matches through the hole and then resumes listening with the stethoscope. She hears the slash of a knife and calls Paul's name. Looking up into the hole, a drop of blood falls onto her face. The woman relays to Dan how she wiped the blood from her face to see an eye staring at her through the hole, an eye "filled with hatred, madness, fear." In this moment of recollection, the woman demands that Dan leave her apartment.

Beyond the breath and blood of the apartment building in *The Strange Color of Your Body's Tears*, the surveillance videos that are viewed by the bearded man connect rooms in the building, as much as, the bearded man tells Dan, the old walls behind new walls and secret passageways between apartments do. *Giallo* is known for its use of elaborate architecture. Argento's Three Mothers trilogy of *Suspiria* (1977), *Inferno* (1980), and *La terza madre/Mother of Tears* (2007) also includes themes of passageways and spaces between walls (Landy 2016, 103). Most poignantly, in *Inferno*, Rose's (Irene Miracle) neighbor, Elise (Daria Nicolodi), shows Mark (Leigh McCloskey) open pipes that connect the apartments and which amplify the voice when spoken into. These open pipes, like blood vessels in the body, connect rooms in the building.

Apartment buildings in *giallo* are not simply the site for the aesthetic staging of murders in bloody tableaus. Architecture in these films comprise the aesthetics of breath and blood by assimilating the apartment building's passageways to blood vessels in the body as though these buildings are living scenes. Such an architecture of aesthetics also alludes to an "architecture" of trauma and the passageways that are made when passing from traumatic past to present. Thus, what is found in *giallo* film is that the red of blood extends from bloody tableaus in scenes of murder to encapsulate the architecture of the apartment building and the psychological "architecture" of the characters' trauma. However, red also extends from the image to enclose the spectator: blood is both within the spectator and without. The red of blood at once seizes and absorbs, while bleeding into the interstices between walls in the apartment building, between past and present, and between image and spectator.

Conclusion

The red of blood in *giallo* film demonstrates affect. *Giallo* and neo-*giallo* is a blood-red cinema with "freshness, life, freedom" (Peirce 1960, 148). The blood of life is the blood that flows from murder victims in the film. Spaces behind walls in the Brussels apartment building connect the apartments mirroring arterial passageways, and apartment walls seem to breath and bleed such that there is life where there wouldn't usually be. The blood of life is also the menstrual blood of young women in *The Strange Color of Your Body's Tears*, which exposes the encounter with a traumatic past for the men. If blood in Cattet and Forzani's film is "freshness, life, freedom" (Peirce 1960, 148), this freedom also has a violence ascribed to it, as the man dressed as Napoleon Bonaparte in Godard's *Weekend* (1967) pronounces: "Freedom is violence." Such freedom and violence are expressions of the red of blood in Cattet and Forzani's neo-*giallo* film, and, in the end, also *The Strange Color of Your Body's Fears*.

Notes

1. In *Cinema 2*, Deleuze refers to an "architecture of vision" to describe the "perspectives and projections" of the body and its shadows (1989, 144).

2. In a similar vein to that of the un/endurable, Deleuze writes in *Cinema 2*: "[I]mages like those which bring together Golda Meir and Hitler in *Ici et ailleurs* would be intolerable" (1989, 179).

Works Cited

Bitel, Anton. 2014. "The Strange Color of Your Body's Tears." *Sight and Sound* 24, no. 5 (May): 66–67.

Chappell, Sophie Grace. 2013. "Plato on Knowledge in the *Theaetetus*." In *The Stanford Encyclopaedia of Philosophy* (Winter), edited by Edward N. Zalta. https://plato.stanford.edu/archives/win2013/entries/plato-theaetetus/.

Deleuze, Gilles. 1986. *Cinema 1: The Movement-Image*. Translated by Hugh Tomlinson and Barbara Habberjam. Minneapolis: University of Minnesota Press.

Deleuze, Gilles. 1989. *Cinema 2: The Time-Image*. Translated by Hugh Tomlinson and Robert Galeta. Minneapolis: University of Minnesota Press.

Deleuze, Gilles. 2003. *Francis Bacon: The Logic of Sensation*. Translated by Daniel W. Smith. London and New York: Continuum.

Edmond, John, and Alexandra Heller-Nicholas. 2018. "Split/Screen Cattet/Forzani." In *Cattet & Forzani: The Strange Films of Hélène Cattet and Bruno Forzani*, edited by John Edmond and Alexandra Heller-Nicholas, 5–8. Brisbane: Queensland Film Festival.

Ellinger, Kat. 2018. "Vice and Vision: Magnifying Sergio Martino for *The Strange Color of Your Body's Tears*." In *Cattet & Forzani: The Strange Films of Hélène Cattet and Bruno Forzani*, edited by John Edmond and Alexandra Heller-Nicholas, 45–48. Brisbane: Queensland Film Festival.

Koven, Mikel J. 2006. *La Dolce Morte: Vernacular Cinema and the Italian Giallo Film*. Lanham, Maryland: Scarecrow Press.

Lacan, Jacques. 1981. *The Four Fundamental Concepts of Psycho-Analysis*. Edited by Jacques-Alain Miller and translated by Alan Sheridan. New York and London: W. W. Norton & Company.

Landy, Marcia. 2016. "The Argento Syndrome: Aesthetics of Horror." In *Italian Horror Cinema*, edited by Stefano Baschiera and Russ Hunter, 93–110. Edinburgh: Edinburgh University Press.

Lowenstein, Adam. 2016. "The *Giallo*/Slasher Landscape: *Ecologia del delitto*, *Friday the 13th* and Subtractive Spectatorship." In *Italian Horror Cinema*, edited by Stefano Baschiera and Russ Hunter, 127–44. Edinburgh: Edinburgh University Press.

Needham, Gary. 2003. "Playing with Genre: Defining the Italian *Giallo*." In *Fear Without Frontiers: Horror Cinema Across the Globe*, edited by Steven Jay Schneider, 135–44. Godalming: FAB Press.

Peirce, Charles Sanders. 1960. *Collected Papers of Charles Sanders Peirce, Vols. I–II*. Edited by Charles Hartshorne and Paul Weiss. Cambridge, MA: The Belknap Press of Harvard University Press.

Ricoeur, Paul. 1966. "Preface." In Mikel Dufrenne, *The Notion of the A Priori*. Translated by Edward S. Casey. Evanston, IL: Northwestern University Press.

Chapter 12

ALMODÓVAR MEETS GAY PORN MEETS *GIALLO*

Rewriting Argento's *L'uccello dalle piume di cristallo* in *Un couteau dans le Coeur*

FERNANDO GABRIEL PAGNONI BERNS

Now considered a "master of horror," Dario Argento is the man who gave Euro-horror—as well as Italian exploitation cinema—deserved respectability. Yet, as Andrew Cooper argues, it was not until after the re-evaluation of Argento's work as a director belonging to what the *Cahiers du cinéma* critics called *politique des auteurs* that "Argento's language" was recognized as having an "auteurist bent" (Cooper 2012, 94). Furthermore, "with the advent of new media technologies like DVD and Blu-ray, Eurocult films are enjoying a renaissance, with films long unseen now available in unedited, original versions, released and sold in special editions that are both popular and profitable" (Shipka 2011, 7). This has provided film scholars and academia with pristine, non-dubbed, uncut copies of examples of Euro-horror for critical re-evaluation. The main consequence was that Argento would become one of the most imitated directors across the globe, from the US to Latin America, to the point that phrases such as "Argento style" are commonly used. In brief, after decades of being perceived merely as an exploitation director, Argento is now renowned as an auteur.

Euro-horror, on the other hand, has not been highly esteemed. Trashy and exploitative, filled with gore, nudity, and preposterous dubbing, Euro-horror has been left at the margins of film studies. Only recently, with the shift in academia towards cultural studies and with the availability of DVD technology and uncut copies, has Euro-horror begun to receive some kind of recognition as a cinema venturing daringly into the dark corridors of the human psyche. The exploitative nature of many of these films seems far removed from the art film subversive nature, yet, as Joan Hawkins argues, the aesthetics and narratives of Euro-horror, paracinema, trash culture, and sleazy psychotronic films are not foreign to the spheres of art filmmaking. Both, horror and avant garde cinema share the status of being non-mainstream, "subversive" (Hawkins 2000, 7), nonlinear, oneiric films filled with "shocking" (Hawkins 2000, 23) sequences and scenes that work almost autonomous from the main narrative. Further, since Argento is inextricably linked to the cycle of *giallo* films, all neo-*gialli* make, albeit in different degrees, reference to the works of the Italian master.

Certainly, many Euro and Hollywood horror films do reference Argento's work. Some offer just passing nods to Argento; some go so far as to rewrite the films, dismantling the narratives to make explicit what in Argento was implicit or foreground as text what in Argento was subtext. Argento is thus reinvented by global cinema, his ideas and images filtered by very different aesthetics and ideologies.

Dario Argento began his career as a horror and *giallo* auteur with *L'uccello dalle piume di cristallo* (*The Bird with the Crystal Plumage*, 1975). An international hit, the film's plot is simple: Sam Dalmas (Tony Musante), an American writer vacationing in Italy prevents a murder at an art gallery. Something in what he saw in the crime scene (a black-clad killer whose face remains obscured attacking a vulnerable woman) is problematic. Dalmas explicitly acknowledges that something is wrong in how he remembers the crime scene. Obsessed with the crime, he becomes amateur detective and starts tracing the killer's identity. As a witness, however, he finds himself a pawn in the killer's deadly game.

In 2018, French film *Un couteau dans le Coeur* (*Knife+Heart*) opened at the Cannes Film Festival. Directed by Yann González, the film takes place in 1979 Paris, where lesbian filmmaker Lois (Vanessa Paradis), who makes arty gay porn, suddenly attracts the attention of a masked serial killer who begins murdering her cast. The film pays homage to *giallo* both in visual (saturated primary colors) and narrative (the black-clad killer, sexual trauma) terms. The reference to *giallo*, however, runs deep, as the film is, basically, a rewriting of Argento's *The Bird with the Crystal Plumage* filtered through a queer lens. Unlike Argento's film, González's *Un couteau dans le Coeur* makes emphasis on queer sex, desire, and identity through positive hues, thus becoming the reverse of Argento's *opera prima*. Furthermore, I will argue, queerness is always lurking at the margins of the *giallo* film due the cycle predisposition to excess, kitsch, transvestism, and homoerotic desire. Unlike the traditional *giallo* film that uses queer tropes as a form of transgression from the norm and with the intention of producing ambiguity, in *Un couteau dans le Coeur* the homoerotic imagination is inflamed not to transgress but to show gay love and care, topics largely absent in the Italian cycle. The film destabilizes the generic codes of the horror genre, specifically the *giallo* horror film, and, through the use of melodrama tropes, critiques the naturalization of heterosexual violence against women and queer people—a staple in the *giallo* film.

Understanding adaptation not as a unidirectional process progressing from an original source to cinematographic illustration, but rather as a process of feedback between works and social and cultural contexts, I use this rewriting as a case of adaptation from film to film, to show how González's film queers Argento's work by revealing its indebtedness to queer desire and identity.

Adaptation, Rewriting, Queerness

As Eduardo Grüner argues, when we, viewers, find inspirations or echoes of other works in a film, we cannot just turn our heads and look the other way as if that relationship was not there due to a principle "of intellectual honesty" (2006, 113) The author of a concrete artistic text has willingly connected his or her work to another time/nation/ideology/aesthetic/culture, inviting us to read it from our socially and culturally located point of view. Thus, the practice of adaptation is both a strategy of hermeneutic intervention and a form of "political reading" (Grüner 2006, 114) that affects the production, circulation, and reception of the film in question.

To this hermeneutic philosophy, there is *no original source*, but only interpretations. The "original" source loses its aura as a unique piece floating amidst a sea of imitative work. Even the primary text—the so-called source—is related to other different texts that precede it chronologically. The "source" already is an interpretation. For instance, Argento's *The Bird with the Crystal Plumage* (allegedly, the source) is a film based on *The Screaming Mimi*, a novel wrote by Edgar Award-winning author Fredric Brown in 1949. The novel, in turn, was first adapted as a noir film, *The Screaming Mimi* (Gerd Oswald, 1958). This first film adaptation is strikingly different from Argento's work, even if both are mostly faithful to the "source" book. So each artistic work answers to the politics of readership and interpretation, mediated by both, the social and cultural contexts and nationalities of production and the directors' interests. In other words, a movie is a rewriting that speaks about itself and the society and culture that produced it rather than referring solely to a previous work through a relationship of mirroring. In this sense, both Oswald's *The Screaming Mimi* and Argento's *The Bird with the Crystal Plumage* are crime texts, but while the former fits squarely into the noir ideology (hard-as-nails reporters with alcohol problems, seedy night clubs, a sense of hopelessness pending above the main characters) and aesthetics (chiaroscuros, striking black-and-white photography, decaying urbanism), the latter is a landmark on the *giallo* cycle closer to horror than "crime." Each text contains zones of ambiguity and indeterminacy, *lacunae* that allows or, better said, ask for interpretations or emphasis. Every narrative choice shuts down other possibilities that do not evaporate but remain there, haunting the work. Thus, a rewriting (another interpretation) is a form of materializing the unsaid potentialities haunting a previous work. For example, the topic of sexual trauma presented in both Brown's novel and Argento's adaptation is completely reworked by Yann González with the purpose of avoiding the misogyny explicitly embodied in the artistic piece "the screaming Mimi" (a theme I will explore later).

Like adaptation itself, queerness is also "a zone of possibilities" (Edelman 1994, 114), always "inflected by a sense of potentiality that it cannot yet quite articulate" (Jagose 1992, 2). Queerness resists patriarchal ideologies that are presented as "natural" and it opens the possibility of alternative ways of existence, counter-hegemonic to the canonical reading just as adaptation does. It can be argued, thus, that the process of adaptation always includes a queer component, since it points, inevitably, to the potential for a new way of being, of read, of interpretation. Readers can open the most heteronormative texts to playful queer interpretations because the text offers spaces of ambiguity that ask for adaptation, rewriting, and liberating transformation.

The *giallo* film is also aligned with sexuality and queerness, albeit in a perfunctory, sometimes misogynistic, and homophobic way. Mostly, the *giallo* film is predicated upon the image of the tortured, mutilated, raped, and killed women. Ian Olney acknowledges that *giallo* films "have a reputation for being deeply and unrepentantly misogynistic" as the cycle finds new, varied, and "spectacularly nasty methods of dispatching women" (2013, 117). Olney, however, remarks that "a review of some of the most popular and well-known *giallo* films reveals that they foster spectatorship-as-drag by deploying a variety of local strategies for engaging the unnatural" (ibid.) in ways that might lead to the denaturalization of the gender binary. Mikel Koven argues that "it would be fairer to argue that, rather than misogynistic, the *giallo* is a misanthropic genre," since the cycle is "fairly egalitarian in its choice of victims" (2006, 66).

Furthermore, the *giallo* cycle carries a reputation for being homophobic or, at least, of staging scenarios where the prejudices against homosexuality are sustained and reinforced (Koven 2006, 56). The cycle, however, is also known for playing with gender stereotypes, rigid gender roles, and expectations. It is not uncommon in *giallo* cinema that the identity of the killer is ambiguous—as is his/her voice (when making a menacing warning through a telephone, for example) and general aspect, before the film's climax—remains oblique and sexless. "Emasculated" men such as priests are common killers in the cycle (*Non si sevizia un paperino*, Lucio Fulci, 1972), thus furthering the dissolution of "proper" ways of being man and woman. Argento is fond of the mixing of gender identities, as his killers "are generally constructed as perverse in their reluctance or inability to undergo 'correct' heterosexual Oedipal trajectories" (Hunt 2000, 329).

It is interesting that issues about non-legitimate sex (such as sadomasochism, transvestism, transgender bodies, or prostitution) "implicitly questioned the hegemonic binarism of 'heterosexuality' and 'homosexuality'" (Jagose 1992, 64) while discussing cultural and social difference. As Harry M. Benshoff notes in his groundbreaking book *Monsters in the Closet: Homosexuality and the Horror Film*, "most classical horror films make little or no distinction between homosexuality and any other form of 'sex perversion'" (1997, 69): all forms of non-normative sex are connected and thus overlap with each other, becoming forms of abnormal monstrosity. In this scenario, any form of deviant sex may be read as both, monstrous and queer. As such, any sexual pervert in *giallo* film may be read as queer.

Un couteau dans le Coeur exhibits queer qualities since the film speaks of homosexual desire while being cluttered with references to Argento, creating thus something new from previous texts. It does so through a process of queering: not just rewriting a previous film but also through the evocation of a whole genre (the *giallo*) through the intersection with art film, melodrama, porn film, kinkiness, and rearticulation of the (hetero)normative narrative of the classic European film. Further, the references do not cease on Argento and *giallo*, as Yann González also adapts and transforms other images related to camp, violence, and the kitsch such as Pedro Almodóvar's aesthetics of passion or Spanish director Jesús Franco's mixing of violence with eroticism.

Queering Argento

One reason critics and reviews in general have not acknowledged the presence of Argento's *The Bird with the Crystal Plumage* in González's film may be that *Un couteau dans le Coeur* is not a remake in the usual sense. The French film is, rather, a rewriting from one cultural realm (sleazy Italian *giallo*) to another (French art film that works in a postmodern mode using pastiche of previous genres, aesthetics, and films). Yet *Un couteau dans le Coeur* refers to the *giallo* cycle explicitly and implicitly. It does explicitly in the use of its bold color palette (lighting composed by saturated primary colors), baroque set design, and a black-clad psychopathic killer, all of which are trademarks of the cycle (Kendrik 2017, 323). Furthermore, the film's official poster evokes the main aesthetics of the traditional Italian *giallo*: a bloody knife is at the center of the composition, a woman in red, a woman in blue, and a man in green, all three occupying the borders. A masked serial killer lurks above. A crow cries above the knife, blending its blackness with splattered blood. The poster heavily references Argento's film. The official poster of *The Bird with the Crystal Plumage* is divided in two horizontal sides, the top half occupied with a woman bathed in red screaming while the segment above is occupied by a black-clad hand holding a shining knife. The poster is completed with the figure of a bird (the animal of the title) silhouetted at the bottom. Second, and implicitly, the film references Argento's *The Bird with the Crystal Plumage* through the ideas and narratives—especially in relation with sexual trauma—that circulate between the two films.

Unlike Argento's film, revolving around the heterosexual relationship between male hero Dalmas and his girlfriend Julia (Susy Kendall), *Un couteau dans le Coeur* is set in Paris in the summer of 1979, where Anne Parèze (Vanessa Paradis), a producer of gay porn movies, wants to lure back her editor and lover Lois (Kate Moran), who had just ended the relationship. Lois chose to end the relationship due to Anne's excessive behavior (the latter drinks too much). After several unsuccessful attempts to get her lover back, Anne embarks on another porn film with her assistant (Nicolas Maury). Even the attempt to make a masterpiece is another way through which Anne tries to momentarily forget the state of her love life. However, as shooting proceeds, actors, past and present, are murdered by a sadistic killer in a black, S&M leather mask.

The Bird with the Crystal Plumage establishes all its themes in the opening sequence. A young woman walks the street while a nursery lullaby acts as the soundtrack. Some anonymous party is taking photos of the girl. The scene is interrupted by briefs inserts of black-gloved hands manipulating a series of shining knives that sit within a drawer lined with deep red velvet. Argento was creating, with this opening sequence, the iconography and main architecture of the genre, building upon what Mario Bava did with *La ragazza che Sapeva Troppo* (1963), arguably, the first Italian *giallo*. The young woman walking the streets wears red, and red is the casing of the knives, establishing a clear connection between colors and emotions, femininity and violence, at the same time that the color red anticipates the bloodshed that will come later. The way the girl is photographed enhances the complex engagement of *giallo* with the role of spectatorship and the gaze. The camera photographing the girl takes the role/place of Argento's camera. Spectators see the girl walking the streets, then hear a click and the image freezes, simulating the effect of a photo being taken. Thus, the killer's camera and that of Argento are one and the same. The photographic camera becomes a subjective point of view, inviting spectators to assume the role of the anonymous party surreptitiously taking photos. As it is revealed seconds later, the person taking the photos is also the killer; thus, viewers and the killer share for a brief moment the same voyeuristic point of view. Even more striking is the use of extra-diegetic music. The lullaby suggests a traumatic past.

Like *The Bird with the Crystal Plumage*, González's film begins with a murder set piece while, at the same time, evoking the opening of Argento's film. Argento's opening, however, is reconstructed to better serve González's ideas of homosexual desire, melodrama, and porn aesthetics. A woman's hand places a roll of film into a projector. The woman's nails are painted deep red, thus establishing a clear connection with the woman wearing red at the opening of Argento's film and the casing of knives (later in González's film, it will be revealed that they are Lois's hands). Also, the color red prefigures future bloodletting, a trademark in the *giallo* cycle. Rather than a man watching a young woman (as audiences assumed when Argento's film opened, to be truly surprised with the twist ending, when the killer is revealed to be a psychopathic woman), here is a woman fully assuming the voyeuristic gaze. The film projected is a "blue movie," more specifically, a gay porn film. Two young men—twinks, in the porn language—passionately kiss each other at what seems to be the countryside. One of them gets on his knees, ready for oral sex. The camera zooms—the zoom another trademark of the *giallo* film and the Italian cinema of the 1970s—to a brunette man watching the boys from the safety of the foliage. He is masturbating. Thus, the young men having sex are voyeuristic observed from two vantage point of views: the woman projecting the film is one of the spectators—from the "front," may be said—while the furtive man is watching them from the "back," obscured by the forest.

At this point, viewers are obliged to assume not a heterosexual, heteronormative gaze that frames a beautiful girl walking the street as happened in Argento's film (a gaze choosing a victim, it must be added, as the killer caresses both the photos and the knives alike, thus associating femininity with vulnerability and predation), but a transsexual, queer position. Arguably, this drag identification is present in Argento's film, but it is only fully disclosed at the story's end, when the killer is revealed to be a female. In *Un couteau dans le Coeur*, this "transsexual" intersecting is fully queer: the one managing the film and watching it is a woman. Thus, a woman is the bearer of the gaze, obliging audiences to share with her what she is watching: gay porn. All of this produces a rupture of the hegemonic patriarchal gaze, the one that Laura Mulvey (1989) sees as constitutive of the woman as being the object to be-looked-at and the man as the bearer of the gaze. In mainstream cinema (such as in Alfred Hitchcock's 1954 *Rear Window*), the story is constructed through the male gaze; the female eye remains at the margins. Dario Argento plays with audiences' expectations, suggesting a male aggressor voyeuristically choosing his victim, to, at the end, pull the rug through a reverse of gender roles. Arguably, Dalmas's confusion springs from his own gender prejudices: he has seen a woman attacking a man. However, his mind rearranged the story to better fit gender expectations, meaning, a man attacking a hapless woman. González, however, gives the next step and completely queers the gaze. *Un couteau dans le Coeur* invites (heterosexual and homosexual alike) viewers to see gay porn through the eyes of a woman. The anonymous woman reveals herself as the master of the narrative, as, after a moment, she starts to accelerate and later slow the speed of the film, making the men within the porn film to behave—quickly, slower—as she commands.

The action cuts to a night club where one of the performers of the porn film, Karl (Bastian Waultier), is dancing on the dance floor. The club is populated with semi-naked men cruising through the space. Some men are depicted having sex in the dark corners of the room but still, within sight of everyone, including spectators. The scene basically reproduces, now as "real," the simulated gay sex from the previous scene. Rich Cante and Angelo Restivo argue that "gay male pornography differs from straight pornography precisely insofar as its public/ private phantasmatics are somehow different," meaning, like the "open secret" of homosexuality itself, the sex at gay night clubs "is at once well known and, nonetheless, invisible to the untutored eye" (Cante and Restivo 2004, 155). The film's gay softcore imagery "opens the eyes" to the heterosexual gaze, obliged to follow, with careful slowness and detail, the narratives and aesthetics of the gay porn film.

Karl is, again, the center of the action and the gaze. He is depicted dancing at the middle of a group of men whom seem to be sexually interested solely in the young man. As in the film-within-the-film, the young man is observed from many angles; his dancing partners lust after him, and someone wearing a leather mask is intently watching Karl from the bar. The mask is a mix of desire and horror, Eros and Thanatos. It is, basically, an S&M black leather mask; it looks, however, rugged and worn, more the face of a satyr or a wild boar than completely human. It is his intent gaze what attracts the blonde boy, who leaves his companions on the dance floor to accompany the stranger to a private room. The *giallo* influence is striking in these first scenes, as the spaces are bathed in hues of deep red and blue, evoking the work of Argento or Mario Bava.

There is "a seemingly reactionary connection between sex and violent death" (Kendrik 2017, 323) in the *giallo* cycle, as victims, especially women, are killed in spectacular, brutal ways while wearing little, if any, clothes. Further, *giallo*'s obsession with models and fashions, cabarets and erotic performances link sleaziness with horror from a patriarchal point of view as men are those carefully watching and, in most cases, killing girls. *Un couteau dans le Coeur* takes this erotization of violence to new extremes but through a queer perspective in the first murder scene. Karl is tied up to a bed by the masked stranger. The young man wears just white briefs that the black-clad man rips and stuff into Karl's mouth. Before that, a close-up of the boy's mouth depicts him licking his own lips with his tongue, a commoditized image of female lust as circulated by (hetero)normative imagery crucial in the model of heterosexual porn and general advertising. The displacement of heterosexual performers by gay performers produces a deep perturbation in a doubly way. First, the sensual lips and tongue belongs to a young man rather than a woman; second, there is not really a significant difference, as the shot is filled with the sensuous mouth. The male mouth framed in close-up can pass for a female mouth "acting" to excite heterosexual men. Thus, sexual iconography does not fit as easily into gender binarism as one would think, becoming rather mobile and fluid—in other words, becoming queer, indeterminate. To add further gender confusion, Anne is seen (in the scene that follows) walking the streets, surrounded by walls covered by the publicity of a new toothpaste. The posters depict sensuous, red lips encasing white teeth. It can be safely assumed that the mouth is that of a woman, as women are traditionally objects to be-looked-at in advertising; however, after the last scene, the assumption is put under question, as the mouth could easily belong to a young man. Interestingly, Anne does not hire "manly" men (i.e., hypermasculine) but young men with "angel faces."

Stopping at a construction zone, she passes all the "macho," muscular men to get Nans (Khaled Alouach), a young man with a "baby face," the film thus finding eroticism on gender fluidity or androgyny.

Returning to the first murder scene, the masked man takes out from his pants not his penis but a black dildo. The scene is interrupted by brief inserts of the porn film-within-the-film seen in the first sequence: the man watching from the safety of the forest reappears, now, thanks to editing and inserting, voyeuristically watching this new scene, thus deepening the power of the queer gaze. Violence and horror mix with eroticism when a sharp, shining blade protrudes from the dildo. Rather than "stabbing" the young man with his penis or the dildo, the masked man penetrates his victim with a knife, killing him. If long knives, axes, and machetes were considered as "phallic" weapons in horror cinema in virtue of their longitude, capacity to penetrate the (female, mostly) human body and embody "the killer's phallic purpose" (Clover 2015, 47), here, both the weapon and the purpose are literally "phallic" as the killer stabs the victim presumably (it remains out of frame) in his butt with the dildo/knife. The nexus between sex and violence so present in the traditional Italian *giallo* is unpacked and brought to the spotlight but via a homosexual lens that disturbs the heteronormative gaze that finds pleasure in the butchering of women. Later in the film, Anne gets angry when one scene she is filming is deemed too boring, as the actors "cannot get hard." She demands passion and lust; she asks the actors to "bite" each other, a new reference to sex as violence, as pain.

Even if a neo-*giallo* due to references to *giallo* aesthetics (colorful staging) and narrative (sexually charged murders), *Un couteau dans le Coeur* shows other influences. Some of them are brief but help in the construction of a nexus that mix violence with sex through a queer perspective. A brief sequence at a lesbian night club shows a kitsch, erotically charged performance: a woman dressed with a mesh bodysuit that evokes a spider-web—complete, with a black spider at the belly—is "killed" on the stage by a fake-looking monster with long fingernails. The scene and the performance is a clear reference to Spanish director Jesús Franco, a man widely recognized in the circuits of lowbrow Euro-horror for his erotic horror films. In one of Franco first films, *Miss Muerte* (*The Diabolical Dr. Z*, 1966), a young female dancer (Estella Blain) with a see-through black lace garment that evokes a spider-web crawls across the stage to finally, at the end of the performance, "kill" a male dummy with her long, black fingernails. The gender reverse—in González's film, it is the woman who ends being killed—highlights violence against women rather than enthroning the figure of the sensuous *femme fatale*, the latter basically being a recipient of patriarchal fantasies and fears.

Figure 1. A mouth in advertising loses its heterosexual assumptions.

Other influences, however, are less explicit. For instance, Yann González taps from the cinema of Spanish director Pedro Almodóvar, widely known for his modern melodramas. Arguably, *Un couteau dans le Coeur* could be read as a modern melodrama with positive queer sensibilities, the kind of film Almodóvar does. Even if both intertexts—Almodóvar's melodramas and the *giallo*—seems to be at odds at first, in fact, they complement each other. Almodóvar was not indifferent to the *giallo* film. Almodóvar's film *Matador* (1986, arguably, a neo-*giallo*, complete with stylized and eroticized murders) opens with a character masturbating while watching Mario Bava's *Sei Donne per' L'Assasino* (1964). Further, Almodóvar stated in interviews that *giallo* film occupies a space among his many cinematic references and influences (together with the films made by Hammer Studios, Fritz Lang, or Alfred Hitchcock). What interested most to Almodóvar was the kitsch—one of the director's trademarks—elements found in many *gialli* (Zurian 2013, 267). Kitsch, like the aesthetics of camp, is recognizable as inextricably linked to "gay sensibility and humor" (Fisiak 2014, 46) and "excess." Kitsch and camp are crucial components of melodrama, a genre that informs *Un couteau dans le Coeur* as well. Melodrama as a genre is built on excess: excess of passion, of desire, of impossible loves, of aestheticism, of pain and suffering, of camp and kitsch. After the opening scene and the brutal killing, González's film cuts to Anne calling from a telephone booth to Lois, her ex-lover. Their dialogue is pure passion, as Anne's love is excessive and poisonous for Lois. Anne is in a fragile state, completely dependent on Lois's love. Anne tells Lois she has woke up "totally alone" and scared (as Lois bitterly states, it is 5 a.m.) and needs her ex-lover voice to calm down. As in classical melodrama, the characters succumb to passion: "The most beautiful melodramas, like those of Sirk and Ophuls, are the ones that show how the worlds in which those characters live—and the happy endings foisted on them—are wrong. And like all those shimmering objects crowding the screen, the answer always lies in what's missing" (Goldberg 2016, 35). What is missing is the other person, the lover, the one who allows the main character to work properly, to exist even. "Let me smell your skin one more time," Anne tells Lois, revealing that she has no will of her own; she needs, morbidly, her lover to justify her life. Unlike what happens in traditional *gialli*, the lesbian relationship is not depicted as deviance and titillation, but as love, toxic as it is. The previous scene seems lifted from an Almodóvar's film, an auteur recognized by his excess—of color, set design, and performances—rather than from a *giallo*. However, like Almodóvar's cinema, *giallo* is predicated in queer excess (one negatively—*giallo*; the other through positive notes—Almodóvar). Linda Williams points how Almodóvar's "queering" of the melodrama "offers novel objects of sympathy: sadomasochists, drag queens, male whores, pregnant nuns" (2009, 167), arguably, all characters that could easily fit within the narratives of *giallo* cinema. Queerness and melodrama are always lurking at the borders of the excesses of the *giallo* film. The queer lens offered by González's film allowed this "discovering" of queer melodrama through the emphasis of aspects that remain oblique in traditional Italian *giallo*. It is through the intersection with melodrama that this "positive queerness" can flux. In this sense, female nails painted deep red fit perfectly well within the aesthetics of both the *giallo* and Almodóvar's film, in each meaning the same: excess of passion, violence, and gender fluidity. After the talk between Anne and Lois goes awry, the film cuts abruptly to the filming of a porn scene: three young men are dancing and kissing each other, each one of them wearing different-colored briefs: red, yellow, and green, the popping colors and the nudity referring to both *giallo* films and Almodóvar. Of course, *giallo* film presents only female nudity, while González's film offers a new disruption of the imagery of the "proper" (heterosexual and male) gaze.

Adapting *The Bird with the Crystal Plumage*

As seen, *Un couteau dans le Coeur* heavily borrows from both *giallo* and melodrama, emphasizing thus the queerness—thanks to the intersecting with

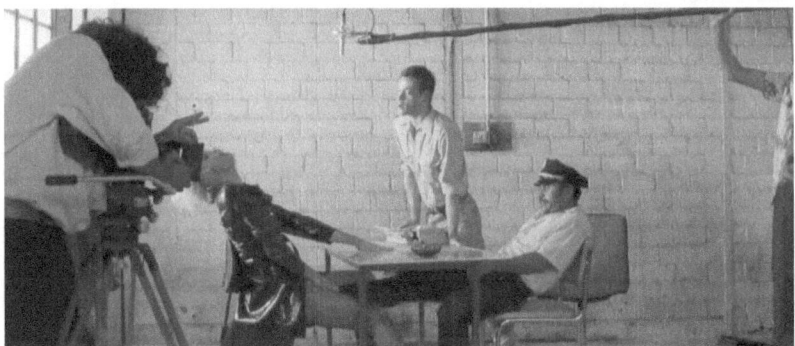

Figure 2. The violence of interrogation is reconfigured in an act of erotic arousal.

Almodóvar's melodrama—that lies, hidden, behind the Italian cycle. Adapting in particular *The Bird with the Crystal Plumage*, González plays with a film that works on gender confusion to unpack all its queer melodramatic possibilities. The first major change is, clearly, the romantic couple. Here, two women are the ill-fated lovers who must struggle not only with their toxic relationship, but also with a serial killer. Further, as in Argento's film, the inspectors in charge of the investigation are well intentioned, but slow in their deductions, obliging the heroine to play amateur detective to find out who is killing her cast of porn performers.

The scene in which Anne is interrogated by the police—male detectives acting slightly dismissive towards a woman who makes "blue films"—is playfully followed by its queer reverse. A transvestite is interrogated by a "macho" inspector and a beautiful, hunky blond male officer. The scene, which ends with everyone masturbating, is a porn scene filmed by Anne, who found inspiration on her own interrogation. After being mistreated by the cops, Anne empowers herself and reconstructs the scene through a queer gaze. The fact that, at first, viewers are in the dark about this new "interrogation" (it seems authentic) blurs the divisions between reality and fiction and, more provocatively, between "normal" (heterosexual) behavior and queer conduct. The new "suspect," a transvestite in Anne's porn film, wears a black vinyl coat, thus referring to the killer in Argento's film (and countless other *giallo* films). The sex confusion (man/woman) refers explicitly to *The Bird with the Crystal Plumage*, where the male killer turns out to be a female killer. Rather than a psychopath, it is Anne's assistant who occupies the role of the "suspicious transvestite" in the fictional world of the porn film. In real life, the man is seen sometimes in drag and is one of Anne's best friends, a person who really cares for her and her crew. Thus, this "suspicious transvestite" is one of the most loyal, sympathetic characters within the film, disrupting the nexus of prejudices, so appreciated in *gialli*, that link sexual "deviance" with criminality and evilness.

While the killer continues murdering past and present performers of Anne's staff—always using his knife-dildo as his weapon in increasingly violent sexual encounters (a man practicing oral sex, for instance, is killed when the sharp edge of the knife drills through his skull)—porn actors stop working with Anne. As in Argento's film, the main heroine is obliged to act due to her personal attachment with the case. Dalmas knows the resolution of the case lies solely in his mind, while Anne faces bankruptcy as nobody wants to work with her any longer (since her performers are killed one by one) and her studio is at the brink of shutting down.

Transvestite killers and a *mise-en-scène* bathed in saturated colors are tropes of the *giallo* film in general. Still, the explicit references to Argento's *The Bird with the Crystal Plumage* begin with the only clue left in the murder scenes: a bird feather is found close to each corpse. The feather belongs to a rare species that is difficult to identify. This explicitly connects with the main clue (and the trigger of the film's resolution) in Argento's film. Indeed, it is the cry of a rare bird—the bird with the crystal-like plumage of the title—that points to where the killer is hiding. It is this only clue that pushes Anne to become amateur detective, as the case of killed gay porn actors "is not a priority" for the cops, as stated by one of the inspectors. As in Argento's film, the cops are useless, obliging those in danger (Dalmas, Anne) to act to end the nightmare.

After consulting experts in birds—including a young beautiful man with a bird claw-like hand—Anne learns that the feathers belong to a Chaladre Grackle or "white-eyed grackle," a rare, almost extinct species. It was said that the bird had healing powers, and the last recorded sight was in the forest that gave the animal its name: Chaladre. As in *The Bird with the Crystal Plumage*, where Dalmas goes to the countryside to find clues about the killer's identity, Anne travels to the French countryside (Chaladre) in search of any lead on the bird or the killer. At a cemetery in Chaladre, Anne finds a tomb marked with the name of Guy Favre and learns about a young man who died in a fire in a barn. His body was never found, only that of a friend who was with him at the moment, the coffin buried at the cemetery containing only clothes.

Back in Paris, Lois is murdered by the masked killer and Anne is able, deep in her depression, to fit together the pieces of the puzzle. Watching one of her old movies in a porn theater, she realizes that the plot closely follows that of Guy's murder at the burning barn. While in the film-within-the-film the ending is a happy one—a father discovers his young son having sex with another man and decides to join the action through an incestuous *ménage* à trois—the real event ended with the father castrating his son and stabbing both teens. He later burns the barn to ashes with his son and his lover inside. Guy survived, his face completely disfigured by the fire. After a long period where he forgot everything about his past, Guy goes to see a gay porn film at Paris, the one made by Anne with a story that resembles the teen's cruel past. This encounter with his history reawakens trauma, unleashing a deep psychosis and pushing Guy to start a killing spree on all the actors depicted in the porn film.

As happens with *The Bird with the Crystal Plumage*, the resolution of the film lies in a piece of art that triggers the return of sexual trauma. In Argento's film, a painting depicting a woman being sexually attacked wakes up memories in Monica Ranieri (Eva Renzi), who was equally attacked in her past. The trauma triggers a cycle of violence in which she needs to enact violence on others as a way to exorcise her inner demons. This conclusion follows Brown's novel, where the climax is given by a different work of art: a sculpture representing "the screaming Mimi," a woman being sexually attacked that wakes up traumatic memories in the novel's main female character, turning her into a killer. In *Un couteau dans le Coeur*, the work of art that contains the answer of the enigma is a porn film that adapts and reconstructs the story, now with a happy ending. Rather than portraying the rape of a woman as a piece of art to see by (male) eyes in art galleries (where it is displayed), Anne's film tells of a tender love story where gay love and happiness prevails. If the hetero-centric Brown novel and Argento film emphasize violence towards women as something turned into art, something to be seen as spectacle, González and Anne's film, in turn, transforms horrifying, homophobic past into something beautiful, full of passion, love, and joy. History has been reconstructed as herstory.

It may be argued that *Un couteau dans le Coeur*, certainly, mixes sex with horror and homophobic violence. Indeed, the film ends in the porn theater, where Guy is killed by the attendants when they realize he is responsible for the string of killings within the gay community. Still, the final titles roll over images of Anne's new porn gay film: an orgy of satyrs and humans where everyone is happy and enjoying freely their sexuality. Anne is depicted happy, still dreaming of Lois but now in pleasant dreams.

Conclusions

Unlike with traditional *giallo* films and following Pedro Almodóvar's queer cinema, gay love and passion is not seen as something sick and ill-fated, but as another, counter-hegemonic way to love. At the heart of the film lies a warning against homophobia, as hate against sexual freedom is the source of all the proceeding horrors.

Yann González takes the *giallo* cycle and constructs a film revolving around sex and trauma. Furthermore, beyond the general tropes of the cycle, the director rewrites Dario Argento's *The Bird with the Crystal Plumage* (in turn, based on a novel) with a main difference: the piece of art is queer in a double way—first, because the film is a porn movie, a product of lowbrow culture rather than "high" art such as sculpture (Brown's novel) or painting (Argento's film). Second, because the piece of art does not depict violent heterosexual assault, but a sweet gay love story filmed to the enjoyment of a group of "secretive" viewers. Anne's art tries to sexually arouse, not to disgust or excite with violence.

Through a queer adaptation that emphasizes all the occluded homoerotic aspects of traditional *giallo*, and with a combination with one of the "queerest" directors working today, Pedro Almodóvar, Yann González rewrote *The Bird with the Crystal Plumage* as a melodrama of horror and homosexual, unquenched desire. While Guy is dying in the porn theater (where everyone group together to protect the gay community), his memories, as depicted in the film (and closing the story until the final credits), is that of love and tenderness. Guy remembers his days with his male lover, kissing and caressing each other in the barn, happiness on their young faces as they embrace each other in deep love.

Works Cited

Benshoff, Harry. 1997. *Monsters in the Closet: Homosexuality and the Horror Film*. Manchester: Manchester University Press.

Cante, Rich, and Angelo Restivo. 2004. "The Cultural-Aesthetic Specificities of All-Male Moving-Image Pornography." In *Porn Studies*, edited by Linda Williams, 142–66. Durham, NC: Duke University Press.

Clover, Carol. 2015. *Men, Women and Chainsaw: Gender in the Modern Horror*. Princeton: Princeton University Press.

Cooper, Andrew. 2012. *Dario Argento*. Urbana and Chicago: University of Illinois Press.

Edelman, Lee. 1994. *Homographesis: Essays in GayLiterary and Cultural Theory*. New York: Routledge.

Fisiak, Tomasz. 2014. "Hag horror Heroines: Kitsch/Camp Goddesses, Tyrannical Females, Queer Icons." In *Redefining Kitsch and Camp in Literature and Culture*, edited by Justyna Stepien, 41–52. Newcastle: Cambridge Scholars Publishing.

Goldberg, Jonathan. 2016. *Melodrama: An Aesthetics of Impossibility*. Durham, NC: Duke University Press.

Grüner, Eduardo. 2006. *El Sitio de la Mirada: Secretos de la Imagen y Silencios del Arte.* Buenos Aires: Norma.

Hawkins, Joan. 2000. *Cutting Edge: Art-Horror and the Horrific Avant-Garde.* Minneapolis: University of Minnesota Press.

Hunt, Leon. 2000. "A (Sadistic) Night at the Opera." In *The Horror Reader*, edited by Ken Gelder, 324–35. New York: Routledge.

Jagose, Annamarie. 1996. *Queer Theory: An Introduction.* New York: New York University Press.

Kendrik, James. 2017. "Slasher Films and Gore in the 1980s." In *A Companion to the Horror Film*, edited by Harry M. Benshoff, 310–28. Malden, MA: Blackwell.

Koven, Mikel. 2006. *La Dolce Morte: Vernacular Cinema and the Italian Giallo Film.* Lanham, MD: Scarecrow Press.

Mulvey, Laura. 1989. *Visual and Other Pleasures.* New York: Palgrave.

Olney, Ian. 2013. *Euro Horror: Classic European Horror Cinema in Contemporary American Culture.* Bloomington: Indiana University Press.

Shipka, Danny. 2011. *Perverse Titillation: The Exploitation Cinema of Italy, Spain and France, 1960–1980.* Jefferson, NC: McFarland and Company.

Williams, Linda. 2009. "Melancholy Melodrama: Almodóvarian Grief and Lost Homosexual Attachments." In *All about Almodóvar: A Passion for Cinema*, edited by Bradley Epps and Despina Kakoudaki, 166–92. Minneapolis: University of Minnesota Press.

Zurian, Francisco. 2013. "La piel que habito: A Story of Imposed Gender and the Struggle for Identity." In *A Companion to Pedro Almodóvar*, edited by Marvin D'Lugo and Kathleen M. Vernon, 262–78. Malden, MA: Blackwell.

Chapter 13

WARPED NESTS

Domestic Architecture, Transgressive Female Bodies, and the Dissolution of the Patriarchal Domain in 1970s American *Gialli*

BRENDA S. GARDENOUR WALTER

Cult cinema of the 1970s, including grindhouse, horror, and *gialli*, capitalized on conservative fears of modernity, among them women's liberation, the sexual revolution, and the dissolution of the patriarchal family home. Characterized by graphic violence, fragmentation, doubling, and the failure of patriarchal authority, three American *gialli*—*Alice, Sweet Alice* (Alfred Sole, 1976), *Private Parts* (Paul Bartel, 1972), and *The Eyes of Laura Mars* (Irvin Kershner, 1978)—center on single women in alternative families who live in non-traditional and communal housing in city neighborhoods (Koven 2006). Unlike the mid-century construction of the suburban cis-het nuclear family home as a site of patriarchal ordering and containment, the urban domestic scenes in each of these films is a site of matriarchal disorder and slippage. This female-coded domestic architecture is not only leaky, but also duplicitous in its structure, with seemingly placid façades masking fragmented and misshapen interiors—warped nests that reflect the disordered bodies hidden within (Shildrik 1997). In *Alice, Sweet Alice*, a pubescent girl lives with her divorced mother in an urban apartment building owned by an agoraphobic pedophile. Subject to an irrational matriarch and a set of failed patriarchs, Alice lives in a transgressive space containing secret rooms and apertures that allow her to slip silently within and beyond the building's walls. In *Private Parts*, a teenaged girl named Cheryl runs away from her family home in suburban Ohio and takes up residence at the King

Edward Hotel in Los Angeles. Dominated by a duplicitous matriarch, this communal domestic structure maintains a conservative exterior in order to hide a slippery interior wormed through with peepholes, concealed rooms, and illicit passageways. In *The Eyes of Laura Mars*, a middle-aged divorced woman, the successful photographer Laura, lives alone in a New York City penthouse dominated by mirrors and windows. A microcosm of her apartment, Laura is a vessel of reflections, her mind channeling the visions of a serial killer. Drawn into the mind of an unstable patriarch, she penetrates the homes and bodies of his victims and projects them through the aperture of her camera, revealing a world of domestic horrors cloaked beneath duplicitous concrete exteriors.

Though a set of nested lenses, including that of the camera, the human eye, and apertures in buildings, viewers both on- and off-screen in each film penetrate architectural and human anatomies, slicing into the private spaces of women at three stages of life: menarche, adolescence, and adulthood. This fragmented visual penetration of matriarchal domestic structures becomes a sort of architectural body horror that carries complex messages about female embodiment, the vulnerability of independent women in urban spaces, and the role of women in the mid-century family. Like the genre of the *giallo* itself, these films are duplicitous, at first appearing to reveal the horrors of patriarchal structures and their destructive effect on women, but ultimately reinforcing the misogynist belief that vulnerable young girls and women at every stage of life must be contained within a well-ordered family home, preferably in a suburban bubble, and governed by a strong patriarch for her own safety, the safety of her children, and that of the greater community (Lazzaro-Weis 1993, 159).

Domestic Architecture:
The Patriarchal Myth at Mid-Century

The deconstruction of architectural space in mid-century American *gialli* is rooted in the reciprocal relationship between the human body and the built environment. Architectural theorists have long argued that buildings are deeply intertwined with cultural constructions of embodiment. The first-century CE author Vitruvius argued that the foundation of all architecture should be the male human body, the balance and proportions of which were deemed perfect in the agnatic world of Ancient Rome (Granger, 1934). Feminist architectural theorists such as Diana Agrest (1988, 28–41) and Leslie Kanes Weisman (1992) argue that this patriarchal body, with its symmetrical exterior and well-ordered interior devoid of superfluous parts or chaotic spaces, continues to dominate architectural design, in particular that of domestic architecture. The structure and function of the detached American home, for example, parallels the Cartesian construction of male anatomy and physiology as rational and mechanistic (Des Chene 2001, 28–29). Exterior surfaces serve as a protective dermis, while the façade serves as a face with window eyes and a front door mouth. Within its timber-framed skeleton, a house breathes through ventilation systems, regulates heating and cooling through thermostatic hypothalamuses, sends electrical impulses through nerve-like wiring, and excretes waste through intestinal sewer pipes hidden in bowel-like basements (Hepworth 2006, 149). Because domestic architecture is a projection of the culturally constructed body, to enter into and dwell within a house is an intimate act, a haptic and sensual experience. Juhani Pallasmaa argues that our experience of space is one of touch, the movement of hands on walls and feet on floors tracing patterns, skin on skin (2012). According to Sarah Robinson, body and building are engaged in a reciprocal process of imprinting (2011). In a healthy house, our bodies settle into space, creating a customized nest where we are nurtured and can dream in safety and bliss (Bachelard 1994). Not all spaces are nurturing, however. Embodied experiences within a hostile home can range from feelings of uncanny displacement and revulsion to physical abuse and dysmorphia. This is of particular concern for those who resist the patriarchal structures upon which domestic architecture remains largely based.

American domestic architecture reflects not only male anatomy and physiology but also the cultural myth of the cis-het patriarchal family. Leslie Weisman writes that "in patriarchal societies where men are by definition the dominant group, social, physical, and metaphysical space are the products of male experience, male consciousness, and male control" (1992, 10). As a vessel for the nuclear middle-class family, the suburban home is a structure designed as a space of rational ordering and production governed by the father as head of household. It is at once a space of exclusion and containment, its thick walls meant to protect inhabitants from chaotic external forces, thereby serving as a container for "safety, privacy, and family" (Weisman 1992, 87). The interior of the home is divided into communal spaces, such as kitchens and family rooms, and private spaces, such as bedrooms and bathrooms (Rosner 2008, 2). In keeping with Victorian architectural norms, communal areas tend to be located towards the front of the house and private areas removed toward the back or hidden upstairs, away from prying eyes (Sensual City Studio 2018, 41). In private areas of the home, family members are segregated into hermetically sealed compartments where bodily activities long considered shameful—intercourse, masturbation, defecation, urination, emesis—are cloaked behind doors (Rosner 2008, 1). The parental bedroom is associated with appropriate sexual contact and potential reproduction, while children's bedrooms are the site of illicit sexual activity. Because of this obsessive control over bodily functions, sexual desire, and reproduction, Henri Lefebvre has argued that the family home is grounded in "genitality," a place where "fertility and fulfillment are identical" (Lefebvre, Brown 2000, 59) The family home is not only a space of cis-het sexual ordering, but also a patriarchal domus where the "king of his castle," governs his house-body and its perimeter while regulating the bodies of those dwelling within it (Weisman 1992, 87). Family members who do not submit to patriarchal authority are punished, sequestered, or "shunted outdoors" beyond the picket fence to restore order within the home (Rosner 2008, 2). Whether peaceful or turbulent, the private lives that unfold within the patriarchal domus are hidden behind the façade of the family house, which functions as a mask of propriety presented to those viewing it from the curb.

Embedded in the design of domestic architecture, the construct of the patriarchal family home was projected as a cultural "norm" through midcentury mainstream media (Johnston 2019, 39–40). Advertisements for suburban ranch homes, domestic appliances, and grocery stores propagated the myth of white suburban bliss, while television programs such as *Father Knows Best* (1954–60) fed a growing nostalgia for a perfect family, one defined by and for hegemonic white men, that never truly existed (Wright 1983). By the late 1960s, countercultural forces actively contested the validity of the patriarchal domus as a space of safety, arguing that "man-made space encodes and perpetuates white male power and superiority and the inferiority and subordination of women and minorities." (Weisman 1992, 10). Patriarchal authorities had long defined the female body as slippery, transgressive, and irrational, a construction that rendered women dangerous and necessitated their constraint in the home, most notably in the bedroom and the kitchen (Bergren 1996, 77–96). Second-wave feminist activists and scholars contested this construction of the female body and its role in the home. In 1972, for example, artists Judy Chicago and Miriam Shapiro gathered together members of the Feminist Art Program at CalArt to create Womanhouse, an installation that, following Betty Friedan, contested "the myth of the white, middle-class housewife as a satisfied, fulfilled, domestic goddess" (Balducci 2006, 17; Friedan 1963). The advent of effective oral contraception further distanced women from their prescribed roles as mothers, thereby rupturing the cultural construction of the home as a reproductive unit in which she was merely a biological servant. As the myth of the self-contained patriarchal domus rapidly dissolved, conservative forces clung to the traditional family home as a source of privilege, power, and identity.

Three 1970s American *gialli*, *Alice, Sweet Alice*, *Private Parts*, and *The Eyes of Laura Mars*, reflect conservative fears about liberated women, in particular those running urban households beyond patriarchal control. Unlike suburban homes, in which "the domestic sphere was closed off, hermetically sealed from the poisonous air of the outside world," apartment blocks were seen as "porous" and "impermanent" spaces marked by "ongoing contact with hallways, neighbors, the surrounding city, and whatever else just exceeds the visible walls" (Hepworth 2006, 152; Fitzpatrick 2018, 129). The setting of these apartment buildings in urban areas magnifies this loss of privacy while exploiting conservative associations of cities with "the breakdown of community," anonymity, poverty, instability, and violence (Koven 2006, 53). Far from the culturally constructed bliss and safety of predominantly white suburbs, redlined urban neighborhoods, stripped of financial resources by white flight, were subject to urban decay and increased crime (Holmes 2018, 2). Through this lens, cities themselves were macrocosmic collective domiciles, crumbling places where strangers, criminals, and non-conforming "others" mixed and mingled—a dangerous place for single woman to live alone, and even more perilous for her to raise a family.

Alice, Sweet Alice: Menarche and Menopause in Jersey

Alice, Sweet Alice (1976) is set in 1961 in a seemingly normal and blue-collar urban neighborhood in Patterson, New Jersey. The epicenter of dysfunction in the film is Alice, a pubescent girl who lives with her divorced mother, Catherine Spages, and her little sister in a one-bedroom walk-up apartment. All three females, and later just two, sleep in the single bedroom. The only other room revealed to the viewer is the combined kitchen and living area, dimly lit and windowless. Unobserved by her distracted mother, Alice often slips away from the claustrophobic apartment and into the building's basement, a space associated with the body's lower functions, including defecation, sexual desire, and the female grotesque (Russo 2012). Within this space, Alice has claimed a hidden room where she keeps a trunk containing her sister's baby doll, her communion veil, a butcher's knife, and a mask of a woman wearing whorish makeup. On the edge of menarche, Alice uses her trunk to navigate her desire for womanhood and blood, both menstrual and murderous. Like menstrual blood, Alice does not remain in her dark basement womb but flows out like a toxin into the community (Lemay 1992, 131; Moss and Cappannari, 1976,

1–15). Through an open bulkhead in the apartment's basement, Alice leaves the building and roams the streets, sometimes slipping through a broken fence and playing in an abandoned factory. In addition to her fluidity, Alice's duplicity enables her to move through architectural spaces with near-invisibility, her chaotic and determinedly adult desires unperceived. In the film's opening scenes, for example, Alice slinks around the church unseen, appearing only after her sister's murdered body is found folded into a pew. Similarly, Alice is off on her own when her aunt, who has just chastised Alice's mother for being too lenient with her daughter, is brutally murdered on the apartment building's stairs. Alice's slipperiness does not suggest the innocence of a sweet young girl off playing with dolls, but rather the culpability of a manipulative young woman determined to get away with murder.

The porous nature of domestic architecture in *Alice, Sweet Alice* is a manifestation of matriarchal failure to contain a chaotic child. It is likewise a reflection of patriarchal impotence. The film features three men who fail to control female chaos: the landlord, Mr. Alphonso, Alice's father, Dom Spages, and the priest, Father Tom. The transgressive apartment building in which Alice lives is a reflection of Alphonso's unique embodiment. An inversion of culturally constructed masculine ideals, Alphonso is obese, physically weak, and emotionally delicate, with his agoraphobia forcing him into confinement with his cats. Like a bird's nest, his apartment reflects the shape of his physical being—greasy, dark, and stained with urine. Bound within this fetid womb, he relies on women and children to run his errands while subsisting on their rent money. Weak and effeminate, Alphonso is neither able to control the boundaries of his body nor those of his own apartment. Alice routinely accosts him, sometimes assaulting him verbally in his doorway, sometimes penetrating his space to play pranks. Alphonso's domestic impotence is paralleled by that of Alice's father who abandoned his wife and daughters in order to start a new life with another woman. After Alice's sister is murdered, Dom's temporary return to his first wife's apartment should signal the reinstatement of domestic order, but because he is bifurcated—torn between two households—he is unable to navigate his ex-wife's emotions or to recognize his daughter's psychopathy. Even as detectives begin to implicate Alice in a recent string of murders, including that of her sister, Dom refuses to believe that a young girl could cause violence. Against the advice of institutional authorities, Dom fights for his daughter's release from confinement. Without a rational patriarchal presence, Alice continues to slip through buildings and bodies without reprimand. As a failed father, Dom cannot discipline his household, thereby endangering the greater community. Dom pays the ultimate price for his impotence when he is killed by a menopausal madwoman in an abandoned factory. Having destroyed him, she leaves his shattered body at the building's entrance—a broken fetus dropped from a crumbling womb.

The third failed patriarch in *Alice, Sweet Alice* is Father Tom, a Catholic priest who acts as a surrogate husband to Catherine and father to Alice. As patriarch, Tom is meant to bring order to the rectory where he lives and the church that he presides over, yet he fails in both contexts. As head of the rectory, Father Tom supervises Mrs. Tredoni, who performs many of the traditional functions of a housewife. On the surface, Tredoni appears to be a submissive and devoted caretaker; she is, however, Alice's adult double, a woman who moves invisibly through architectural spaces. Unlike Alice in her moist basement, a place often associated with "negative remembrances, pushed outside of consciousness," Mrs. Tredoni lives in the rectory's attic, a dusty room in which she stores the artifacts of her murders hidden in albums and boxes (Pallasmaa 2001, 27; Punter 2002). Emerging from her desiccated womb-room, Tredoni dons the same communion veil and harlot's mask worn by Alice as she stalks and kills those who do not uphold the gender roles and sexual morals prescribed by the Catholic Church. At first, Father Tom fails to see her as dangerous, believing instead that she is merely an overwrought woman whose servitude has earned her sainthood. Made aware of her murderous nature, Father Tom fails to contain her. The film ends, as it began, in the church during Holy Communion, the apogee of patriarchal ritual. When Father Tom denies Tredoni the Host, she screams, "But you give it to that whore!" as she points to Alice's mother. Removing a phallic knife from her paper bag and penetrating Father Tom in the neck, Tredoni forces him to kneel and collapse on his own altar, his body and church transformed into spaces of abject slippage by a woman beyond his control (Clover 1987, 187–228).

In *Alice, Sweet Alice*, the reading of domestic architecture, patriarchal family structures, and the role of women within both is fragmented and contradictory. As depicted in this late-1970s film, the social mores of the early 1960s, including the total subordination of women, appear backwards. Through a feminist lens, one could argue that the oppression of women and the suffocation of female sexual desire were catalysts for the murderous behavior of both Alice and Tredoni, strong-willed women who defied social control. The overall message of the film, however, plays on conservative and misogynistic fears of irrational mothers as heads of household and their purported inability to contain their pubescent daughters. Alice and Tredoni represent transformative stages in a woman's life cycle, menarche and menopause, periods that are culturally associated with emotional instability, the leakage of fluids, and chaotic bodily change. While the three patriarchs in this film fail to contain the bodies of these women in domestic space, order is restored by an outside patriarchal force—the police—that neither trivializes nor patronizes Alice or Tredoni. Unavailable to manipulation, the police arrest the menopausal Tredoni and confine her to prison. Alice, however, slips out of their grasp, suggesting that pubescent girls on the edge of sexual awakening—hiding behind masks of innocence—are as dangerous as "old witches." As manifestations of the monstrous feminine, these young women have the power to corrupt patriarchal bodies and buildings invisibly from within, thereby transforming rational, once-male structures into irrational, female messes (Creed 1993, 2002; Lindsey 1996).

Private Parts: Runaway Adolescence in Los Angeles

The transformative power of the monstrous feminine is at the dark heart of Paul Bartel's 1972 American *giallo*, *Private Parts*, a film that plays on conservative, cis-het fears of matriarchal disorder, the slippage of gender identities, and same sex desire. In setting the film in the King Edward, a subversive residential hotel in downtown Los Angeles, Bartel manipulates suburban fears of cities as dangerous places of violent bodily mixing. The owner and manager of the King Edward is Aunt Martha, a duplicitous matriarchal figure who takes in her niece, Cheryl, a teenager who has run away from a traditional family home in suburban Ohio. A widowed mother of one, Martha appears to be a paradigmatic housewife who tends to her residents as adopted children. Despite her grey bun, flowered frock, and apron, her husky body and dodgy account of childbirth call her gender into question. One day, while watching her aunt haul large garbage bins, Cheryl comments, "You handle that almost as good as a man!" Martha is a stern matriarch, carefully controlling access to the hotel and monitoring the activity of its residents. She attempts to order Cheryl's appearance and behavior, demanding that she remove her makeup and conform to female gender conventions, including obedience and modesty. Martha is particularly concerned with containing Cheryl's burgeoning sexuality, chastising her as a slut and warning her that desire can lead to danger. Martha's old-fashioned appearance and values as well as her desperate displays of control are nevertheless a false façade, a mask designed to protect her transgressive embodiment and desire, both of which are projected onto the hotel's architecture.

The hotel's exterior is unremarkable, its brick façade typical of early-twentieth-century urban buildings. Stepping across the threshold, the hotel's lobby is immaculate, its front desk dominated by Martha and flanked by a grand staircase. Upon first inspection, the dimly lit hallways seem neatly maintained and all of the doors are locked. Despite this projection of an orderly building, with neatly separated rooms containing the private lives of strangers, the hotel is in fact a slippery structure connecting all residents into a single organic space. As she unpacks her bags, Cheryl hears footsteps and scratching coming from the locked room adjoining hers. One night, she discovers a pornographic screenplay called "Desire in the Shadows" that has been hidden in her nightstand. A note inside reads, "Are you enjoying it so far, Cheryl?" Later in the film, she returns to her locked room to find black lingerie and a satin mask on her bed with a note reading, "You would drive me crazy if you would let me see you with these things on." Realizing that her room is not secure, Cheryl determines to discover the true nature of the building. Stealing the master keys from her aunt, Cheryl opens the locked room next to hers to discover a decrepit liminal space, its window papered over, with two peepholes in opposing walls. One peephole looks into Cheryl's room, another into a grimy bathroom shared by several residents. Glory holes for the phallic eye, these peepholes are surrounded by claw marks, creating a sort of vulva in each wall (Petit 2010, 168–75). Using her master key, Cheryl continues her sexually charged exploration of the building, discovering a statue of Jesus covered in BDSM gear in a gay priest's room and puddles of lubricant leaking from the room of an old woman. In another room, a drunk man covered in urine stains and grease is passed out on a carpet of empty beer bottles. Each room is a projection of its inhabitant's body, with only tissue-thin walls and the thrust of a key temporarily separating one from the other.

While the entire hotel is an interconnected and fluid body, two spaces provide the key to its fundamentally queer secret. The first is the building's basement, which contains a photographer's darkroom and a furnace, both of which are used for disposing bodies of murdered trespassers. The second is the room occupied by Martha's son, George, a voyeuristic photographer who sells pictures to a pornographic magazine called *The Prying Eye*. George's room is filled with cameras and tape recorders, equipment for capturing and possessing other people's private moments. His walls are papered over with photographs of women's fragmented bodies, including breasts, buttocks, and open mouths. On the bed is a sex doll made of transparent vinyl papered over with Cheryl's face. George's masturbatory routine includes injecting the doll with blood to give it life—a practice approved of by Martha because "they can't hurt you, George, and you can't hurt them." When Cheryl breaks into his room, George attempts to inject her with a blood-like substance laced with a sedative. In his attempt to penetrate her with his phallic needle, a light falls and knocks him out. The noise awakens Martha, who opens his shirt to check for a heartbeat—an invasion of bodily privacy that reveals George as a biological woman. When police arrive on the scene, they discover Aunt Martha covered in blood and wearing black lingerie, revealing an absence of breasts and a manly paunch.

As a manifestation of Martha's queer embodiment, the domestic architecture of the King Edward Hotel speaks to the oppressiveness of gender binaries and the imperative to maintain a cis-het façade in order to protect one's own private parts. The hotel's exterior suggests that it is a well-ordered domestic space that conforms to suburban ideals of privacy, propriety, and gender normativity. Beneath this façade, behind each of its closed doors, and below each occupant's clothing and skin, however, lie unexpected holes, hidden rooms, and twisted pathways to transgressive desire, all of which are dominated by a womanly man and her masculinized daughter. In stating that "the body is a prison that bends us to its will. It makes us ugly or pretty, men or women, whether we like it or not," Martha is participating in a protective performance of gender, one that belies the fact that "desire is not biological destiny, and neither is our social role" (Betsky 1995, 201). In a society dominated by cis-het norms, "women can dress like men, and men can be sensitive, as long as both still engage in games of power and accept environments in which they have to create a world for themselves according to rules they don't set" (Bestky 1995, 174). Both Martha and the hotel must conform to external gender expectations for bodies and houses in order to protect the gender-non-conforming worlds of queer desire that have been carved out within. Unlike the apartment block in *Alice, Sweet Alice*, a porous body that contaminates the community, the slippage within the hotel is tightly contained within its walls. Only those who trespass in search of discovering the building's secrets are at risk of violent death and dissolution in the basement—with the exception of Cheryl who, as a member of the family, replaces her aunt as matriarch. In this role, Cheryl will have to maintain a façade of rationality and gender-normativity in order to protect the hotel's secrets, and those of its indwelling family, from prying eyes.

Open to complex interpretations, *Private Parts* not only highlights the games of power that non-gender conforming people must play in cis-het spaces, but also plays upon conservative fears about gender duplicity and sexual exploration in the dark corners of liberal cities. Cheryl runs away from conservative Ohio to Los Angeles, an ultra-liberal city associated with sexual experimentation, gender fluidity, and alternative families—all of which were seen as a threat to the suburban, cis-het, and patriarchal family ideal.

As worlds of close bodily contact, conservatives imagined cities as places of chaotic mixing and transformation, deemed especially dangerous for "irrational" adolescent girls unable to recognize or protect themselves from sexual "others." Cheryl's inability to sustain herself in Los Angeles drove her to a hotel, a structure associated with transience, contamination, and furtive sexual contact, "not a place of rooted life" (Betsky 1995, 175). Unable to control her desire and unaware of any danger, Cheryl's sexual exploration of the hotel's queer architectural body resulted in her transformation into a duplicitous matriarch, a misshapen woman who can never return to innocence or to her home in Ohio, and who will never marry and bear children as expected by society, but must instead remain forever trapped in an urban liminal space with a strange and impermanent family not of her own making.

The Eyes of Laura Mars: Divorced and Middle-Aged in New York

Written by John Carpenter and directed by Irvin Kershner, the 1978 film *The Eyes of Laura Mars* follows a divorced female photographer as her life shatters and dissolves in the chaotic milieu of New York City. The film's domestic architecture, like its protagonist, is marked by doubling, fragmentation, and fluidity. As a famous photographer and published author, Laura Mars lives in a penthouse apartment in a Manhattan high-rise apartment. While these accommodations are often associated with luxurious decadence, Laura's apartment is minimalist and monochromatic (Vidler 1992). Her drab grey interior creates a cold atmosphere, suggesting that the cement of the outside city has somehow crept into her home. This grey space is dominated by large windows that frame the cityscape, giving the effect of a store-window display. This sense of being out in the street while still in the living room is enhanced by the raised grey dais in front of the window, a carpeted platform evoking a sidewalk and curb. The projection of the city into this interior space is mitigated by blinds; when closed, Laura's apartment becomes a nest, seemingly sealed off from urban chaos. Within this nest are two intimate spaces. The first is her library, which is crowded with books and photographs; the second is her bedroom, which is dominated by a central bed flanked by symmetrical mirrors. These mirrors transform Laura's bedroom into an architectural camera obscura, with the large windows on the opposite wall (or the eye of the viewer) serving as an aperture. By panning the room, these mirrors become single frames on a strip of film, fragmented images of fractured time. The result is a multiplicity of Lauras, even as she sits alone

Figure 1. A multiplicity of Lauras evokes a film strip.

on her bed, illuminated by a track-lit heart on the wall. Despite her closed blinds, Laura's high-rise nest is continually connected to the city around it, its most intimate spaces subject to intrusion by ill-intentioned men (her ex-husband, Neville), urban crime and violence projected through the television, the homicidal visions of a serial killer, and the eye of the viewer. This doubled, fragmented, and porous domestic space is a reflection of Laura's mental and physical instability.

Laura, like her apartment and the urban world that she inhabits, is a loosely bound collection of contradictions. Having mastered the male gaze, Laura has found fame as a photographer who uses violence and misogyny to sell products (Mulvey 1975, 6–18; Mulvey 1989). Her photographs, many of which reproduce murder scenes, objectify women, depicting them as blood-hungry perpetrators or sexualized victims. Laura presents herself as aloof and unemotional, cool as concrete—behavioral qualities culturally associated with male rationality. As a woman working in a job traditionally held by men, Laura retains these masculine qualities as a part of her façade, even when dressed in ultra-feminine clothing. At home in her apartment, or in the company of her few close friends, however, Laura reveals herself to be emotionally and mentally delicate, qualities culturally associated with female irrationality. Laura's vulnerability is magnified as she begins to receive violent visions of murders as they are committed, as seen through the eyes of the killer. In these moments, both she and the viewer experience tunnel vision, as if witnessing events through a contracted pupil, following the killer as he penetrates the intimate spaces of buildings and bodies. The increasing frequency of these uncontrollable visions disrupts Laura's narrative of hyper-rationality, leaving her colleagues to wonder if she is having "female troubles" or experiencing a mental breakdown (Butler 2006). Laura's loss of mental stability marks her as a "pathological heroine" whose eyewitness testimony—the *testamonio oculare* that is a hallmark of *giallo*—cannot be trusted (Needham 2007, 298).

At once penetrating in her gaze and penetrated by the gaze of the killer, Laura's doubled and contradictory nature mirrors that of her apartment, which is at once self-contained and open to unpredictable penetration by external forces. Growing increasingly unsure of her own visions, Laura comes to rely on a police detective, John Neville, as a source of stability. Stoic in the face of intense violence, Neville presents as a hyper-rational male authority figure, a man charged with bringing legal order to urban criminal chaos. Believing this to be his true nature, Laura trusts him, falls in love with him, and submits to his protective authority. Neville, however, is duplicitous, his rational façade concealing his inner identity as a madman and serial killer, all of which is revealed in the film's final scene. Alone in her apartment and believing that she is safe, Laura is suddenly penetrated by a vision in which she is stalked by the killer, indicating that she will be his next victim. As she deadbolts her door against the killer, Neville breaks through her apartment window, pretending to protect her. As he consoles her, he reveals that his mother was a "hysterical woman, a hooker," who left him alone in a dark room sitting in filth while she worked the streets of Washington, DC. One day, his father returned and slit her throat. As a result of his witnessing this violence, Neville developed a "split personality." Realizing that she has fallen for a false patriarch, that her apartment-body has been penetrated by the killer, Laura attempts to lock herself in her bedroom but is unable to keep Neville out. Once again unable to control her own boundaries, Laura lunges forward and hugs Neville violently, telling him over and over again that she loves him. This irrational outpouring of emotion, "a woman's only weapon," blindsides the killer, who stabs his own reflection in multiple mirrors, an image repeated around the room. Ultimately, Laura takes his gun and shoots him, his death echoed across shattered shards of glass, penetrating him in her inner sanctum. Rather than a safe nest, Laura's home is revealed to be a space of exposure, alienation, and "foreboding . . . a generator and container of fear" (Pallasmaa, 2001, 25). Her bedroom is now a crime scene, the mean city at last fully insinuated into her most intimate domestic space.

The Eyes of Laura Mars speaks to conservative fears about the vulnerability of single women living alone in big cities, especially New York. By the mid-1970s, New York was suffering from a "severe financial and municipal crisis," and this was projected into homes through the national news and into the imagination through television shows and films (Wojcik 2010, 31).

For many suburbanites, New York had become synonymous with poverty, housing projects, seedy bars, sex work, and rampant crime—a place to be visited only through the sanitized tourism offered by visual media (Webb 2014, 85–86). While this mental cityscape persisted throughout the decade, by 1975, the financial and social structures within New York were changing rapidly. Drawn in by the promises of career advancement, large salaries, and bourgeois metropolitan lifestyles, professionals began to leave the suburbs and relocate to Manhattan. In order to accommodate this influx, brownstones, lofts, and high-rise apartments were renovated or constructed to cater to the needs of a wealthier and more discerning clientele. While breezing through gentrified spaces, many professionals imagined themselves to be living urban lives of "grit and authenticity" (Webb 2014, 86). In the suburban imagination, these professionals, especially single women, were living in danger. While Laura is initially depicted as a successful, intelligent, street savvy woman who can take care of herself—the cultural paradigm of the mid-seventies liberated professional woman—she is ultimately unable to control her own bodily or domestic boundaries. Despite living in a secure high-rise apartment with a masculine interior accentuated by a statue of a rooster in her living room, the city creeps into her apartment. Urban violence pours in through her television screen, and the visions of a killer penetrate her mind. Meanwhile, Laura invites the killer-in-disguise into both her body and her domestic space. Both Laura and Neville are scarred by broken relationships, and Neville is the product of a broken urban family. Searching for love, they find each other in the ever-shifting urban world of late 1970s New York, where a traditional happy ending is denied them.

Conclusions

"Cinema illuminates the cultural archaeology of both the time of its making and the era it depicts" (Pallasmaa 2001, 14). Released in the 1970s, *Alice, Sweet Alice*, *Private Parts*, and *The Eyes of Laura Mars* reveal cultural fears about the autonomy of women within and beyond the home, the purported breakdown of patriarchal authority, the horrors of the American family, same-sex desire, gender fluidity, and the slippery boundaries of the human body—all of which are reflected in the collective architectural spaces depicted in each film (Williams 2013). They likewise speak to suburban fears of urban spaces as places of unpredictable intimate contact, sometimes non-consensual, involving fluid exchange between strangers through sex and/or violence. Through this lens, the city becomes a body, with blood-traffic flowing through arteries, massive sewage systems excreting the waste of millions, and countless collections of memories and desires, all in continual and chaotic motion (Grosz 1992, 241–54). This macrocosmic urban body contains myriad homes, from high-rises and hotel rooms to cardboard boxes in the alleyways, integrating them into a single collective domicile, and the bodies within them into a single slippery organism—interdependent, alive, and vulnerably human.

Works Cited

Agrest, Diana I. 1988. "Architecture from Without: Body, Logic, and Sex." *Assemblage*, no. 7: 28–41.
Bachelard, Gaston. 1994. *The Poetics of Space*. Boston: Beacon Press.
Balducci, Temma. 2006. "Revisiting Womanhouse: Welcome to the (Deconstructed) Dolhouse," *Woman's Art Journal*: 17–23.
Bergren, Ann. 1996. "Female Fetish, Urban Form." In *The Sex of Architecture*, edited by Diana Agrest, Patricia Conway, and Leslie Kanes Weisman, 77–96. New York: Harry N. Abrams.
Betsky, Aaron. 1995. *Building Sex: Men, Women, Architecture, and the Construction of Sexuality*. New York: William and Morrow.
Brown, Michael P. 2000. *Closet Space: Geographies of Metaphor from Body to the Globe*. New York: Routledge.
Butler, Judith. 2006. *Gender Trouble: Feminism and the Subversion of Identity*. New York: Routledge.
Clover, Carol. 1987. "Her Body, Himself: Gender in the Slasher Film," *Representations*, no. 20: 187–228.
Creed, Barbara. 1993. *The Monstrous Feminine: Film, Feminism, and Psychoanalysis*. New York: Routledge.
Creed, Barbara. 2002. "Horror and the Monstrous-Feminine: An Imaginary Abjection." In *Horror: The Film Reader*, edited by Mark Jancovich, 66–76. New York: Routledge.
Des Chene, Dennis. 2001. *Spirits and Clocks: Machine and Organism in Descartes*. Ithaca: Cornell University Press.
Fitzpatrick, Veronica. 2018. "Home's Invasion: Repulsion and the Horror of Apartments." In *The Apartment Complex: Urban Living and Global Screen Cultures*, edited by Pamela R. Wojcik, 126–44. Durham, NC: Duke University Press.
Friedan, Betty. 1963. *The Feminine Mystique*. New York: Dell.
Grosz, Elizabeth. 1992. "Bodies-Cities." In *Sexuality and Space*, edited by Beatriz Colomina et. al., 241–54. Princeton: Princeton University Press.
Hepworth, Mike. 2006. "Privacy, Security, and Respectability: The Ideal Victorian Home." In *Housing and Dwelling: Perspectives on Modern Domestic Architecture*, edited by Barbara M. Lane, 150–54. New York: Routledge.
Holmes, Nathan. 2018. *Welcome to Fear City: Crime Film, Crisis, and the Urban Imagination*. Albany: SUNY Press.
Johnston, Lynda. 2019. *Transforming Gender, Sex, and Place: Geographies of Gender Variance*. New York: Routledge.

Koven, Mikel J. 2006. *La Dolce Morte: Vernacular Cinema and the Italian Giallo Film*. New York: Scarecrow Press.

Lazzaro-Weis, Carol. 1993. *From Margins to Mainstream: Feminism and Fictional Modes in Italian Women's Writing, 1968-1990*. Philadelphia: University of Pennsylvania Press.

Lefebvre, Henri. 1992. *The Production of Space*. Oxford: Blackwell.

Lemay, Helen Rodnite. 1992. *Women's Secrets: A Translation of Pseudo Albertus Magnus' De Secretis Mulierum with Commentaries*. Albany: SUNY Press.

Lindsey, Shelley Stamp. 1996. "Horror, Femininity, and Carrie's Monstrous Puberty." In *The Dread of Difference: Gender and the Horror Film*, edited by Barry Keith Grant, 329-45. Austin: University of Texas Press.

Moss, Leonard W., and Stephen C. Cappannari. 1976. "Mal'occhio Ayin ha ra, Oculus fascinus, Judenblick: The Evil Eye Hovers Above." *The Evil Eye*, edited by Clarence Maloney, 1-15. New York: Columbia University Press.

Mulvey, Laura. 1975. "Visual Pleasure and Narrative Cinema," *Screen* 16:3, 6-18.

Mulvey, Laura. 1989. *Visual and Other Pleasures*. Bloomington: Indiana University Press.

Needham, Gary. 2007. "Playing with Genre: An Introduction to the Italian Giallo," *The Cult Film Reader*, eds. Ernest Mathijs and Xavier Mendik, 294-300. Maidenhead: Open University Press.

Pallasmaa, Juhani. 2002. *The Architecture of Image: Existential Space in Cinema*. Helsinki: Rakennustieto.

Pallasmaa, Juhani. 2012. *The Eyes of the Skin: Architecture and the Senses*. Hoboken, NJ: Wiley.

Petit, Emmanuel. 2010. "On the Entrails of Architecture's Organism," *Perspecta* 42, 168-75.

Punter, David. 2002. "Spectral Criticism." In *Introducing Criticism at the 21st Century*, edited by Julian Woffreys, 259-278. Edinburgh: Edinburgh University Press.

Robinson, Sarah. 2011. *Nesting: Body, Dwelling, Mind*. Richmond, CA: William Stout Publishers.

Rosner, Victoria. 2008. *Modernism and the Architecture of Private Life*. New York: Columbia University Press.

Russo, Mary. 2012. *The Female Grotesque: Risk, Excess, Modernity*. New York: Routledge.

Sensual City Studio. 2018. *A History of Thresholds: Life, Death, and Rebirth*. Berlin: JOVIS.

Shildrick, Margrit. 1997. *Leaky Bodies and Boundaries: Feminism, Postmodernism, and Bioethics*. New York: Routledge.

Vidler, Anthony. 1992. *The Architectural Uncanny: Essays in the Modern Unhomely*. New York: MIT Press.

Vitruvius. 1931. *On Architecture*: Books I-V: Loeb Classical Library. Translated by Fred Granger Harvard: Harvard University Press.

Vitruvius. 1934. *On Architecture*: Books VI-X: Loeb Classical Library. Translated by Fred Granger. Harvard: Harvard University Press.

Webb, Lawrence. 2014. *The Cinema of Urban Crisis: Seventies Film and the Reinvention of the City*. Amsterdam: Amsterdam University Press.

Weisman, Leslie Kane. 1992. *Discrimination by Design: A Feminist Critique of the Man-Made Environment*. Urbana: University of Illinois Press.

Williams, Tony. 2013. *Hearths of Darkness: The Family in the American Horror Film*. Jackson: University of Mississippi Press.

Wojcik, Patricia. 2010. *The Apartment Plot: Urban Living in American Film and Popular Culture, 1945–1975*. Durham, NC: Duke University Press.

Wright, Gwendolyn. 1983. *Building the Dream: A Social History of Housing in America*. New York: MIT Press.

Chapter 14

"BEAUTY IS THE ONLY THING"

Sex and Fantasy in American *Giallo* Cinema

CONNOR JOHN WARDEN

Introduction

The growth of *giallo* cinema outside the confines of Italy represents a fertile ground for cultural cross-pollination. As the genre moved beyond the immediate climate that produced it, it would naturally begin to pick up elements of the myriad cultures into which it spread. Perhaps nowhere is this more evident than in the United States, where it was tied more heavily into existing Hollywood crime-thriller traditions; the neo-*giallo* cinema produced in the United States from the 1980s onwards owes as much to Alfred Hitchcock as to Mario Bava. This represents an interesting cycle of mutual influence between the two regions: American crime-noir influenced *giallo* cinema in Italy, which in turn would be a source for the slasher genre in the following decades. This interplay between the two filmmaking traditions leads to a constant dialogue between the two cultures through their shared medium, and places American neo-*giallo* as a genre unto itself.

As Mackenzie notes, much of the previous academic work on *giallo* has placed a large emphasis on the sexual aspects of the genre (2013, 34), and in some ways has come to hyperfocus analysis of the genre onto one aspect of it—often failing to engage with the political themes of many *giallo* films entirely. There is certainly some truth to this, to the extent that "psychosexual trauma" has been identified as one of the key defining characteristics of academic discourse around the genre (Koven 2014, 206). However, simply because discussion of sexual content has played a significant role in the literature does not mean it is unworthy of discussion; indeed, it suggests that there is ground for debate within this field. I therefore leave discussion of the oft-neglected elements of the genre to other contributors in this collection, and instead propose a reappraisal of the American neo-*giallo*.

We must recognize that much of the common interpretation of *giallo* as being a sex-obsessed genre comes from an earlier era of criticism where it was discarded by (largely American) scholarly discourse; as Sanjek had it, "dismissed as grindhouse fodder" (1990, 151). We see the dismissive attitude among American scholars persist through until the twenty-first century, only changing with the emergence of a new wave of horror scholarship (Hunt 1992, 67). This popular perception of *giallo* in the English-speaking world can be attributed to Italy's "grindhouse" reputation—particular thanks for which can be attributed to the United Kingdom's "Video Nasties" list but which held just as well across the Atlantic. This perception of the *giallo* genre as seedy, or an "exploitation" genre, has been allowed to exist by an academic discourse which singles out individual auteurs as being worthy of discussion (cf. McDonagh 1991)—for instance, the idea that Argento is a "good exception" in an otherwise sleazy and scurrilous genre. This not only does a disservice to the artistic merit of other filmmakers within the field, but it also stifles academic discourse. Indeed, by placing a small number of Italian directors (Bava, Argento, and to a lesser extent Fulci) on a pedestal, it should come as no surprise that other directors, or filmmakers in other nations, have been excluded from previous discourse.

The analysis undertaken in this chapter comes from a number of lenses, each of which overlaps to help build a picture of what sex means within the American *giallo* tradition: firstly, a consideration of power dynamics, including how protagonist gender influences them; secondly, a consideration of "unreality," encompassing fantasy and dreams; and finally, a materialist analysis of how sex and capitalism overlap within the genre.

Choosing Our Victims

In selecting films to analyze for this chapter, two examples of the American neo-*giallo* genre (hereafter referred to as simply "*giallo*," for sake of ease) provide us with a wealth of content with which to discuss sex. These are *Body Double* (Brian De Palma, 1984) and *The Neon Demon* (Nicolas Winding Refn, 2016). These may be controversial choices to single out above others, especially those that better fit the traditional *giallo* mold, such as *Eyes of Laura Mars* (Irvin Kershner, 1978), but both can be explained as fitting into the *giallo* stable in ways which emphasize particular elements.

The two selected films epitomize the archetypal "M" and "F" *gialli* proposed by Mackenzie (2013, 34–39); thus, each allows a different lens through which to view menace, violence, and their relationships with sex on the screen. It is therefore with debt to Mackenzie's framework for gendered *giallo* that we proceed. To elaborate, this analysis suggests that *gialli* with female protagonists often place their central woman in a fragile and passive state—as in *Il dolce corpo di Deborah* (Romolo Guerrieri, 1968), the main characters of "Female" or "F" *gialli* are frequently witnesses to crimes, or else an object in a larger plot, but rarely take up the investigative role of solving the crime themselves. Instead, these films focus on their self-doubt as the world shifts around them, as well as the emotional drive of fear. Conversely, "Male" or "M" *gialli* under Mackenzie's framework tend to place their hero as a bystander-turned-sleuth, an active participant towards solving the violent crimes underpinning the narrative. Compared to the introspective focus on personal fear within the F-*giallo*, the archetypal M-*giallo* is outward facing, more concerned with the plot and less with the emotions of the protagonist.

Briefly summarizing the plots of our chosen films, we can already start to see how they fit into the "M" and "F" archetypes, respectively. *Body Double* focuses on a struggling actor, Jake Scully (Craig Wasson), who stays in a friend's house after his relationship ends. While there, he becomes infatuated with his next-door neighbor, Gloria (Deborah Shelton), whom he watches through a telescope each night. Ultimately, this leads to him witnessing her murder and then becoming a suspect in her death by the police. After discovering that he had not in fact watched his neighbor but rather actress Holly Body (Melanie Griffith)—the titular body double—Scully surmises that he was set up to witness the murder, leading suspicion away from the actual killer, Sam (Gregg Henry).

The Neon Demon tells the story of Jesse (Elle Fanning), an aspiring model freshly moved to Los Angeles. She quickly works her way up through the modeling industry, gaining prominence at the expense of more established competitors, led by Ruby (Jena Malone), who ultimately plots to kill her. Throughout the film, Jesse experiences a number of vivid nightmares and hallucinations, questioning her own perspective and stability, and being unable to shake the feeling of dread menace stalking her.

While the killer in *Body Double* may not be completely concealed from the audience, he is in many ways the standard *giallo* murderer: his identity is hidden, his gloves are black leather, and he is able to physically overpower his victim with relative ease. In its handling of the central crime, *Body Double* follows Koven's interpretation of the *giallo* protagonist: an amateur who is thrown into the investigation by accident, and who becomes embroiled in a mission to solve the crime (Koven 2014, 204–205). Certainly, De Palma's film takes heavy prompts from Hitchcock, but his cinematography and use of music are much more in common with the Italian tradition. While we do not see point-of-view shots for the villain leading up the murder, we are treated to a different kind of in-universe perspective: the build-up to the killing is seen through the telescope. The choice of an in-universe view rather than the omniscience of the film camera is a crucial step towards the *giallo* camp of directing.

To define *The Neon Demon* as an American *giallo* is controversial on both counts. In the first instance, the Scandinavian provenance of Winding Refn, and his English co-writer, Polly Stenham, brings into question whether the film can be called American or not. Without becoming bogged down in the multiple units of production for the film, the answer that it is American comes from the choice of setting. That the film is based in Los Angeles, and that its core locales include a roadside motel, are deliberate choices to place the film into the American tradition of direction rather than a European one; were they not, Paris or Milan would have been more traditionally *giallo* locations for a film about fashion models. The film makes deliberate use of an American setting, pulling on tropes of a small-town girl traveling across the continent to attempt fame; such a division from support networks, and such a great distance traveled within one's own country, are distinctly American rather than European themes. *The Neon Demon* is, regardless of its director's country of birth, a film which sits more comfortably in the American *giallo* genre than the European one.

Secondly, there is the question of whether *The Neon Demon* constitutes a *giallo* film at all. After all, the most prominent part of a *giallo* film is surely the murders? With the only one of those coming at the climax, how can this be meaningfully called a *giallo* picture? But a string of murders are not essential for a *giallo* horror; the core elements are menace and beauty—the constant creeping sense of threat, told through vivid lighting, set design, and camerawork. These are things which *The Neon Demon* has in abundance. It fulfills easily the criteria set out in Mackenzie's "F-giallo" framework: it focuses on a young woman, isolated and beset by omnipresent if unclear menace, while her mental fragility is at the core of her experience (Mackenzie 2013, 118–19). While the eventual killer is not concealed, there are multiple elements of anonymous threats within the film; the fumbling of an attacker with Jesse's motel door harks back to similar scenes in *Suspiria* (Dario Argento, 1977).

While it may not appear a *giallo* in terms of its plot, *The Neon Demon* appears to clearly fulfill the sense of fear which underpins the genre and supplements this with aesthetics unmistakably taken from Argento or Lamberto Bava.

The core point of contention with each of these films is that they are "not *giallo*" because they lack a few stylistic or plot elements seen in Italian *giallo* films. However, this notion is ultimately overly restrictive: the American *giallo* is inspired by its Italian predecessor, but will add, remove, or adapt elements to suit the cultural sensibilities of its audience. As discussed above, the academic corpus of defining what *giallo* is has tended to focus overtly on European efforts of a specific era—and thus necessarily exclude works produced at later dates, or in different regions. When we discuss American *giallo*, then, we should not expect it to look the same as other nations' *giallo* traditions, but rather be another branch of the same family, drawing from the same lineage and adding parts of its own contemporary culture. This is most clearly seen in the season Winding Refn curated for Picturehouse Cinemas in the United Kingdom, in which he clearly shows a range of influences from European *giallo* and American cult-horror traditions (Picturehouse Blog 2016). For the purposes of our analysis, we understand that when we discuss American *giallo*, we are talking about a genre which has multiple roots—aiming not to imitate Italian *giallo*, but rather to create a distinct genre influenced by it.

Sexual Power and the Gender Divide

At the heart of the American *giallo* comes one question, summed up by Sarah (Abbey Lee) in four words early into *The Neon Demon*: "Who are you fucking?" This question is what the entire film's world is implied to center upon—the use of sex as connection, as leverage to reach a higher position and establish oneself in the industry. In *Body Double*, the question can be turned on its head: exactly who Scully is sleeping with is the key to solving the mystery of Gloria's murder. Likewise, the lure of sexual arousal is used to pull Scully into the conspiracy at the heart of the film, and is a trap for the antagonist's own ends. At the heart of each piece, the notion that sex is power, or has power over others, is crucial.

For Jesse, the heroine of *The Neon Demon*, her sex appeal is the key to her success in Los Angeles. Her entire career and her sharp ascent to stardom arise from the fact that others find her attractive. As her awareness of her own beauty increases, so too does her arrogance and mental instability, until it eventually peaks in the film's closing act. However, when placed within the sexual arena itself, she is unfamiliar and uncomfortable: Jesse rejects Ruby's advances both from fear and inexperience. The power she has gained throughout the film, then, is shown to be contingent on her never actually entering the space of sex; the power she has gained through sex appeal ultimately dissipates when she rejects sex, and becomes vulnerable within Ruby's house. In this reading, the power of sex within *The Neon Demon* is illusory—a value assigned by others based on assumption and desire, rather than concrete ability. That is to say that Jesse's value in the eyes of others does not come from her ability to actually supply sex itself, but rather the idea that she might. Fundamentally, Jesse's inability to turn that illusory power into substance leads to her downfall.

Similarly, Sam's ploy as the villainous husband in *Body Double* is predicated upon the illusory power of sexual desire: the notion that Scully will watch and be aroused enough to gain his attention, but will never attempt to realize sexual contact with Gloria. Indeed, the point at which Scully comes closest to finally having sex with Gloria is the closest Sam's murder plan comes to failure—as it places him close enough to almost stop her handbag from being stolen. One assumes that had Scully and Gloria had chance to speak longer, Sam's deception with the window dance would have been revealed, and his plan foiled. While Scully still watches through the apartment telescope, and maintains sexual desire to keep watching, Sam's plan can progress and he maintains power over the situation. As soon as Scully attempts to move beyond desire and actually engage Gloria, Sam's scheme is endangered and his grasp is lost. Again, we see that sexual power only exists so long as the fragile desire remains untouched, unengaged—as soon as that desire is brought towards the realm of actual sex, the power held begins to rapidly dissipate.

Gender

It would be incomplete to discuss power dynamics and sex without a discussion of the gender of protagonists and how this affects their relationship with sex. *Giallo* is not only frequently a sexual genre, it is also a highly gendered one. As discussed under Mackenzie's framework of "M" and "F" *gialli*, the experiences and story arcs of *giallo* protagonists can vary alongside their sex. Male protagonists often come into a plot by accident, often witnessing something incriminating, and become targets of menace through their investigation; female protagonists, conversely, frequently first come into contact with the plot of menace by being a victim of it—either directly or through

Figure 1. A roaring lion in the naïve girl's bed.

the targeting of their friends, family, etc. In short, men become part of a *giallo* plot through their *action*, while women are drawn in by their *being*. This active versus passive relationship to plot has an obvious sexual parallel, particularly when read within the context of mid-twentieth-century Italy and its social mores; the rigidity of gender roles, and expected behavior, is on full show in these films where men act upon the world, and women are acted upon (Mackenzie 2013, 35–39).

We can of course take this a step further in examining how the protagonists of these films actually participate in or relate to the act of sex. It is clear that American *gialli* follow these gendered divides of activity versus passivity. The events and plot progression of *Body Double* stem from Scully seeking out Gloria and, later, Holly; these events are part of his investigation and a key part of developing the plot. Indeed, his pursuit of Gloria goes hand-in-hand with the development of sustained menace, manifested here in the Indian. Sex is something which Scully actively pursues, and which draws him into the plot. In *The Neon Demon*, by contrast, Jesse has sex brought to her—through the amorous advances of others, through her nightmares, and through the praise of those in the fashion industry. Unlike Scully, Jesse does not choose sex nor does he pursue it; unlike Scully, it does not bring her closer to the plot—it rather reinforces that she is the plot, the thing to be sought and captured by others. The relationships here are inverse, and for our protagonists, it appears the view of sex as something done by men to women holds up in the context of the American *giallo*.

Indeed, Jesse's role in *The Neon Demon* is as the object of menace, which manifests throughout the film in explicitly or implicitly sexual ways. The destruction of her bedroom by a mountain lion, a stalking savage beast, is an obvious instance of this; particularly as it comes after she has politely rejected Dean's (Karl Glusman) advances on a date. The image of a teenage girl finding something primal which she does not fully understand waiting in her bedroom is the perfect microcosm of sexual anxiety and fear of predation by older or more powerful men.

Likewise, there is the sense of the demonic in the neon triangle during the fashion show, a building force inside Jesse which has entered without her will—some force which life in Los Angeles has ultimately thrust inside her and she must now live with. That the increasing severity and proximity of these threats grows alongside Jesse's sexual profile and desirability is not coincidental—and comes to a head with her body being literally broken and consumed by others because of their wants. Throughout *The Neon Demon*, Jesse's story is one of being a target for desire, a target for sexual pursuit—and while she rises through the modeling industry, and gains power because of her sexual attributes and beauty, there is always a lurking threat looking to harm her specifically because of those attributes. To Jesse, sex is the source of her power, but also the root of her deepest vulnerability. In Scully, by contrast, there is no such vulnerability: sex is something he can do to others, but cannot himself be threatened with as a vector for attack. This core imbalance is the center of the gendered difference between male and female protagonists.

Rejection and Power

Much as the ability to display sexual desirability, or to consummate sex, is a form of a power gain within the American *giallo*, its denial is likewise a power dynamic. Both *The Neon Demon* and *Body Double* present us with clear moments of sexual rejection or spurning, and each reaction comes with dramatic consequences; each represents a loss of power for the individual, and the reaction is a means by which the rejected character seeks to redress that loss.

For Ruby, who is rejected by Jesse towards the end of *The Neon Demon*, the spurning is responded to in two ways. The first of these is the act of necrophilia she commits in the morgue the following day, seeking to return her ability to perform sexual action. The corpse is unable to refuse or spurn; it can neither add nor detract from the sexual experience, which is fundamentally masturbatory. By performing this action, Ruby consummates through a Jesse-surrogate what she had been unable to do with the actual target of her affections: transferring the sexual desire onto a new, accessible target. This action does not redress the power imbalance between Ruby and Jesse, however; it simply heals over the immediate wounding to Ruby's pride. The response to the perceived power imbalance on a larger scale, of course, is the murder of Jesse. By choosing to destroy the target of her affections, Ruby chooses a drastic interpretation of power-imbalance redress. In this interpretation, the power dynamics are clearly on display, and rejection is seen as something to be "won" against.

By contrast, Scully experiences sexual rejection at the beginning of *Body Double*, setting the film's events in motion. When he is cuckolded, Scully's confidence and ability to engage normally with sexuality is damaged; it is that precise attribute which causes him to be singled out by Sam. The voyeurism Scully partakes in is a reaction to his cuckolding on two fronts. In the first instance, viewing Gloria through the telescope allows Scully to experience arousal without a sense of investment: he can be gratified without the threat of further rejection—his viewing is without consent, and without the ability to be denied, and thus serves a parallel to Ruby's necrophilia. Secondly, Scully is reconciled to the breakdown of his relationship, and his rejected state, by his watching a woman he will likely never sleep with; this is taken further with his pornography use after Gloria's death, wherein he starts willingly watching women have sex with other men, effectively embracing his cuckoldry. Much like his claustrophobia, however, Scully is only able to move on and achieve his goals by overcoming this—by seeking out Holly and beginning a relationship with her. While in *The Neon Demon*, rejection is ultimately an ending, in *Body Double* it is presented as a setback which can be overcome positively, bringing the spurned lover out stronger. In part, this is likely due to a personal versus interpersonal understanding of the power loss: Scully's loss of power through his rejection is taken as personal and thus, like his phobia, can be overcome through his own internal action; Ruby's rejection, conversely, is interpersonal, and therefore must be addressed through "taking back" the lost power in the exchange. The myriad presentations of sexual power dynamics nonetheless evidently form a core element in American *giallo* cinema.

Unreality, Detachment, and Fantasy

A core element of many *giallo* films is the role played by dream sequences, fantasy, and the unreliability of the senses. Such storytelling elements have a pedigree stretching back to the roots of gothic horror, and it is the combination of these elements with crime-noir that plants the seeds of the *giallo* genre. American *giallo* places an additional perspective upon this unreliability, or this separation of narrative into layers: frequently, it makes use of plays-within-plays, in-universe films, and similar devices to toy with the nature of storytelling. In the case of sexuality as presented in these films, this perhaps goes even further.

Cinema is inherently detached from the viewer, and there will always be a barrier for interaction between the audience and screen, but American *gialli* push further with this notion, using the restricted nature of cinema to their advantage. The beginning of *Body Double*, for instance, is a cold open into what appears to be another film—before it is revealed to be a film in which Scully is acting. This playing with audience perception is key to establishing the themes of the film: namely, that things are often not as they seem, and that theatricality and performance will play a large part in what is to follow. This serves to create "layers" of reality: that while the events of *Body Double* are presented to us as the film's reality, the events of *Vampire's Kiss* are a fictional layer beyond that. This essentially establishes a separate stage on which certain things play out and the film carries forward by having its sexual activity on this separate stage.

With the exception of a brief, unconsummated tryst between Scully and Gloria, all the sexual content of *Body Double* is indirect: it is seen through in-universe objects, through telescopes and film cameras. It is almost never witnessed directly. In *Body Double*, sex is something happening out of reach—in front of a camera, through a telescope, in a house across the valley—inaccessible, out of reach to both audience and character. In this sense, sex is something distant and unattainable so that even when it happens, it is placed into the theater of the unreal, into that additional layer beyond. Likewise, nudity in *The Neon Demon* only occurs before an in-universe camera; it is again detached another layer from our experience. Rather than seeing nudity through a screen, we watch nudity through a screen-on-a-screen: it is distant, intangible, unreal.

The question is whether such a presentation elevates or relegates things to that status. One could argue that by separating sex from the ordinary, *giallo* mythologizes it and places it on a pedestal above the real events. By detaching sex in this way, we remove it from the brutish considerations of the rest of the film; such scenes, then, can be viewed as though the camera was an omniscient voyeur, and thus the scenes can be brought to a new aesthetic height, their separation intentional. However, if we take Linda Williams's understanding of idealized voyeurism, this cannot hold. That understanding suggests that voyeurism in its ideal form comes from viewing a male surrogate who can perfectly stand in for the viewer (Williams 1999, 90). The single scene of male penetrative sex in *Body Double* takes place in the context of creating a pornographic film—a film in which Scully could feasibly be a surrogate for in-universe viewers, but necessarily cannot be for us the audience. We see him performing this act within the context of his broader journey outside of this encounter; he cannot be our surrogate because there is no believability—we have seen the layers of unreality in which this scene takes place—and once again, the sheet of glass has come up between us and events, causing us to view them indirectly. Even when sex occurs, it is fundamentally detached and unreal.

Fantasy

When discussing detachment from the reality, and separation of storytelling space, we cannot help but consider the role played by fantasy. Dream sequences have been a longstanding feature of both of the American *giallo*'s major influences: the Italian *giallo*, as in the sleep focus of *Una lucertola con la pelle de donna* (Lucio Fulci, 1971); and the American crime-thriller genre, such as *Spellbound* (Alfred Hitchcock, 1945). There is therefore a pedigree to dream sequences as key to storytelling in the American *giallo*, and these are often key to interpreting the sexual nature of these films.

Let us first consider what is probably the most visceral dream sequence in *The Neon Demon*, in which Jesse dreams of her motel manager, Hank (Keanu Reeves), holding her down to a bed and forcing her to swallow a knife in a forced-fellatio motif. On the face of it, this scene is an exploration of Jesse's fear of predation: after all, it was Hank who got rid of the mountain lion, the previous threat to her, but if he, the even more powerful force, chooses to become predatory, she has little chance of escape. It serves to drive home the notion of the modeling industry, and Los Angeles as a whole, as being a place in which no figure is completely trustworthy, and no relationship entirely safe—themes that become crucial as the film unfolds into its final act after her waking from the nightmare.

This is perhaps the first point at which Jesse's power in the sexual realm is taken away from her—the scene takes place at the height of her building confidence, as it follows on from Sarno's (Alessandro Nivola) explanation that "beauty is the only thing"—as it is the first time Jesse is pushed beyond the realm of being distantly desirable, and into the physical space of the sexual act. It clearly foreshadows her later discomfort with Ruby, and begins the third-act decline into powerlessness. This nightmare is an anxiety-fantasy, illustrating once again the fragile illusion that is sexual power in *The Neon Demon*.

For *Body Double*, the voyeuristic fantasies of Jake Scully are used not only to explore the sexual psyche of the character but also to play further with the notions of reality versus unreality. Fantasy acts not only as a filter through which the film's events are viewed, but frequently as a source of driving conflict within the plot. Primarily, we should discuss Scully's attraction to Gloria, which comes from a place of sexual fantasy. After all, the two characters have never met at the point Scully begins following her; any connection he feels to her exists solely within his own head. That pursuit of Gloria is driven by a desire to act upon those sexual fantasies. After her death, his subsequent research into and pursuit of Holly Body exists to even more deeply embrace that fantasy, seeking to transfer his neutered sexual advances onto a similar target. Notably, the two points where Scully's fantasies are forced into conflict with reality both cause significant negative events: his first face-to-face encounter with Gloria leads to her handbag and keycard being stolen, setting in motion the events leading to her murder; and his ending the playboy-pornographer fantasy with Holly leads to her leaving the apartment and being placed likewise in harm's way. De Palma's work is an exploration of how ingrained fantasy will inevitably either be unrealized, as the circumstances never occur (e.g., the subject of fantasy is never met) or will clash with reality negatively (e.g., the subject of fantasy is met but does not act as imagined). In this sense, sexual fantasy as presented in *Body Double* is a route to conflict and downfall: either for oneself, being drawn into the plot and investigation; or for others, placing them into harm's way as a result of attempting to enact fantasies.

Scully's fantasies go beyond the bare bones of sexual desire, though. They are wrapped up in a romantic heroic fantasy. Scully never knows Gloria, but only imagines her; even so, he still spends an entire day tracking her through the city in an attempt to rescue her from a perceived threat. This heroic fantasy is broken once people outside of Scully are involved: the store clerk at the mall, the security guard, even the homicide detective, all treat Scully's actions as what they appear to be—the actions of a stalker and pervert, fixated on Gloria. Indeed, it is hard to call such an appraisal unfair, as Scully's actions are driven by sexual motives towards the woman he spied on and followed without her knowledge. Again, fantasy in *Body Double* cannot survive contact with the external world; while the fantasy is insular, a justifying narrative which makes sense of and excuses actions taken, the external reality is incompatible with it. The shattering of Scully's fantasies by other characters not only serve to reinforce the themes of this film—and promote the *giallo* trope of the protagonist not being believed by authorities—but also give the audience members pause to reconsider the events they have watched. We become acutely aware in these moments of conflict between fantasy and reality that we are seeing from the perspective of one character; and that we are not an omniscient, idealized voyeur, but restricted. The interplay of fantasy and reality by De Palma helps keep the film within the confines of our own telescope lens.

In each case, the role of fantasies is to make points about the reality of their respective films. For *The Neon Demon*, it serves to reinforce and foreshadow Jesse's powerlessness within the realm of the actual-sexual, maintaining the importance of her distance from others to stay as desirable-sexual. In *Body Double*, fantasy is used to heighten awareness of voyeurism and viewpoint, playing with the audience's perception of events, as well as to bring into criticism the sexual actions of the protagonist.

The Commodification of Fantasy

Beyond merely exploring fantasy on a meta-level, fantasy is a plot device within these films—and in two films concerned with different media industries, the commodification and exploitation of sexual fantasy plays a major role. Within *Body Double*, we are shown the workings of a pornographic industry that creates and sells fantasies, and the film examines how fantasy interplays with notions of passivity and powerlessness on the part of the beholder. *The Neon Demon* inverts this, presenting us with characters who actively cultivate themselves as fantasy-objects in order to gain power and position.

During an initial questioning after the death of Gloria, Scully is reprimanded by a homicide detective, suggesting that he was "so busy peeping on her [he] didn't bother to warn the poor woman." At its core, this is an accusation of passivity. From the initial rejection onwards, Scully's sexuality throughout *Body Double* is shown as something passive; not in the sense of "having sex done to him," as we have considered female sexuality in the *giallo*, but in the sense of consuming sexual material rather than producing it. This begins through watching Gloria from afar. After her death, he is drawn into pornography use—an inherently consumption-led model of sexual experience. Scully becomes the beholder of fantasy, and a passive actor in both sex and influence.

From that stage onwards, Scully is left in thrall to the pornography industry—his only sexual experience being either watching it or, later, participating in its production himself. His access to sex is therefore within the grasp of created fantasy. Even the trailer for the in-universe film *Peepers*, which draws him to Holly Body, is an allusion to this; that the film shows a peeping Tom is a statement that even Scully's previous experiences have now been assimilated by the pornography industry. Even before stepping in front of the camera, Scully's sexual identity has been eroded and commodified. Once he joins the pornography studio, his only consummated sexual experiences are within the context of that industry; it now monopolizes his sex. Hence, after the death of the "real" in Gloria, Scully's access to sex comes only through the fantasy-producing machine. Crucially, even despite taking a physical role in proceedings, Scully is never in control of these encounters; he has merely become a tool by which the producers, scripting and directing his actions, seek to create fantasies for others and thereby gain other passive dependents.

When Scully attempts to act of his own accord, rather than on the command of the pornographers, he is reprimanded. That Scully ejaculates inside of Holly is a cause for concern among the crew of the film set; they wish to see a "money shot," an act separated from the normal, real experience of sex as lived, but one which is more befitting the manufactured scene they are putting together. By ejaculating within her, Scully fails to maintain the detached nature of the piece; his natural act intrudes upon the artificial set-up the film crew requires. This state of affairs persists until the denouement, which implies Scully has begun a relationship with Holly, thus achieving the "real" to free himself from the fantasy-pornographic framework. For De Palma, so long as the individual remains a slave to fantasy—even an active participant in creating fantasy—he remains powerless, only regaining that power once he begins to act within the theater of the real.

Holly Body, meanwhile, represents the individual already ingrained within the fantasy-pornographic system. Her existence is tied into several layers of meta-fantasy. Our first introduction to the character is within a trailer-within-a-film, another of De Palma's layered statements emphasized by the trailer showing her through binoculars. This follows into seeing her through the lens of a pornographer's camera with Scully, which is on the same layer of detachment as seeing her perform through a telescope during her nightly dancing. Even when she attends a Hollywood party with Scully, she is still a layer detached from the film's reality; she is "switched on," networking, and behaving as she believes she should to secure the promised job from Scully. In essence, Holly perceives her existence to be tied to the fantasy-construct version of herself and becomes powerless once detached from that affected persona. After being thrown into the murder case outside of her persona, and overcoming real danger using real rather than fantasy power, however, she develops beyond this learned dependence on fantasy. Holly begins being attuned to fantasy-as-commodity and treats this as her source of worth, but she only begins to exercise true power once she breaks from the fantastical paradigm.

By contrast, sex as presented within the modeling industry of *The Neon Demon* is at once less explicit and more unattainable than the sex industry of *Body Double*. Jesse's photoshoot with gold paint may lack the interpersonal contact of *Body Double*'s sexual media, but is undeniably intended as sexual; yet it is untouched and untouchable, behind the camera lens. Her body is one which is idealized, but held unattainable for both the in- and out-of-universe viewer. Modeling is presented, then, as something that thrives off pushing sex into a space of the unreal—as a way to elevate the image of its models—and as another fantasy-creation machine.

Sex-as-commodity is seen in *The Neon Demon* as a transactional expectation, evidenced in Sarah and Gigi's (Bella Heathcote) discussion of "casting couches" as a way to get ahead. Of course, the only reason sex can exist as a commodity in that situation is due to the other party—the predominantly male authority figure—wanting it. The cultivation of fantasy around oneself is a necessary aspect of allowing it to be realized as sexual capital. Hence, consciously created fantasy is seen within a capitalistic framework.

Moreover, the characters of *The Neon Demon* have a second layer of fantasy: the belief that these objects of sexual fantasy exist within a zero-sum game for their audience's attention. This plays out in Jesse's elevation in a restaurant, for which Gigi is humiliated to bolster that praise. Sarah cuts open Jesse's hand and drinks blood from it because the latter is taking Sarno's finite attention. Even Ruby's reaction to rejection, and the violent means she employs, comes from this same underlying assumption: that when she cannot attain her fantasy, she must be on the losing side of a game. The assumption of zero-sum, of desirability being treated as a physical commodity, is brought out most clearly in Jesse's ultimate fate: her consumption by others is the assumption that her loss must mean their gain, and that her sexual appeal and currency can be stolen as though it were a physical resource. Eating someone's flesh to gain their charisma and fame may be absurd to us, but within the context of the film—in which onlookers desire and demand that their perceived fantasies be made real—it is an extreme conclusion to the actions of characters driven by fantasy.

This reading of sexual fantasy as a zero-sum game lends itself to embracing the competitive aspects of the film. The capitalistic setting of Los Angeles emphasizes the material angle, with concerns about professional survival. The arrival of a new figure of higher sexual desirability threatens Gigi and her cohort to the point that they worry for their survival. Fantasy is not a thing with objective value, but is weighed against other fantasies. Once again, the perception of what is real—the fantasy of the sex-appeal market—does more to drive characters' actions than what actually exists. Sex in *The Neon Demon* exists only inasmuch as people fantasize about its existence, and when that fantasy is found incompatible with reality, its characters resort to necrophilia and bloodshed.

Conclusions

The American *giallo* presents an interesting conundrum in which sex appears to be on display in lurid detail, but is never accessible: always visible, but never seen for what it is. For all that previous literature has too often dismissed the genre as simply being about sex and violence, such a reduction can be useful to help us pull together our final thoughts—particularly as a comparison. In short, violence in the American *giallo* genre has a reality to it, which sex does not. Consider the sounds and action which come in *Body Double* with the Indian's murder of Gloria—what we see, what we hear. The whirr of the murderer's drill, the screams of the victim, the barking and noise of her dog; these noises lend a weight and presence to the scene, stationing it firmly within the film's reality. By contrast, even the closest sex comes to being real, when Scully and Gloria meet on the beach, lacks diegetic sound, instead sinking into a sea of soundtrack. This only becomes truer for the music video/pornographic film starring Scully and Holly. The penetration of an oversized drill through flesh is shown to us a hundred times more real than the penetration of a man's flesh into a woman's. Sex does not have a voice in *Body Double*, but violence certainly does.

Sexual presence in *The Neon Demon* takes place on the other side of a camera, or else with a lifeless corpse. The violence, meanwhile, is graphic, and the scenes of cannibalism given weight; the violence is allowed to exist within the main reality of the film, while sexuality is only ever seen through a detached glass. The sexuality of Jesse is only in photographs and fantasy, while she remains virginal until her death; the sex, therefore, is never allowed to manifest while the closing scenes show that the violence is only too real.

What sex does occur in these films is sterile, stripped away from the context and reality of sex-as-lived. Let us consider again the sex scene between Scully and Holly. That the scene requires a "money shot" is crucial. There can be no fecundity, not even an illusion of the means by which conception occurs. The design of the piece requires it to be detached from life, detached from the natural consequences of sex. The key to stopping sex having a voice is to cut it out from its context. In making it sterile, incapable of bearing fruit, sex is silenced completely—and made unreal.

Clearly, we can question why it is that sex is so detached in the American *giallo*, while violence is so prevalent by contrast. One interpretation would be the well-documented imbalance American filmmakers and audiences have, where they are more comfortable with violence than sexuality.

Further work could be done to better understand the mutual relationship between the American *giallo* and its close cousin, the slasher movie—particularly in the way they emerged from similar influences only to diverge. Indeed, much has already been written about the sexual mores of that genre (Cowan and O'Brien 1990; Menard et al., 2019). I believe that an answer to understanding the American *giallo*'s lack of real sex can be found through this; that by keeping the female lead away from the realm of sex, in death, she may maintain her purity forever. In this reading, the same social moralizing which characterized boom-era slashers had resonating effects within Hollywood's take on the *giallo* film.

In pulling together the threads of power and fantasy, we seem faced with sex as a paradox in American *gialli*: ever-present yet never really there. The creators of *Body Double* and *The Neon Demon* present to us worlds where sex controls so many aspects of people's lives, and yet is always kept in the theater of the unreal. They remark upon the cultural context in which they exist. These films have been produced under a modernist system that commodifies sex, and particularly within a film industry in which sex permeates and corrupts the major power structures. To fail to read this context would be to fail to understand the point of these films: that De Palma and Winding Refn are making films about the entertainment industry, and about the multifaceted role sex plays within this culture, exaggerated to its extreme by the filmmaker.

Sex in Hollywood's *gialli* is best summed up by the credits sequence of *Body Double*: before the sex scene begins, there is a cut as an actress is switched. There is no illusion of reality for us, the audience, though there will be one for the eventual in-universe audience who see Scully's film. The layers of detachment are shown to us one final time, by a director who has made his case. This leads us to reconsider everything we have seen prior, and is the final indictment: that sex in the American *giallo* does not really exist. It is an illusion. Sex is power, it is fantasy, it is fetish and obsession and commodity; but it is never sex.

Works Cited

Cowan, Gloria, and Margaret O'Brien. 1990. "Gender and Survival vs. Death in Slasher Films: A Content Analysis." *Sex Roles* 23 (August): 187–96.

Hunt, Leon. 1992. "A (Sadistic) Night at the Opera: Notes on the Italian Horror Film." *Velvet Light Trap* (Fall): https://go.gale.com/ps/i.do?p=AONE&u=googlescholar&id=GALE|A90190287&v=2.1&it=r&sid=AONE&asid=da9b4c98.

Koven, Michel. 2014. "The *Giallo* and the Spaghetti Nightmare Film." In *The Italian Cinema Book*, edited by Peter Bondella, 203–210. New York: Bloomsbury.

Mackenzie, Michael. 2013. "Gender, Genre and Sociocultural Change in the Giallo: 1970–1975." PhD thesis, University of Glasgow. https://theses.gla.ac.uk/4730/1/2013Mackenziephd.pdf.

McDonagh, Maitland. 1991. *Broken Mirrors/Broken Minds: The Dark Dreams of Dario Argento*. London: Sun Tavern Fields.

Menard, Dana, Angela Weaver, and Christine Cabrera. 2019. "'There are Certain Rules one must Abide by": Predictors of Mortality in Slasher Films." *Sexuality and Culture*, no. 23 (June): 621–40.

Picturehouse (blog). June 27, 2016. https://picturehouses.wordpress.com/2016/06/27/nicolas-winding-refn-presents/.

Sanjek, D. 1990. "Fans' Notes: The Horror Film Fanzine." *Literature/Film Quarterly* 18, no. 3 (July): 150–59.

Williams, Linda. 1999. *Hard Core: Power, Pleasure, and the "Frenzy of the Visible."* California: University of California Press.

Chapter 15

THE CANADIAN *GIALLO*, OR HOW THE ITALIAN THRILLER INFLUENCED THE CANADIAN SLASHER FILM

MIKEL J. KOVEN

Quite a few years ago, I wrote about the relationship between certain kinds of slasher films and their relationship to urban legends (Koven 2003). To differentiate between urban legend-based slasher films from what I saw as *typical* slasher films, I referred to those horror films as being more like murder mysteries; actually, I called them "Scooby-Doo movies," because at their conclusions, the killer is revealed to be one of the group being murdered. Often these films end with the killer being unmasked with great surprise. In preparing that essay for publication, a connection was suggested, by one of the article's reviewers, that there was a link between what I was calling "Scooby-Doo movies" and the Italian *giallo*. Once this article had been published, I began exploring the Italian *giallo* in more detail, and the result was *La Dolce Morte: Vernacular Cinema and the Italian* Giallo (Koven, 2006), what I have subsequently learned to be the first book-length academic study of the *giallo*. I am now picking up where I started from and looking in more detail at the relationship between the *giallo* and the slasher film, particularly those I referred to as "Scooby-Doo movies." However, the "Scooby-Doo movies" I shall be discussing here were all produced in Canada between 1980 and 1982, and many are recognized as classics of the sub-genre: *Prom Night* (Paul Lynch, 1980), *Happy Birthday to Me* (J. Lee Thompson, 1981), *Terror Train* (Roger Spottiswood, 1981), *Visiting Hours* (Jean-Claude Lord,

1982), and *Curtains* (Jonathan Stryker [Richard Ciupka], 1983). And all these films, I argue, feature strong connections to the *giallo*.

The connection between the *giallo* and the slasher film was noted as early as 2002; Adam Rockoff, in his seminal book on the slasher film, *Going to Pieces*, noted that the slasher film owed much to the Italian thriller, and while he does offer a brief discussion about the *giallo*, he does not make the connections beyond vague fuzzy allusions (2002, 30). But the relation between the *giallo* and the slasher film is entirely missing from Vera Dika's *Games of Terror* (1990, 29), although she does grant that there is a playful quality to the slasher film. Dika notes that in some films, like those discussed below, "the spectator is implicated by a number of conventionalized formal strategies, ones that encourage a play with the film itself, rather than ones that merely allow the events to unfold for the spectator's observation" (1990, 22). In other words, although she does not make the connection herself, the ludic challenge to the audience is to try and solve the film's central mystery; one sees this in the *giallo* too. Kim Newman, in *Nightmare Movies* (1988, 105), likewise discusses the *giallo vis a vis* Dario Argento as an auteur, but when it comes to discussing the slasher film, the author did not see, or did not comment, on the connection made here (Newman 1988, 143–57).

And yet, other critics *did* see the connection as more than vague. Jim Harper, writing about the same time I was writing *La Dolce Morte*, made the connection unambiguous: "the *giallo* films of the sixties and the seventies paved the way for the stalk and slash movies of the eighties" (2004, 9). He continues noting that "it's possible to see the seeds of the *giallo* in almost every aspect of *Halloween* and the multitude of films that followed" (2004, 10). While I have argued elsewhere that *Halloween* is a different animal than the *giallo*-influenced slasher films I will be discussing, here, what is most significant is Harper's connection between the two film cycles/genres/*filone* (Koven 2003).

The black leather and the masks may give Argento's murders a supernatural appearance, but ultimately they are revealed to be coherent and seemingly normal people. The endless repetition of this device in slasher movies has robbed it of any impact—no one is surprised when the killer turns out to be another 'normal' student, teacher, journalist, whatever—but ultimately it has been derived from the *gialli* (Harper 2004, 10).

Harper also distinguishes between those killers whose identities are hidden from the audience until the film's final act and those who, due to physical deformity or another disfiguration, are continually killing (Jason Vorhees, Michael Myers, etc.). And it is in this sense that the horror film more closely resembles a murder mystery, and therefore, *giallo*. Martin Rubin

(1999, 163–64) distinguishes between those slasher films which follow a "whodunit format" from those which feature the "cipher format": as argued below, Rubin's "whodunit format" have a distinct connection to the *giallo*. "There is a teasing, gamelike quality to stalker films, filled with red herrings, practical jokes, false alarms, and false alarms that turn out to be real alarms" (Rubin 1999, 167). Harper notes that these "whodunit format" slasher films' killers "are articulate and agile, and usually engage in conversation at some point. Although obviously deranged, they tend to bear no physical disfigurement that would prevent them from mixing in civilized society" (2004, 42). And a surprising number of what we, retrospectively, call "classic" slasher films follow this "whodunit format," rather than the "cipher."

In more recent years, the *giallo*-slasher connection has been more widely recognized. Wickham Clayton sees the *giallo* as explicitly a "prototype" to the slasher film (2015, 7), a point echoed by David Roche in the same volume (2015, 35n2). Ian Conrich notes the oft-cited connection between the *giallo* and slasher film in that the couple pinioned by a skewer through both of their bodies while making love appears in both *Friday the 13th Part Two* (Steve Miner, 1981) and *Bay of Blood* (Mario Bava, 1971) (2015, 111). Conrich also sees these films as "essentially whodunits that are closer to Agatha Christie or Scooby-Doo and can include an end-of-film unmasking and explanation" (2015, 113). Finally, despite not name-dropping the *giallo*, per se, Jessica Balanzategui notes the following in accounting for the marked change in tone between *Halloween* and *Friday the 13th*, with the more ratiocination of *Prom Night* or *Terror Train*:

> This thematic shift involves a level of generic hybridity, as the slasher began drawing on plot elements from the mystery and detective genre to flesh out the narrative and amplify anxieties about the identity of the killer. As a result, viewers and protagonists became tasked with solving the mysteries of the killer's existence by uncovering clues surrounding each of the murders. (2015, 170)

What Balanzategui sees as a change in the narrative structure of the films, has, instead, always been part of the continuity between the *giallo* and the slasher film. Balanzategui is correct in identifying the playful, ludic game these films have with their audiences.

But why Canada? Why did Canada produce so many classic slasher films in the wake of the successes of *Halloween* (John Carpenter, 1978) and *Friday the 13th* (Sean S. Cunningham, 1980)? The question is particularly worth asking since, as Canadian film critic John Harkness (1982, 27) noted,

The crazed killer is an American phenomenon ... [and] these stories are native to the American psychology.... When we [Canadians] try to imitate a foreign genre, we wind up with a *Visiting Hours*, a *Terror Train*, a *My Bloody Valentine*, where artistic decisions are based solely on commercial factors.

To be sure, "commercial factors" play an instrumental role in these films' production. Andrew Dowler also noted that Canadian filmmakers were particularly poor at imitating the earlier American successes. Dowler (1985, 16) notes, "and we've never made them worse: ... just cold, pallid and relentlessly dull simulacra [of the American films]," and he concludes, much as Harkness did, that Canada just does not have the tradition of crime and mystery fiction which our American cousins do (1985, 17). However, as Richard Nowell (2011, 57–78) noted in detail, it was not *Halloween* which lit the fuse for the slasher film to explode, but a Canadian shocker made a few years earlier, *Black Christmas* (Bob Clark, 1974) (see also Constantineau, 2010). The cultural relationship between Canada and the United States creates a permeable membrane of mutual influence, which Suzie Young (2005) also noted.

However, calling these films out as commercial prospects only, as Harkness and Dowler do, is an oversimplification. Certainly, these films were produced to make money, more than they were to as an artistic expression of Canadian identity, but that is only part of the picture. In 1967, the Canadian Film Development Corporation (CFDC) was founded as a government body to partially fund and offer tax incentives to Canadian filmmakers exploring topics of a national interest. While, in the first few years of the CFDC, several films were produced which today are recognized as classics of Canadian national cinema (Don Shebib's *Going Down the Road* [1970] and Peter Carter's *The Rowdyman* [1972] are two examples), they failed at the Canadian box office, due, in part, as Christopher Gittings notes (2002, 95), to American companies' monopoly on distribution in Canada. By 1974, the Canadian government felt that CFDC-funded films needed an explicitly commercial orientation; that the films needed to stand, at least a chance, of competing with American films. To facilitate this, the CFDC enabled eligible film producers to write off 100 percent of investment against the film's profits on their personal income tax, so long as certain key factors were maintained (see Pednekar, 2985). "The Tomkins Report of 1976 ... pushe[d] the Canadian industry towards making Hollywood-style films, films 'with a mass audience appeal beyond the boundaries of any one country'" (Gittings, 2002, 96). And it was in this context that *Black Christmas* was born; as Richard Nowell (2011, 63) notes, "*Black Christmas* was seen by CFDC executives to be capable of proving Canada with its first genuine US box-office success." Due to the amount of investment that independent producers could write off in this period, the mid-to-late-1970s and early 1980s became known as "the tax shelter" period, and this is the context which birthed the slasher films being examined here. Canadian horror film historian Caelum Vatnsdal noted (2004, 121): "The tax shelter period was a deeply ignoble time in Canadian history. Abuse was rampant; not just of the tax laws, but of cinema itself. Films were made the wrong way by the wrong people for the wrong reasons."

So "ignoble" was this period that the slasher films discussed here do not appear in mainstream textbooks on Canadian cinema (see Elder, 1989; Gittings, 2002; and Beard and White, 2002); the tax shelter years produced films which, it appears, Canadian film studies wishes to ignore even existed! Vatnsdal noted (2004, 122) that "[t]hese are the movies that . . . undermined Canada's position in the film world simply by being so awful." And Canadian film history would rather focus on those films which articulated "a Canadian cultural identity" (Ted Magder, cited by Nowell 2011, 62), and not those cheapened by the (perceived) stench of commercial opportunism.

The job of establishing continuity between the *giallo* and the slasher film would be substantially easier if we could uncover an interview with one of the slasher film directors, screenwriters, or producers who fully admits that so-and-so saw *Deep Red* (Dario Argento, 1975) at the Rio Cinema (or the Biltmore, or the Coronet) in Toronto in 1978, on a double bill with *Halloween*. This continuity would be more easily established if we could put anyone who worked on these slasher films in the same room screening a *giallo*. But I have yet to find such a connection. Instead, I need to put together small pieces of discussion, much like a jigsaw puzzle, to create the picture. Of course, simply by identifying that slasher films are murder mysteries, whodunits, by their very definition makes them *gialli*; the word, in Italian, refers to the murder mystery genre. So, any whodunit is, by definition, a *giallo*. But were any of these filmmakers watching Italian exploitation cinema? Raiford Guins notes (2005, 16) that "prior to videocassette and its large-scale 'home penetration' in the mid-1980s, Italian horror 'films' (when distributed and shown on US screens [and by extension, Canadian screens]) were exhibited in limited release, or found on the midnight movie circuit, or at paracinema festivals, or at drive-in cinemas after their postwar glamour period had run its course." So, via Guins, we know that some of these Italian thrillers were screened in North America during this period at less-than-reputable venues. Again according to Dowler (1885, 18), "as far as I can gather from back issues of *Cinema Canada*, none of our *schlockmeisters* is a rabid film fan (I could be wrong about this; I don't know these guys personally and what I'm doing here is speculating), at least not the sort of junkie who's spent great chunks of his life sprawled in some three-for-a-dollar fleapit drinking it all in." Despite the limited release of Italian thrillers in North America, critics such as Dowler suggest that no one involved in the making of these Canadian slasher films ever watched any, despite the speculative nature of his conclusion.

Returning to Richard Nowell (2011, 59), he recognizes that the *giallo* film goes back to the early 1960s and continued right up to the late 1970s (and beyond), and therefore, audiences would be acclimatized to films wherein psychotic killers murder a bunch of beautiful people for their own, often, psychosexual needs. But Nowell also notes that the Motion Picture Association of America (MPAA), whose membership consists of the major (and a few minor) American studios and distribution companies, would often pick up Italian exploitation films (among others) for North American distribution. "For example, Dario Argento's giallo film *Quattro Mosche di Velluto Grigio* (1971) was released by Paramount as *Four Flies on Grey Velvet* and MGM had issued *La Tarantola dal Ventre nero* (1971) as *The Black Belly of the Tarantula*" (Nowell 2011, 66). Never mind questioning whether the Canadian slasher filmmakers watched *gialli* at the drive-in or urban grindhouse cinemas, the major studios were distributing Italian pick-ups across the continent. Film audiences had a better chance of watching a foreign import film (whether subtitled or dubbed) in the early 1970s during a period of low production "famine" (Nowell 2011, 69); demand for films outweighed the supply due to the major studios cutting back on production. And with international hits like Argento's *Bird with the Crystal Plumage* there was a certain demand for these horror-mystery hybrids: quoting Nowell again (2011, 130),

> On the back of Dario Argento's 1969 international hit *The Bird with the Crystal Plumage*, MPAA-members had imported Italian *giallo* films into the US to alleviate the production shortage of the early 1970s ... The *giallo* films were not hits in the US, but the production of American versions [of *giallo*-like films] ... suggests that they resonated deeply with some American filmmakers.

With Canadian filmmakers, too. What Nowell identifies as "American *giallo*" are mainstream studio pictures such as *Dressed to Kill* (Brian de Palma, 1980), *Cruising* (William Friedkin, 1980), and *The Eyes of Laura Mars* (Irvin Kershner, 1978), which "relocated the grisly murder-mysteries of Dario Argento and his contemporaries from urban Italian locations to the upper-middle-class neighbourhoods of New York City" (2011, 118). So, even if we cannot say with any certainty that *Prom Night* director Paul Lynch saw *The Bird with the Crystal Plumage,* or that *Terror Train*'s director, Roger Spottiswood, spent the 1970s sitting in the Toronto's Biltmore cinema, we can begin to look at the complexity of influences the *giallo* had on North American genre cinema in the late 1970s and early 1980s. Of course, this is not to suggest that the *giallo* was the only influence on the slasher film, but, as I hope to demonstrate now, the influences are sufficiently pronounced to call these films Canadian *gialli.*

But first, a note on the analyses: the discussions below textually examine the six key Canadian-made slasher films that most resemble the Italian *giallo*: *Prom Night, Terror Train, My Bloody Valentine, Happy Birthday to Me, Visiting Hours,* and *Curtains.* Each of these films will be looked at considering a list of typical *giallo* attributes: *testamone occulare,* the amateur detective, ineffectual police, sexualized murders, any discourse on modernity, sexualized trauma (of the killer), the black-gloved killer, the use of the I-camera, diverse methods of killing, gory set pieces, sequences of ratiocination, a range of suspects, and occasionally a fading Hollywood star. In much the same way that not all *gialli* feature all these aspects, some will be more relevant than others in the application to the slasher films. There will be spoilers.

Prom Night

Prom Night can be easily summarized as a killer, dressed all in black, is hunting the students at Hamilton High School's senior prom. But the film opens, indeed spends ten full minutes, six years in the past. Twins Robin (Tammy Bourne) and Alex Hammond (Dean Bosacki), and their older sister Kim (Debbie Greenfield), come across a group of schoolmates playing an extreme form of "hide and go-seek" called "Killer" in an old, abandoned building: the person who is "it" hunts down the others who are hiding, but once found, joins the killer in tracking down those yet to be discovered. Robin wants to join in on the game and runs off to play, while Kim continues home, and Alex vacillates about whether to follow Kim or Robin. The older kids playing the game team up against Robin and frighten her so badly she steps backwards and crashes through a window to her death. The other children swear never to talk about this tragedy to anyone. Jump ahead six years later, and the anniversary of Robin's death coincides with Hamilton High's senior prom, and those kids—Jude (Joy Thompson), Kelly (Mary Beth Rubens), Nick (Casey Stevens),[1] and Wendy (Anne-Marie Martin), the "leader" of this group—are getting ready for the big dance. Throughout the day, the teenagers responsible for Robin's death receive threatening phone calls asking them if they "can

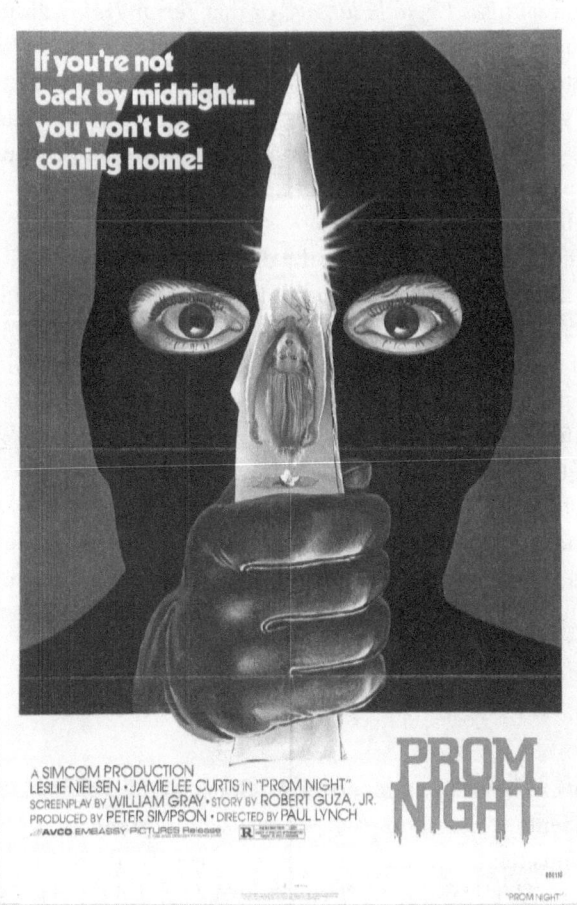

Figure 1. The *giallo*-influenced poster for *Prom Night* (Paul Lynch, 1980).

... come out to play tonight" and warning that "I'll see you at the prom." Of course, the killer is true to his word, and one by one murders the other teens.

While *Prom Night* maintains several motifs from *Halloween*—notably the teenage/high school age milieu and the casting of Jamie Lee Curtis in the lead role (as the teenaged Kim)—that suggest continuity with the emerging slasher film cycle, the film also features several *giallo*-like aspects. Most obvious, and illustrated by the film's original poster, is the costume of the killer: black balaclava, black turtle-neck top, black trousers, and most importantly, black gloves.

Of course, as Martin Rubin (and others) have pointed out, the killer's disguise is entirely "for the purpose of keeping the killer's identity hidden" (1999, 164). But otherwise, the film uses its formal construction to also keep the killer's identity a secret until the end. Vera Dika notes (1990, 89), "while Who is the killer? is the narrative question that supposedly dominates the film, the frameline has been used to mask the killer's identity, as does the skintight black suit and the face mask he wears." It is not that the killer is wearing a disguise that is important, but that the disguise is essential to maintain the whodunit format. In *Halloween* or *Friday the 13th*(s), and others of Rubin's "cipher format," once one encounters Michael or Jason (or Jason's mom), there is no respite before one is killed. The game, such as it is, is more often *where* is the killer? With these *giallo*-inspired films, as already noted, we are playing a more active game of *who* is the killer?

The killer's taunting phone calls to the teenagers also have *giallo*-esque qualities. In these sequences, we are presented with extreme close-up shots of the telephone cord, the phone, a(n ungloved) hand holding the receiver, and most threateningly, the pencil crossing off the names of Jude, Kelly, Nick, and Wendy, violently. The killer's voice is raspy and clearly disguised to further delay the revelation of the killer's identity. Caelum Vatnsdal dismisses any anxiety this sequence might have on an audience (2004, 139); noting that these calls are "less-than-frightening [and] . . . from an irritated mystery man with a whispery voice and a good supply of pencils, which he taps endlessly as he sibilates vaguely threatening messages." But when seen through the lens of the *giallo*, these sequences have a certain Argento-esque quality, given the Italian penchant for extreme close-ups in the killer's world, and the same purpose: to delay the revelation of the killer's identity.

It is the mystery element that most clearly aligns *Prom Night* to the *giallo*: the film's entire formal set up is to hide whodunit. We are given a variety of suspects as red herrings too: the killer might be Robin's still-grieving father (Leslie Nielsen), who also happens to be Hamilton High's principal, it could be the creepy school caretaker, Mr. Sykes (Robert Silverman), or it could be the escaped pedophile, Leonard Merch, who was wrongly convicted of murdering young Robin. Significantly, the Merch plot line is more expanded on in the television cut of the film, replacing some of the film's excised gore when originally broadcast on US television. By removing this aspect from the theatrical cut of the film, the whodunit aspect is diminished in favor of increasing the closer affinity with *Halloween* and thus the emergent slasher film. The differences between these two cuts of the film are suggestive: to be reinstated in the television cut of the film, those Merch-focused sequences would have been originally written, shot, and edited before being removed from the theatrical cut. This suggests the film's mystery components were more pronounced originally, and the film was cut back to be close to the style of the slasher before theatrical release. Interestingly, the police presence in the film is entirely focused on hunting down Leonard Merch, the red herring, and *giallo*-like, presents law enforcement as ineffectual.

The murders are sexualized insofar as Kelly was about to lose her virginity to Drew (Jeff Wincott), but decided not to at the last minute,[2] Jude and Slick (Sheldon Rybowski) are both killed after losing *their* virginities (and smoking some weed), and Wendy, it is suggested, lost her virginity long ago, and she is chased down by the killer with an axe. Significantly, neither Kim's nor Nick's virginity is ever questioned in the film, which may be why they survive. While the punishment-for-sex motif is rampant throughout slasher movies, and *Prom Night* makes that connection particularly clear, it is different only in degree to the *giallo*.

Despite the absence of any *testemone occulare*, or anyone occupying an amateur detective role (no one knows these murders are happening), and while the police, in hunting down the known pedophile, Merch, assume there to have been sexual trauma, *we* know Merch was not responsible for Robin's death. And except for Lou (David Mucci) getting decapitated with an axe and having his severed head roll out into the middle of the disco dance floor, the set pieces are weak. There is still sufficient connection to the *giallo* to see *Prom Night* as an extension and reinterpretation of these Italian thrillers.

The unmasking of the killer at the film's conclusion, the revelation that the killer has always been Alex Hammond (Michael Tough), is the epitome of the "Scooby-Doo" ending: had he not been dying, it stands to reason Alex would have cursed that he might have gotten away with his crimes if it were not for those kids.

Terror Train

Even by slasher standards, *Terror Train* is a minor film (see Harkness 1980). It opens with the past trauma sequence (as did *Prom Night*, and *Halloween* before that): Kenny Hampson (Derek McKinnon) is pledging the Sigma Phi fraternity, and as part of a prank, he is enticed into losing his virginity with Alana (Jamie Lee Curtis). Instead of Alana, however, Kenny slips into bed with a purloined cadaver from the Medical School; the shock of this sexually tinged trauma drives Kenny insane. As a result of the prank, fraternity parties have been banned on campus. Jumping ahead three years, and the soon-to-be graduating class have hired out an antique train as the venue for an elaborate New Year's fancy-dress party. Unbeknownst to the university students, Kenny Hampson has returned and is stalking the party, murdering those who partook of the prank years earlier. The device of the fancy-dress costume party means that Kenny can continually change his costume. As Vera Dika noted (1990, 97),

> because of the disguise element in *Terror Train*, Who is the killer? becomes the central question toward the end of the film. Although we know the killer's identity from the opening sequence, his changing use of costume and the length of time that has elapsed from the past event makes us unsure in our recognition of him.

Our chief suspect for "who is Kenny now?"—we barely see him clearly in the past trauma sequence—is the stage magician hired to entertain the kids (played by illusionist David Copperfield). Throughout the film, he has a flirtation with Alana: we see him staring at her (established through shot-reverse-shot editing), and she enjoys the attention. All of which echoes Kenny's unresolved feelings for Alana, particularly as it was her seduction which lured him into the prank to begin with. We discover, about halfway through the film, that Kenny was heavily into magic, and at one point, the magician's assistant refers to him as "Ken." The magician remains the film's chief suspect until he is murdered with a sword through the head in one of his magic tricks. We are led to conclude that not only is Kenny Hampson the killer (which is true), but that Kenny is the magician (which is false). The killer turns out to be the magician's assistant; as a member of the trans community, actor McKinnon can hide right under our noses because we are not looking for Kenny disguised as a woman.

While the revealed identity of Kenny Hampson and his/her ever-changing series of disguises underlines the murder-mystery elements of the narrative, murders on a train are a staple milieu for mystery novels and *giallo* films. Agatha Christie's *Murder on the Orient Express* (originally published in 1934) may be the template for this narrative, or its filmed version from 1974 (directed by Sidney Lumet); or, as I suggested in *La Dolce Morte* (2006, 17n5), there may be a connection to *Murder She Said* (George Pollock, 1961), based on Christie's *4:50 from Paddington* (1957). *Gialli* set on a train include *Night Train Murders* (Aldo Lado, 1975) and *Death Steps in the Dark* (Maurizio Pradeaux, 1977), both of which may have indirectly inspired *Terror Train*. While the setting and the game of "who is the killer?" underline this *giallo* connection, the film's diegetic timeline occurs over just one night, which makes the film more a slasher, than *giallo*.

Both Alana and the train's conductor, Carne (played by fading Hollywood veteran Ben Johnson), know something is amiss and play amateur detectives; the police absence is explained by being on a moving train. Carne comes across the bodies, but they disappear whenever he returns with others for confirmation, while Alana is the one who puts the pieces together fingering Kenny Hampson as the killer. While the murders are not particularly sexual, the trauma Kenny experienced certainly was. Both amateur detectives could have killed Kenny: Alana initially pushes him off the train, after stabbing him with a sword, but he holds on until Carne is able to smack him off the train with a shovel. Kenny plummets to his (presumed) death into an icy river, as so many *giallo* killers have before him.

Happy Birthday to Me

The plot to *Happy Birthday to Me* is intricate, and in this sense, is one of the most *giallo*-like of the Canadian produced slasher films. Adam Rockoff (2002, 114), for example, calls it "a complicated and confusing film." *Cinema Canada* published a brief report from the set of the film in 1981, noting that "no one from the press is permitted on set for fear a reporter will see and record something which could spoil the surprise for theater audiences. In fact, after roughly half the shooting, neither cast nor crew are aware of the identity of the killer, not even the killer him/herself" (Goldberg 1981, 6; see also Reiter 1981, 32). *Birthday* sees the "top ten" (a self-labeled clique of the elite) at Crawford Academy bumped off one by one in some highly original ways which evoke the set pieces in *gialli*.

The film opens in classic *giallo* style: Bernadette (Lesleh Donaldson) is attacked in her car by a black-gloved killer hiding in the back seat. While a chase ensues, she is killed with a straight razor across the throat.

Each murder is accomplished by diverse and creative means: Etienne (Michel-René Labelle) is garroted with his own scarf in the wheel of a motorcycle, Greg (Richard Rebiere) is crushed while weightlifting, and Steve (Matt Craven) is skewered with a shish kabob. All this mayhem appears to focus on Ginny (Melissa Sue Anderson), who is not only playing amateur detective, trying to figure out what is happening to her friends, but also reconstructing the past event trauma which saw her in hospital undergoing serious brain surgery. In Ginny trying to remember what happened to her, we can see, if not an explicit *testemone occulare*, then at least something similar: an attempt to visually express how the mind tries to reconstruct broken memories. These memories are clearly linked to the current spate of murders, but until Ginny can fully recall what happened to her, and the incidents surrounding her mother's death, neither we nor our protagonist will understand the connection. And while these past events are not explicitly sexualized, there is an

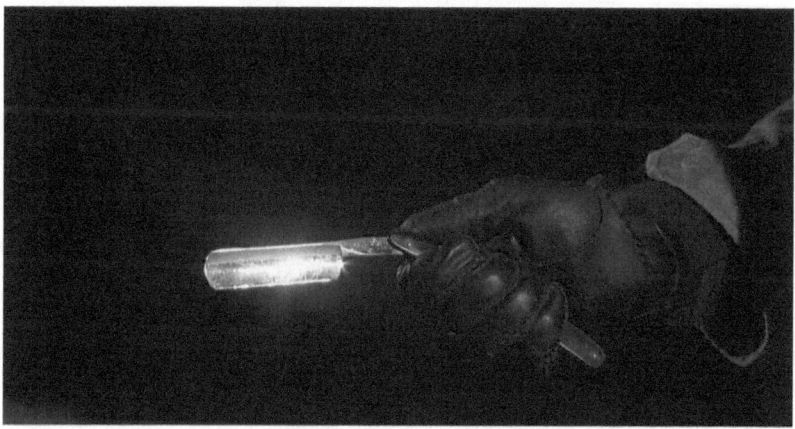

Figure 2. *Happy Birthday to Me* (J. Lee Thompson, 1981)—the *giallo*'s black-gloved killer.

underlying sexual motive: Ginny's mother, who was "from the wrong side of the tracks," had an affair with a married man and Ginny was the result. This also gives Ginny a previously unknown half-sister. But the actual cause of Ginny's mother's death, while related, was not directly causal with the affair.

Gialli based in elite private schools suggest films like *Suspiria* (Dario Argento, 1977), *What Have You Done to Solange? (Cosa avete fatto a Solange?*, Massimo Dallamano, 1972), or *The Young, the Evil and the Savage* (*Nude ... si muore*, Antonio Margheriti, 1968). And, in focusing on such a privileged milieu, *Birthday* resonates with the jet-setting, wealthy characters one often finds in the Italian thrillers. Ginny's mother (Sharon Acker) is characterized as a social climber, as someone who did not belong in the world which houses Crawford Academy, and by extension, that taint spread to Ginny herself, making her a suspect in these murders. While we "see" Ginny murder both Alfred (Jack Blum) and Steve, our own vision as audience is compromised by misdirection: Anne (Tracey Bregman), the film's actual killer and Ginny's half-sister, is wearing an elaborate rubber mask to resemble Ginny. But there is a plethora of other suspects throughout the film, including Ginny's father (Lawrence Dane), her psychiatrist (played by Hollywood veteran Glenn Ford), another of the "top ten," Rudi (David Eisner), and creepy Alfred, who is into such macabre hobbies as taxidermy (shades of Norman Bates) and special horror effects; we even see Alfred wearing the tell-tale black gloves of a *giallo* killer. And, while very few of these films include set pieces on the scale of an Argento or Fulci film, the final tableau in *Birthday*, of a grisly birthday party where all the accumulated corpses from the film are set up around a table, including a recently dug up Ginny's mom, plays with the kind of spectacle we often find in Italian genre cinema.

What these three films—*Prom Night*, *Terror Train*, and *Happy Birthday to Me*—have in common, among other things, is that they feature "young" people: either high school or university students. And while some *gialli* obviously do center on young student-types, many of them have more adult protagonists: professionals and other working folk, long past their carefree student days. Slasher films, on the other hand, tend to feature (and are marketed to) the late teen/early twenties audience. So, despite narrative and stylistic similarities with the *giallo*, one of the critical differences between these two types of horror films is the group of protagonists: slasher films are about the young while *gialli* tend to be about adults. However, the Canadian slasher films I am discussing here tend to focus on more adult protagonists rather than teenagers, and in the discussions which now follow, this focus on adult characters strengthens this claim that such films are indebted to the *giallo*.

My Bloody Valentine

To be sure, *My Bloody Valentine* is not the strongest *giallo*-inspired slasher movie under consideration here; however, as a murder mystery investigating who the actual killer might be, it nicely illustrates some of the differences and continuities between these two forms. Nowell identifies that *Valentine* resembles *Terror Train* to the extent that it was marketed specifically *as* a murder mystery that tried to capture a broader market share than a straight up horror movie might (2011, 231; see also Dowler, 1981, 67).

Twenty years earlier, in the town of Valentine Bluffs (filmed in Sydney Mines, Nova Scotia), a mine accident caused five miners to be trapped while the rest of the town celebrated Valentine's Day with a community dance. One miner, Harry Warden (Peter Cowper), survived for several weeks before being rescued by eating the other four. Warden, now clearly insane, was committed to the local asylum but escaped the following year, returned to Valentine Bluffs, and murdered anyone celebrating Valentine's Day in retribution for the mine accident. Legend has it that Harry Warden returns every year to ensure the town never celebrates another Valentine's Day. Twenty years later, Valentine Bluffs is about to celebrate its first Valentine's Day dance in two decades when it appears that Warden has returned and begins killing off the residents. As far as the police are concerned, Warden is the logical suspect, but eventually they discover that he has been dead for the past five years. Another suspect is T. J. (Paul Kelman), a local miner who tried his luck "out west" but has returned in disgrace trying to pick up his old life and his old girlfriend, Sarah (Lori Hallier), who is now seeing someone else. This new

"Harry Warden" turns out to be fellow miner, Axel (Neil Affleck), Sarah's new beau: as a child, he saw Warden murder his father, which scarred him for life. The significant aspect is that, when not disguised in his full mining gear as "Harry Warden," Axel is the likable work colleague, a controlling boyfriend to Sarah, and the love rival for T. J.; unlike the real Warden, Axel is never the crazed lunatic miner all the time.

While the past trauma is not a sexual one,[3] the film opens with two miners deep underground. One miner strips down and is revealed to be a beautiful woman in her underwear under the protective boiler suit (Pat Hemingway) who has a heart-shaped tattoo over her heart. She suggestively fondles her lover's protective gear, including the air hose on his face mask. The still-disguised miner (who is presumably male) impales her on a pickaxe right through the heart (both literally and through her tattoo). It is never explained whether this sequence is in the past during Warden's initial rampage or is somehow and in some way part of the current rampage (although I would be hard pressed to find a young woman in a rural mining town with a heart tattoo on her chest in 1961). So, while the original trauma is not a sexual one, a sexualized murder is part of the story. Axel, as the new "Warden," can stalk and kill those others who go off on their own to make love away from the pack of the others partying in the mine.

While much of the cast are "young," none of them are "kids"; these are twenty-somethings in the working world, not at school or university. *Valentine* is also noteworthy in this respect in featuring an entirely working-class setting and characters. Modernity is addressed not only in the lax sexual mores of the young people, but also in T. J. looking for work outside of the community he was born into. And, at least while T. J. is suspected of committing the murders (for us, playing the game of "whodunit," not necessarily diegetically), we never find out what happened to him "out west"; the world outside of Valentine Bluffs may have corrupted him into becoming a killer. And in this regard, modernity—here recognized as young people moving away from the community for better work opportunities—is deeply suspicious.

Richard Nowell's *Blood Money* paints a vivid picture of the business concerns effecting the release of these slasher movies. In particular, he outlines how mainstream Hollywood films like *Cruising* or *Dressed to Kill* were heavily criticized for their misogyny and violence, and that such criticism caused a backlash against the violence in the slasher film. "Misogynistic films were highly susceptible to the X-rating, the receipt of which would have made the negotiation of an MPAA-member distribution deal all but impossible and left the filmmakers facing the distinct prospect of incurring substantial financial loses" (Nowell 2011, 221). The upshot of which is that Paramount, the studio that picked up the distribution deal on *Valentine*, heavily cut back some of the gorier moments in the film. More recently, some of the previously cut footage has been restored to the print of the film, and the two versions are worth comparing. While the almost blood-less theatrical release of the film forgoes the horror spectacles in favor of telling its story as quickly as it can, the "director's cut" of the film reinstates the spectacle of the murders. Because the overall flow of the film is interrupted for gory spectacle in this new cut of the film, these moments work like set pieces in the Italian films: moments where the camera lingers on the destruction of the human body longer than is necessary for its narrative purpose.

Curtains

The only explicit production connection to the Italian thrillers is a movie Andrew Dowler calls (1985, 17) "a film so bad that they gave the director's credit to one of the characters (an inept and repulsive director played by John Vernon)," *Curtains* (Jonathan Stryker [Richard Ciupka], 1983) (see also Dowler, 1984, 33). Due to interference by the producer, the film's original director took his name off the film, and rather than use the industry standard "Alan Smithee," chose to give directing credit to the fictional Stryker. As for the connection to the *giallo*, actress Lesleh Donaldson, who plays the figure skater Christie in the film, noted in an interview with James Burrell for the Canadian horror magazine *Rue Morgue*, "Richard wanted it [*Curtains*] to be very artistic, *giallo*-like and European" in opposition to what producer Peter Simpson (who produced *Prom Night*) wanted: another slasher film (Burrell, 2015, 73). This *giallo* connection was also noted by Jim Harper, who commented that "the murders themselves are a nod to the *gialli* rather than *Friday the 13th*" (2004, 77).

Curtains opens with actress Samantha Sherwood (Samantha Eggar) committed to an asylum by her lover and director, Jonathan Stryker (Vernon). While ostensibly this committal is research for a role, Stryker abandons Sherwood in the asylum while he tries to recast the role with a younger actress. As an audition process, Stryker and his six ingénues relocate to a country house as the actresses vie for the role. Sherwood escapes from the asylum bent on revenge. A killer begins knocking off the competition, dressed in a hag-mask and black (*giallo*) gloves. While most of the evidence points towards Sherwood as the film's obvious killer, including a cut from Sherwood to the hag-mask in a suitcase, and then to a black-gloved hand taking down a sickle and sharpening it, this immediately precedes Christie being killed

Figure 3. The Bava-inspired use of color in *Curtains* (Richard Ciupka, 1983).

with the sickle while skating. All such editing points towards the conclusion that Sherwood is the killer, until she is murdered by the film's actual killer, Patti (Lynne Griffin).

Ironically, in the sequence which most evokes the *giallo*, the killer chases Tara (Sandee Currie) through a props store, the lighting casts pools of distinct color, thereby suggesting some of Mario Bava's work, but this was *not* directed by Ciupka, despite Donaldson's comment that he wanted it to be *giallo*-like: "that whole prop house chase scene, isn't mine, either" (quoted in Burrell, 2015, 73).

In an "in progress" report from the set of *Curtains*, Thérèse Beaupré (1981, 43) notes that "with a background in cinematography, Ciupka is obviously sensitive to the visual aspects of the film." So who knows? Perhaps the lighting in the sequence *was* Ciupka's, but as the sequence continues into a more traditional slasher film set-up, *that* is what Ciupka denies is his. In any case, this is pure speculation on my part.

Visiting Hours

Visiting Hours is the only film under consideration here to appear on the British Department of Public Prosecution's notorious "video nasty" list, and therefore, has always had something of an unsavory reputation. And it is this reputation which underlines my claim that *Visiting Hours* is the most *giallo*-like of the slasher films produced in Canada. Rarely is *Visiting Hours* even considered a "slasher" film, despite Kate Egan quoting Alexander Walker in the British *Evening Standard* newspaper identifying the film as the epitome of the label (Egan, 2007, 31). Richard Nowell, for example, calls it a "violent adult-centered thriller" (2011, 241), and Anna Fudakowska calls it "a fresh variation on the psychodrama theme" (1980, 6). Both of which suggest a more *giallo*-inflected narrative than a slasher horror movie.

Typical of the *giallo*, the film's plot is labyrinthian: Deborah Ballin (Lee Grant) is a crusading television journalist who is publicly defending a case of self-defense against an abusive spouse. Her position provokes a dangerous misogynist, Cole Hawker (Michael Ironside), to attack her in her home. Ballin survives the attack, and while recovering in hospital, Hawker tries to finish the job as she can identify him to the police. Hawker is a vicious sociopath and killer of (predominantly) older women; he photographs his victims in the act of raping and murdering them and has built himself a small shrine in the closet at his apartment. He has some kind of strange relationship with his older landlady, and sends racist and abusive letters to the press and judiciary. His mother abandoned him, and he grew up with his abusive father. All of this points to a portrait of a deeply disturbed individual. In his attempt to finish off Ballin, he accidentally murders the wrong patient (Ballin had changed rooms); as he sneaks out of the hospital, he has an exchange of looks with a protective young nurse, Sheila Munroe (Linda Purl). It does not take much for Munroe to make the connection between the woman murdered in Ballin's old room and the man she saw slipping out: both she and Ballin try to recall enough information about Hawker to aid the police (*testemone occulare*, by any definition). Hawker take his frustrations out on a young woman he picks up in a coffee shop, Lisa (Lenore Zann); but she too gets away from him, though not before she has been savagely beaten. Three women can now identify Hawker, and they effectively join forces to stop this maniac.

While Hawker does rack up a significant body count, without any disguise, there is no ambiguity as to the killer's identity. By 1982, Michael Ironside was a sufficiently identifiable screen presence, at least since David Cronenberg's *Scanners* (1980), so there is sufficient facial recognition for the film's audience. While Ballin is incapacitated in hospital, it is up to Munroe to be the film's amateur detective, assisted by Lisa. Lisa discovers Hawker's sick shrine when she returns to his apartment to trash it. The police are useless and dismiss Ballin's and Munroe's accounts as hysterical and paranoid, further challenging the legitimacy of what they saw. The police's attitude towards the women eyewitnesses underlines the film's reflection of societal misogyny; Hawker's violence against women is merely an extreme form of how society continually undermines women's voices and experiences. In the Janet Macklin case that Ballin is so outspoken about, the evidence is clear that had anyone paid attention to the evidence of domestic abuse, she would not be on trial for her husband's murder.

Visiting Hours is a veritable checklist of *giallo* attributes: we have the *testemone occulare* of Ballin, Munroe, and Lisa; Munroe and Lisa acting in the roles of amateur detectives; ineffectual police; a series of sexualized murders; reflections on modern society (particularly as it effects women); moments of subjective camera positions while Hawker stalks his victims—the so-called "killer-cam" shots; the processes of ratiocination as Ballin and Munroe, and Munroe and Lisa, try to figure out how to track down Hawker; and while I have mentioned Lee Grant playing Deborah Ballin, her former partner and TV producer, Gary Baylor, is played by "fading Hollywood legend" William Shatner.[4] Missing from seeing *Visiting Hours* as a classic *giallo* are the black gloves and disguise of the killer, a range of suspects, or diverse methods of killing. But thematically, and stylistically, the similarities are sufficient to see the connection.

Conclusions

Kate Egan, in her book *Trash or Treasure?* (2007), visits a concept which lies at the heart of this current project and my approach in the comparison between the *giallo* and the slasher film. In her book, she notes (31),

> Such an approach, in Dick Hebdige's terms, can be conceived as a "fixing of a chain of associations," where a new strain of horror is identified fashionable and commercial and thus, regardless of its actual national origins, is perceived by critics as emerging from America (the "paradigm" of consumerism and the traditionless).

In this regard, while the slasher films discussed herein may disguise their Canadian national origins as a generic "America," so too did the Italian *giallo*, particularly as they circulated in internationally dubbed versions. To a grindhouse or drive-in audience, watching a horror film from anywhere fixes that "chain of associations" in such a way as it all becomes "American," and therefore indistinguishable from one another. The *giallo* films circulated throughout North American through the 1970s in forms that only a discerning cineaste might distinguish its national origins.

While Lesleh Donaldson is the only industry person to even name-drop the *giallo*, there are sufficient connections between the Italian thrillers and the

Canadian-made slasher films. From black-gloved killers to the controversial sexualized murders, from incompetent police officers to the emergence of amateur detectives, and from subjective "killer-cam" cinematography to fading Hollywood stars and directors, all of these films also function as discourse on contemporary social issues, including feminism, unemployment, childish pranks, and childish behavior. And, of course, simply by being murder mysteries, these films are *gialli* by definition.

Notes

1. He is Kim's date for the prom.
2. I think, in this light, it is significant that Drew is not killed, only Kelly is.
3. One might be able to make the psychoanalytic case that, in *seeing* Warden murder his father, Axel is somehow channeling the Oedipal guilt that Warden did what Axel could only desire and therefore subconsciously represses his own identification with the killer.
4. Although Shatner is, in fact, Canadian.

Works Cited

Balanzategui, Jessica. 2015. "Crises of Identification in the Supernatural Slasher: The Resurrection of the Supernatural Slasher Villain." In *Style and Form in the Hollywood Slasher Film*, edited by Wickham Clayton, 161–79. Basingstoke: Palgrave Macmillan.

Beard, William, and Jerry White, eds. 2002. *North of Everything: English-Language Cinema Since 1980*. Edmonton: University of Alberta Press.

Beaupré, Thérèse. 1981. "In Progress: *Curtains*." *Cinema Canada*, no. 73 (April): 43.

Burrell, James. 2015. *Rue Morgue Magazine's Horrorwood North: The Extraordinary History and Art of Canadian Genre Cinema*. Toronto: Marrs Media.

Clayton, Wickham. 2015. "Introduction: The Collection Awakes." In *Style and Form in the Hollywood Slasher Film*, edited by Wickham Clayton, 1–14. Basingstoke: Palgrave Macmillan.

Conrich, Ian. 2015. "Puzzles, Contraptions and the Highly Elaborate Moment: The Inevitability of Death in the Grand Slasher Narratives of the *Final Destination* and *Saw* Series of Films." In *Style and Form in the Hollywood Slasher Film*, edited by Wickham Clayton, 106–17. Basingstoke: Palgrave Macmillan.

Constantineau, Sara. 2010. "*Black Christmas*: The Slasher Film was Made in Canada." *Cineaction*, no. 82 (January): 58–63.

Dika, Vera. 1990. *Games of Terror: Halloween, Friday the 13th, and the Films of the Stalker Cycle*. Rutherford: Fairleigh Dickinson University Press.

Dowler, Andrew. 1981. "George Mihalka's *My Bloody Valentine*." *Cinema Canada*, no. 74 (May): 67.

Dowler, Andrew. 1984. "'Jonathan Stryker's' *Curtains*." *Cinema Canada*, no. 113 (December): 33.

Dowler, Andrew. 1985. "Canadian Gothic, Eh? A Glib Overview of Current Schlock." *Cinema Canada*, no. 123 (October): 16–18.

Egan, Kate. 2007. *Trash or Treasure? Censoring and Changing Meanings of the Video Nasties*. Manchester: Manchester University Press.

Elder, R. Bruce. 1989. *Image and Identity: Reflections on Canadian Film and Culture*. Waterloo: Wilfred Laurier University Press.

Fudakowska, Anna. 1980. "In Progress: *The Fright*." *Cinema Canada* 69 (January-February): 5–6.

Gittings, Christopher E. 2002. *Canadian National Cinema*. London: Routledge.

Goldberg, Howard. 1981. "In Progress: *Happy Birthday to Me*." *Cinema Canada*, no. 68 (September): 6–7.

Guins, Raiford. 2005. "Blood and Black Glovers on Shiny Discs: New Media, Old Tastes, and the Remediation of Italian Horror Films in the United States." In *Horror International*, edited by Steven Jay Schneider and Tony Williams, 15–32. Detroit: Wayne State University Press.

Harkness, John. 1980. "Roger Spottiswoode's *Terror Train*." *Cinema Canada*, no. 70 (December): 34–35.

Harkness, John. 1982. "Jean-Claude Lord's *Visiting Hours*." *Cinema Canada*, no. 86 (July): 27.

Harper, Jim. 2004. *Legacy of Blood: A Comprehensive Guide to Slasher Movies*. Manchester: Headpress/Critical Vision.

Koven, Mikel J. 2003. "The Terror Tale: Urban Legends and the slasher film." *Scope: An On-line Journal of Film Studies*, May. https://www.nottingham.ac.uk/scope/documents/2003/may-2003/koven.pdf.

Koven, Mikel J. 2006. *La Dolce Morte: Vernacular Cinema and the Italian Giallo Film*. Lanham, MD: Scarecrow Press.

Newman, Kim. 1988. *Nightmare Movies: A Critical History of the Horror Film, 1968–88*, 2nd ed. London: Bloomsbury.

Nowell, Richard. 2011. *Blood Money: A History of the First Teen Slasher Film Cycle*. New York: Continuum.

Pednekar, Manjunath. 1985. "Economic Relations Between Selected Canadian Film Producers and American Major Distributors: Implications for Canada's National Film Policy." *Canadian Journal of Communication* 11, no. 2 (Spring): 149–79.

Reiter, Anne. 1981. "J. Lee Thompson's *Happy Birthday to Me*." *Cinema Canada*, no. 75 (July): 32.

Roche, David. 2015. "(In)Stability of Point of View in *When a Stranger Calls* and *Eyes of a Stranger*." In *Style and Form in the Hollywood Slasher Film*, edited by Wickham Clayton, 17–36. Basingstoke: Palgrave Macmillan.

Rockoff, Adam. 2002. *Going to Pieces: The Rise and Fall of the Slasher Film, 1978–1986*. Jefferson, NC: McFarland and Company.

Rubin, Martin. 1999. *Thrillers*. Cambridge. Cambridge University Press.

Vatnsdal, Caelum. 2004. *They Came from Within: A History of Canadian Horror Cinema*. Winnipeg: Arbeiter Ring Publishing.

Young, Suzie. 2005. "Snapping Up Schoolgirls: Legitimation Crisis in Recent Canadian Horror." In *Horror International*, edited by Steven Jay Schneider and Tony Williams, 235–56. Detroit: Wayne State University Press.

ABOUT THE CONTRIBUTORS

Donald L. Anderson has a PhD from the University of Washington. He currently teaches writing, literature, and film studies at Mt. Hood Community College outside of Portland, Oregon. His publications include a recent chapter on *Twin Peaks: The Return* in the anthology *Make America Hate Again: Trump-era Horror and the Politics of Fear* (Routledge). Other articles have appeared in *Horror Studies*, *Situations*, *Gothic Studies*, and *Studies in the Fantastic*. He is the former lead guitarist of the heavy metal band Agalloch who recorded and toured for twenty years and now writes progressive metal under the band named Sculptured.

Brian Brems is professor of English at the College of DuPage. His academic work on cinema is varied, with numerous chapters appearing in edited collections. He is coeditor of *ReFocus: The Films of Paul Schrader* (2020), and he publishes regularly in online film magazines and websites, including *Bright Wall/Dark Room*, *Vague Visages*, and *Film Inquiry*. He has also contributed to *Film School Rejects* and *Little White Lies*.

Eric Brinkman has a master's degree from the Shakespeare Institute and a PhD from the Ohio State University's Department of Theatre, Film, and Media Arts. His current research focuses on how the affect generated by the performances of female actors shapes the reception of theatre and film productions. He also has a forthcoming book chapter on genderfluid Shakespeare and a journal article on how the character of Iago in productions of *Othello* functions as a scapegoat for white racial anxieties. He currently works as an instructional consultant for the Michael V. Drake Institute for Teaching and Learning.

Matthew Edwards is author and editor of many books on cult/horror cinema, including *The Atomic Bomb in Japanese Cinema* (2015), *Klaus Kinski, Beast of Cinema* (2016), and *Twisted Visions: Interviews with Horror Filmmakers* (2017), *The Rwandan Genocide on Film* (2018), and *Murder Movie Makers: Directors Discuss their Killer Flicks* (2020). He has also contributed booklet notes for 88 Films releases, including *Schizoid*, *Disciples of Shaolin*, and *Robotrix* and written extensively on Hong Kong/world cinema for various books and magazines.

Brenda S. Gardenour Walter holds a PhD in medieval history from Boston University. Her research areas include medievalism in dark popular culture, kink studies, and the intersections between the human body, architecture, and the environment in the Anthropocene. She was professor of History at the Saint Louis College of Pharmacy, where she taught classes in cultural competency and global health. She has worked with non-governmental organizations to serve communities in Honduras and Haiti, and is now a full-time horticulturalist for Forest Park Forever, an urban nonprofit serving Saint Louis, Missouri.

Andrew Grossman is editor and coauthor of the anthology *Queer Asian Cinema: Shadows in the Shade*, an editor of and contributor to *Bright Lights Film Journal*, and a columnist for *Popmatters.com*. He has contributed book chapters to numerous anthologies, including *24 Frames: Korea and Japan*; *New Korean Cinema*; *Chinese Connections: Critical Perspectives on Film, Identity, and Diaspora*; *Film and Literary Modernism*; *Directory of World Cinema: China, Vol. 2*; *Asexualities: Queer and Feminist Perspectives*; *Transnational Chinese Cinema: Corporeality, Desire, and the Ethics of Failure*; *Movies in the Age of Obama*; *Hong Kong Horror Cinema*; *100 Years of Soviet Cinema*; and *The Routledge Handbook of Male Sex Work*. He also produced and directed a feature documentary, *Not That Kind of Christian!!*, which was featured at the 2007 Montreal World Film Festival.

Lisa Haegele, Phd, is assistant professor of German at Texas State University. Her research focuses on German, Austrian, and Swiss cinema from the postwar period to the present, with a special focus on genre films. She has published her work in various edited volumes, including *Berlin School Glossary: An ABC of the New Wave in German Cinema* (Intellect, 2013), *The Berlin School and Its Global Contexts: A Transnational Art Cinema* (Wayne State University Press, 2018), *Celluloid Revolt: German Screen Cultures and the Long 1968* (Camden House, 2019), *Cold War Spy Stories from Eastern Europe*

(University of Nebraska Press, 2019), *German #MeToo* (Camden House, 2022), and in a special issue of the peer-reviewed journal *The Sixties: A Journal of History, Politics, and Culture* (2017). She received a Berlin Program Fellowship for Advanced German and European Studies in 2010/2011. She is currently working on her book project "From Pop to Punk: West German Genre Films in the Long 1968," which explores long-forgotten genre films in West Germany from the late 1960s to the early 1980s.

Gavin F. Hurley, PhD, is assistant professor of composition and director of the writing program at Ave Maria University in Florida, where he teaches writing, rhetoric, journalism, and supernatural literature. His scholarship has appeared in academic journals such as *Journal for the History of Rhetoric*, *Horror Studies*, *Journal of Communication and Religion*, and *Metal Music Studies*. He has published on the rhetoric of horror fiction in essay collections such as *Virtual Dark Tourism: Ghost Roads* (Palgrave, 2018), The Spaces and Places of Horror (Vernon, 2019), and *Horror Literature from Gothic to Post-Modern: Critical Essays* (McFarland and Company, 2020). Dr. Hurley is a member of the Rhetoric Society of America and the Horror Writer's Association.

Mikel J. Koven is senior lecturer and course leader for film studies at the University of Worcester. He has written extensively on all manner of exploitation cinema and the relationship between film and folklore studies. He is the author of *La Dolce Morte: Vernacular Cinema and the Italian Giallo Film* (2006), *Film, Folklore and Urban Legends* (2008), and *Blaxploitation Films* (2010).

Sharon Jane Mee, PhD, is adjunct lecturer in film studies at the University of New South Wales, Australia. Her recent book is *The Pulse in Cinema: The Aesthetics of Horror* (Edinburgh University Press, 2020) and she is coeditor of the collection *Sound Affects: A User's Guide* (Bloomsbury, forthcoming). She has published in journals *Screening the Past*, *SubStance*, and *Film-Philosophy*, among others. Her research interests include poststructuralism and biopolitics; the sensory and sensuous cinematic experience; rhythm, movement, and affect in early cinema and horror cinema; and aesthetics and ethics.

Fernando Gabriel Pagnoni Berns (PhD in Arts, PhD candidate in History) works as professor at the Universidad de Buenos Aires (UBA), Facultad de Filosofía y Letras (Argentina). He teaches courses on international horror film. He is director of the research group on horror cinema "Grite" and has published chapters in the books *To See the Saw Movies: Essays on Torture Porn and Post 9/11 Horror*, edited by John Wallis; *Critical Insights: Alfred Hitchcock*, edited by Douglas Cunningham; *Dreamscapes in Italian Cinema*, edited by Francesco Pascuzzi; *Gender and Environment in Science Fiction*, edited by Christy Tidwell; and *Doubles and Hybrids in Latin American Gothic*, edited by Antonio Alcalá (Routledge); among others. He has authored a book about Spanish horror TV series *Historias para no Dormir* (Universidad de Cádiz, 2020) and has edited a book on Frankenstein bicentennial (Universidad de Buenos Aires) and one on director James Wan (McFarland and Company, 2021). He is currently editing a book on horror comics for Routledge.

Émilie von Garan is a Toronto-based critical writer and researcher exploring the intersection of the body, technology, and architecture in film and moving image art. She received her bachelor of arts from Concordia University in Montreal and holds a master of Arts from Toronto's OCAD University. She is now a PhD candidate in Film Studies at the University of Toronto. Her interests include continental philosophy, horror theory, art criticism, and the ways in which art and horror share aesthetic, structural, and conceptual strategies. Her dissertation explores the instability of the gaze in postwar Italian cinema through the works of filmmakers Michelangelo Antonioni and Dario Argento.

Connor John Warden is a research student in history in Oxford Brookes University. He is a Catholic academic, specializing in twentieth-century church history and the sociology of religion. He is based at HPC, Oxford Brookes. He is an alumnus of St Edmund Hall, Oxford.

Sean Woodard is a doctoral student in English at the University of Texas at Arlington. He also serves as film editor for *Drunk Monkeys*, which houses his "Finding the Sacred Among the Profane" and "The Magic of Film Scoring" columns. He has contributed book chapters to forthcoming edited anthologies. He has also presented conference papers on horror and *giallo* cinema, fairy tales, and film scoring. His film criticism, fiction, and other writing has been featured in *Los Angeles Review of Books*, *South Broadway Ghost Society*, *NonBinary Review*, *Horrorbuzz*, and *Los Angeles Magazine*, among other publications.

INDEX

Abrakadabra, 3
adaptation, 9, 164, 201–2, 214
Ai sha (Love Massacre), 148, 152, 154–56
Alice, Sweet Alice, 9, 216, 220–22, 225, 229
Almodóvar, Pedro, 209–10, 214
Altman, Robert, 14
Amer, 7, 104, 165, 184
American *giallo*, 9, 216–17, 220, 223, 234, 236–37, 239–43, 248–49, 256
anime, 166, 168, 178
architecture, 4, 9, 33, 36, 39, 41, 43, 45, 62, 183, 186, 194–96, 216–19, 221–23, 225–26
Argentina, 3–4
Argento, Dario, 3–4, 6–9, 15–19, 31–37, 40–45, 52, 69, 84, 106, 130, 144–46, 151, 157–58, 162n2, 162n8, 162n12, 164–66, 169, 174–76, 185–88, 196, 199–207, 211–14, 234, 236–37, 252, 255–56, 259, 263
art film, 52, 62, 64, 68–69, 200, 203–4
Artaud, Antonin, 154–56

Bartel, Paul, 216, 223
Baudrillard, Jean, 64, 85
Bava, Lamberto, 22–23, 145, 237
Bava, Mario, 5–6, 15–17, 19, 23–25, 30–31, 40–43, 55, 68–69, 84, 99, 102, 106, 108, 117–19n2, 146, 149, 166, 169, 188, 205, 207, 209, 233–34, 253, 267
Bhabha, Homi, 31
Bianchi, Andrea, 15, 23–26

Bido, Antonio, 8, 129–37
Birds, The, 16
"Black Cat, The" (short story), 21
Black Christmas, 254
Body Double, 9, 234, 235–46, 248–49
Bolkan, Florinda, 108–9
Bouchet, Barbara, 8, 99, 103, 105–19, 187
Brown, Fredric, 201–2, 213

Canadian horror film, 255, 266
capitalism, 49, 52, 55–56, 60, 70, 141, 159, 161, 234
Cattet, Hélène, 7–8, 104, 183–87, 189, 194, 197
Cavara, Paolo, 107, 187
Chi l'ha vista morire? (Who Saw Her Die?), 20
Christie, Agatha, 40–43, 143–44, 166, 253, 262
Clover, Carol, 27, 177, 208, 222
colonialism, 36, 43, 45n6, 76
Cosa avete fatto a Solange? (What Have You Done to Solange?), 22, 69, 263
Creed, Barbara, 174, 180n5, 223
Cruising, 22, 255, 265
Curtains, 252, 257, 266–67

Dallamano, Massimo, 22, 69, 142, 262
De Palma, Brian, 22, 158, 234, 245–46, 249, 256
Del Toro, Guillermo, 165

Deleuze, Gilles, 110, 182–83, 188–94, 197n1, 197n2
Dian zhi bing bing (Cops and Robbers), 146, 149–50
Dressed to Kill, 22, 158, 256, 265

Ecologia del delitto (Bay of Blood), 55, 146, 188–89
economic miracle, 54–55, 61
Ercoli, Luciano, 21, 84–85, 89, 92–93, 95–96, 99, 106
Euro-horror, 122, 199–200, 208
Eyes of Laura Mars, The, 9, 216–17, 220, 226, 228–29, 235, 256

fascism, 55–56, 63, 68, 188–89
Fassbinder, Rainer Werner, 70, 72, 146
female body, 219
Filone, 4, 6, 15–16, 23, 51–52, 54, 61, 65, 81, 167, 169, 179, 252
"Final Girl," 165–66, 177–78
5 bambole per la luna d'agosto (Five Dolls for the August Moon), 40
Forzani, Bruno, 184
Foto de Gioia (Delirium), 145
4 mosche di velluto grigio (Four Flies on Grey Velvet), 5, 144, 186, 256
Francesca, 3
Franco, Jesús, 7, 67–68, 71–72, 75, 81–82, 106, 194, 203, 208
Freud, Sigmund, 144–45, 149–50
Friday the 13th (franchise), 253, 259, 266
Fulci, Lucio, 61, 69, 103, 105–7, 109, 113, 145, 165, 176, 187, 194, 203, 234, 243, 263
Fung gip (The Secret), 148, 152–53, 156

Gatti rossi in un labirinto di vetro (Eyeball), 5, 109
Godard, Jean-Luc, 50–51, 61
González, Yann, 7, 9, 200–201, 204–5, 208–10
Grindhouse, 3, 216, 234, 256, 269
Gritos en la noche (The Awful Dr. Orlof), 68
grotesque, the, 35, 131, 171, 220

Hai shi chu shi (The Red Panther), 142, 148, 151, 156–57, 159
Halloween, 154, 252–55, 258–60
Happy Birthday to Me, 251, 257, 262, 264
Hitchcock, Alfred, 13, 15–17, 26, 28, 144, 164, 170, 179n2, 206, 209, 233, 236, 243
Holmes, Sherlock, 30, 144, 160
homoerotic themes, 153, 201, 214
homophobia, 202, 213
Hong Kong cinema, 8, 141–42, 146, 149, 160–62

Kon, Satoshi, 164–65, 168–71, 178–79n2
Krimi films, 4, 69

I corpi presentano trace di violenza carnale (Torso), 103, 145–46
Il gatto dagli occhi di giada (Watch Me When I Kill), 129–37
Il tuo vizio è una stanza chiusa e solo io ne ho la chiave (Your Vice Is a Locked Room and Only I Have the Key), 5, 20, 106
Inferno, 196
Italian communism, 53

La casa con la scala nel buio (A Blade in the Dark), 6, 22–23, 145, 147
La dama rossa uccide sette volte (The Red Queen Kills Seven Times), 107
La morte ha fatto l'uovo (Death Laid an Egg), 7, 49–50, 52, 54–56, 58, 61–65
La polizia chiede aiuto (What Have They Done to Your Daughters?), 103, 142
La ragazza che sapeva troppo (The Girl Who Knew Too Much), 6, 30–31, 68, 117, 166, 205
La tarantola dal ventre nero (The Black Belly of the Tarantula), 107, 187, 256
La terza madre (Mother of Tears), 196
Lado, Aldo, 20, 23, 106, 187, 261
Le foto proibite di una signora per bene (The Forbidden Photos of a Lady above Suspicion), 8, 21–22, 84–86, 89–91, 96–100, 106

Lenzi, Umberto, 5, 109, 166
L'étrange couleur des larmes de ton corps (The Strange Color of Your Body's Tears), 8, 183, 185–86
Lo strano vizio della Signora Wardh (The Strange Vice of Mrs. Wardh), 15, 84, 184, 187
L'uccello dalle piume di cristallo (The Bird with the Crystal Plumage), 3, 5–7, 9, 16, 31–32, 35, 37–41, 44–45, 52, 69, 84, 103, 169, 175, 187, 199–201
Lyotard, Jean-François, 36–37

Martino, Sergio, 15, 20–21, 23, 69, 84, 106, 145, 166, 184, 186–87, 194
melodrama, 151, 154, 201, 203, 205, 209–11, 214
menstrual blood, 188, 197, 220
Milano calibro 9 (Caliber 9), 105
misogyny, 28, 150, 173, 176, 202, 222, 227, 265, 268
modern city, 32, 43
Mulvey, Laura, 27–28, 206, 227

Nazism, 55–56, 107
Neon Demon, The, 9, 234–43, 245–49
Nicolodi, Daria, 41, 106
Night Caller, 142, 148, 150–51, 158
Night of the Living Dead, 48
Non si sevizia un paperino (Don't Torture a Duckling), 103, 105–7, 109, 112–13, 116, 118–19, 145, 187, 203
Nude per l'assassino (Strip Nude for Your Killer), 15, 19, 23, 26–28, 103

Oedipal theme, 150, 153, 203, 270n3
Onetti, Luciano, 3–4

Pâfekuto burû (Perfect Blue), 8, 164–66, 169–70, 172, 174–79
Paroxismus (Venus in Furs), 68, 75, 80
Perche' quelle strane gocce di sangue sul corpo di Jennifer? (The Case of the Bloody Iris), 5, 84, 187

Poe, Edgar Allan, 21, 146, 166, 176
poliziottesco film, 105, 107, 142, 147–49
pornography, 118, 170, 172, 174–75, 200, 203–8, 210–14, 224, 242, 244–46, 248
postcolonial theory, 31–32, 43, 141
Private Parts, 9, 216, 220, 223, 225, 229
Profondo rosso (Deep Red), 103, 144–47, 186, 205, 255
Prom Night, 251, 253, 256–60, 264, 266
Psycho, 13–17, 23, 25–26, 144, 170

queer themes, 200–203, 206–11, 213–14, 224–26
Questi, Giulio, 49–56, 58, 60–64

Rear Window, 17, 206
Red Brigades, 56–57
Refn, Nicolas Winding, 9, 234, 236–37, 249
Romero, George, 48, 56
rural *giallo*, 61

Sartre, Jean-Paul, 86–87
Scavolini, Romano, 8, 122–28
scopophilia, 35, 162n4
Screaming Mimi, The (book), 40, 201
Screaming Mimi, The (film), 201–2
Sei donne per l'assassino (Blood and Black Lace), 6, 16, 18–19, 22–23, 55, 68–69, 99–100, 103, 108, 209
Sette note in nero (The Psychic), 165, 176, 179n1
sexploitation, 5, 73
Shaw Brothers Studios, 142, 151
Shi yao (Corpse Mania), 142, 151–53
Shōjo, 165, 171, 177, 179
slasher genre, 4, 6, 9, 15, 23, 25, 68, 148, 150, 158, 174, 177, 180n5, 233, 248, 251–70
Solamente nero (The Bloodstained Shadow), 129–30, 133, 135, 137
Sole, Alfred, 216
Sonno Profondo, 3
Spain, 67, 69
split screen, 183–84, 192–94

Strange Color of Your Body's Tears, The, 8, 104, 165, 184–91, 193–94, 196–97
Suspiria, 158, 176, 186, 196, 236, 263

Tenebrae, 32, 39, 41–43, 146, 162n2, 162n12
Terror Train, 251, 253–54, 257, 260–61, 264
Texas Chain Saw Massacre, The, 48–49, 58
tourism, 30, 33–35, 38, 229
transnational perspective, 4, 67–69, 141–42, 156, 159, 161, 168
Tutti I colori del buio (*All the Colors of the Dark*), 20, 103, 105–6, 186–87

Un bianco vestito per Marialé (*A White Dress for Marialé*), 122–28
Un couteau dans le Coeur (*Knife+Heart*), 7–8, 200–201, 203–4, 206–10, 213

Una Lucertola con la Pelle di Donna (*A Lizard in a Woman's Skin*), 69, 103, 243
urbanity, 31–33, 39, 43, 45n6, 55, 62, 64, 147, 151, 202, 216–17, 220, 223, 226–30, 256

Vertigo, 15, 17
Video Nasties, 234, 267
Visiting Hours, 251, 254, 257, 267, 269
voyeurism, 8, 17, 35, 97, 107, 165, 170, 174, 205–6, 208, 224, 241–45

Wallace, Edgar, 4–5, 69, 166
Williams, Linda, 118, 172, 174, 210, 242

Ye ging wan (*He Lives by Night*), 142, 149, 151, 156, 158–59, 162n12

www.ingramcontent.com/pod-product-compliance
Lightning Source LLC
Chambersburg PA
CBHW021835220426
43663CB00005B/259